The
Baker's Book
of Essential
Recipes

Easy Plum Crostata (page 157)

The
Baker's Book
of Essential
Recipes

HEARST BOOKS
New York

DARK CHOCOLATE–RASPBERRY LAYER CAKE (PAGE 92)

Contents

Chocolate Chip, Drop Sugar, and Peanut Butter
Cookies (pages 3, 5, 10)

FOREWORD

Close your eyes and imagine your kitchen warmly perfumed with cinnamon and nutmeg; you kids' faces sweetly glazed with chocolate icing; your guests' eyes alight as you spoon into a lofty soufflé.

If these simple pleasures sound inviting, *Good Housekeeping*'s test kitchens are here to help you discover (or rediscover) the joys of baking. In *Baker's Book of Essential Recipes*, we share 185 of our all-time favorites, each chosen to enhance your baking repertoire and your enjoyment of all things baked.

And, in our experience, a big portion of the joy comes from mastering the special techniques associated with each baked good. So, alongside delectable recipes for everything from cookies to cakes, pies to pastries, we've included dozens of step-by-step techniques—we call it Test Kitchen Know-How— to help ensure your baking success.

Fill up your cookie jar with old-fashioned favorites like Lemon Slice-'n'-Bakes, Crunchy Chocolate Biscotti, and Gingerbread Cutouts; our how-to photos demonstrate how to shape and cut out the dough. Or learn how to bake puddings in a hot water bath known as a *bain-marie*, so you can whip up Crème Caramel, Mocha Pots de Crème, and other creamy and comforting desserts with confidence.

Perhaps you've always wanted to bake pie from scratch. Whether you choose to make a Pear Pie with a Cookie-Cutter Crust or a Pumpkin Pie with Pecan Brittle, we walk you through the essential techniques, from rolling a piecrust to making decorative edges and tops. Or maybe you're in the mood for a homemade pizza. Our basic recipes for pizza dough and sauce, plus instructions on rolling a crust, will have you making Pizza Puttanesca or Sausage Calzones in time for tonight's dinner.

If you're already a skilled baker (or just want to expand your horizons), our specialty pastries are just the thing. Learn to make choux pastry dough and you can master cream puffs, éclairs, even piping a showstopping Caramel Christmas Wreath. Or use store-bought phyllo dough to shape baklava or spanakopita, filled with a savory spinach and ricotta cheese mixture.

But before you preheat your oven, be sure to check out Baking Basics: We offer an overview of all the equipment you'll need to make these delights (many of which you probably already have in your kitchen), along with an overview of essential ingredients you'll want in your pantry.

We hope that you'll take pleasure in the process of baking these luscious treats—and the many delicious results.

—Susan Westmoreland
Food Director, *Good Housekeeping*

BAKING BASICS

Fine baking is undoubtedly an art, but it also calls for a more scientific approach. While adding a "pinch of this and a splash of that" is a wonderfully intuitive way to cook up a stew, baking requires attention to detail.

Light-as-a-feather, fully risen cake depends on accurate measurement of the leavening and use of the right size pan. For a successful soufflé, you must separate the eggs carefully so that not the smallest speck of yolk sullies the whites. This glossary of baking basics covers many of the utensils and ingredients you'll encounter in our recipes. Take a little time to browse these pages. Even experienced bakers are likely to learn a few things they didn't know before.

Equipment

Our great-grandmothers baked with not much more than a bowl, a wooden spoon, and a rolling pin—and you don't have to invest your life savings in kitchen equipment in order to bake well. However, a few well-chosen tools and gadgets will make the job easier and more pleasurable. In many cases, inexpensive kitchen tools function just as well as top-of-the-line products, but a really good mixer and high-quality baking pans are two cases where the extra cost is well worth it. For ideas on what to do when you don't have exactly the right tool for the job, see "Savvy Swaps" on page xii.

Appliances

A hundred years ago, "baking day" was a test of endurance that could last from dawn till dusk. Today, electrical kitchen appliances save time and muscle power. Using a stand mixer to beat egg whites, a food processor to make graham-cracker crumbs, or a bread machine to knead dough frees you for the more creative aspects of the baking process—icing a cake, braiding a yeast dough, or adorning a piecrust with pastry cutouts.

BLENDER A blender does some jobs better than a food processor—for example, mixing very liquid batters. Use your blender to make popover and pancake batter (as well as smoothies and shakes, of course). You can also chop nuts very fine, puree fruits for dessert sauces, and crush ice in a blender. A machine with a "pulse" button helps you get precisely the results you're after.

ELECTRIC MIXER A regular hand mixer is fine for making frostings, cake batters, and light- to medium-density cookie doughs. But for the greatest versatility, you will need a heavy-duty stand mixer. Its powerful motor can handle stiff cookie doughs and knead pizza and bread doughs; and because you don't have to hold a stand mixer, it saves your energy and leaves both hands free for adding ingredients. You can even walk away for a moment and let the mixer work completely on its own (keep an eye on things, though!). Heavy-duty stand mixers come with large stainless-steel bowls, a flat paddle for mixing batters, a wire whip attachment for beating cream or egg whites, and a dough hook for kneading bread dough.

FOOD PROCESSOR Fitted with a metal blade, this machine is a serious time-saver for cutting fat into flours for pie dough and for mixing and kneading pastry and bread doughs. A food processor with a 6-cup work bowl can knead dough made with up to 4 cups of flour. A larger machine, with an 8-cup capacity, can handle a dough made with 6 to 8 cups of flour. The machine also excels at chopping or grinding nuts, making cookie or bread crumbs, chopping onions, or grating hard cheeses. Mini processors are handy for small jobs, such as chopping a handful of nuts, and they take up little counter space.

IMMERSION BLENDER Also called a hand blender, this small appliance can be used for whipping cream. The blender consists of a handle (which contains a small motor) and a long shaft with a mixing blade at the end (partially enclosed for safety). If your options for whipping cream are by hand or by immersion blender, the blender will save you some time. (An electric mixer will be the fastest of all.)

Baking Pans, Sheets & Dishes

Before you get serious about baking, take an inventory of your pans. If they're warped or rusted, it's time for new ones. Good-quality aluminum pans are among the best. You don't need nonstick pans for most recipes, but a durable nonstick finish is useful for some pans (see below). Be sure you have enough of each pan shape and size to bake, for instance, a few dozen cookies (the pans need to cool down before reuse), muffins for brunch, or a three-layer cake.

BAKING STONE Short of building a brick oven, a baking stone is your best bet for achieving a perfect crust on breads and pizzas. You position the round or rectangular ceramic "stone" on the oven rack and place the bread dough directly on it. The stone draws moisture from the dough so that the bottom crust browns and crisps. A set of thick terra-cotta tiles from a building-supply center works equally well; you can also buy sets of baking tiles that come fitted into a metal tray.

BUNDT PAN This one-piece tube pan is curved on the bottom and deeply fluted, so it turns out cakes that look decorative even when you don't frost them. Standard Bundt pans come in 6-cup and 12-cup sizes. If you don't have one, you can substitute a tube pan.

COOKIE SHEETS These are flat baking pans that do not have sides, although one or both ends may be slightly turned up to make it easier to handle the pans. In addition to baking cookies, these pans are used for loaves of bread that are shaped by hand. You'll definitely need heavy pans for bread. Cookie sheets should also be placed under two-part pans (such as springform or tart) that may leak during baking. Insulated cookie sheets, which have a cushion of air between two layers of metal, help keep cookie bottoms from overbrowning. You can duplicate this effect by stacking two pans. To ensure good air circulation, choose cookie sheets that fit your oven rack with 2 inches to spare on all sides.

COOLING RACKS Baked goods should be cooled on a wire rack both before and after you turn them out of the pan, or moisture may condense in the pan. Racks speed cooling, too, because air circulates all around. Round 10-inch racks are perfect for cooling cake layers; a nice big rectangular rack is good for cookies and breads. A rack is also useful when you're applying a thin glaze or icing: the drips will fall through the wire grid (place a sheet of waxed paper underneath to catch them) instead of pooling around the cake, cookies, or pastry.

CUPCAKE PANS *see* Muffin pans.

JELLY-ROLL PAN/HALF SHEET PAN These rectangular pans with low sides typically measure 15½" by 10½" to 18" by 13" respectively. Use for sheets of sponge cake destined to become rolled cakes, and for baking rolls and pastries. Turned upside down, these pans can serve as an extra cookie sheet.

LAYER CAKE PANS It's worth the investment to buy layer cake pans made of medium-weight aluminum. You'll need both 8- and 9-inch round pans and 8- and 9-inch square pans. The latter are used for bar cookies as well as square layer cakes. Round layer cake pans should be at least 1½ inches deep. Square pans are about 2 inches deep.

LOAF PANS These deep rectangular pans, made in both metal and glass, are used for yeast breads, quick breads, and loaf cakes. They come in standard sizes of 8½" by 4½" and 9" by 5". A loaf will bake faster in a glass pan than in a metal pan because of the radiant heat. Adjust your baking times accordingly.

MUFFIN PANS Also called cupcake pans, these come in a range of sizes. The standard size, which measures 2½ inches across the top of an individual cup, holds about ½ cup batter. With these traditional muffin pans, it's easiest to remove the finished baked goods if you line the pans with fluted paper cups. You can also buy special pans made of heavy cast iron or aluminum to make muffins in fanciful shapes, such as flowers, fruits, or ears of corn (corn sticks).

PIE PLATE Made of ovenproof glass, ceramic, or metal, pie plates come in 8-, 9-. and 10-inch sizes and deep-dish options. A clear glass plate lets you check on how the bottom of the pie is browning, and the crust will actually brown better in glass. Decorative stoneware pie plates may be of nonstandard sizes, so be sure to measure them beforehand to see if they'll work with your chosen recipe. Similarly, disposable foil pie pans, so useful when baking pies for gifts, have a smaller capacity than standard pie plates.

PIZZA PAN This shallow round pan is useful but not necessary for making pizza: You can simply mark a circle on a cookie sheet or baking stone and pat and stretch the dough to the right size. Some pizza pans have a perforated or mesh bottom to allow air to circulate and help crust crisp.

POPOVER PANS Popovers can be baked in muffin pans, but there are also special pans for them. These have deeper cups that are flared at the top.

SHEET-CAKE PAN This 13" by 9" by 2" rectangular pan could prove to be the most versatile one in your repertoire. Use it for single-layer cakes and large batches of bar cookies, or as a *bain-marie*, or water bath, for custards. Available in both metal and glass.

SPRINGFORM PAN A springform is a deep, round, two-piece pan; you'll need one if you're planning to bake cheesecakes or other cakes that are too delicate to turn out. The bottom and the side (or "collar") are separate pieces, and the side unlatches so that it can be removed from the cake for serving. Our recipes call for a 9-inch springform, the most common size.

TART PAN Choose "loose bottom" tart pans, which come in two parts. The fluted rim has just a slight edge around the inside bottom, and the flat bottom rests on this edge. To remove the tart from the side of the pan, stand the pan on a heavy can and ease the side down, leaving the tart on the pan bottom for serving. Tart pans come in many sizes and shapes.

TUBE PAN Sponge cakes and angel-food cakes require a pan with a "chimney" in the middle. This gives the batter something to latch onto as it rises. Tube pans come in one-piece and removable-bottom styles. The pan usually has little feet around the edge to allow you to stand it upside down for cooling, although many people like to invert the pan by slipping the center tube over the neck of a bottle.

Basics, Utensils & Gadgets

When you bake, it seems that you can never have too many bowls. And if you have too few (or too few wooden spoons or spatulas), you'll constantly need to wash them in the middle of whatever you're doing. We're not suggesting that you buy every single item listed here: Take into consideration the kinds of things you bake before buying gadgets and specialty supplies. The following, though, are true essentials: bowls, a chef's knife, dry and liquid measuring cups, measuring spoons, a rubber spatula, wooden spoons, a vegetable peeler, and a timer.

BOWLS A set of nesting bowls in graduated sizes from 1 to 3 quarts will see you through most baking projects; you may need a larger bowl for bread making. A deep bowl is best for mixing, and a heavy one is less likely to skate around the counter. (Placing a damp kitchen towel under any bowl will also help.) Plastic bowls absorb fat, which is a problem when you need a grease-free bowl (for beating egg whites, for instance). Heatproof glass, ceramic, and stainless-steel bowls are good choices. A collection of smaller bowls is useful for holding premeasured ingredients (cereal or dessert bowls, or custard cups can double in this role).

CAKE TESTER Many cooks use a toothpick or bamboo skewer for testing whether cakes are done. But there is also a gadget sold specifically for this purpose. It consists of a small handle attached to a length of rigid metal wire that is inserted into the center of the cake. If few to no crumbs are clinging to the wire when you remove it, the cake is done.

CITRUS JUICER The simplest citrus juicer is a one-piece gadget (of glass, ceramic, metal, or plastic) with a grooved, pointed dome in the center. You press and turn the halved citrus fruit on the dome, and out flows the juice. Some juicers come in two parts, the bottom portion being a dish to catch the juice. Electric citrus juicers work on the same principle, but the reamer revolves automatically. The most economical juicer for lemons and limes is a reamer—a small, hand-held device that you push into the halved fruit and twist.

COOKIE CUTTERS Made of tin, copper, aluminum, or plastic, these fanciful forms are used for cutting rolled-out dough into all sorts of shapes. Cookie cutters should have a smooth, sharp cutting edge; on metal cutters, the other side should have a finger-friendly rolled edge for safe handling.

COOKIE PRESS This tool, used for making spritz cookies from rich buttery dough, works something like a pastry bag. The press consists of a squat metal cylinder with a wide nozzle at the bottom. Perforated metal plates are fitted to the nozzle to make variously shaped cookies. A screw-operated plunger and a tight cover allow you to press out the dough onto the cookie sheet. Nowadays you can also buy electric cookie presses.

DOUGH SCRAPER Also called a bench scraper or bench knife, this functions like a big spatula: It's a rectangle of rigid metal or hard plastic about 4" by 5", with a rolled top to serve as a handle. The metal edge is thin but not sharpened. Use this tool to clean your counter of bits of dough and mounds of flour; it also helps you turn and lift sticky dough at the start of kneading and is good for transferring small pastries to a baking sheet.

DRY MEASURING CUPS Used for measuring flour, sugar, cornmeal, cocoa, and the like, these come in sets of graduated sizes, usually ¼, ⅓, ½, and 1 cup. The cups are often joined with a ring but are easier to handle if you separate them. When measuring flour, confectioners' sugar, and other light, powdery items, spoon the ingredient into the cup (do not tamp or pack down), then level it by sweeping across the top with the back of a knife. Granulated sugar can be measured by dipping; brown sugar should be packed into the cup. Never use dry measuring cups for liquid (or vice versa); you won't get an accurate measurement.

EGG SEPARATOR Rather than separating the yolk from the white by dropping the yolk from half-shell to half-shell (a time-honored but tricky process), you can use an egg separator. These may be saucer- or spoon-shaped; they have a little cup in the center to catch the yolk while the white slips through slots at the sides.

FLOUR SIFTER Resembling a big metal mug, the flour sifter has a wire-mesh bottom and, most commonly, a spring-action agitator that moves when you squeeze a trigger in the handle. The agitator aerates the flour, and the mesh strainer eliminates lumps. (You'll need to stir the ingredients after sifting.) You can also sift with a fine-mesh strainer, tapping the edge with a spoon to shake the dry ingredients through.

GRATER A one-piece *box grater* has perforations of different sizes for shredding chocolate, cheese, carrots, citrus zest, or nutmeg all on one utensil. You can place the grater on a plate, cutting board, or sheet of waxed paper while you use it. *Flat graters* are like one side of a box grater, with a handle at the top. They come in different styles for different jobs, and you may need several. You can lay a flat grater across the top of a bowl for a neat job. We especially love *Microplane graters* for their sharpness and ease of use; they are perfect for grating citrus peel and fresh ginger. For easy cleanup when grating sticky foods, spritz the face of the grater with nonstick spray before you begin.

SAVVY SWAPS

Don't have exactly the right tool for the job? Repurpose one of these multi-taskers to get the job done.

- **IF YOU MISPLACED YOUR COOKIE CUTTER COLLECTION,** use the rim of a glass or cup—or the edge of a jar or can—to cut out cookie dough.

- **DON'T OWN A FLOUR SIFTER?** Use a whisk to aerate flour or confectioners' sugar.

- **FOR AN ECONOMICAL ALTERNATIVE** to a pastry bag, use a heavy-duty resealable plastic bag. Fill the bag half full with frosting, snip off one corner, and get piping.

- **INSTEAD OF A SPRING-ACTION COOKIE DOUGH SCOOP,** use a melon baller to scoop perfectly round mini cookies. Just reduce the baking time by 1 or 2 minutes.

- **YOU DON'T HAVE TO OWN A FOOD PROCESSOR** to grind cookies or graham crackers for a crumb crust. Instead, enclose the cookies in a resealable plastic bag and pound them with a meat mallet.

- **IF YOU DON'T OWN A SET OF RAMEKINS** to make mini cakes and soufflés, a cupcake pan fitted with foil liners can be used as a stand-in.

- **A Y-SHAPED PEELER IS NOT JUST FOR GRATING CARROTS.** Use it to shave decorative curls from a block of chocolate. Chocolate curls make an elegant garnish for cakes and pies.

KNIVES For serious chopping, you'll need a *chef's knife*, which has a broad, wedge-shaped blade. An 8-inch chef's knife suits most home cooks. Look for a knife with a full tang—this means that the metal of the blade extends all the way through the handle. A knife made this way is stronger, better balanced, and safer to use. A *small paring knife*, with a blade about 4 inches long, is right for peeling and cutting up fresh fruit, peeling onions, and trimming vegetables. Though small, the knife should be strong and well made. Knives should be sharpened often. A dull knife is frustrating and dangerous to use, because it will slip rather than bite into what it is meant to be cutting. To slice bread and light-textured cakes, and to split cake layers horizontally, use a long knife with a *serrated blade*, working it through with a firm or gentle sawing motion, depending on the texture of the bread or cake.

LIQUID MEASURING CUPS Made of clear heatproof glass or plastic, these beaker-shaped cups have measurements marked on the sides. For accurate measurement, place the cup on the work surface, pour in the liquid, and then bend so you can check the amount of liquid at eye level. Liquid measures in 1- and 2-cup sizes will serve most purposes. There are also 8-cup glass measuring cups that make excellent batter bowls (complete with a handle for pouring). Don't measure dry ingredients in cups meant for liquids; it's not possible to level off the contents.

MEASURING SPOONS These can be used for both dry ingredients (baking powder, salt, spices) and liquid ingredients (lemon juice, vanilla extract); it's a good idea to have two sets. Stainless-steel spoons with smooth edges (for leveling) are the best choice. These come in sets usually with ¼, ½, and 1 teaspoon, plus 1 tablespoon. Some sets have a ⅛-teaspoon measure as well.

PARCHMENT PAPER Also called kitchen parchment or baker's parchment, this translucent, dull-finished paper is used for lining baking pans. Parchment paper comes in sheets and rolls.

PASTRY BAG For making cream puffs and éclairs, shaping meringue, and adorning cakes with whipped cream, you'll need a pastry bag with assorted tips. Nylon bags are easier to keep clean than canvas bags; they dry more quickly, and the fabric retains its flexibility better than canvas. A basic set of tips (also called tubes) will see you through the recipes in this book. A *decorating bag* is recommended when small quantities of icing or frosting are used on cakes and fine pastries.

PASTRY BLENDER You can use two knives to cut fat into dry ingredients to make crumbly dough for pastry, but if you find this difficult, try a pastry blender. Its straight handle is fitted with a curved sweep of tines or wires that are used with a punching/chopping motion. It's especially helpful for making biscuits and scones.

PASTRY BOARD This large, sturdy wooden board makes an excellent work surface. Look for a board (hardwood or acrylic) with a deep lip at the front and back. The front lip, which faces down, hooks over the edge of the counter to keep the board from sliding away as you knead or roll dough; the lip at the back is turned up to act as a backsplash and keep flour from going everywhere. A marble pastry board is a luxury, but the smooth surface is a pleasure to work on, and it stays cooler than any other material, so it's worth the investment if you make pastry often. Alternatively, you can simply use a clean countertop—or line your counter with parchment paper.

PASTRY BRUSH For smoothing on glazes and brushing off crumbs or excess flour, natural-bristle brushes should be set aside for baking (apart from brushes you use for basting savory foods). A 1-inch-wide brush is best for glazing; a wider brush works well for sweeping a surface clear of flour. A brand-new natural-bristle paintbrush can also be used.

PASTRY CLOTH AND ROLLING-PIN COVER Dusting your work surface and dough with a lot of flour to keep dough from sticking will turn pastry crust tough. Instead, consider purchasing a pastry cloth (a sheet of canvaslike cotton) and cover, sometimes called a sleeve, for your rolling pin. These need only a light dusting of flour. Some pastry cloths even have measured rounds marked on them to help you roll dough to just the size you need.

PASTRY WHEEL, CUTTER, OR JAGGER Like pizza cutters (which you can substitute if you already have one), these consist of a sharp-edged metal wheel mounted on the end of a wooden handle. These rolling cutters work much better than a knife for cutting uncooked dough. A jagger has a fluted wheel that produces a zigzag edge, as if you'd cut the dough with pinking shears; it's pretty for piecrust edges and crackers.

PIE WEIGHTS A piecrust baked blind (without a filling) needs to be weighted in the center to keep it from shrinking, buckling, and bubbling. Small, bean-shaped aluminum or ceramic weights are sold for this purpose; you can also buy a 6-foot rope of stainless-steel beads to coil in the crust before baking. Or use real dried beans or uncooked rice (and reuse them again and again). Line the bottom of the crust with a square of foil before placing pie weights inside.

ROLLING PINS First, the *American-style rolling pin* with handles and a free-spinning roller: You want the weight of the pin to do the work, so choose a heavy one (at least 4 pounds). The roller should turn smoothly on ball bearings; it should be of hardwood and nicely finished. If you prefer a *European-style wooden pin*—the one-piece kind—experiment with the tapered design as well as the straight style. These are inexpensive, and it's nice to have both on hand.

RULER An 18-inch wooden ruler with a steel edge (or a steel ruler) will help you roll piecrust to the right size, trim sheets of phyllo to fit a pan, and cut even-sized bar cookies and loaf-cake slices. And while some baking pans do have the size of the pan marked on the bottom, many do not. Estimating pan size can be risky; measuring with a ruler is foolproof.

SCALE A kitchen scale is useful for weighing out 3 ounces of chocolate from a large bar or 2 pounds of peaches from the half bushel you've brought home. When dividing cake batter between two pans, weighing them ensures that they're filled equally; the same goes for dividing a batch of bread dough. Although American recipes call for ingredients by volume measures (e.g.

cups), British and Continental recipes give them by weight. If you bake from foreign recipes, you'll need a kitchen scale. A battery-operated digital scale that shows both grams/kilograms and ounces/pounds, and can handle weights up to 5 pounds, is a good choice.

SPATULAS *Silicone, nylon, or plastic spatulas* in several sizes are a must; the narrower ones are great for getting the last bit of honey out of the jar. Choose flexible spatulas with sturdy handles and heat-resistant blades. You'll also need a *wide metal spatula* for removing hot cookies from cookie sheets; it should have a thin edge to slip under fragile cookies without breaking them. You'll need *icing spatulas* for frosting cakes—one about 10 inches long overall and a smaller one, with a blade about ½ inch wide and 4 inches long. An *offset or angled spatula*, on which the blade has a bend in it close to the handle, makes it easier to ice the sides of a cake.

SPOONS Wooden spoons are nonreactive and won't burn your fingers when you're stirring hot liquids. They also cut down on clatter when you're stirring in a pot or stainless-steel bowl. Choose spoons made of hardwoods such as maple; they should be smoothly finished and free of rough patches that may splinter. Metal cooking spoons should have heatproof handles so they can be used for stirring hot sauces as well as batters.

STRAINER/SIEVE A wire-mesh strainer or sieve can be used to strain liquids and sift dry ingredients together like flour, confectioners' sugar, baking powder or soda, and cocoa powder. Buy a few sizes with different mesh gauges.

THERMOMETERS Precise temperatures are important in baking. If you proof yeast in water that's too hot or bake popovers in an oven that's too cool, neither will succeed. Every kitchen should be equipped with an *instant-read thermometer:* About the size of a pen (complete with sheath and pocket clip), it is used to check the temperature of liquids (up to 220°F), rising dough, roasting meat, or the inside of your freezer. Oven thermostats are sometimes inaccurate, so the number you set on the control may be far from the actual temperature. Check it with an *oven thermometer* that you can leave in while you're baking.

TIMER Timing is too important in baking to risk relying on a glance at your watch. Many ranges and microwave ovens come equipped with timers—or you can use the timer on your smartphone. If you work on several baking projects simultaneously, consider buying an electronic timer with multiple settings.

WAX PAPER This semitransparent paper with a thin coating of wax on both sides is sold in rolls. Because it is moistureproof and nonstick, it has many applications in baking. Use it to roll up a log of icebox cookie dough or to separate layers of sticky brownies or bars for storage. You can also sift together dry ingredients on a small piece of waxed paper; when it's time to add them to the batter, just pick up two sides of the paper and dump the ingredients in. Brush off and reuse.

WHISK These days, most bakers do their mixing with an electric mixer, but a whisk still has its uses. This classic French tool—a straight handle most commonly with looped wires—is intended for stirring sauces, quickly combining ingredients, and beating eggs and cream. Whisks come in a variety of sizes and types, with the largest, the balloon whisk, designed to be used for beating egg whites until they're stiff.

ZESTER This tool is made to order for removing the thin top portion of peel from citrus fruits. You can use a fine grater for grating peel, but a zester cuts long, thin strips for garnishes.

Ingredients

Baking is scientific, but it is also part magic. When carefully combined, an assortment of ingredients can be transformed into a toothsome cake, irresistible cookie, or crusty loaf. Silky flour, moist brown sugar, freshly shelled nuts, plump raisins, a molten pour of melted chocolate—all should be of the best possible quality. Most baking ingredients are products you can keep on hand, whether in the cabinet, refrigerator, or freezer. Buy baking ingredients in a store with a good turnover and check freshness dates on any products that bear them.

Chocolate & Cocoa

Chocolate is the favorite flavor of millions, and fortunately there are many different ways to use it in baking. Chocolate starts out as cocoa beans, which are dried, hulled, and roasted. The resulting pieces, called cocoa nibs, are then crushed to produce chocolate liquor—a mixture of cocoa butter and particles of cocoa. To make solid chocolate, the two elements are separated, refined, and then recombined in various proportions; other ingredients, such as flavorings or emulsifiers, may be added. Cocoa powder is made by removing most of the cocoa butter from chocolate liquor, resulting in a fine powder.

UNSWEETENED CHOCOLATE Sold in packages of squares (and sometimes labeled baking chocolate), this is virtually pure chocolate liquor in solid form, with no sugar added. Sometimes flavoring and lecithin (an emulsifier) are incorporated.

SEMISWEET CHOCOLATE Some sugar (between 40 and 65 percent) has been added to this type of dark chocolate; the amount varies from one brand to another. Additional cocoa butter and vanilla flavor may be added as well. In general, American semisweet chocolate is sweeter than European brands. This chocolate is available in bulk or squares for baking, and in the form of bars for eating. The bars can, of course, be used for baking too, and are generally of better quality. Semisweet chocolate, chopped into chunks, can be substituted for semisweet chocolate chips.

WORKING WITH CHOCOLATE

If you consider chocolate a treasure, you'll want to use it with care. Here's how we do it in the Test Kitchen.

STORING Store solid chocolate, well wrapped, in a cool place (65°F is ideal). High temperatures are harder on chocolate than low ones, so if your kitchen is very warm, double-wrap the chocolate and keep it in the refrigerator.

CHOPPING Use a large chef's knife or heavy serrated knife to cut chocolate into pieces. Be sure the cutting board is perfectly clean and dry. To finely chop chocolate, cut it into small chunks (about ¼ inch) by hand, then pulse it in a food processor fitted with the metal blade.

MELTING The winning way to melt chocolate? Microwave it. A solid square softens swiftly, and because it's not exposed to direct heat, there's less chance that you'll scorch it. Best of all, there's no pot to scrub. To melt masterfully, use a glass measure with an easy-to-grasp handle. Melt the chocolate on High just until it looks soft and shiny (it may retain its shape rather than becoming liquid— don't overdo the heating, or the chocolate will scorch); stir until smooth.

BITTERSWEET CHOCOLATE This dark chocolate contains added sweetener too, but less than semisweet; bittersweet chocolate typically contains at least 65 percent cocoa solids. As with semisweet, the amount of sugar varies from brand to brand. Look for the percentage on the label: a higher proportion of cocoa assures a more intense chocolate flavor.

MILK CHOCOLATE This type of chocolate, sold for eating out of hand, is made with milk solids, heavy cream, or other dairy products added and is usually quite sweet and soft-textured, with a mild cocoa flavor. Milk chocolate can't be substituted for other kinds of chocolate to flavor a cake batter or cookie dough, but it can be used in the form of chunks or chocolate chips in place of other types of chocolate.

DARK SWEET CHOCOLATE Most notably used in German's chocolate cake, this is the sweetest type of chocolate that does not have milk added. Look for bars in the baking aisle.

WHITE CHOCOLATE Most of what's sold as "white chocolate" is not, technically speaking, chocolate at all. It contains no chocolate liquor and is commonly made with a fat other than cocoa butter, usually palm kernel oil. Only recently have the rules been relaxed to allow manufacturers to label these products as "chocolate." Look for white chocolate made with cocoa butter to get the best flavor.

CHOCOLATE CHIPS OR MORSELS Originally available only in semisweet, chocolate chips now come in milk, dark, mint, and white versions, as well as in different sizes. Try different brands until you find a favorite. Don't use chips when a recipe calls for melted squares or bars: Chips are formulated to hold their shape during baking and will behave differently in a batter or frosting.

COCOA Cocoa powder is made by removing most of the fat from chocolate, drying the resulting paste, and then grinding it to a powder. Dutch-process or European-style cocoa has been treated with alkali to neutralize some of the acid. Use Dutch-process cocoa only if the recipe specifies it, as it reacts differently with leavenings.

Dairy Products & Eggs

Creamy cheesecakes, delicate custards, mouthwatering shortcakes, towering soufflés—all depend on fresh, wholesome products from the dairy case. It's easy to check that you're getting fresh dairy products and eggs, because they are all are marked with a sell-by date.

BUTTER *see* Fats, page xxiv.

MILK The dairy case presents lots of alternatives when it comes to milk—lactose-reduced, calcium-enriched— but for baking, the plain old-fashioned variety is perfect. *Whole milk*, naturally, brings the most richness to custards, puddings, and sauces; *reduced-fat milk* (2 percent fat) has nearly as much fat and can be substituted. You'll probably notice a difference in creamy desserts if you substitute *low-fat milk* (1 percent fat) or *skim milk*, now labeled nonfat. *Buttermilk*, made by culturing low-fat or skim milk, brings a hint of a tangy flavor to biscuits, muffins, and cakes. It also helps produce baked goods with a tender crumb. Don't substitute buttermilk or yogurt for whole milk. However, you can substitute yogurt for buttermilk, if necessary, in most recipes.

CREAM With a butterfat content of between 36 and 40 percent, *heavy cream* whips up to the dense, dreamy stuff of toppings, fillings, and frostings. *Medium or whipping cream*, which can also be whipped, has 30 to 36 percent fat. *Light cream*, also called coffee cream, contains a mere (!) 18 to 30 percent fat. *Half-and-half*, with a fat content between 10.5 and 18 percent, can be substituted for light cream. Making whipped cream is much easier if the cream, bowl, and beaters are all ice cold. Chill them in the freezer beforehand.

SOUR CREAM Nothing can match the thickness and tangy richness of real dairy sour cream, which is made by culturing whole milk with lactic add. Light sour cream can be substituted in some recipes, but don't bake with nondairy "sour dressings."

YOGURT This fermented dairy product is available plain or flavored, in whole-milk, low-fat, and nonfat versions. Low-fat yogurt—but not nonfat—can be substituted for full-fat in most recipes.

Tomato Phyllo Tarts (page 297)

CREAM CHEESE The main ingredient in cheesecakes and some frostings is a snowy white, soft but solid cheese. Use the kind that comes in a block, rather than in a tub. In addition to regular, *full-fat cream cheese*, you can buy *Neufchâtel*, which has about one-third less fat, and *light cream cheese*, with about half the fat. (Fat-free cream cheese bears little resemblance to the real thing.) It's best not to substitute anything else for full-fat cream cheese unless the recipe suggests it.

EGGS Our recipes call for large eggs, which weigh approximately 2 ounces each. Substituting other sizes, such as small or jumbo, is not recommended because the results will be different. To store eggs in the refrigerator, use their original container, rather than putting them in the egg holder cups in the refrigerator door; this will keep them colder and also prevent them from picking up flavors from other foods (eggshells are porous). Eggs will keep for up to five weeks.

Flavorings

Spices, herbs, and extracts play important roles in dessert making. Vanilla extract is not only a lovely flavor on its own—it enhances the flavor of chocolate. Apple pie minus cinnamon would be bland, and without ginger, there would be no gingerbread. Keep an assortment of these flavorings in your kitchen, ready for use in our recipes.

EXTRACTS It takes just a spoonful of these concentrated flavorings to perfume a cake or quick bread. Use pure—not imitation—extracts whenever you can. Vanilla is the extract most used in American recipes. Try a few different brands and see which you prefer; they do vary. Other extracts to keep on hand are almond, orange, lemon, and peppermint.

HERBS AND SPICES Beginning life as humble leaves, twigs, seeds, roots, and stalks, these supply a world of flavors for baking. Sweet spices for cookies, pungent herbs for pizza—they're all as close as your supermarket.

If a recipe calls for fresh herbs and you have only dried, the usual substitution ratio is three to one—if the recipe calls for 3 tablespoons of chopped fresh oregano, use 1 tablespoon of dried instead. Spices such as nutmeg and cardamom will stay fresh longer if you buy them whole and crush or grind them as needed. Herbs and spices lose their power over time. Before you use any dry seasoning, rub a bit between your fingers to be sure that the aroma and flavor are still vivid. Keep dried herbs and spices in tightly closed containers in a cool, dark place (not in a rack over the stove where they'll be exposed to heat and moisture).

Here are some of the herbs and spices you'll encounter in this book: allspice, anise seeds, basil, caraway seeds, cardamom, cinnamon, cloves, crushed red pepper, cumin, fennel seeds, ground ginger, nutmeg, mace, oregano, rosemary, thyme. Apple-pie spice and pumpkin-pie spice are blends that you can buy ready-made; you can also prepare the same blends yourself, to taste.

PEPPER Any recipe that calls for pepper deserves freshly ground pepper, either black or white. Both come from dried berries of the same plant, but white pepper is made from hulled berries. Use a peppermill to grind whole peppercorns as needed, and you'll always enjoy this spice at its flavorful best.

SALT If you've ever tasted bread made without salt, you know what even a pinch of this vital seasoning does for baked goods, and yeast bread needs salt to rise properly. Without a pinch of salt, sweet baked goods can taste flat. When the type of salt is not specified, use *table salt* for the recipes in this book. *Kosher salt*, specified in some recipes, is much coarser grained. Because of the difference in texture, a teaspoon of one is not equal to a teaspoon of the other.

Flours & Meals

What would baking be without flour? A hot oven and an empty pan! The right kind of flour (bread, cake, whole wheat) is the key to fine baking, so be sure to use the type specified in the recipe. When you bring flour home from the store, transfer it from the bag or box to a canister or wide-mouth jar with a tight lid. Store flour in a cool place. Whole-grain flours and meals, which contain more fat than refined products, should be stored in the refrigerator or freezer to keep them from becoming rancid (in hot climates, store all flour in the refrigerator). Let flour return to room temperature before using it. If the recipe says to sift the flour, do. If not, just stir the flour to aerate it slightly before measuring.

WHEAT FLOUR *All-purpose flour* is a blend of soft and hard wheats, giving it a balanced content of protein and starch that works in most recipes. *Cake flour* is made from soft wheat and ground very fine. Low in protein, it produces tender, fine-grained cakes. To substitute all-purpose flour for cake flour, subtract 2 tablespoons all-purpose flour from each cup. Do not substitute self-rising cake flour for plain cake flour; the self-rising type contains leavening in addition to the wheat. *Bread flour* is made from hard wheat; its higher protein content is needed to support the structure of the dough as it rises. *Semolina* is a coarse-grained flour made from durum wheat, which is very hard. It's used for making pasta and some Italian breads and cakes. *Whole-wheat flour* is made from the entire wheat kernel, with both the bran (outer covering) and germ (protein- and oil-rich nucleus) included.

CORNMEAL Dried kernels of field corn (different from the sweet corn we eat fresh) are ground into meal for baking. When metal grinders are used, most of the hull and germ are removed, and the meal emerges very smooth but somewhat characterless. Stone-ground cornmeal retains some of the hull and germ and because of that is coarser. It brings a more interesting flavor and texture to baked goods. *Yellow cornmeal* and *white cornmeal* are ground from different varieties of corn. Choosing one or the other will affect only the color of the finished product.

WHOLE-WHEAT FLOUR THAT'S WHITE

If you don't like the flavor and texture of whole-wheat flour, try baking with white whole-wheat flour instead. Gold Medal and King Arthur Flour make it, and there are also health-food-store options to choose from.

Milled from an albino variety of wheat, it's as healthy as traditional whole wheat—with the same levels of fiber, nutrients, and minerals—but it lacks the heartier taste and grainy heft. It's ideal for all whole-grain recipes and can be substituted for up to half of the all-purpose flour in many other recipes without substantially changing the taste.

CORNSTARCH Made from the endosperm (the starchy portion) of the corn kernel, cornstarch is as fine and light as talcum powder. In baking, cornstarch is used in combination with wheat flour for very fine-textured cookies and cakes. It also serves as a thickener for puddings and sauces. If you are using cornstarch in quantity, sift it before adding it to the other ingredients.

OATMEAL Oats come in several forms. *Steel-cut oats* are whole oat kernels that have been chopped. *Old-fashioned oats* are steamed to soften them, then rolled into flakes. *Quick-cooking oats* are a similar product, but cut into smaller pieces. *Instant oatmeal* is made from the whole oat, but further processed, so that it softens immediately when moistened. Old-fashioned and quick-cooking oats are suitable (and interchangeable) for most cookie and bread recipes.

MEYER LEMON PUDDING CAKES (PAGE 213)

Dried Fruit & Nuts

From moist, spicy cookies studded with bits of pecan and apricot to a fluffy coconut frosting to a sophisticated hazelnut-chocolate cake, there are countless good reasons to keep dried fruit and nuts on hand. Buy them in boxes, bags, or bulk (health-food stores usually have a good selection); store them airtight so they'll stay fresh and delicious longer.

COCONUT Grating coconut from a whole nut is quite a project; fortunately, flaked coconut (both unsweetened and sweetened) is sold in bags, ready to use. Refrigerate any leftovers. Unless a recipe calls for fresh coconut, do not substitute it; use the fresh only for garnish.

DRIED FRUIT Joining old-fashioned favorites like raisins, dates, currants, figs, dried apricots, and prunes are chewy dried apple, peach, pear, pineapple, and mango, as well as sweet dried cherries and tart cranberries. To keep dried fruit moist, store it in tightly closed bags or jars; it will keep longer in the refrigerator. When chopping dried fruit, lightly oil the blade of the knife or kitchen shears, and the fruit won't stick. To soften fruit that has gotten too dry and hard, place it in a bowl, sprinkle it with water, then cover and microwave it for about 30 seconds.

TOASTING COCONUT

Shredded (or flaked) coconut becomes lightly golden and even more flavorful when you toast it.

Spread the coconut in a shallow pan in a single layer. Bake in a preheated 350°F oven for about 10 minutes, stirring frequently. Watch closely—coconut can go from toasted to burnt quickly.

NUTS AND SEEDS Rich in fat, nuts and seeds are quite perishable. If the fat turns rancid, the nuts or seeds will have an unpleasant smell rather than their usual rich, toasty fragrance—and you should discard them. Buy shelled (but not chopped) nuts in airtight packaging if possible. Unless you're going to use them immediately, store nuts and seeds in the freezer, in sealed food-storage bags. For optimal flavor, toast nuts and seeds briefly before using them. A final tip: when chopping nuts in a food processor or blender, run the machine in very quick pulses and watch carefully, as the nuts can quickly turn from finely chopped to nut butter.

Leavenings

Bakers owe a huge thank-you to their forebears who discovered and developed techniques for turning a soupy bowl of batter into a lofty cake, or a damp lump of dough into a tender loaf of bread. Yeast has been in use since ancient times, but baking powder dates back only to the mid-nineteenth century. Today, yeast and other leavenings come in convenient, ready-to-use forms for nearly foolproof baking. Measure baking powder and baking soda carefully, leveling off the top of the spoon with the back of a knife or a metal spatula.

BAKING POWDER This seemingly magical compound, works by releasing carbon dioxide gas into the batter. *Double-acting baking powder* is made from baking soda (see opposite) plus an acid ingredient (in most brands, sodium aluminum sulfate). When mixed with liquid, the baking powder begins to release carbon dioxide bubbles, and more is released when the batter is heated in the oven. Baking powder must be stored airtight. To test baking powder for freshness, stir ½ teaspoon into 1 cup of warm water: It should foam up instantly. If not, discard it and buy a fresh can.

BAKING SODA The chemical sodium bicarbonate, a base (the opposite of an acid), has long been used as a leavening. When combined with an acidic liquid, such as molasses, buttermilk, or fruit juice, or an acidic dry ingredient like brown sugar or cocoa powder, it releases carbon dioxide. Once baking soda starts to work, you must get the batter into the oven promptly,

TOASTING NUTS

An easy way to make nutty cookies, bars, and other baked goods taste even better is to toast the nuts—they become more flavorful.

Toast nuts whole and let them cool before chopping. These instructions work for walnuts, pecans, almonds, macadamia nuts, hazelnuts (see Tip) and even sesame seeds. Check (and stir) nuts often as they toast, as they can go from golden-and-fragrant to black-and-burnt in just moments.

Preheat the oven (or a toaster oven) to 350°F and spread out the nuts on a rimmed baking sheet in a single layer. Bake them until they are fragrant and lightly browned, 10 to 12 minutes, stirring several times. (Small nuts or pieces like sliced almonds will take less time. Check them after 4 to 5 minutes.) Immediately transfer the toasted nuts to a plate to cool. If you're toasting just a few nuts, heat them in a dry skillet over low heat for 3 to 5 minutes, stirring frequently.

TIP Toast hazelnuts as directed above until any portions without skin begin to brown. Transfer the nuts to a clean, dry kitchen towel and rub them until the bitter skins come off.

before it loses its fizz. Store the opened box in an airtight container.

CREAM OF TARTAR A by-product of winemaking, this fine white powder is a chemical called potassium acid tartrate. It is sometimes added to egg whites while they're being beaten to help stabilize them, which makes them a more effective leavening.

YEAST This is a living organism, a one-celled fungus that has the power to puff a ball of dough to many times its original size. To do this, the yeast needs to be combined with liquid at just the right temperature (105°F to 115°F) and given some starch to feed on. The yeast takes in the starch, turns it into sugar, and releases bubbles of carbon dioxide—which gets trapped within the dough, causing it to rise. Cold stops the action of yeast, so be sure that all ingredients are at room temperature, and put the dough in a warm, draft-free place to rise. The recipes in this book use *active dry* and *quick-rise yeast*, both sold in ¼-ounce packages and in jars. Store yeast in the refrigerator and check the freshness date on the package before you use it. If you're not sure the yeast is still good, stir it into the warm water called for in the recipe, and add a good pinch of sugar. After 5 to 10 minutes, the mixture should be bubbly.

Fats

If you've ever tried to cut down on the fat in a baking recipe, you know that it's no simple trick. That's because butter, oil, shortening, and other fats play several different roles in achieving delicious results. In pastry crust, fat coats particles of the protein in flour; if the dough is mixed properly (so that it's not totally blended), the fat will also separate the layers of dough to create a flaky texture. Fat keeps cookies, cakes, and quick breads soft and moist, traps the air bubbles that make them rise, and acts as a flavor carrier.

BUTTER The queen of all baking fats, butter brings a rich, sweet flavor to baked goods that nothing else can duplicate. Salted butter has been used in the development of all the recipes in this book, unless otherwise noted. Butter should be at room temperature if it is to be creamed with sugar or blended into an already-mixed dough; it will soften more quickly if you cut it into pieces. It is better not to try to soften butter over heat; once melted—even if it is then chilled—it will not have the same properties for baking. For flaky pie and tart crusts, the butter should be well chilled. Always keep it covered in the refrigerator. You can store butter in the freezer for up to six months, but it must be well wrapped or it will take on off flavors.

MARGARINE Although it looks a lot like butter, even the finest margarine cannot approach butter's taste. If you choose to bake with margarine (many of our recipes suggest it as an acceptable alternative to butter, while a few recipes specify butter only), use a solid stick type, with a fat content of at least 80 percent, not one that comes in a tub or squeeze bottle. Avoid diet or light margarines, which contain additional water that will greatly affect the outcome of the recipe.

OIL For some recipes, oil is the fat of choice. There are many different vegetable oils available, but for baking, the main point is to

use a flavorless oil. For most recipes, corn, safflower, sunflower, canola, soybean, and light olive oil are good choices. Like any fat, oil can become rancid, so store it in a cool place—not near the stove. Don't substitute oil for solid shortening in any baking recipes.

VEGETABLE SHORTENING Made by treating vegetable oil with hydrogen to solidify it and make it stable at room temperature, shortening has a texture akin to that old-fashioned favorite, lard. Both shortening and lard are pure fat (butter and margarine contain some milk solids), which makes them ideal for pastry crusts. Vegetable shortening melts more slowly than butter, so cookies baked with it will be "taller" than those made with butter. Shortening will keep longer if stored in the refrigerator.

Sweeteners

The pleasing sweetness of our favorite desserts has several sources: It may come from sugarcane, sugar beets, maple trees, or beehives. Each type of sweetener has its own delightful flavor and unique properties that affect the texture—crisp, crunchy, moist, smooth—of baked goods and other desserts.

SUGAR There's more to sugar than just sweetness. In baking, sugar helps batters and doughs to rise by allowing more air to be captured as the mixture is beaten. Sugar also helps keep cakes and cookies tender and moist. *Granulated white sugar* is the baking basic; *superfine sugar*, also sold as bar sugar, dissolves more quickly, which is desirable for recipes in which a very smooth texture is desired. *Confectioners' sugar* (also called powdered sugar) is very finely ground and sifted white sugar, it's used for mixtures where a smooth texture is of primary importance, as in uncooked frostings. The designation 10X, often seen on confectioners' sugar packaging, denotes the finest possible texture. A little cornstarch is added to confectioners' sugar to reduce clumping;

still, the sugar is usually lumpy from being packed tightly in the box and should be sifted and stirred before use. Many people think that *brown sugar* is somehow more natural than white sugar, but it is, in fact, simply granulated white sugar with varying amounts of molasses added to it. Dark brown and light brown sugar are interchangeable in our recipes.

MAPLE SYRUP Not just for pancakes, maple syrup is also a fine sweetener and flavoring for desserts. Be sure to buy pure maple syrup—not "table syrup" or "pancake syrup," which may contain no maple at all. Maple syrup's grade gives you an indication of its flavor, with AA or "Fancy" being the palest in color and most delicate in flavor. If you're a true maple fan, you may want to use a darker (and less expensive) grade, which will have a bolder maple flavor.

MOLASSES Originally a by-product of sugar refining, the best (unsulfured) molasses is now made by refining boiled-down sugarcane juice. Molasses is a very thick, brown syrup with a tangy undertone to its sweetness. The lighter the molasses, the milder and sweeter its flavor. Molasses is often used in spicy, old-fashioned desserts such as gingerbread and Indian pudding. Baked goods made with molasses have a tendency to brown quickly, so check their progress in the oven regularly. Store molasses in a cool place; if it's too cold to pour, heat the jar of molasses in a pan of warm water.

HONEY Beloved for its old-country fragrance and flavor, honey, like all liquid sugars, helps keep baked goods moist. Depending on its source (what kinds of flowers the bees fed on), honey can vary in flavor. Sample a few and find a favorite. Because honey is acidic, baking recipes in which it is used will also include some baking soda to balance the acid.

CORN SYRUP This sweetener is a thick, barely pourable liquid made from cornstarch. It comes in light (nearly colorless) and dark (clear brown) versions. In baking, corn syrup is used to help breads and cookies retain moisture; it also contributes to the satiny texture of some frostings and icings by preventing the crystallization of the sugar.

Cookies

CRANBERRY–CHOCOLATE CHUNK COOKIES

DROP COOKIES

Making drop cookies is a snap if you keep these pointers in mind: They will bake more evenly if they're all the same size. Also be sure the cookie sheets are cool when you drop the dough on them. If they're warm, the cookies may spread too quickly and bake up flat.

Chocolate Chip Cookies

Hands down, these are America's favorite cookie—and so open to interpretation. Use one of our variations, or make up your own!

Active time: 15 minutes
Bake time: 10 minutes per batch
Makes: about 36 cookies

1¼ cups all-purpose flour
½ teaspoon baking soda
½ teaspoon salt
½ cup butter or margarine (1 stick), softened
½ cup packed light brown sugar
¼ cup granulated sugar
1 large egg
1 teaspoon vanilla extract
1 cup (6 ounces) semisweet chocolate chips
½ cup walnuts, chopped (optional)

1. Preheat oven to 375°F. On sheet of waxed paper, combine flour, baking soda, and salt.

2. In large bowl, with mixer on medium speed, beat butter and both sugars until light and creamy. Beat in egg and vanilla until well combined. Reduce speed to low; beat in flour mixture until blended. With spoon, stir in chocolate pieces and walnuts, if you like.

3. Drop dough by rounded tablespoons, 2 inches apart, on two ungreased large cookie sheets. Bake 10 to 12 minutes, until edges are golden, rotating sheets between upper and lower oven racks halfway through. With wide metal spatula, transfer cookies to wire racks to cool completely. Repeat with remaining cookie dough.

4. Store cookies in airtight container up to 1 week, or freeze up to 3 months.

Each cookie: about 80 calories, 1g protein, 11g carbohydrate, 4g total fat (2g saturated), 1g fiber, 13mg cholesterol, 80mg sodium

WHITE CHOCOLATE-MACADAMIA COOKIES Prepare dough as instructed, but substitute ¾ *cup white chocolate chips* for the semisweet chocolate chips and *1 cup macadamia nuts*, chopped, for the walnuts. Bake cookies as directed.

Each cookie: about 110 calories, 11g protein, 11g carbohydrate, 7g total fat (3g saturated), 0g fiber, 13mg cholesterol, 85mg sodium

CRANBERRY-CHOCOLATE CHUNK COOKIES Prepare dough as instructed, but in addition to semisweet chocolate chips, add ¾ *cup white chocolate chips* and *1 cup dried cranberries*, and increase nuts to *1½ cups walnuts*, toasted (see page xxiii) and chopped. Bake 11 minutes per batch.

Each cookie: about 170 calories, 2g protein, 21g carbohydrate, 9g total fat (4g saturated), 1g fiber, 21mg cholesterol, 75mg sodium

Grandma's Oatmeal-Raisin Cookies

If you like crisp oatmeal cookies, bake these until the tops are golden. For softer, chewier cookies, bake only about 12 minutes, or just until the edges change color. You can use either old-fashioned or quick-cooking oats, but don't use instant oatmeal, which is so fine that the cookies will not have much texture.

Active time: 15 minutes

Bake time: 15 minutes per batch

Makes: about 24 cookies

3/4 cup all-purpose flour

1/2 teaspoon baking soda

1/4 teaspoon salt

1/2 cup butter or margarine (1 stick), softened

1/2 cup granulated sugar

1/3 cup packed brown sugar

1 large egg

2 teaspoons vanilla extract

1 1/2 cups old-fashioned or quick-cooking oats, uncooked

3/4 cup dark seedless raisins or chopped pitted prunes

1. Preheat oven to 350°F. On sheet of waxed paper, combine flour, baking soda, and salt.

2. In large bowl, with mixer on medium speed, beat butter and both sugars until creamy. Beat in egg and vanilla until smooth. Reduce speed to low; beat in flour mixture. With spoon, stir in oats and raisins.

3. Drop dough by heaping tablespoons, 2 inches apart, on two ungreased large cookie sheets. Bake 15 minutes or until golden, rotating cookie sheets between upper and lower oven racks halfway through. With wide metal spatula, transfer cookies to wire racks to cool completely. Repeat with remaining cookie dough.

4. Store cookies in airtight container up to 3 days, or freeze up to 3 months.

Each cookie: about 115 calories, 2g protein, 17g carbohydrate, 4g total fat (2g saturated), 1g fiber, 19 mg cholesterol, 95 mg sodium

OATMEAL CHOCOLATE-CHIP COOKIES Prepare dough as instructed, but stir in *1 cup (6 ounces) semisweet chocolate chips* with the oats and raisins. Bake as directed.

Each cookie: about 145 calories, 2g protein, 22g carbohydrate, 6g total fat (4g saturated), 1g fiber, 19mg cholesterol, 95mg sodium

FORMING DROP COOKIES

With practice, you'll become expert at scooping equal-size dollops of dough.

Use one tablespoon to scoop the dough and, with a second, scrape each dollop onto the prepared cookie sheet. Leave about 2 inches of space between the balls of dough so the cookies don't spread into each other during baking. If you make a lot of drop cookies, purchase a tablespoon-size cookie scoop with a trigger handle; it makes this job a cinch.

Vegan Oatmeal-Raisin Cookies

Be sure to use vegan margarine in the stick form, not spread, or your cookies will be tough and dry.

Active time: 35 minutes
Bake time: 13 minutes per batch
Makes: about 36 cookies

1 cup all-purpose flour
1 teaspoon ground cinnamon
1/2 teaspoon baking soda
1/2 teaspoon salt
3/4 cup vegan stick margarine
3/4 cup packed brown sugar
1/3 cup granulated sugar
1/2 cup plain unsweetened soy milk
1 teaspoon vanilla extract
3 cups old-fashioned oats, uncooked
1 cup dark seedless raisins
1 cup walnuts (4 ounces), chopped

1. Preheat oven to 350°F. Line three large cookie sheets with parchment. In bowl, whisk flour, cinnamon, baking soda, and salt.

2. In large bowl, beat margarine and both sugars until fluffy. Beat in soy and vanilla (mixture will look curdled). Beat in flour mixture. Stir in oats, raisins, and nuts.

3. Drop dough by heaping tablespoons onto prepared pans, 2 inches apart. Bake one sheet at a time until cookies look dry and are browned at edges, 13 to 15 minutes. Let stand on sheet 1 minute; transfer cookies to wire rack to cool completely.

4. Store cookies in airtight container up to 3 days, or freeze up to 1 month.

Each cookie: about 135 calories, 2g protein, 18g carbohydrate, 6g total fat (2g saturated), 9g fiber, 0mg cholesterol, 93mg sodium

Drop Sugar Cookies

If you don't have the time (or the inclination) to make roll-and-cut sugar cookies, try this simple old-fashioned drop cookie recipe. The cookies can be varied by stirring in 1/2 cup chopped nuts or mini chocolate chips, or 1 tablespoon freshly grated lemon peel. You can also decorate them with icing after baking, if you like.

Active time: 25 minutes
Bake time: 14 minutes per batch
Makes: about 42 cookies

2 cups all-purpose flour
1 teaspoon baking powder
1/4 teaspoon salt
3/4 cup butter or margarine (11/2 sticks), softened
1 cup sugar
1 large egg
3 tablespoons milk
2 teaspoons vanilla extract

1. Preheat oven to 350°F. On sheet of waxed paper, stir together flour, baking powder, and salt.

2. In large bowl, with mixer on medium-low speed, beat butter and sugar until creamy. Add egg, milk, and vanilla: beat until well blended. Reduce speed to low; beat in flour mixture just until blended.

3. Drop dough by rounded teaspoons, 2 inches apart, onto two ungreased large cookie sheets. Bake 14 minutes, or until browned at edges, rotating cookie sheets between upper and lower oven racks halfway through. With wide metal spatula, transfer cookies to wire racks to cool completely. Repeat with remaining cookie dough.

4. Store cookies in airtight container up to 1 week, or freeze up to 3 months.

Each cookie: about 70 calories, 1g protein, 9g carbohydrate, 3g total fat (2g saturated), 0g fiber, 14mg cholesterol, 60mg sodium

Chewy Molasses Spice Cookies

What are ground mustard and black pepper doing in a cookie recipe? These seasonings, time-honored ingredients in German and Scandinavian recipes for gingerbread and spice cookies, add a lively hotness that plays against the sweetness.

Active time: 15 minutes
Bake time: 13 minutes per batch
Makes: about 42 cookies

2 cups all-purpose flour
1½ teaspoons baking soda
1 teaspoon ground ginger
½ teaspoon ground cinnamon
¼ teaspoon salt
¼ teaspoon finely ground black pepper
⅛ teaspoon ground cloves
⅛ teaspoon ground mustard
½ cup butter or margarine (1 stick), softened
¾ cup packed dark brown sugar
½ cup light (mild) molasses
1 large egg
1 teaspoon vanilla extract

1. Preheat oven to 350°F. On sheet of waxed paper, stir together flour, baking soda, ginger, cinnamon, salt, pepper, cloves, and mustard.

2. In large bowl, with mixer on medium speed, beat butter and brown sugar until smooth. Beat in molasses until combined. Reduce speed to low; beat in egg and vanilla until blended. Beat in flour mixture until combined, scraping bowl occasionally with rubber spatula.

3. Drop dough by rounded tablespoons, 3 inches apart on two ungreased large cookie sheets. Bake cookies 13 to 15 minutes, until flattened and evenly browned, rotating cookie sheets between upper and lower oven racks halfway through. Cool on cookie sheets on wire rack 2 minutes. With wide metal spatula, transfer cookies to racks to cool completely. Repeat with remaining dough.

4. Store cookies in airtight container up to 1 week, or freeze up to 3 months.

Each cookie: about 70 calories, 1g protein, 11g carbohydrate, 2g total fat (1g saturated), 0g fiber, 11mg cholesterol, 85mg sodium

SUGAR-COATING SHAPED COOKIES

For a sparkly finish, roll cookie dough in plain or cinnamon sugar.

Roll one ball of cookie dough at a time in cinnamon sugar (or granulated sugar), then transfer to the prepared cookie sheet, leaving at least 2 inches between the balls.

Snickerdoodles

These cinnamon-spicy cookies are probably Pennsylvania-Dutch in origin—although nobody has come up with a definitive explanation of their name. Because the balls of dough are rolled in cinnamon sugar, the cookies come out with crinkly, crackly tops.

Active time: 25 minutes
Bake time: 12 minutes per batch
Makes: about 54 cookies

3 cups all-purpose flour
2 teaspoons cream of tartar
1 teaspoon baking soda
1 cup butter or margarine (2 sticks), softened
1¹/₃ cups plus ¹/₄ cup sugar
2 large eggs
1 teaspoon vanilla extract
1¹/₂ teaspoons ground cinnamon

1. Preheat oven to 375°F. On sheet of waxed paper, stir together flour, cream of tartar, and baking soda.

2. In large bowl, with mixer on medium speed, beat butter and 1¹/₃ cups sugar until light and fluffy. Beat in eggs, one at a time, beating after each addition. Beat in vanilla. Reduce speed to low; beat in flour mixture until well combined.

3. In small bowl, combine cinnamon with remaining ¹/₄ cup sugar. With hands, shape dough into 1-inch balls. Roll in cinnamon sugar to coat (see opposite). Place balls, at least 2 inches apart, on two ungreased large cookie sheets. Bake 12 minutes, or until set, lightly golden, and slightly crinkly on top, rotating cookie sheets between upper and lower oven racks halfway through. Cool on cookie sheets on wire racks 1 minute. With wide metal spatula, transfer cookies to wire racks to cool completely. Repeat with remaining cookie dough.

4. Store cookies in airtight container up to 1 week, or freeze up to 3 months.

Each cookie: about 80 calories, 1g protein, 11g carbohydrate, 4g total fat (2g saturated), 0g fiber, 17mg cholesterol, 60mg sodium

---

Wheat-Free Almond Butter Cookies

These gluten-free cookies are not only wholesome, they're delicious too. They're also egg-free, so they're suitable for vegans as well.

Active time: 10 minutes
Bake time: 11 minutes per batch
Makes: about 36 cookies

1 tablespoon ground flaxseeds or flaxseed meal
3 tablespoons water
1 cup smooth almond butter
1 cup packed brown sugar
1 teaspoon baking soda
¹/₂ teaspoon pure vanilla extract
Pinch salt
¹/₂ teaspoon pumpkin pie spice (optional)
Sliced almonds (optional)

1. Preheat oven to 350°F. Line two cookie sheets with parchment paper. In small bowl, mix flaxseeds with water. Let stand 5 minutes.

2. In bowl of stand mixer, combine almond butter, brown sugar, baking soda, vanilla, salt, soaked flaxseeds, and pumpkin pie spice if using; mix on low speed until thoroughly combined.

3. Using a 1-tablespoon measure, form dough into balls and place on prepared cookie sheets, 1¹/₂ inches apart. If desired, top balls with sliced almonds.

4. Bake 11 to 12 minutes or until slightly golden, rotating cookie sheets between upper and lower oven racks halfway through. Transfer to wire racks to cool.

5. Store cookies in airtight container up to 5 days, or freeze up to 1 month.

Each serving: about 70 calories, 1g protein, 8g carbohydrate, 4g total fat (1g saturated), 13g fiber, 0mg cholesterol, 72mg sodium

CHOCOLATE CRINKLES

Chocolate Crinkles

As the rich, sugar-coated dough bakes, it spreads into puffy rounds, then forms crinkles on the surface.

Active time: 25 minutes plus chilling
Bake time: 8 minutes per batch
Makes: about 48 cookies

1³/4 cups all-purpose flour

1/2 cup unsweetened cocoa

1 teaspoon baking soda

1/2 teaspoon baking powder

1/4 teaspoon salt

1/2 cup butter or margarine (1 stick), softened

1¹/4 cups granulated sugar

2 tablespoons light corn syrup

2 ounces unsweetened chocolate,
   melted and cooled

2 large eggs

2 teaspoons vanilla extract

1/2 cup confectioners' sugar

1. On sheet of waxed paper, stir together flour, cocoa, baking soda, baking powder, and salt.

2. In large bowl, with mixer on medium speed, beat butter, granulated sugar, and corn syrup until combined. Reduce speed to low and beat in chocolate, eggs, and vanilla until well blended. Beat in flour mixture until combined, scraping bowl occasionally with rubber spatula. Cover dough and refrigerate 1 hour.

3. Preheat oven to 350°F. Place confectioners' sugar in small bowl. Shape dough by level teaspoons into 1-inch balls; roll in confectioners' sugar.

4. Place cookies, 1 inch apart, on two ungreased large cookie sheets. Bake 8 minutes, or until set, rotating cookie sheets between upper and lower oven racks. With metal spatula, transfer cookies to wire racks to cool. Repeat with remaining dough and sugar.

5. Store cookies in airtight container up to 1 week, or freeze up to 1 month.

Each cookie: about 35 calories, 1g protein, 6g carbohydrate, 1g total fat (1g saturated), 1g fiber, 7 mg cholesterol, 35 mg sodium

Chocolate Wows

The name says it all. Three kinds of chocolate plus pecans make a spectacular cookie.

Active time: 20 minutes
Bake time: 12 minutes per batch
Makes: about 48 cookies

1/3 cup all-purpose flour

1/4 cup unsweetened cocoa

1 teaspoon baking powder

1/4 teaspoon salt

6 ounces semisweet chocolate, chopped

1/2 cup butter or margarine (1 stick)

2 large eggs

3/4 cup sugar

1¹/2 teaspoons vanilla extract

2 cups pecans (8 ounces), chopped

1 cup (6 ounces) semisweet chocolate chips

1. Preheat oven to 325°F. Grease two large cookie sheets. In small bowl, combine flour, cocoa, baking powder, and salt.

2. In heavy 2-quart saucepan, melt chocolate and butter over low heat, stirring frequently, until smooth. Cool.

3. In large bowl, with mixer on medium speed, beat eggs and sugar until light, about 2 minutes, scraping bowl with rubber spatula. Reduce speed to low. Add chocolate mixture, flour mixture, and vanilla; beat just until blended. Increase speed to medium; beat 2 minutes. Stir in pecans and chocolate chips.

4. Drop batter by rounded teaspoons, 2 inches apart, onto prepared cookie sheets. With small metal spatula, spread batter into 2-inch rounds. Bake until tops are shiny and cracked, about 12 minutes, rotating cookie sheets between upper and lower oven racks halfway through. Cool 10 minutes on cookie sheets. With metal spatula, transfer cookies to wire racks to cool. Repeat with remaining batter.

5. Store cookies in airtight container up to 3 days, or freeze up to 3 months.

Each cookie: about 100 calories, 1g protein, 9g carbohydrate, 7g total fat (3g saturated), 1g fiber, 14mg cholesterol, 45mg sodium

Peanut Butter Cookies

Kids adore these cookies—and they love to help make the crisscross pattern on top (see box).

Active time: 25 minutes
Bake time: 10 minutes per batch
Makes: about 48 cookies

1¹/2 cups all-purpose flour
¹/2 teaspoon baking soda
¹/2 cup butter or margarine (1 stick), softened
³/4 cup creamy or chunky peanut butter (see Tip)
¹/2 cup packed brown sugar
¹/2 cup granulated sugar
1 large egg
¹/2 teaspoon vanilla extract

1. Preheat oven to 375°F. Grease two large cookie sheets. In small bowl, combine flour and baking soda.

2. In large bowl, with mixer on medium speed, beat butter until creamy. Add peanut butter and both sugars; beat until well blended. Beat in egg and vanilla. Reduce speed to low; beat in half of flour mixture until blended. With wooden spoon, stir in remaining flour mixture until combined.

3. With hands, shape dough into 1-inch balls. Place balls, at least 2 inches apart, on prepared cookie sheets. Using floured tines of fork or potato masher, press each ball into disk ³/8 inch thick. Bake 10 to 12 minutes, until lightly browned at edges, rotating cookie sheets between upper and lower oven racks halfway through. Place cookie sheets on wire racks to cool 2 minutes. With wide metal spatula, transfer cookies to racks to cool completely. Repeat with remaining cookie dough.

4. Store cookies in airtight containers up to 1 week, or freeze up to 3 months.

Each cookie: about 75 calories, 2g protein, 8g carbohydrate, 4g total fat (2g saturated), 1g fiber, 10mg cholesterol, 55mg sodium

PEANUT BUTTER JUMBLES Prepare recipe as instructed, but stir in *¹/2 cup Mini M&Ms* after incorporating all of the flour mixture in step 2.

Each cookie: About 85 calories, 2g protein, 10g carbohydrate, 5g total fat (2g saturated), 1g fiber, 10mg cholesterol, 55mg sodium

PEANUT BRITTLE COOKIES Prepare recipes as instructed, but stir in *8 ounces peanut brittle candy*, coarsely chopped, after incorporating all the flour mixture in step 2.

Each cookie: About 95 calories, 2g protein, 12g carbohydrate, 5g total fat (2g saturated), 1g fiber, 10mg cholesterol, 72mg sodium

TIP For more wholesome cookies, chose natural peanut butter.

MAKING CROSSHATCH MARKS

There's no mistaking the tic-tac-toe pattern on these cookie-jar favorites.

Arrange balls of cookie dough on a prepared cookie sheet, then use the tines of a fork (or one quick move with a potato masher) to flatten and mark the dough with a crisscross pattern.

Gluten-Free Peanut Butter Cookies

Sink your teeth into these old-fashioned favorites, made with natural peanut butter and our easy gluten-free flour blend. Make sure to use a gluten-free cornstarch like Bob's Red Mill brand and pure vanilla extract, as artificial extracts may contain gluten.

Active time: 35 minutes plus cooling • Bake time: 12 minutes per batch • Makes: about 24 cookies

1 cup All-Purpose Gluten-Free Flour Blend
(see below)
1/4 cup cornstarch
1 teaspoon baking powder
1 teaspoon baking soda
1/2 teaspoon salt

1 cup natural creamy peanut butter
4 tablespoons butter, softened
1/2 cup packed brown sugar
1/2 cup granulated sugar
2 large eggs
1 teaspoon pure vanilla extract

1. Preheat oven to 350°F. Grease two large cookie sheets with nonstick cooking spray. In small bowl, whisk together flour blend, cornstarch, baking powder, baking soda, and salt.

2. In large bowl, with electric mixer on low, beat peanut butter, butter, and both sugars until creamy. Beat in eggs, one at a time. Beat in vanilla. Beat in flour mixture just until combined.

3. Using heaping measuring tablespoons, shape dough into balls and place 2 inches apart on prepared cookie sheets. Press with fork to create crisscross pattern (see opposite). Bake one sheet at a time until golden brown at edges, 12 to 15 minutes. Let stand on baking sheet 1 minute; with wide metal spatula, transfer cookies to wire racks to cool completely.

4. Store in airtight container up to 5 days, or freeze up to 1 month.

Each cookie: about 150 calories, 3g protein, 17g carbohydrate, 8g total fat (2g saturated), 1g fiber, 21mg cholesterol, 188mg sodium

ALL-PURPOSE GLUTEN-FREE FLOUR BLEND

If you or a loved one has gluten sensitivities, mix up a batch of our blend and keep it on hand. Or, for a shortcut, swap in a store-bought version such as Cup4Cup or Gluten-Free Pantry brands. (Note that you cannot substitute a gluten-free blend for the all-purpose flour called for in other recipes in this book.)

Active time: 5 minutes
Makes: about 6 cups

2 cups sorghum flour
1 1/2 cups potato starch
1 cup tapioca flour
1 cup corn flour

In large bowl, whisk sorghum flour, potato starch, tapioca flour, and corn flour until thoroughly blended. Refrigerate in airtight container up to 1 month.

Each 1/2 cup: about 230 calories, 4g protein, 53g carbohydrate, 1g total fat (0g saturated fat), 4g fiber, 0mg cholesterol, 0mg sodium

Coconut Macaroons

These cookies are traditional for Passover, when baked goods must be made without flour or leavening. But they're delicious any time of year (and a welcome treat for those avoiding wheat or gluten).

Active time: 10 minutes
Bake time: 25 minutes per batch
Makes: about 42 cookies

3 cups (9 ounces) sweetened flaked coconut
4 large egg whites
3/4 cup sugar
1 teaspoon pure vanilla extract
1/2 teaspoon salt
1/8 teaspoon pure almond extract

1. Preheat oven to 325°F. Line two large cookie sheets with parchment paper or foil.

2. In large bowl stir together coconut, egg whites, sugar, vanilla, salt, and almond extract until evenly combined.

3. Drop batter by rounded teaspoons, 1 inch apart, on prepared cookie sheets. Bake 25 minutes, or until set and lightly golden, rotating cookie sheets between upper and lower oven racks halfway through. Cool 1 minute on cookie sheets. With wide metal spatula, transfer cookies to wire racks to cool completely. Repeat with remaining batter.

4. Store cookies in an airtight container up to 3 days, or freeze up to 1 month.

Each cookie: about 40 calories, 1g protein, 6g carbohydrate, 2g total fat (2g saturated), 1g fiber, 0mg cholesterol, 35mg sodium

CHOCOLATE COCONUT MACAROONS Prepare as instructed, but add *2 tablespoons unsweetened cocoa* and *1 ounce semisweet chocolate*, grated, to batter. Bake as directed.

Each cookie: about 45 calories, 1g protein, 7g carbohydrate, 2g total fat (2g saturated), 1g fiber, 0mg cholesterol, 35mg sodium

DEEP CHOCOLATE MACAROON TRUFFLES Prepare Chocolate Coconut Macaroons as instructed, but instead of semisweet chocolate, substitute *1 ounce bittersweet (60% to 70% cacao) chocolate*, grated, to batter. Bake as directed. Shortly before serving, in microwave-safe bowl, microwave *5 ounces bittersweet chocolate* on High in 30-second increments until melted and smooth, stirring frequently. Dip tops of macaroons in chocolate to coat. Let harden on wire racks. Drizzle with *2 ounces melted white chocolate* if desired.

Each cookie: about 70 calories, 1g protein, 8g carbohydrate, 4g total fat (3g saturated), 1g fiber, 0mg cholesterol, 50mg sodium

Chocolate Macaron Sandwiches

Macarons have the most tempting texture: crisp on the outside and soft and chewy on the inside. (See "Macaroons versus Macarons" on page 45 to learn about their origins.) These almond-chocolate macarons are made even more fabulous, as they are sandwiched with a heavenly chocolate and cream filling.

Active time: 20 minutes plus chilling
Total time: 13 minutes per batch
Makes: about 36 sandwich cookies

MACARONS
1 cup blanched slivered almonds (4 ounces)
1 cup sugar
2 tablespoons unsweetened cocoa
Pinch salt
1/3 cup egg whites
2 ounces unsweetened chocolate, melted and cooled
1/2 teaspoon pure vanilla extract

CHOCOLATE FILLING
1/4 cup heavy cream
1 1/2 teaspoons sugar
1 teaspoon butter or margarine
3 ounces bittersweet or semisweet chocolate, chopped
1/4 teaspoon pure vanilla extract

1. Preheat oven to 350°F. Line two large cookie sheets with parchment paper.

2. Prepare macarons: In food processor with knife blade attached, combine almonds, sugar, cocoa, and salt; process until almonds are ground to a powder. Add egg whites, melted chocolate, and vanilla; process until paste is formed.

3. Transfer batter to large pastry bag fitted with ¾-inch round tip. Pipe batter into 1-inch mounds, 2 inches apart, on prepared cookie sheets. Bake until almost firm, 13 to 14 minutes, rotating cookie sheets between upper and lower oven racks halfway through. Set cookie sheets on wire racks to cool 1 minute. With wide metal spatula, carefully transfer macarons to wire racks to cool completely.

4. Prepare filling: In 1-quart saucepan, combine cream, sugar, and butter; heat to boiling over medium-high heat. Remove from heat. Add chocolate to cream mixture; stir until melted and smooth. Stir in vanilla. Pour into small shallow bowl; refrigerate until firm and spreadable, at least 1 hour.

5. Turn half of macarons so flat bottoms face up. With small metal spatula, spread scant 2 teaspoons chocolate filling on each flat surface. Place remaining macarons on top to make sandwiches.

6. Store cookies in airtight container, with waxed paper between layers, up to 3 days, or freeze up to 1 month.

Each sandwich cookie: about 290 calories, 3g protein, 31g carbohydrate, 18g total fat (11g saturated), 1g fiber, 66mg cholesterol, 95mg sodium

TOP: COCONUT MACAROONS; BOTTOM: CHOCOLATE MACARON SANDWICHES

ICEBOX COOKIES

It's hard to make a case for buying refrigerated cookie dough when you can make your own— in a scrumptious variety of flavors—and have it on hand for baking any time the spirit moves you.

Lemon Slice-'n'-Bakes
Using half confectioners' sugar and half granulated sugar gives these cookies a melt-in-your-mouth texture. For a special treat, sandwich them with lemon frosting or melted bittersweet chocolate.

Active time: 30 minutes plus chilling
Bake time: 12 minutes per batch
Makes: about 60 cookies

2 cups all-purpose flour
1/4 teaspoon baking powder
1/4 teaspoon salt
2 to 3 large lemons
3/4 cup butter or margarine (1 1/2 sticks), softened
1/2 cup plus 2 tablespoons granulated sugar
1/2 cup confectioners' sugar
1/2 teaspoon vanilla extract

1. On sheet of waxed paper, stir together flour, baking powder, and salt. From lemons, grate 1 tablespoon peel and squeeze 2 tablespoons juice.

2. In large bowl, with mixer on medium speed, beat butter, 1/2 cup granulated sugar, and confectioners' sugar until creamy. Beat in lemon peel and juice and vanilla until blended. Reduce speed to low and beat in flour mixture just until combined.

3. Divide dough in half. Shape each half into 6-inch-long log. Wrap each log in waxed paper and refrigerate overnight (if using margarine, freeze overnight), or label, date, and freeze up to 3 months.

4. Preheat oven to 350°F. Keeping remaining log refrigerated, cut 1 log into scant 1/4-inch-thick slices. Place slices, 1 1/2 inches apart, on two ungreased large cookie sheets. Sprinkle lightly with 1 tablespoon granulated sugar. Bake 12 minutes, or until lightly browned at edges, rotating cookie sheets between upper and lower oven racks halfway through. Cool on cookie sheets on wire racks 2 minutes. With wide metal spatula, transfer to racks to cool completely. Repeat with remaining cookie dough and granulated sugar.

5. Store cookies in airtight container up to 1 week, or freeze up to 3 months.

Each cookie: about 50 calories, 0g protein, 6g carbohydrate, 2g total fat (1g saturated), 0g fiber, 6mg cholesterol, 35mg sodium

LEMON POPPY SEED SLICES Prepare as instructed, but add *2 tablespoons poppy seeds* along with lemon peel and juice and vanilla. Bake as directed.

Each cookie: about 50 calories, 1g protein, 6g carbohydrate, 2g total fat (1g saturated), 0g fiber, 6mg cholesterol, 35mg sodium

MINI LEMON SLICES Prepare dough as instructed; divide into 4 pieces. Roll each piece into 12-inch-long log; wrap in waxed paper and refrigerate. Cut into 1/4-inch-thick slices and place, 1 inch apart, on two ungreased large cookie sheets. Bake 10 to 12 minutes, until lightly browned at edges, rotating sheets between upper and lower oven racks halfway through. Repeat with remaining dough. Makes about 16 dozen cookies.

Each cookie: about 15 calories, 0g protein, 2g carbohydrate, 1g total fat (0g saturated), 0g fiber, 2mg cholesterol, 11mg sodium

Coconut Thins

Toasting the coconut lends these crisps rich, nutty flavor.

Active time: 30 minutes plus chilling

Bake time: 8 minutes per batch

Makes: about 96 cookies

1¾ cups all-purpose flour

¼ cup cornstarch

½ teaspoon baking powder

⅛ teaspoon ground nutmeg

⅛ teaspoon salt

¾ cup butter or margarine (1½ sticks), softened

1 cup sugar

1 large egg

½ teaspoon vanilla extract

¼ teaspoon almond extract

2 cups (6 ounces) sweetened flaked coconut, toasted
  (see page xxii)

1. On sheet of waxed paper, stir together flour, cornstarch, baking powder, nutmeg, and salt.

2. In large bowl, with mixer on medium speed, beat butter and sugar until light and fluffy. Beat in egg and both extracts until well combined. Reduce speed to low and beat in flour mixture and coconut until well combined.

3. Divide dough in half. On separate sheets of waxed paper, shape each half into 14" by 1½" log. Wrap each log tightly in waxed paper. Refrigerate several hours until very firm, or label, date, and freeze up to 3 months.

4. Preheat oven to 350°F. Keeping remaining dough refrigerated, cut 1 log into ¼-inch-thick slices. Place slices, 1 inch apart, on two ungreased large cookie sheets. Bake 8 to 9 minutes until edges are golden brown, rotating cookie sheets between upper and lower oven racks halfway through. Cool on cookie sheets on wire racks 1 minute. With wide metal spatula, transfer to racks to cool completely. Repeat with remaining cookie dough.

5. Store cookies in airtight container up to 1 week, or freeze up to 3 months.

Each cookie: about 30 calories, 4g protein, 1g carbohydrate, 2g total fat (1g saturated), 0g fiber, 5mg cholesterol, 20mg sodium

---

SHAPING AND SLICING ICEBOX COOKIES

Icebox cookie dough can be refrigerated in waxed-paper-wrapped logs for three hours. For longer storage, up to three days, place the wrapped logs in resealable plastic bags until you're ready to slice and bake them.

Form the dough roughly into a log shape, then use the waxed paper to roll and smooth it into a cylinder of even thickness. Refrigerate until very firm.

As you slice the log of chilled dough, turn it every few cuts so that the bottom doesn't become flattened.

Lime Slice-'n'-Bakes

A drift of powdered sugar tops these thin, crisp citrus squares. For even more delicate cookies, slice the dough 1/8 inch thick and bake for 10 to 12 minutes.

Active time: 30 minutes plus chilling
Bake time: 12 minutes per batch
Makes: about 48 cookies

2 to 3 limes
1/2 cup butter or margarine (1 stick), softened
3/4 cup granulated sugar
1 large egg
1 3/4 cups all-purpose flour
About 1/2 cup confectioners' sugar

1. From limes, grate 1 teaspoon peel and squeeze 3 tablespoons juice. In medium bowl, with mixer on medium speed, beat butter and granulated sugar until creamy. Reduce speed to low; beat in egg and lime peel and juice until blended. Beat in flour until combined.

2. Divide dough in half. On separate sheets of waxed paper, shape each half into 6" by 2" by 2" brick. Wrap each brick tightly in waxed paper and freeze 3 hours, or label, date, and freeze up to 1 month.

3. Preheat oven to 350°F. Slice 1 brick into 1/4-inch-thick slices. Place slices, 1 inch apart, on two ungreased large cookie sheets. Bake cookies 12 to 15 minutes, until edges are golden brown, rotating cookie sheets between upper and lower oven racks halfway through. With wide metal spatula, transfer to wire racks. Sift confectioners' sugar over hot cookies. Repeat with remaining cookie dough and confectioners' sugar.

4. Store cookies in airtight container up to 1 week, or freeze up to 3 months.

Each cookie: about 50 calories, 1g protein, 8g carbohydrate, 2g total fat (1g saturated), 0g fiber, 10mg cholesterol, 20mg sodium

TOP: LIME SLICE-'N'-BAKES; BOTTOM: CHOCOLATE ICEBOX COOKIES

Chocolate Icebox Cookies

To make elegant sandwich cookies, pair two of these thin rounds with your favorite frosting, ice cream, or a thin layer of raspberry jam. Crushed, they'd make a great crust for a chocolate cream pie; see our recipe on page 173.

Active time: 25 minutes plus chilling
Bake time: 10 minutes per batch
Makes: about 120 cookies

1²/₃ cups all-purpose flour

¹/₂ cup unsweetened cocoa

1 teaspoon baking powder

¹/₂ teaspoon baking soda

¹/₄ teaspoon salt

³/₄ cup butter or margarine (1¹/₂ sticks), softened

¹/₂ cup packed light brown sugar

¹/₂ cup granulated sugar

2 ounces semisweet chocolate, melted and cooled

1 teaspoon vanilla extract

1 large egg

1. On sheet of waxed paper, stir together flour, cocoa, baking powder, baking soda, and salt.

2. In large bowl with mixer on medium speed, beat butter and both sugars until light and fluffy. Beat in chocolate and vanilla until well combined. Beat in egg. Reduce speed to low and beat in flour mixture until well combined.

3. Divide dough in half. On separate sheets of waxed paper, shape each half into 12" by 1½" log. Wrap each log tightly in waxed paper and slide onto small cookie sheet for easier handling. Refrigerate dough at least 2 hours or overnight, until firm enough to slice (if using margarine, freeze overnight). For longer storage, label, date, and freeze up to 3 months.

4. Preheat oven to 350°F. Cut 1 log crosswise into scant ¼-inch-thick slices; keep remaining log refrigerated. Place slices, 1 inch apart, on two ungreased large cookie sheets. Bake 10 to 11 minutes, rotating sheets between upper and lower oven racks halfway through. Set cookie sheets on wire racks to cool 1 minute. With wide metal spatula, transfer cookies to racks to cool completely. Repeat with remaining dough.

5. Store cookies in airtight container up to 1 week, or freeze up to 3 months.

Each cookie: about 25 calories, 0g protein, 4g carbohydrate, 1g total fat (1g saturated), 0g fiber, 5mg cholesterol, 25mg sodium

CHOCOLATE SPICE COOKIES Prepare cookies as instructed, but add *¼ teaspoon finely ground black pepper*, *¾ teaspoon ground cinnamon*, and *⅛ teaspoon ground allspice* to flour mixture in step 1.

Each cookie: about 25 calories, 0g protein, 4g carbohydrate, 1g total fat (1g saturated), 0g fiber, 5mg cholesterol, 25mg sodium

SHAPED COOKIES

Whether shaping balls, logs, pretzels, or tartlets, don't work in a lot of extra flour—it will make the cookies tough. If the dough is too soft or sticky, instead chill it to firm it up.

Walnut Biscotti

These buttery, nutty biscotti are perfect for dunking. For a fancy flourish, dip them in white chocolate.

Active time: 40 minutes plus cooling
Bake time: 50 minutes
Makes: about 36 biscotti

2 cups all-purpose flour
1¹/2 teaspoons baking powder
¹/4 teaspoon salt
¹/2 cup butter (1 stick), softened (do not use margarine)
¹/3 cup granulated sugar
¹/3 cup packed brown sugar
2 large eggs
1 tablespoon vanilla extract
1 cup walnuts (4 ounces), toasted (see page xxiii) and coarsely chopped
12 ounces white or dark chocolate, melted (optional)

1. Preheat oven to 325°F. Line large cookie sheet with parchment paper.

2. On waxed paper, mix together flour, baking powder, and salt.

3. In large bowl, with mixer on medium speed, beat butter and both sugars until creamy. Add eggs, one at a time, beating well after each addition. Beat in vanilla. Reduce speed to low; gradually beat in flour mixture just until blended, occasionally scraping bowl. Stir in walnuts.

4. On lightly floured surface, divide dough in half. Form each half into 1¹/2-inch-wide log and place on prepared sheet, spacing logs 3 inches apart. Bake 30 minutes or until golden brown. Cool on pan on wire rack 5 minutes.

5. Carefully slide logs onto large cutting board. With serrated knife, cut each log crosswise into ¹/2-inch-thick diagonal slices; place slices, cut side down, on same sheet. Bake 20 to 25 minutes or until golden brown and crisp. Cool completely on pan on wire rack.

6. If desired, dip half of each cooled biscotti into melted chocolate. Place on cookie sheet lined with waxed paper to let chocolate harden. Store biscotti in airtight container up to 1 week, or freeze up to 1 month.

Each biscotto (without chocolate): about 90 calories, 2g protein, 10g carbohydrate, 5g total fat (2g saturated), 0g fiber, 17mg cholesterol, 45mg sodium

TEST KITCHEN KNOW-HOW

SHAPING AND SLICING BISCOTTI

Biscotti dough is first baked in a log, then sliced to create cookies and baked again.

To form the log, drop the dough by spoonfuls down the length of the cookie sheet. With lightly floured hands, flatten and shape it into a cylinder of even thickness. After the first baking, slice the slightly cooled loaf with a serrated knife, using an even sawing motion.

Crunchy Chocolate Biscotti

We've given this biscotti recipe a low-fat makeover, using egg whites instead of whole eggs and vegetable oil instead of butter to decrease the saturated fat.

Active time: 30 minutes plus cooling • Bake time: 50 minutes • Makes: about 48 biscotti

3 large egg whites
1/3 cup vegetable oil
2 tablespoons strong brewed coffee
1 teaspoon vanilla extract
1²/3 cups all-purpose flour
3/4 cup sugar
1/2 cup unsweetened cocoa

1 teaspoon baking powder
1/4 teaspoon baking soda
1/4 teaspoon salt
1/3 cup chopped hazelnuts or other nuts, toasted
  (see page xxiii)
1/3 cup dried tart cherries

1. Preheat oven to 350°F. Lightly grease two large cookie sheets.

2. In small bowl, beat together egg whites, oil, coffee, and vanilla.

3. In large bowl, stir together flour, sugar, cocoa, baking powder, baking soda, salt, nuts, and cherries until well mixed. Pour egg mixture over dry ingredients and stir until combined. Shape dough into two 12" by 1" logs; place both on prepared cookie sheet, spaced well apart, and flatten slightly. Bake 30 minutes or until toothpick inserted in center comes out clean. Cool logs on cookie sheet on wire rack 10 minutes.

4. Transfer 1 log to cutting board. Cut diagonally into scant ½-inch-thick slices. Arrange slices, cut side up, on ungreased cookie sheet. Repeat with remaining log, using second cookie sheet. Bake until slices are dry, 20 minutes, rotating cookie sheets between upper and lower oven racks halfway though. Using wide metal spatula, transfer biscotti to rack to cool.

5. Store biscotti in airtight container up to 2 weeks, or freeze up to 3 months.

Each biscotto: about 50 calories, 1g protein, 8g carbohydrate, 2g total fat (1g saturated), 1g fiber, 0mg cholesterol, 30mg sodium

Pecan Tassies

The South is home to these diminutive pecan tarts. In a pinch, bake the nut filling in store-bought miniature tart shells rather than making the pastry yourself.

Active time: 40 minutes plus chilling
Bake time: 30 minutes
Makes: about 24 cookies

1 small package (3 ounces) cream cheese, softened
1/2 cup plus 1 tablespoon butter or margarine, softened
1 cup all-purpose flour
2 tablespoons granulated sugar
1 cup pecans (4 ounces), toasted (see page xxiii) and finely chopped
2/3 cup packed light brown sugar
1 large egg
1 teaspoon vanilla extract

1. Preheat oven to 350°F. In large bowl, with mixer on high speed, beat cream cheese with ½ cup butter until creamy. Reduce speed to low and add flour and granulated sugar; beat until well mixed. Cover bowl with plastic wrap; refrigerate 30 minutes.

2. In medium bowl, with spoon, combine pecans, brown sugar, egg, vanilla, and remaining 1 tablespoon butter.

3. With floured hands, divide chilled dough into 24 equal pieces (dough will be very soft). With floured fingertips, gently press each piece of dough evenly onto bottom and up side of twenty-four 1¾" by 1" ungreased miniature muffin-pan cups. Spoon equal amounts pecan filling into all pastry cups.

4. Bake 30 minutes, or until filling is set and crust is golden. With small thin knife, loosen cookie cups from muffin-pan cups and transfer to wire rack to cool.

5. Store cookies in airtight container, with waxed paper between layers, up to 1 week, or freeze up to 3 months.

Each cookie: about 135 calories, 1g protein,12g carbohydrate, 9g total fat (4g saturated), 1g fiber, 24mg cholesterol, 60mg sodium

Brown Sugar and Pecan Fingers

This shortbread-style dough is rolled directly onto the cookie sheet, then cut into fingers after baking.

Active time: 25 minutes
Bake time: 20 minutes
Makes: 24 cookies

3/4 cup butter or margarine (1½ sticks), softened
1/3 cup packed dark brown sugar
1/4 cup granulated sugar
1 teaspoon vanilla extract
1/4 teaspoon salt
1¾ cups all-purpose flour
1/2 cup pecans (2 ounces), chopped

1. Preheat oven to 350°F. In large bowl, with mixer on medium speed, beat butter, both sugars, vanilla, and salt until creamy, about 2 minutes. At low speed, gradually beat in flour until just evenly moistened. With hand, press dough together to form ball.

2. Divide dough in half. On one side of ungreased large cookie sheet, roll half of dough, covered with waxed paper, lengthwise into 12" by 5" rectangle. On other side of same cookie sheet, repeat with remaining dough, leaving 1½ inches between rectangles. With fork, prick dough at 1-inch intervals. Press tines of fork along long sides of rectangles to form decorative edge. Sprinkle pecans evenly over rectangles; press gently to make nuts adhere.

3. Bake until edges are lightly browned, 20 to 25 minutes. While pastry is still warm, cut each rectangle crosswise into 12 thin "fingers." Using wide metal spatula, transfer to wire rack to cool.

4. Store cookies in airtight container up to 1 week, or freeze up to 3 months.

Each cookie: about 120 calories, 1g protein, 12g carbohydrate, 8g total fat (4g saturated), 0g fiber, 15mg cholesterol, 90mg sodium

BROWN SUGAR AND PECAN FINGERS

Hermits

Originating in New England in clipper-ship days, these moist and wonderfully chewy cookies most likely got their name because they keep so long. Sailors would stow them away "like hermits" as snacks on extended voyages. Although they're sometimes made as drop cookies, the dough is more traditionally formed into long slabs that are cut into cookie-size pieces after baking, as we've done below.

Active time: 20 minutes plus cooling
Bake time: 22 minutes per batch
Makes: 36 cookies

2 cups all-purpose flour

1 teaspoon baking powder

$1/2$ teaspoon baking soda

$1/4$ teaspoon salt

1 teaspoon ground cinnamon

$1/2$ teaspoon ground ginger

$1/4$ teaspoon ground nutmeg

$1/8$ teaspoon ground cloves

$1/2$ cup butter or margarine (1 stick), softened

1 cup packed light brown sugar

$1/4$ cup light (mild) molasses

1 large egg

1 cup dark seedless raisins

1 cup pecans (4 ounces), toasted (see page xxiii)
     and coarsely chopped

1. Preheat oven to 350°F. Grease and flour two large cookie sheets.

2. On sheet of waxed paper, stir together flour, baking powder, baking soda, salt, cinnamon, ginger, nutmeg, and cloves.

3. In large bowl with mixer on medium speed, beat butter and sugar until light and fluffy. Beat in molasses until well combined. Beat in egg. Reduce speed to low and beat in flour mixture until blended. With rubber spatula, fold in raisins and pecans.

4. Divide dough in thirds. With lightly floured hands, on prepared cookie sheets, shape each third into 12" by 1½" log. On one prepared cookie sheet, place 2 logs spaced widely apart; place third log on remaining cookie sheet. Bake 22 minutes, rotating sheets between upper and lower oven racks halfway through, until logs are set and tops are firm to touch. Cool on cookie sheets on wire racks 15 minutes.

5. Transfer logs to cutting board. With serrated knife, slice each log in half lengthwise, then cut crosswise into 2-inch pieces. Transfer to wire racks to cool completely. Store bars in an airtight container up to 1 week, or freeze up to 3 months.

Each cookie: about 115 calories, 1g protein, 17g carbohydrate, 5g total fat (2g saturated), 1g fiber, 13mg cholesterol, 80mg sodium

Oatmeal Chocolate-Chip Cookie Pizza

Supersizing chocolate chip cookie batter to pizza proportions is faster—and more fun—than dropping the dough by the spoonful. We've replaced some of the flour with oats to ensure crisp edges and a chewy center.

Active time: 15 minutes
Bake time: 18 minutes
Makes: 1 large cookie or 12 servings

3/4 cup all-purpose flour
1/4 teaspoon baking soda
1/4 teaspoon salt
6 tablespoons butter or margarine
1/3 cup packed brown sugar
1/3 cup granulated sugar
1 large egg
1 teaspoon vanilla extract
1 cup old-fashioned oats, uncooked
3/4 cup semisweet chocolate chips
1/2 cup walnuts (2 ounces), chopped

1. Preheat oven to 375°F. Line large cookie sheet with parchment paper. On sheet of waxed paper, mix flour, baking soda, and salt until well blended.

2. In 3-quart saucepan, melt butter over low heat. Remove pan from heat; with wire whisk, stir in both sugars until blended. Whisk in egg and vanilla extract. With wooden spoon, stir in flour mixture, then oats, chocolate chips, and walnuts until combined.

3. Spoon batter into center of prepared cookie sheet. With spatula, spread batter to form even 8-inch round. Bake 18 minutes, or until golden brown. Set sheet on wire rack to cool 15 minutes. Transfer to cutting board lined with waxed paper; cut into wedges and serve warm.

4. Store leftovers in airtight container up to 3 days, or freeze up to 3 months.

Each wedge: about 240 calories, 4g protein, 29g carbohydrate, 14g total fat (6g saturated), 2g fiber, 34mg cholesterol, 145mg sodium

TOP: HERMITS; BOTTOM: OATMEAL CHOCOLATE-CHIP COOKIE PIZZA

Sicilian Sesame Cookies

Here are cookies you can serve as a snack or any time of day, even early morning, because they're not too sweet.

Active time: 30 minutes
Bake time: 30 minutes per batch
Makes: about 48 cookies

2¼ cups all-purpose flour
2 teaspoons baking powder
¾ cup sugar
¼ teaspoon salt
3 large eggs, beaten
4 tablespoons butter or margarine, melted
1 teaspoon vanilla extract
1 cup sesame seeds (5 ounces), toasted and cooled
   (see page xxiii)

1. Preheat oven to 350°F.

2. In large bowl, stir together flour, baking powder, sugar, and salt. In small bowl, stir together eggs, melted butter, and vanilla. Add to flour mixture, stirring just until blended.

3. Transfer dough to lightly floured surface. With hands, knead dough 5 or 6 times until smooth. Divide dough in quarters. Roll 1 piece into 24-inch-long rope; with knife, cut into twelve 2-inch logs.

4. Fill small bowl with *water*, and place sesame seeds in second small bowl. Dip each log in water and roll in sesame seeds until completely covered. Place logs, 1 inch apart, on two ungreased large cookie sheets. Bake 30 to 35 minutes, until golden brown, rotating sheets between upper and lower oven racks halfway through. With wide metal spatula, transfer cookies to wire racks to cool completely. (Cookies will harden as they cool.) Repeat with remaining cookie dough and sesame seeds.

5. Store cookies in airtight container up to 1 week, or freeze up to 3 months.

Each cookie: about 65 calories, 2g protein, 9g carbohydrate, 3g total fat (1g saturated), 1g fiber, 16mg cholesterol, 45mg sodium

Raspberry Linzer Thumbprint Cookies

Our hazelnut drop cookies deliver all the flavor of traditional Austrian Linzer torte in a bite-size package. A food processor makes them a cinch to prepare. Raspberry jam is the classic filling, but you could use cherry, or any other jam.

Active time: 45 minutes
Bake time: 20 minutes per batch
Makes: about 48 cookies

1⅓ cups hazelnuts (6½ ounces)
½ cup sugar
¾ cup butter or margarine (1½ sticks), cut up
1 teaspoon vanilla extract
¼ teaspoon salt
1¾ cups all-purpose flour
¼ cup seedless red raspberry jam

1. Preheat oven to 350°F. Set aside ⅓ cup hazelnuts. Toast and skin remaining 1 cup hazelnuts (see page xxiii).

2. In food processor with knife blade attached, process toasted hazelnuts with sugar until nuts are finely ground. Add butter, vanilla, and salt and process until blended. Add flour and process until evenly combined. Remove knife blade and press dough together with hands.

3. Finely chop remaining ⅓ cup hazelnuts; spread on sheet of waxed paper. With hands, shape dough into 1-inch balls (dough may be slightly crumbly). Roll balls in nuts, gently pressing nuts onto dough. Place balls, about 1½ inches apart, on two ungreased large cookie sheets.

4. With thumb, make small indentation in center of each ball. Fill each indentation with ¼ teaspoon jam. Bake 20 minutes, or until lightly golden around edges, rotating cookie sheets between upper and lower oven racks halfway through. With wide metal spatula, transfer cookies to wire racks to cool completely. Repeat with remaining balls and jam.

5. Store cookies in airtight container up to 1 week, or freeze up to 3 months.

Each cookie: about 75 calories, 1g protein, 7g carbohydrate, 5g total fat (2g saturated), 1g fiber, 8mg cholesterol, 40mg sodium

Tiny Jewel Tartlets

Kids will love using their little fingers to make perfect thumbprints in these jammy buttons.

Active time: 50 minutes plus chilling
Bake time: 12 minutes per batch
Makes: about 144 miniature cookies

1 large egg yolk
1/2 teaspoon vanilla extract
11/2 cups all-purpose flour
1/2 cup sugar
1/4 teaspoon salt
1/2 teaspoon freshly grated lemon peel
3/4 cup cold butter (11/2 sticks), cut into small pieces
   (do not use margarine)
1/2 cup jam, such as raspberry, strawberry, or apricot

1. In small bowl, beat egg yolk and vanilla. In food processor, pulse flour, sugar, and salt to blend. Add lemon peel and butter and pulse until coarse crumbs form. With processor running, add yolk mixture. Pulse until large, moist clumps form.

2. Press dough together and pat into flat, 3/4-inch-thick square. Wrap tightly with plastic and refrigerate at least 2 hours and up to 3 days.

3. Unwrap dough and cut crosswise into 1/2-inch-wide strips, then cut lengthwise to form 1/2-inch squares. Let stand 15 minutes to soften. Line two cookie sheets with parchment paper.

4. Roll 1 dough piece into ball and place on prepared sheet. With finger or end of wooden spoon, make indentation in center. If dough cracks, roll again. Repeat with remaining pieces, spacing balls 1 inch apart on cookie sheets. Refrigerate 15 minutes or until dough is firm.

5. Preheat oven to 350°F. If jam has seeds or chunks, strain through fine-mesh sieve. Place in resealable plastic sandwich bag and snip tiny hole in one corner. Squeeze jam into indentations in all cookies.

6. Bake until golden brown, 12 to 15 minutes, rotating cookie sheets between upper and lower oven racks halfway through. Transfer cookies to wire racks to cool completely. Repeat with remaining dough and jam.

7. Store cookies in airtight container up to 1 week, or freeze up to 1 month.

Each cookie: about 20 calories, 0g protein, 2g carbohydrate, 1g total fat (1g saturated), 0g fiber, 4mg cholesterol, 5mg sodium

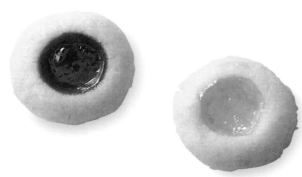

Walnut Cookie Balls

Walnut Cookie Balls

A traditional choice for the holiday cookie tray, we think these delicious mouthfuls ought to be enjoyed all year long.

Active time: 45 minutes
Bake time: 13 minutes per batch
Makes: about 78 cookies

1 cup butter (2 sticks), softened (do not use margarine)
6 tablespoons granulated sugar
1/2 teaspoon vanilla extract
2 cups all-purpose flour
1/8 teaspoon salt
2 cups walnuts (8 ounces), chopped
1 1/4 cups confectioners' sugar

1. Preheat oven to 325°F.

2. In large bowl, with mixer on medium speed, beat butter, granulated sugar, and vanilla until creamy, occasionally scraping bowl with rubber spatula. On low speed, gradually beat in flour and salt just until blended, continuing to scrape bowl occasionally. Stir in walnuts.

3. With hands, shape dough into 1-inch balls. Place balls, 1 inch apart, on two ungreased large cookie sheets. Bake until bottoms are lightly browned, 13 to 15 minutes, rotating cookie sheets between upper and lower oven racks halfway through.

4. Place confectioners' sugar in pie plate. While cookies are hot, with wide metal spatula, transfer 4 or 5 cookies at a time to plate with sugar. Gently turn cookies with fork to generously coat. Transfer to wire rack to cool completely. Repeat with remaining dough and confectioners' sugar.

5. Store cookies in airtight container, with waxed paper between layers, up to 1 week, or freeze up to 3 months.

Each cookie: about 65 calories, 1g protein, 6g carbohydrate, 4g total fat (2g saturated), 0g fiber, 7mg cholesterol, 30mg sodium

Mexican Wedding Cookies

These two-bite pastelitas de boda *may be made with almonds, walnuts, or toasted, skinned hazelnuts instead of pecans. The cookies should be rolled in confectioners' sugar twice: once while they're still slightly warm (so that the sugar sticks) and again after they've cooled, for a pristine, snowy finish.*

Active time: 25 minutes
Bake time: 20 minutes per batch
Makes: about 48 cookies

1 cup pecans (4 ounces)
1 3/4 cups confectioners' sugar
1 cup butter (2 sticks), cut into 16 pieces, softened (do not use margarine)
1 teaspoon vanilla extract
2 cups all-purpose flour

1. Preheat oven to 325°F.

2. In food processor with knife blade attached, pulse pecans and 1/4 cup sugar until nuts are finely chopped. Add butter and vanilla and pulse until smooth, scraping down sides of processor with rubber spatula. Add flour and process until ingredients are combined and dough holds together.

3. With floured hands, shape dough into 1-inch balls. Place balls, 1 1/2 inches apart, on two ungreased large cookie sheets. Bake 20 to 22 minutes, until bottoms are lightly browned and cookies are very light golden brown, rotating cookie sheets between upper and lower oven racks halfway through. With wide metal spatula, transfer to wire racks to cool.

4. Place remaining 1 1/2 cups sugar in pie plate. While cookies are still warm, roll in sugar until coated and place on wire racks to cool completely. When cool, reroll cookies in sugar until thoroughly coated. Repeat with remaining dough and confectioners' sugar.

5. Store cookies in airtight container, with waxed paper between layers, up to 1 week, or freeze up to 3 months.

Each cookie: about 85 calories, 1g protein, 9 carbohydrate, 5g total fat (3g saturated), 1g fiber, 10mg cholesterol, 40mg sodium

Four-Ingredient Palmiers

Palmiers (palm trees) are clever French pastries made by cutting slices from a doubly scrolled sheet of puff-pastry dough. Unlike the classic, which you'll find on page 329, this version uses a simple but rich sour-cream dough instead of puff pastry; just a quartet of ingredients required!

Active time: 35 minutes plus chilling
Bake time: 15 minutes per batch
Makes: about 72 cookies

1½ cups cold butter (3 sticks), cut up
  (do not use margarine)
3 cups all-purpose flour
¾ cup sour cream
1 cup sugar

1. In large bowl, with pastry blender or two knives used scissor-fashion, cut butter into flour until mixture resembles coarse crumbs. Stir in sour cream. On lightly floured surface, knead just until dough holds together. Flatten dough to 8" by 6" rectangle. Wrap in waxed paper and refrigerate until firm enough to roll, at least 2½ hours, or overnight.

2. Preheat oven to 400°F. Cut dough in half and return 1 piece to refrigerator. Place dough on work area and sprinkle ½ cup sugar on surface. With floured rolling pin, roll dough into 14-inch square. Using side of hand, make indentation down center of dough. Starting at one side, roll dough tightly up to indentation. Repeat with other side until second roll meets first in center, incorporating as much of sugar as possible into dough. Refrigerate scroll.

3. Repeat process with remaining chilled dough and ½ cup sugar. With serrated knife, cut scroll crosswise, into ¼-inch-thick slices. (Refrigerate scroll if too soft to slice.) Place slices, 2 inches apart, on ungreased cookie sheet. Bake 10 minutes. With wide metal spatula, carefully turn cookies over and bake 5 minutes longer, or until sugar has caramelized and cookies are deep golden. Cool on cookie sheet 1 minute. With wide metal spatula, transfer palmiers to wire racks to cool completely. Repeat with remaining scroll and sugar.

4. Store cookies in airtight container, with waxed paper between layers, up to 1 week, or freeze up to 3 months.

Each cookie: about 70 calories, 1g protein, 7g carbohydrate, 4g total fat (3g saturated), 0g fiber, 11mg cholesterol, 40mg sodium

Almond Tuiles

Gracefully arched French terra-cotta roof tiles—tuiles—inspired the curved shape of these cookies. If curling the cookies seems too time-consuming, serve them flat as wafers.

Active time: 30 minutes
Bake time: 5 minutes per batch
Makes: about 30 cookies

3 large egg whites
3/4 cup confectioners' sugar
1/2 cup all-purpose flour
6 tablespoons butter, melted (do not use margarine)
1/4 teaspoon salt
1/4 teaspoon almond extract
2/3 cup sliced natural almonds

1. Preheat oven to 350°F. Generously grease large cookie sheet.

2. In large bowl, with wire whisk, beat egg whites, sugar, and flour until blended and smooth. Beat in melted butter, salt, and almond extract.

3. Drop 1 heaping teaspoon batter on prepared cookie sheet. With back of spoon, as shown, spread batter in circular motion to make 3-inch round. Repeat to make 3 more rounds, about 3 inches apart. Bake only 4 rounds at a time because baked cookies must be shaped quickly before they harden. Sprinkle with sliced almonds, but do not allow almonds to overlap.

4. Bake 5 to 7 minutes, until edges are golden. With wide metal spatula, quickly remove cookies from cookie sheet and drape over rolling pin to create curved shape, as shown, before transferring to a wire rack to cool. (If you like, omit shaping cookies and cool flat.) Repeat with remaining batter and almonds. Batter will become slightly thicker upon standing.

5. Store cookies in airtight container up to 1 week, or freeze up to 1 month.

Each cookie: about 60 calories, 1g protein, 5g carbohydrate, 4g total fat (2g saturated), 0g fiber, 6mg cholesterol, 50mg sodium

TEST KITCHEN KNOW-HOW

SHAPING ALMOND TUILES

Working quickly, while the cookies are still hot is the key to shaping these pretty arched cookies, which pair perfectly with tea.

Using the back of a spoon, spread the batter into even 3-inch rounds on well-greased cookie sheet (batter will spread further during baking to fill in any thin areas).

While the cookies are still hot, carefully drape them over a rolling pin or other cylindrical object to create a curved shape. (If cookies become too hard to shape, return to oven briefly to soften.) When firm, transfer the tuiles to wire racks to cool completely before serving—or stacking and storing.

Tulipes

Tulipes are delicate cookies that are shaped like the blossom of a tulip, so they're perfect for filling with a scoop of sorbet.

Active time: 30 minutes plus cooling
Bake time: 5 minutes per batch
Makes: about 12 cookies

3 large egg whites
³/₄ cup confectioners' sugar
¹/₂ cup all-purpose flour
6 tablespoons butter, melted (do not use margarine)
¹/₂ teaspoon vanilla extract
¹/₄ teaspoon salt
1 quart sorbet or ice cream

1. Preheat oven to 350°F. Grease large cookie sheet.

2. In large bowl, with wire whisk, beat egg whites, sugar, and flour until blended and smooth. Beat in melted butter, vanilla, and salt.

3. Drop 1 heaping tablespoon batter on prepared cookie sheet. With small metal spatula or back of spoon, spread in circular motion to form 4-inch round. Repeat to make 2 cookies 4 inches apart on cookie sheet. Bake until edges are golden, 5 to 7 minutes.

4. Place two 2-inch-diameter glasses upside down on work surface. With wide metal spatula, quickly lift 1 hot cookie and gently drape over bottom of glass, then shape into bowl. Shape second cookie. When cool, transfer to wire rack. If cookies become too firm to shape, return pan to oven to soften cookies slightly.

5. Repeat steps 3 and 4 with remaining batter. (It will become thicker upon standing.) To serve, place tulipes on dessert plates and fill with scoop of sorbet.

6. Store unfilled tulipes in single layer in airtight container up to 1 week.

Each tulipe with sorbet: about 225 calories, 2g protein, 42g carbohydrate, 6g total fat (4g saturated), 2g fiber, 15mg cholesterol, 63mg sodium

Top: Tulipes; Bottom: Madeleines

Madeleines

These classic shell-shaped sponge cakes must be baked in a special pan, but they taste so good it's worth the investment. A madeleine pan can also be used as a candy or butter mold.

Active time: 25 minutes plus cooling
Bake time: 10 minute per batch
Makes: about 24 cookies

1 cup all-purpose flour
1/2 teaspoon baking powder
10 tablespoons butter, softened (do not use margarine)
3/4 cup sugar
3 large eggs
1 large egg yolk
1 1/2 teaspoons vanilla extract

1. Preheat oven to 400°F. Generously grease and flour madeleine pan. On sheet of waxed paper, mix flour and baking powder.

2. In large bowl, with mixer on medium speed, beat butter and sugar until creamy, about 2 minutes. Add eggs, egg yolk, and vanilla. Increase speed to high; beat until pale yellow, about 3 minutes. Reduce speed to low and beat in flour just until blended, scraping bowl with rubber spatula.

3. Spoon batter by rounded measuring tablespoons into prepared pan. Bake 10 to 12 minutes, until madeleines are browned at edges and tops spring back when lightly pressed. Let madeleines cool in pan 1 minute. With tip of table knife, release onto wire rack to cool completely.

4. Wash, grease, and flour pan. Repeat step 3 with remaining batter.

5. Store madeleines in airtight container, with waxed paper between layers, up to 2 days, or freeze up to 3 months.

Each cookie: about 105 calories, 2g protein, 11g carbohydrate, 6g total fat (3g saturated), 0g fiber, 48mg cholesterol, 65mg sodium

---

THE LITERARY COOKIE

Madeleines have associations that go well beyond your usual cookie. These small French sponge cakes, baked in a pan with shallow, shell-shaped cups, were made world-famous by Marcel Proust (1871–1922) in his four-volume novel, *Remembrance of Things Past*. The novel opens with the writer having madeleines with afternoon tea. The shape and flavor of the little cakes evoke long-forgotten events of his youth and life.

Pretzel Cookies

To give these clever cookies the look of salted pretzels, sprinkle them with coarse grains of pearl sugar, which remain crystalline, rather than melting, when baked. You can purchase this special decorating sugar at baking supply shops or online.

Active time: 20 minutes
Bake time: 25 minutes per batch
Makes: 20 pretzels

1/2 cup butter or margarine (1 stick), softened
1/3 cup granulated sugar
1 teaspoon freshly grated lemon or orange peel
1/4 teaspoon salt
1 large egg
2 large egg yolks
2 cups all-purpose flour
1/2 teaspoon water
Coarse or granulated sugar for sprinkling
2 ounces semisweet chocolate, melted (optional)

1. Preheat oven to 350°F.

2. In large bowl with mixer on medium speed, beat butter and granulated sugar until creamy. Add lemon or orange peel, salt, egg, and 1 egg yolk; beat until well blended. Add flour and beat until combined.

3. Gather dough into ball and knead on lightly floured surface. With hands, divide dough by heaping tablespoons into 20 pieces. Roll each piece into 11-inch-long rope. Shape each rope into loop-shaped pretzel (see Tip). Place pretzels, 1 inch apart, on two large ungreased cookie sheets.

4. In small cup, with fork, beat remaining egg yolk with water. Brush on pretzels. Sprinkle with coarse sugar. Bake 25 to 28 minutes, until golden brown, rotating cookie sheets between upper and lower oven racks halfway through. Cool on cookie sheets on wire racks 3 minutes. With wide metal spatula, transfer cookies to rack to cool completely. When cool, drizzle melted chocolate over cookies, if you like; let chocolate set before serving.

5. Store pretzels in airtight container, with waxed paper between layers, up to 1 week, or freeze up to 3 months.

Each pretzel: about 115 calories, 2g protein, 15g carbohydrate, 5g total fat (3g saturated), 1g fiber, 44mg cholesterol, 80mg sodium

TIP To form a pretzel shape, form each rope of dough into an open loop. Then cross the ends and rest each one on the bottom of the loop; press ends lightly to seal.

Chocolate Pretzel Cookies

Making these pretzel-shaped treats is a perfect project for kids and parents. Decorating them with colored sprinkles adds to the fun.

Active time: 1 hour
Bake time: 15 minutes per batch
Makes: 36 pretzels

2 cups all-purpose flour
1/3 cup unsweetened cocoa
2 teaspoons baking powder
1/2 teaspoon salt
3/4 cup butter or margarine (1 1/2 sticks), softened
3/4 cup sugar
1 large egg
1 teaspoon vanilla extract
Assorted sprinkles

1. Preheat oven to 350°F. In medium bowl, combine flour, cocoa, baking powder, and salt.

2. In large bowl, with mixer on medium speed, beat butter and sugar until creamy. Beat in egg and vanilla until well blended. At low speed, beat in flour mixture just until blended, occasionally scraping bowl with rubber spatula.

3. Divide dough in half. Wrap 1 piece in plastic. Place sprinkles in pie plate.

4. Working with unwrapped portion of dough, on unfloured work surface, with hands, break dough into 18 equal pieces and shape into 9-inch-long ropes. Shape each rope into loop-shaped pretzel (see Tip, opposite). Gently press pretzels, top side down, into sprinkles. Place pretzels, decorated side up, 1/2 inch apart, on two ungreased large cookie sheets.

5. Bake until bottoms are lightly browned, about 15 minutes, rotating cookie sheets between upper and lower oven racks halfway through. With wide metal spatula, transfer pretzels to wire racks to cool completely. Repeat with remaining piece of dough.

6. Store pretzels in airtight container, with waxed paper between layers, up to 1 week, or freeze up to 3 months.

Each pretzel: about 80 calories, 1g protein, 10g carbohydrate, 4g total fat (3g saturated), 1g fiber, 16mg cholesterol, 93mg sodium

ROLLED COOKIES

Once you roll out these doughs, you're on your way to lots of different kinds of cookies. Cookie cutters are one option, or try freehand shaping. Rolled dough can also go three-dimensional: Form it into tiny jam-filled crescents or fold it into fruit-filled triangular pastries.

Classic Sugar Cookies

Here's the perfect, all-purpose sugar cookie dough. You can slice it into diamonds with a knife and sprinkle it with colored sugar, or cut it into shapes with cookie cutters and decorate it with frosting.

Active time: 1 hour 30 minutes plus chilling
Bake time: 12 minutes per batch
Makes: about 76 cookies

3 cups all-purpose flour
1/2 teaspoon baking powder
1/2 teaspoon salt
1 cup butter (2 sticks), softened (do not use margarine)
1 1/2 cups sugar
2 large eggs
1 teaspoon vanilla extract
Ornamental Frosting (optional, page 343)

1. In medium bowl, stir together flour, baking powder, and salt.

2. In large bowl, with mixer on low speed, beat butter and sugar until blended. Increase speed to high; beat until light and fluffy, about 5 minutes. Reduce speed to low; beat in eggs and vanilla until mixed, then beat in flour mixture just until blended, occasionally scraping bowl with rubber spatula. Divide dough into 4 equal pieces; flatten each into disk. Wrap each disk in plastic and refrigerate overnight. (Or, to make ahead, wrap each disk in a double layer of plastic and freeze up to 3 months.)

3. Preheat oven to 350°F. Remove 1 piece dough from refrigerator. On lightly floured surface, with floured rolling pin, roll dough until slightly less than 1/4 inch thick. (Or, for easier cleanup, roll out the dough between sheets of floured waxed paper.) With floured 3- to 4-inch cookie cutters, cut dough into as many cookies as possible; reserve trimmings (see Tip). Place cookies, 1 inch apart, on two ungreased large cookie sheets.

4. Bake until edges are golden, 12 to 15 minutes, rotating cookie sheets between upper and lower oven racks halfway through. With wide metal spatula, transfer cookies to wire racks to cool completely. Decorate with Ornamental Frosting, if desired. Repeat, using remaining dough and trimmings to form cookies.

5. Store cookies in airtight container, with waxed paper between layers, up to 2 weeks, or freeze up to 3 months.

Each cookie: about 60 calories, 1g protein, 8g carbohydrate, 3g total fat (2g saturated), 0g fiber, 13mg cholesterol, 47mg sodium

TIP To get the most out of your dough, cut out cookies as close together as possible—you want as little dough as possible left over for rerolling. Overhandling dough can make it tough.

Sour Cream Cutouts

A sprinkle of sugar makes these cookies sparkle. When you reroll the trimmings, press the pieces together to make a flattened rectangle rather than kneading them together—the cookies will be more tender.

Active time: 35 minutes plus chilling
Bake time: 8 minutes per batch
Makes: about 78 cookies

1³/4 cups all-purpose flour
¹/2 teaspoon baking soda
¹/4 teaspoon salt
¹/2 cup butter or margarine (1 stick), softened
1 cup sugar plus additional for sprinkling
1 large egg
1 teaspoon vanilla extract
¹/2 cup sour cream

1. On sheet of waxed paper, stir together flour, baking soda, and salt

2. In large bowl, with mixer on medium speed, beat butter and 1 cup sugar until combined. Reduce speed to low and beat in egg and vanilla until blended. Beat in sour cream. Beat in flour mixture until combined, scraping bowl occasionally with rubber spatula. Shape dough into 4 balls; flatten each slightly. Wrap each ball in waxed paper and refrigerate until firm enough to roll, at least 2 hours or overnight. (If using margarine, refrigerate overnight.)

3. Preheat oven to 350°F. Remove 1 piece dough from refrigerator. On lightly floured surface, with floured rolling pin, roll dough ¹/8 inch thick. With floured 2-inch cookie cutters, cut as many cookies as possible; reserve trimmings. Place cookies about 1¹/2 inches apart on two ungreased large cookie sheets. Sprinkle lightly with sugar. Bake 8 minutes, rotating cookie sheets between upper and lower oven racks halfway through. With wide metal spatula, transfer cookies to wire racks to cool completely. Repeat to form cookies from remaining dough, trimmings, and sugar.

4. Store cookies in airtight container up to 1 week, or freeze up to 3 months.

Each cookie: about 35 calories, 0g protein, 5g carbohydrate, 2g total fat (1g saturated), 0g fiber, 7mg cholesterol, 30mg sodium

ROLLING AND CUTTING OUT SUGAR COOKIES

This favorite holiday activity takes time. Plan ahead and enlist the kids or some friends to join in the fun.

Form the well-chilled dough into a disk. Lightly flour the rolling pin and your work surface, then roll the dough to less than a ¼-inch thickness.

Use cookie cutters to cut out the cookies (simple shapes will be most successful). Reroll the scraps and repeat.

Transfer the cookies to a cookie sheet and decorate with colored sugar before baking, if you like. Or frost the cookies once they are completely cool.

Fig Crescents

These little fruit- and nut-filled cookies are a delightful holiday treat.

Active time: 1 hour 15 minutes plus chilling
Bake time: 15 minutes per batch
Makes: about 66 cookies

COOKIE DOUGH

2 3/4 cups all-purpose flour
1/2 teaspoon salt
1/4 teaspoon baking soda
2 large eggs
1 cup granulated sugar
1/2 cup butter or margarine (1 stick), softened
2 tablespoons heavy cream
1 teaspoon vanilla extract

FILLING

1 large orange
3/4 cup dried Mission figs (5 ounces), stems removed
1/2 cup (2 ounces) walnuts
1/4 cup dark seedless raisins
1/4 cup honey
1 1/2 teaspoons ground cinnamon

1 large egg, whisked
1/4 cup white decorating sugar

1. Prepare dough: On waxed paper, combine flour, salt, and baking soda.

2. In large bowl, with mixer on medium speed, beat eggs, sugar, and butter 2 minutes or until creamy, occasionally scraping bowl. Beat in cream and vanilla until mixed. Reduce speed to low; gradually beat in flour mixture just until blended, occasionally scraping bowl. Divide dough into 4 equal pieces; flatten each into disk. Wrap each disk in plastic; refrigerate at least 2 hours or up to 3 days.

3. Meanwhile, prepare filling: From orange, finely grate 1/2 teaspoon peel and squeeze 3 tablespoons juice. In food processor, pulse orange peel and juice, figs, walnuts, raisins, honey, and cinnamon until coarsely ground.

4. Preheat oven to 350°F. Grease two large cookie sheets. In cup, with fork, lightly beat egg.

5. Remove 1 disk dough from refrigerator. On lightly floured surface, with floured rolling pin, roll dough 1/8 inch thick. With floured 2 1/2-inch fluted round biscuit or cookie cutter, cut out as many cookies as possible. Wrap and reserve trimmings in refrigerator. With spatula, carefully place dough rounds 1 inch apart on prepared sheets. Spoon 1 level teaspoon filling onto 1 side of each dough round. Fold dough in half over filling. Gently press edges to seal. Lightly brush crescents with egg; sprinkle with decorating sugar.

6. Bake 15 to 16 minutes or until tops are golden brown, rotating cookie sheets between upper and lower oven racks halfway through. Transfer to wire racks to cool. Repeat with remaining dough and trimmings, filling, egg, and decorating sugar.

7. Store cookies in airtight container up to 2 weeks, or freeze up to 3 months.

Each cookie: about 70 calories, 1g protein, 11g carbohydrate, 2g total fat (1g saturated), 1g fiber, 13mg cholesterol, 25mg sodium

Gingerbread Cutouts

The warm flavors of molasses, cloves, and ginger meld in these classic holiday cookies. Bring the family together to decorate them with frosting and colored sugar.

Active time: 35 minutes plus chilling
Bake time: 10 minutes per batch
Makes: about 24 cookies

3¼ cups all-purpose flour
2 teaspoons ground ginger
1 teaspoon baking soda
1 teaspoon ground cinnamon
1/2 teaspoon ground nutmeg
1/4 teaspoon ground cloves
1/4 teaspoon salt
3/4 cup butter (1½ sticks), softened (do not use margarine)
3/4 cup sugar
1/2 cup unsulfured molasses
1 large egg
Ornamental Frosting (optional, page 343)
Sanding sugar, for decorating (optional)

1. In medium bowl, whisk flour, ginger, baking soda, cinnamon, nutmeg, cloves, and salt.

2. In large bowl, with mixer on medium speed, beat butter and sugar until creamy. Beat in molasses and egg until well blended, scraping side of bowl occasionally. Beat in flour mixture until combined. Divide dough into 3 equal pieces. Place each portion between two large sheets of waxed paper. With rolling pin, roll dough to 1/3-inch thickness. Refrigerate, on cookie sheet, until firm and cold, at least 2 hours.

3. Preheat oven to 350°F. Remove 1 piece dough from refrigerator; remove waxed paper and place dough on lightly floured surface. With floured 3- to 4-inch cookie cutters, cut out as many cookies as possible. Place cookies 1 inch apart on ungreased cookie sheet.

4. Bake 10 to 12 minutes or until set and just slightly darker at edges. Cool on cookie sheets on wire rack 1 minute. With wide metal spatula, transfer cookies to racks to cool completely. Repeat with remaining dough pieces, continuing to reserve trimmings. Gather all trimmings together, then roll and chill as described above to make as many cookies as possible.

5. When cookies are cool, use Ornamental Frosting and sanding sugar to decorate cookies if desired. Allow frosting to dry completely, about 1 hour, before serving or storing. Store cookies in airtight container (with waxed paper between layers, if decorated) up to 2 weeks, or freeze up to 3 months.

Each cookie: about 160 calories, 2g protein, 24g carbohydrate, 6g total fat (4g saturated), 1g fiber, 23mg cholesterol, 135mg sodium

Classic Rugelach

A specialty of Jewish bakeries (and Jewish grandmothers), rugelach are cookie-size rolled pastries. The dough may be prepared days or weeks ahead of time and frozen; you can also shape the rugelach in advance and refrigerate or freeze them. Bake without thawing.

Active time: 1 hour plus chilling
Bake time: 30 minutes
Makes: about 48 rugelach

DOUGH

1 cup butter or margarine (2 sticks), softened
1 package (8 ounces) cream cheese, softened
1 tablespoon sugar
1 teaspoon vanilla extract
1 teaspoon freshly grated orange peel (optional)
2 cups all-purpose flour

RUGELACH ASSEMBLY

1¹/2 teaspoons ground cinnamon
¹/2 cup sugar
8 teaspoons butter, melted
1 cup walnuts (4 ounces), chopped
1 cup dried currants
1 large egg yolk
1 tablespoon water

1. To make dough, in large bowl, with mixer on low speed, beat butter and cream cheese until blended and smooth. Beat in sugar, vanilla, and orange peel, if using. Beat in flour until blended. Divide dough into 4 equal pieces. Wrap each piece in waxed paper and refrigerate until firm, at least 2 hours or overnight. (If using margarine, freeze overnight.)

2. Preheat oven to 325°F. Line two large cookie sheets with foil; grease foil. When ready to assemble pastries, in small bowl, stir together cinnamon and sugar.

3. On lightly floured surface, with floured rolling pin, roll 1 piece chilled dough into 10½-inch round; keep remaining dough refrigerated. Brush dough with 2 teaspoons melted butter. Sprinkle generous

2 tablespoons cinnamon sugar over dough. Sprinkle one-fourth of nuts and one-fourth of currants over top; gently press filling onto dough.

4. With pastry wheel or sharp knife, cut dough into 12 wedges (see box, below). Starting at curved edge, roll up each wedge jelly-roll fashion. Place, point-side down, about ½ inch apart, on prepared cookie sheets. Repeat with remaining dough, melted butter, and fillings.

5. In cup, stir together egg yolk and water. Lightly brush mixture over rugelach. Bake about 30 minutes, or until golden, rotating cookie sheets between upper and lower oven racks halfway through. Immediately transfer rugelach to wire racks to cool.

6. Store rugelach in airtight container, with waxed paper between layers, up to 1 week, or freeze up to 3 months.

Each rugelach: about 110 calories, 1g protein, 9g carbohydrate, 8g total fat (4g saturated), 1g fiber, 22mg cholesterol, 60mg sodium

FORMING RUGELACH

These little pastries take some time to shape, but are well worth the effort.

Spread the dough with butter and sprinkle on the fillings. Cut the round into wedges and roll each one up, starting from the wide end.

Whole-Wheat Sugar Cookies

Using white whole-wheat flour adds healthy whole-grain goodness to this low-fat take on a classic. For a dressed-up variation, try the Linzer Jewels, pictured below.

Active time: 1 hour plus chilling • Bake time: 10 minutes per batch • Makes: about 72 cookies

1 cup all-purpose flour
1 cup white whole-wheat flour (see page xx)
½ teaspoon baking powder
¼ teaspoon salt
1 cup sugar

½ cup trans-fat-free vegetable oil spread (60% to 70% oil)
1 large egg
2 teaspoons vanilla extract

1. On sheet of waxed paper, combine both flours, baking powder, and salt.

2. In large bowl, with mixer on low speed, beat sugar and vegetable oil spread until blended. Increase speed to high; beat until light and creamy, about 3 minutes, occasionally scraping down bowl with rubber spatula. Reduce speed to low; beat in egg and vanilla, then beat in flour mixture just until blended.

3. Divide dough in half; flatten each half into a disk. Wrap each disk with plastic and refrigerate until dough is firm enough to roll, about 2 hours.

4. Preheat oven to 375°F.

5. Remove 1 piece dough from refrigerator. On lightly floured surface, with floured rolling pin, roll dough ⅛ inch thick. With 2-inch cookie cutters, cut out as many cookies as possible; wrap and refrigerate trimmings. With lightly floured spatula, place cookies 1 inch apart on two ungreased cookie sheets.

6. Bake cookies until lightly browned, 10 to 12 minutes, rotating cookie sheets between upper and lower oven racks halfway through. With wide metal spatula, transfer cookies to wire racks to cool completely. Repeat with remaining dough and dough trimmings.

7. Store cookies in airtight container up to 5 days, or freeze up to 3 months.

Each cookie: about 35 calories, 1g protein, 5g carbohydrate, 1g total fat (0g saturated), 0g fiber, 3mg cholesterol, 20mg sodium

BERRY-ORANGE LINZER JEWELS Prepare cookies as directed, but in step 2, add *1 teaspoon grated orange peel* with egg and vanilla. Chill, roll, and cut as above in steps 3 and 5, but use scalloped 2-inch square or round cookie cutter. Use small star-shaped or other decorative cutter to cut out centers of half the cookies. Bake and cool as above in step 6. When cookies are cool, if you like, sift *confectioners' sugar* through sieve over cookies with cutout centers. Using *¼ cup seedless red raspberry jam*, spread scant ½ teaspoon jam on each whole cookie; top with cookie with cutout center. Makes about 36 sandwich cookies.

Each sandwich cookie: about 70 calories, 2g protein, 10g carbohydrate, 2g total fat (0g saturated), 0g fiber, 6mg cholesterol, 40mg sodium

Pinwheels

You'll be surprised at how easy it is to shape these festive cookies. For more variety in both flavor and color, try using several different kinds of jam.

Active time: 35 minutes plus chilling
Bake time: 9 minutes per batch
Makes: 24 cookies

1⅓ cups all-purpose flour
¼ teaspoon baking powder
⅛ teaspoon salt
6 tablespoons butter or margarine, softened
½ cup sugar
1 large egg
1 teaspoon vanilla extract
¼ cup damson plum, seedless raspberry, or other jam

1. On sheet of waxed paper, stir together flour, baking powder, and salt.

2. In large bowl, with mixer on medium speed, beat butter and sugar until light and fluffy. Beat in egg and vanilla until well combined. Reduce speed to low and beat in flour mixture until combined. Divide dough in half, wrap each half in waxed paper, and refrigerate at least 1 hour, or overnight. (If using margarine, freeze overnight.)

3. Preheat oven to 375°F. Remove 1 piece dough from refrigerator. On floured surface, with floured rolling pin, roll dough into 10" by 7½" rectangle. With jagged-edged pastry wheel or sharp knife, cut rectangle lengthwise into 4 strips, then cut each strip into 3 squares. Arrange squares 1 inch apart on two ungreased large cookie sheets. On each square, use small sharp knife to make 1½-inch cut from each corner toward center. Spoon ½ teaspoon jam in center of each square. Fold every other tip into center to form pinwheel.

4. Bake 9 minutes, or until lightly browned around edges and set, rotating cookie sheets between upper and lower oven racks halfway through. With wide metal spatula, transfer cookies to wire racks to cool completely. Repeat with remaining dough and jam.

5. Store cookies in airtight container, with waxed paper between layers, up to 3 days, or freeze up to 3 months.

Each cookie: about 80 calories, 1g protein, 12g carbohydrate, 3g total fat (2g saturated), 0g fiber, 17mg cholesterol, 50mg sodium

Best Linzer Cookies

A half pound of pecans goes into these tartlike treats filled with raspberry jam.

Active time: 1 hour plus chilling
Bake time: 17 minutes per batch
Makes: about 48 cookies

2 cups pecans (8 ounces)
1/2 cup cornstarch
1 1/2 cups butter (3 sticks), softened (do not use margarine)
1 1/3 cups confectioners' sugar
2 teaspoons vanilla extract
3/4 teaspoon salt
1 large egg
2 3/4 cups all-purpose flour
3/4 cup seedless red raspberry jam

1. In food processor with knife blade attached, pulse pecans and cornstarch until pecans are finely ground.

2. In large bowl, with mixer on low speed, beat butter and 1 cup confectioners' sugar until mixed. Increase speed to high; beat 2 minutes or until light and fluffy, occasionally scraping bowl with rubber spatula. At medium speed, beat in vanilla, salt, and egg. Reduce speed to low; gradually beat in flour and pecan mixture just until blended, occasionally scraping bowl.

3. Divide dough into 4 equal pieces; flatten each into disk. Wrap each disk with plastic and refrigerate 4 to 5 hours or until dough is firm enough to roll.

4. Preheat oven to 325°F. Remove 1 disk dough from refrigerator; if necessary, let stand 10 to 15 minutes at room temperature for easier rolling. On lightly floured surface, with floured rolling pin, roll dough 1/8 inch thick. With floured 2 1/4-inch fluted round, plain round, or holiday-shaped cookie cutter, cut dough into as many cookies as possible. Change to floured 1- to 1 1/4-inch cutter of same shape as larger cutter, and cut out centers from half of cookies. Collect small center pieces along with other dough trimmings to reroll; wrap and return to refrigerator. With lightly floured spatula, carefully place cookies, 1 inch apart, on two ungreased large cookie sheets.

5. Bake cookies until edges are lightly browned, 17 to 20 minutes, rotating cookie sheets between upper and lower oven racks halfway through. Using wide metal spatula, transfer cookies to wire racks to cool. Repeat with remaining dough and trimmings.

6. When cookies are cool, sprinkle remaining 1/3 cup confectioners' sugar through sieve over cookies with cut-out centers.

7. In small bowl, stir jam with fork until smooth. Spread scant measuring teaspoon jam on surface of whole cookies; place cut-out cookies on top.

8. Store cookies in airtight container, with waxed paper between layers, up to 3 days, or freeze up to 3 months.

Each cookie: about 115 calories, 16g protein, 11g carbohydrate, 8g total fat (3g saturated), 1g fiber, 17mg cholesterol, 80mg sodium

PRESSED & PIPED COOKIES

You could call these methods elaborations on the drop cookie—the dough is placed on the sheet by piping it through a pastry bag tip or "extruding" it through the decorative plates of a cookie press. Cookie-press dough is very buttery yet firm so that it neither crumbles nor runs when spritzed onto the baking sheet. Soft, almost batterlike doughs based on almond paste or meringue are better suited for piping with a pastry bag.

Almond Macaroon Fingers
It's hard to believe that cookies as chewy and rich as our chocolate-brushed macaroons are also low in fat, but it's the truth.

Active time: 1 hour 30 minutes
Bake time: 17 minutes per batch
Makes: about 42 cookies

1 can (7 to 8 ounces) almond paste
1/2 cup confectioners' sugar
2 large egg whites
1/2 teaspoon vanilla extract
2 ounces bittersweet or semisweet chocolate,
    broken into pieces

1. Preheat oven to 300°F. Line two cookie sheets with parchment paper.

2. In food processor with knife blade attached, process almond paste and sugar until only occasional small lumps remain. Add egg whites and vanilla; pulse until well combined.

3. Spoon batter into decorating bag fitted with 1/2-inch star tip. Pipe batter into 3-inch-long fingers, 1 inch apart, onto prepared cookie sheets.

4. Bake until edges start to turn golden brown, 17 to 19 minutes, rotating cookie sheets between upper and lower oven racks halfway through. Set cookie sheets on wire racks to cool. Repeat with remaining batter.

5. In microwave-safe cup, microwave chocolate on High until soft and shiny, 1 minute (see page xvi). Stir until smooth. With pastry brush, brush chocolate on half of each macaroon; let set. Or refrigerate 5 minutes to set chocolate. Peel cookies from parchment.

6. Store cookies in airtight container, with waxed paper between layers, up to 3 days, or freeze up to 3 months.

Each cookie: about 30 calories, 1g protein, 5g carbohydrate, 1g total fat (0g saturated), 0g fiber, 18mg cholesterol, 11mg sodium

Christmas Macarons

Bittersweet chocolate is sandwiched between crisp macaroons, festively colored for the holidays.

Active time: 25 minutes plus standing and cooling
Bake time: 18 minutes per batch
Makes: about 36 sandwich cookies

1 cup slivered almonds (4 ounces)
2 cups lightly packed confectioners' sugar
3 large egg whites, at room temperature
¼ teaspoon salt
7 drops green liquid food coloring
¼ teaspoon almond extract
4 ounces bittersweet chocolate, melted

1. Preheat oven to 300°F. Line two large cookie sheets with parchment paper.

2. In food processor with knife blade attached, process almonds and 1 cup sugar until finely ground and powdery, occasionally scraping bowl with rubber spatula. Add remaining sugar; pulse until combined. Transfer to large bowl.

3. In bowl of stand mixer, with mixer on medium speed, beat egg whites and salt until soft peaks form. Beat in food coloring and almond extract. Increase speed to high and beat just until stiff (but not dry) peaks form when beaters are lifted (see page 235). With rubber spatula, fold egg whites into almond mixture until blended. Batter will be just pourable and sticky.

4. Transfer batter to pastry bag fitted with ½-inch round tip. Holding bag about ½ inch above parchment, pipe 1-inch rounds spaced 1½ inches apart (batter will spread). Let stand 20 minutes.

5. Bake, one cookie sheet at a time, 18 to 19 minutes or until bubbles that form around bases of macarons are firm to touch but tops are not browned. Cool on wire rack. Repeat with second cookie sheet.

6. When cookies are cool, spread chocolate on bottoms of half of macarons, using about ½ teaspoon for each. Top each with another macaron, bottom side down. Let stand until chocolate hardens, about 45 minutes.

7. Store cookies in airtight container, with waxed paper between layers, up to 3 days, or freeze up to 1 month.

Each cookie: about 60 calories, 1g protein, 9g carbohydrate, 3g total fat (1g saturated), 1g fiber, 0mg cholesterol, 20mg sodium

MACAROONS VERSUS MACARONS

Chewy sweet lumps of toasty shredded coconut or vibrantly colored meringue-like cookie sandwiches? Although the ingredients used to make these two cookies are basically the same—egg whites, sugar, and coconut or almonds—their looks and textures are worlds apart.

Macaroons trace their origins to Italy, where the flourless, unleavened cookies were originally made with almond paste. A version that swapped shredded coconut for the almond paste became popular with the European Jewish community (the unleavened cookies made a perfect Passover treat). A crispy, meringue-like version made with ground almonds (called *macarons* in French) was developed by the chefs of Catherine de Medici, the French king's Italian wife. We provide recipes for both cookies here and on pages 12 to 13.

SPRITZ COOKIES

Spritz Cookies

Making these molded favorites is easy with one of the new cookie presses, which offer patterns for every season.

Active time: 35 minutes
Bake time: 10 minutes per batch
Makes: about 66 cookies

2¼ cups all-purpose flour
½ teaspoon baking powder
½ teaspoon salt
1 cup butter or margarine (2 sticks), softened
½ cup sugar
1 large egg
1 teaspoon vanilla extract
1 teaspoon almond extract
Candy décors (optional)
Ornamental Frosting (page 343, optional)

1. Preheat oven to 350°F. Place two large cookie sheets in freezer.

2. On waxed paper, combine flour, baking powder, and salt. In large bowl, with mixer on medium speed, beat butter and sugar until pale and creamy. Beat in egg, then beat in both extracts. With mixer on low speed, gradually add flour mixture. Beat just until blended.

3. Spoon one-third of dough into cookie press or large decorating bag fitted with large star tip. Onto chilled cookie sheets, press or pipe dough as desired, spacing 2 inches apart. Sprinkle with décors, if using.

4. Bake until lightly browned around edges, 10 to 12 minutes, rotating cookie sheets between upper and lower oven racks halfway through. Place cookie sheets on wire racks to cool 2 minutes. Using wide metal spatula, transfer cookies to racks to cool completely. Rechill cookie sheets and repeat with remaining dough.

5. Decorate cookies with Ornamental Frosting, if desired. Set aside to allow frosting to dry. Store cookies in airtight container up to 1 week, or freeze up to 1 month.

Each cookie: about 50 calories, 1g protein, 5g carbohydrate, 3g total fat (2g saturated), 0g fiber, 10mg cholesterol, 20mg sodium

Pignoli Cookies

Thanks to the food processor—and prepared almond paste—making these classic Italian cookies, with their topping of pine nuts (or pignoli), is a breeze. To keep your fingers from getting sticky, use a pastry bag to form the rounds.

Active time: 25 minutes
Bake time: 10 minutes per batch
Makes: about 24 cookies

1 tube or can (7 to 8 ounces) almond paste
¾ cup confectioners' sugar
1 large egg white
4 teaspoons honey
½ cup pine nuts (3 ounces)

1. Preheat oven to 350°F. Line two large cookie sheets with parchment paper.

2. Crumble almond paste into food processor with knife blade attached. Add sugar and process until paste is texture of fine meal. Transfer to large bowl. Add egg white and honey. With mixer on low speed, beat until blended. Increase speed to medium-high and beat 5 minutes, or until very smooth.

3. Spoon batter into pastry bag fitted with ½-inch round tip. Pipe ¼-inch rounds, 2 inches apart, on prepared cookie sheets. Brush cookies lightly with *water* and cover completely with pine nuts, pressing lightly to make nuts stick.

4. Bake 10 to 12 minutes, until golden brown, rotating cookie sheets between upper and lower oven racks halfway through. Slide parchment paper onto wire racks and let cookies cool on parchment. Repeat with remaining dough and pine nuts.

5. Store cookies in airtight container up to 5 days, or freeze up to 3 months.

Each cookie: about 75 calories, 2g protein, 9g carbohydrate, 4g total fat (0g saturated), 1g fiber, 0mg cholesterol, 5mg sodium

Peppermint Meringues

Peppermint flavoring (and a little food coloring) lends these melt-in-your-mouth puffs a holiday flair. Don't use peppermint extract that contains peppermint oil—the meringues will quickly deflate. For these cookies, choose imitation peppermint extract instead.

Active time: 1 hour plus standing
Bake time: 2 hours
Makes: about 12 cookies

4 large egg whites
¼ teaspoon cream of tartar
1 cup confectioners' sugar
¼ teaspoon imitation peppermint extract
Red and green food coloring

1. Preheat oven to 225°F. Line two large cookie sheets with foil.

2. In small bowl, with mixer on high speed, beat egg whites and cream of tartar until soft peaks form; gradually sprinkle in sugar, beating until whites stand in stiff, glossy peaks (see page 235). Beat in peppermint extract.

3. Transfer half of meringue mixture to another bowl. Using food colorings, tint meringue in one bowl pale red and meringue in other bowl pale green.

4. Spoon red meringue into large resealable plastic bag, cut ¼-inch opening at corner. Repeat with green meringue in second bag. Fit large pastry bag (we used a 14-inch bag) with basket-weave or large round tip (½- or ¾-inch-diameter opening). Place pastry bag in 2-cup glass measuring cup to stabilize bag, fold top third of bag over top of cup. Simultaneously squeeze meringues from both resealable bags into pastry bag, filling it no more than two-thirds full.

5. Pipe meringue onto cookie sheets, leaving 1 inch between each meringue. If using basket-weave tip, pipe meringue into 3- to 4-inch-long pleated ribbons; if using round tip, pipe meringue into 2-inch rounds. Bake meringues 2 hours, carefully rotating cookie sheets between upper and lower oven racks halfway through. Turn oven off. Leave meringues in oven at least 30 minutes or overnight to dry.

6. When dry, remove meringues from foil with wide metal spatula. Store in airtight container, with waxed paper between layers, up to 3 weeks.

Each cookie: about 10 calories, 0g protein, 2g carbohydrate, 0g total fat (0g saturated), 0g fiber, 0mg cholesterol, 5mg sodium

Meringue Fingers

For a whimsical touch, we've half-dipped these piped cookies into melted semisweet chocolate.

Active time: 25 minutes plus cooling
Bake time: 1 hour
Makes: about 48 cookies

3 large egg whites
1/4 teaspoon cream of tartar
1/8 teaspoon salt
1/2 cup sugar
1 teaspoon pure vanilla extract
2 squares (2 ounces) semisweet chocolate
1 teaspoon vegetable shortening

1. Preheat oven to 200°F. Line two large cookie sheets with foil.

2. In small bowl, with mixer on high speed, beat egg whites, cream of tartar, and salt until soft peaks form when beaters are lifted. Increase speed to high and gradually sprinkle in sugar, 2 tablespoons at a time, beating until dissolved. Add vanilla; continue beating until meringue stands in stiff, glossy peaks when beaters are lifted (see page 235).

3. Spoon meringue into pastry bag fitted with 1/2-inch star tip. Pipe meringue into 3" by 1/2" fingers, about 1 inch apart, on prepared cookie sheets.

4. Bake meringues 1 hour, or until set, rotating cookie sheets between upper and lower oven racks halfway through. Set cookie sheets on wire racks to cool 10 minutes. With small spatula, transfer meringues to racks to cool completely.

5. When meringues have cooled, in small saucepan, heat chocolate and shortening over low heat, stirring occasionally, until melted and smooth. Remove saucepan from heat. Dip one end of each meringue into melted chocolate; let dry on wire racks.

6. Store meringues in airtight container, with waxed paper between layers, up to 1 week, or freeze up to 3 months.

Each cookie: about 15 calories, 0g protein, 3g carbohydrate, 0g total fat (0g saturated), 0g fiber, 0mg cholesterol, 10mg sodium

Lemon Meringue Drops

These melt-in-your-mouth meringues are both crunchy and cloud-light—and require only five ingredients. Bonus: Meringue is naturally gluten-free! Just be sure to chose a gluten-free cream of tartar, such as McCormick, Spice Islands, or Durkee brands.

Active time: 45 minutes plus standing
Bake time: 1 hour 30 minutes
Makes: about 60 cookies

3 large egg whites
1/4 teaspoon cream of tartar
1/8 teaspoon salt
1/2 cup sugar
2 teaspoons freshly grated lemon peel

1. Preheat oven to 200°F. Line two large cookie sheets with parchment paper.

2. In medium bowl, with mixer on high speed, beat egg whites, cream of tartar, and salt until soft peaks form. With mixer running, sprinkle in sugar, 2 tablespoons at a time, beating until sugar dissolves and meringue stands in stiff, glossy peaks when beaters are lifted (see page 235). Gently fold in lemon peel.

3. Spoon meringue into decorating bag fitted with 1/2-inch star tip. Pipe meringue into 1 1/2-inch stars, about 1 inch apart, on prepared cookie sheets.

4. Bake meringues until crisp but not brown, 1 hour 30 minutes, rotating cookie sheets between upper and lower oven racks halfway through. Turn oven off; leave meringues in oven until dry, 1 hour.

5. Remove meringues from oven and cool completely. Remove from parchment with wide metal spatula.

6. Store meringues in airtight container up to 1 month, or freeze up to 3 months.

Each meringue: about 5 calories, 0g protein, 2g carbohydrate, 0g total fat (0g saturated), 0g fiber, 0mg cholesterol, 10mg sodium

Brownies & Bars

Brownies 53

Blondies 61

Shortbread 66

Fruit & Nut Bars 69

BROWNIES

Baking brownies is easy and fun—and yields deliciously chocolaty results. Invite the kids to help. It's a great way to teach them the baking basics: measuring accurately, mixing and combining the wet and dry ingredients, and maybe the hardest skill of all—patience.

Cocoa Brownies with Mini Chocolate Chips

We like to cool these treats before serving, because they are too soft to cut when warm. But if the kids (and you) are swooning from the aroma and can't wait to dig in, let them cool enough that you won't get burned—then cut and enjoy!

Active time: 15 minutes
Bake time: 18 minutes
Makes: 16 brownies

1/2 cup all-purpose flour
1/2 cup unsweetened cocoa
1/4 teaspoon baking powder
1/4 teaspoon salt
6 tablespoons butter or margarine
1 cup sugar
2 large eggs
2 teaspoons vanilla extract
1/3 cup mini chocolate chips

1. Preheat oven to 350°F. Line 8-inch square baking pan with foil (see page 56); grease foil.

2. On waxed paper, combine flour, cocoa, baking powder, and salt.

3. In 3-quart saucepan, melt butter over low heat. Remove saucepan from heat; with rubber spatula, stir in sugar, then eggs, one at a time, and vanilla until well blended. Stir in flour mixture. Spread batter in prepared pan; sprinkle with chocolate chips.

4. Bake 18 to 20 minutes or until toothpick inserted 2 inches from center comes out almost clean. Cool brownies completely in pan on wire rack, about 2 hours.

5. When cool, lift foil, with brownie, out of pan and place on cutting board; peel foil away from sides. Using chef's knife, with gentle sawing motion, cut into 4 strips, then cut each strip crosswise into 4 squares. Refrigerate brownies in airtight container up to 1 week, or freeze up to 3 months.

Each brownie: about 120 calories, 2g protein, 17g carbohydrate, 6g total fat (3g saturated), 0g fiber, 36mg cholesterol, 100mg sodium

COCOA BROWNIES WITH TOASTED WALNUTS Substitute *¼ cup walnuts*, toasted (see page xxiii) and chopped, for mini chocolate chips.

Each brownie about 130 calories, 2g protein, 18g carbohydrate, 6g total fat (3g saturated), 1g fiber, 36mg cholesterol, 100mg sodium

Good Housekeeping's Classic Brownies

Ultrarich, with lots of deep, dark chocolate flavor, these brownies are fabulous, whether you make the plain version or opt for the praline-topped variation. For a moist, fudgy texture, do not overbake them.

Active time: 10 minutes
Bake time: 30 minutes
Makes: 24 brownies

1¼ cups all-purpose flour
½ teaspoon salt
¾ cup butter or margarine (1½ sticks)
4 ounces unsweetened chocolate, chopped
4 ounces semisweet chocolate, chopped
2 cups sugar
1 tablespoon vanilla extract
5 large eggs, beaten

1. Preheat oven to 350°F. Line 13" by 9" baking pan with foil (see page 56); grease foil. In small bowl, with wire whisk, mix flour and salt.

2. In heavy 4-quart saucepan, melt butter and both chocolates over low heat, stirring frequently, until smooth. Remove from heat. With wooden spoon, stir in sugar and vanilla. Add eggs; stir until well mixed. Stir flour mixture into chocolate mixture just until blended. Spread batter evenly in prepared pan.

3. Bake until toothpick inserted 1 inch from edge comes out clean, about 30 minutes. Cool completely in pan on wire rack.

4. When cool, lift foil, with brownie, out of pan and place on cutting board; peel foil away from sides. Using chef's knife, with gentle sawing motion, cut lengthwise into 4 strips, then cut each strip crosswise into 6 pieces. If brownies are sticky, dip blade in warm water and dry off between cuts. Refrigerate brownies in airtight container up to 1 week, or freeze up to 3 months.

Each brownie: about 205 calories, 3g protein, 26g carbohydrate, 11g total fat (6g saturated), 1g fiber, 60mg cholesterol, 121mg sodium

PRALINE-ICED BROWNIES Prepare classic brownies as directed; cool completely. In 2-quart saucepan, heat *5 tablespoons butter or margarine* and *⅓ cup packed brown sugar* over medium-low heat until mixture has melted and bubbles, about 5 minutes. Remove from heat. With wire whisk, beat in *3 tablespoons bourbon* (or *1 tablespoon vanilla extract plus 2 tablespoons water*); stir in *2 cups confectioners' sugar* until mixture is smooth. With small metal spatula, spread topping over room-temperature brownies; sprinkle *½ cup pecans*, toasted (see page xxiii) and coarsely chopped, over topping. Using chef's knife, with gentle sawing motion, cut lengthwise into 8 strips, then cut each strip crosswise into 8 pieces. If brownies are sticky, dip blade in warm water and dry off between cuts. Makes 64 bite-size brownies.

Each brownie: about 110 calories, 1g protein, 15g carbohydrate, 6g total fat (3g carbohydrate, 1g fiber, 23mg cholesterol, 52mg sodium

Brownies

The rich texture and chocolaty goodness of these brownies speak of decadence, but each square has just 95 calories, 3 grams of fat, and no cholesterol. Our cheats? Swapping nonfat cocoa for chocolate and cholesterol-free spread for not-so-heart-healthy butter.

Active time: 15 minutes • Bake time: 22 minutes • Makes: 16 brownies

1 teaspoon instant coffee powder or granules
2 teaspoons vanilla extract
1/2 cup all-purpose flour
1/2 cup unsweetened cocoa
1/4 teaspoon baking powder

1 1/4 teaspoons salt
1 cup sugar
1/4 cup trans-fat-free vegetable oil spread
   (60% to 70% oil)
3 large egg whites

1. Preheat oven to 350°F. Line 8-inch square baking pan with foil (see page 56); grease foil. In cup, dissolve coffee in vanilla extract.

2. On waxed paper, combine flour, cocoa, baking powder, and salt.

3. In medium bowl, whisk sugar, vegetable oil spread, egg whites, and coffee mixture until well mixed; then blend in flour mixture. Spread into prepared pan.

4. Bake 22 to 24 minutes or until toothpick inserted in brownies 2 inches from edge comes out almost clean. Cool completely in pan on wire rack, about 2 hours.

5. When cool, lift foil, with brownie, out of pan and place on cutting board; peel foil away from sides. Using chef's knife, with gentle sawing motion, cut brownies into 4 strips, then cut each strip crosswise into 4 squares. Refrigerate brownies in airtight container up to 3 days, or freeze up to 3 months.

Each brownie: about 95 calories, 2g protein, 17g carbohydrate, 3g total fat (1g saturated), 1g fiber, 0mg cholesterol, 75mg sodium

Hazelnut Brownies

Nutella, that luscious chocolate-hazelnut spread, was created in Italy in the 1940s by Pietro Ferrero. Chocolate was scarce due to the war, so he stretched his supply by adding ground hazelnuts—the result became hugely popular. Look for it in supermarkets near the peanut butter.

Active time: 30 minutes
Bake time: 25 minutes
Makes: 24 brownies

1 cup all-purpose flour
1/2 teaspoon salt
3/4 cup butter or margarine (11/2 sticks)
4 ounces unsweetened chocolate
2 ounces semisweet chocolate
1/2 cup Nutella or other chocolate-hazelnut spread
11/2 cups sugar
1 teaspoon vanilla extract
4 large eggs, lightly beaten
1 cup hazelnuts (4 ounces), toasted and skins removed
    (see page xxiii), coarsely chopped

1. Preheat oven to 350°F. Line 13" by 9" baking pan with foil (see right); grease foil. In small bowl, with wire whisk, mix flour and salt.

2. In 3-quart saucepan, melt butter and both chocolates over low heat, stirring frequently, until smooth. Remove from heat; stir in chocolate-hazelnut spread. Add sugar and vanilla; stir until well blended. Add eggs; stir until well mixed. Stir in flour mixture and nuts just until blended. Spread batter evenly in prepared pan.

3. Bake until toothpick inserted 2 inches from edge comes out almost clean, 25 to 30 minutes. Cool in pan.

4. When cool, lift foil, with brownie, out of pan and place on cutting board; peel foil away from sides. Using chef's knife, with gentle sawing motion, cut brownie lengthwise into 4 strips, then cut each strip crosswise into 6 pieces. Refrigerate brownies in airtight container up to 1 week, or freeze up to 3 months.

Each brownie: about 230 calories, 4g protein, 23g carbohydrate, 15g total fat (6g saturated), 2g fiber, 52mg cholesterol, 125mg sodium

LINING A PAN WITH FOIL

For easy removal of brownies and bars from the pan after baking, we recommend lining the pan with aluminum foil. It also makes cleanup a breeze.

Turn the empty baking pan bottom side up. Cover the outside of the pan tightly with foil, shiny side out. Use enough foil so that it overlaps the edge of the pan by an inch or two (the extra foil will be used as "handles" to help you remove the brownies from the pan after baking). Lift the foil off the pan.

Turn the baking pan right side up and carefully fit the molded foil into the pan, smoothing it to fit into the edges and corners. Follow the recipe's instructions to grease and/or dust the foil with flour.

Vegan Chocolate-Chip Walnut Brownies

Don't be put off by the presence of prunes in this recipe—when going egg-free, fruit purees are often used to provide moistness and that satisfying unctuousness you get from eggs. The triple shot of cocoa, unsweetened chocolate, and chocolate chips will please the most dedicated chocoholic.

Active time: 25 minutes • Bake time: 30 minutes • Makes: 16 brownies

2/3 cup water

1/3 cup pitted prunes

1 cup all-purpose flour

1 teaspoon baking powder

1/2 teaspoon salt

1/4 teaspoon baking soda

1/3 cup quick-cooking oats, uncooked

1/4 cup unsweetened cocoa

3 ounces unsweetened chocolate, melted and cooled

1/3 cup canola oil

2 teaspoons vanilla extract

1 1/3 cups sugar

3/4 cup walnuts (3 ounces), chopped

1/3 cup dairy-free chocolate chips

1. Preheat oven to 350°F. Line 9-inch square baking pan with foil (see opposite); spray foil with nonstick cooking spray. Place water and prunes in microwave-safe bowl. Microwave on High 2 minutes. Let stand 5 minutes.

2. Meanwhile, in small bowl, whisk flour, baking powder, salt, and baking soda.

3. In food processor, process oats until finely ground. Add prunes and soaking water and process until very smooth, about 1 minute. Add cocoa and process until smooth.

4. Scrape prune mixture into large bowl. Stir in chocolate, oil, and vanilla until smooth. Add sugar and stir until well blended. Stir in flour mixture and then walnuts and chocolate chips. Scrape batter into prepared pan.

5. Bake until toothpick inserted in center comes out with moist but not wet crumbs, 30 to 35 minutes. Let cool completely on wire rack. When cool, lift foil, with brownie, out of pan and place on cutting board; peel foil away from sides. Using chef's knife, with gentle sawing motion, cut into 4 strips, then cut each strip crosswise into 4 squares. Refrigerate brownies in airtight container up to 3 days, or freeze up to 3 months.

Each brownie: about 235 calories, 3g protein, 32g carbohydrate, 12g total fat (3g saturated), 3g fiber, 0mg cholesterol, 136mg sodium

Cheesecake Swirl Brownies

A ribbon of creamy almond cheesecake winds its way through the middle of these super-chocolaty brownies.

Active time: 30 minutes
Bake time: 35 minutes
Makes: 24 brownies

1¼ cups all-purpose flour
¾ teaspoon baking powder
½ teaspoon salt
½ cup butter or margarine (1 stick)
4 ounces unsweetened chocolate, chopped
4 ounces semisweet chocolate, chopped
2 cups sugar
5 large eggs
2½ teaspoons vanilla extract
12 ounces (1½ packages) cold cream cheese
¾ teaspoon almond extract

1. Preheat oven to 350°F. Line 13" by 9" baking pan with foil (see page 56); grease foil. In small bowl, with wire whisk, mix flour, baking powder, and salt.

2. In heavy 4-quart saucepan, melt butter and both chocolates over low heat, stirring until smooth. Remove from heat. With wooden spoon, beat in 1½ cups sugar. Stir in 4 eggs and 2 teaspoons vanilla; beat until well blended. Stir in flour mixture just until blended.

3. In small bowl, with mixer on medium speed, beat cream cheese until smooth; gradually beat in remaining ½ cup sugar. Beat in remaining 1 egg and ½ teaspoon vanilla, along with almond extract, just until blended.

4. Spread 1½ cups chocolate batter in prepared pan. Spoon cream-cheese mixture in 6 large dollops on top of chocolate mixture (cream-cheese mixture will cover most of chocolate batter). Spoon remaining chocolate batter over and between cream cheese in 6 large dollops. With tip of knife, cut and twist through mixtures to create marbled effect.

5. Bake until toothpick inserted in center comes out almost clean, 35 to 40 minutes. Cool completely in pan on wire rack.

6. When cool, lift foil, with brownie, out of pan and place on cutting board; peel foil away from sides. Using chef's knife, with gentle sawing motion, cut lengthwise into 4 strips, then cut each strip crosswise into 6 pieces. If brownies are sticky, dip blade in warm water and dry off between cuts. Refrigerate brownies in airtight container up to 1 week, or freeze up to 3 months.

Each brownie: about 240 calories, 4g protein, 26g carbohydrate, 14g total fat (8g saturated), 1g fiber, 70mg cholesterol, 159mg sodium

MARBLING BROWNIE BATTER

This is an easy technique that yields fancy-looking results.

To produce a marbled effect with two different-colored batters, simply pull and swirl a kitchen knife through the batters.

Bake
Sale

BLONDIES

One of the easiest of bar cookies to make, our classic blondie is packed with butterscotch flavor. We've also included a low-fat take on this favorite so everyone can indulge.

Blondies

These favorites go from saucepan to baking pan in one easy step. Make them with pecans as directed or see our ideas at right for other irresistible add-ins. The blondies in the photo feature semisweet chocolate chips.

Active time: 10 minutes
Bake time: 30 minutes
Makes: 24 blondies

6 tablespoons butter or margarine
1³/4 cups packed light brown sugar
2 teaspoons vanilla extract
2 large eggs
1 cup all-purpose flour
2 teaspoons baking powder
1 teaspoon salt
1¹/2 cups pecans (6 ounces), coarsely chopped

1. Preheat oven to 350°F. Line 13" by 9" baking pan with foil (see page 56); grease foil.

2. In 3-quart saucepan, melt butter over low heat. Remove saucepan from heat. With wooden spoon, stir in brown sugar and vanilla. Beat in eggs until well blended. In small bowl, combine flour, baking powder, and salt; stir into sugar mixture just until blended. Stir in pecans.

3. Spread batter evenly in prepared pan. Bake 30 minutes, or until toothpick inserted 2 inches from edge of pan comes out almost clean. Do not overbake; blondies will firm as they cool. Cool completely in pan on wire rack.

4. When cool, lift foil, with blondie, out of pan and place on cutting board; peel foil away from sides. Using chef's knife, with gentle sawing motion, cut lengthwise into 4 strips, then cut each strip into 6 pieces. Store blondies in airtight container up to 3 days, or freeze up to 3 months.

Each blondie: about 160 calories, 2g protein, 21g carbohydrate, 8g total fat (2g saturated), 1g fiber, 25mg cholesterol, 180mg sodium

---

BLONDIE MIX-INS

For extra-special blondies, mix in any of these items in step 2. You can use them instead of the pecans—or add up to 3 cups of mix-ins total.

CHIPS Stir in 1 cup chocolate, butterscotch, toffee, or peanut butter chips.

DRIED FRUIT Stir in 1 cup dried cranberries, cherries, raisins, crystallized ginger, or sweetened flaked coconut.

NUTS Swap in 1½ cups coarsely chopped walnuts, hazelnuts, almonds, or salted peanuts. Toast them first, if you like (page xxiii).

Peanut Butter Bar Cookies

Put on the coffeepot, pour the milk, and get ready for a serious treat. Good as these cookies are just as they come from the oven, you may want to dress them up with a drizzle of chocolate. Use your favorite—milk, semisweet, or dark. See the variation below for how to do it.

Active time: 15 minutes
Bake time: 30 minutes
Makes: 40 bars

2¼ cups all-purpose flour
1 teaspoon baking powder
⅛ teaspoon salt
1 cup chunky or creamy peanut butter
½ cup butter or margarine (1 stick), softened
1 cup packed dark brown sugar
½ cup granulated sugar
1 teaspoon vanilla extract
⅛ teaspoon almond extract
2 large eggs

1. Preheat oven to 350°F. Grease 13" by 9" baking pan with foil (see page 56); grease foil.

2. In medium bowl, stir together flour, baking powder, and salt.

3. In large bowl, with mixer on medium speed, beat peanut butter, butter, and brown and granulated sugars until light and fluffy. Beat in vanilla and almond extracts. Beat in eggs, one at a time, beating well after each addition. Reduce speed to low and beat in flour mixture until well combined.

4. Scrape batter into prepared pan. Bake 30 minutes, or until toothpick inserted in center of pan comes out clean. Cool completely in pan on wire rack.

5. When cool, lift foil, with pastry, out of pan and place on cutting board; peel foil away from sides. Using chef's knife, with gentle sawing motion, cut lengthwise into 5 strips, then cut each strip crosswise into 8 pieces. Store bars in airtight container up to 3 days, or freeze up to 3 months.

Each bar: about 120 calories, 3g protein, 15g carbohydrate, 6g total fat (2g saturated), 1g fiber, 17mg cholesterol, 80mg sodium

CHOCOLATE-TOPPED PEANUT BUTTER BARS Prepare bars as instructed, then drizzle *2 ounces melted chocolate* over baked cake. Allow chocolate to set before cutting into bars.

Each chocolate-topped bar: about 125 calories, 3g protein, 16g carbohydrate, 6g total fat (2g saturated), 1g fiber, 17mg cholesterol, 80mg sodium

Coconut Joy Bars

Rich coconut milk custard is nestled between a layer of toasted coconut crust and smooth chocolate in these decadent bars.

Active time: 20 minutes plus cooling and setting
Bake time: 30 minutes
Makes: 48 bars

1 bag (14 ounces) sweetened flaked coconut
1 1/2 cups all-purpose flour
1/3 cup confectioners' sugar
1/4 teaspoon salt
1 cup butter (2 sticks), at room temperature
   (do not use margarine)
3/4 cup granulated sugar
1/3 cup cornstarch
1 can (14 ounces) coconut milk, shaken
8 ounces bittersweet chocolate, chopped

1. Preheat oven to 350°F.

2. In 13" by 9" baking pan, spread 1 cup coconut. Bake 6 to 8 minutes or until golden, stirring once. Cool. Wipe out pan, line with foil (see page 56); lightly grease foil.

3. In food processor, finely grind toasted coconut. Add flour, confectioners' sugar, and 1/8 teaspoon salt; pulse to blend. Add butter. Pulse until blended.

Top: Peanut Butter Bar Cookies;
Bottom: Coconut Joy Bars

4. With spatula, spread dough into even layer in pan. Bake 30 minutes or until golden brown. Cool on wire rack.

5. Meanwhile, in 2-quart saucepan, whisk granulated sugar, cornstarch, and remaining 1/8 teaspoon salt. Whisk in coconut milk until smooth. Heat to simmering over medium-high, whisking frequently. Simmer 2 minutes or until very thick, whisking. Fold in untoasted coconut. Cool slightly. Spread in even layer over cooled crust.

6. Place chocolate in medium microwave-safe bowl. Microwave on High 2 minutes at 30-second intervals until almost completely melted, stirring between intervals. Stir mixture until smooth. Pour and spread chocolate over coconut filling. Refrigerate until chocolate is set.

7. When chocolate is firm, lift foil, with pastry, out of pan and place on cutting board; peel foil away from sides. Cut pastry into approximately 1" by 2" rectangles. Refrigerate bars in airtight container, with waxed paper between layers, up to 3 days, or freeze up to 3 months.

Each bar: about 145 calories, 2g protein, 14g carbohydrate, 10g total fat (8g saturated), 1g fiber, 10mg cholesterol, 70mg sodium

THE MAGIC OF COCONUT MILK

Unsweetened canned coconut milk is a naturally creamy liquid that lends body and sweet flavor to custards and other desserts.

To make a nondairy coconut whipped cream, refrigerate a can of unsweetened coconut milk overnight. Scoop off the coconut cream that has risen to the top; do not include any of the coconut water below it. Beat the coconut cream and 1/4 cup confectioners' sugar with an electric mixer until soft peaks form. Refrigerate for at least 1 hour or overnight.

Butterscotch Blondies

They'll never guess these chewy bars have only 3 grams of fat per square.

Active time: 15 minutes
Bake time: 35 minutes
Makes: 16 blondies

1 cup all-purpose flour
1/2 teaspoon baking powder
1/4 teaspoon salt
3 tablespoons butter or margarine
3/4 cup packed dark brown sugar
2 large egg whites
1/3 cup dark corn syrup
2 teaspoons vanilla extract
2 tablespoons finely chopped pecans

1. Preheat oven to 350°F. Line 8-inch square baking pan with foil (see page 56); grease foil. In small bowl, with wire whisk, mix flour, baking powder, and salt.

2. In large bowl, with mixer on medium speed, beat butter and brown sugar 2 minutes. Reduce speed to low; beat in egg whites, corn syrup, and vanilla until smooth. Beat in flour mixture just until combined. Spread batter in prepared pan. Sprinkle with nuts.

3. Bake until toothpick inserted in center comes out clean, 35 to 40 minutes. Cool in pan on wire rack.

4. When cool, transfer foil, with blondie, to cutting board; peel foil away from sides. Using chef's knife, with gentle sawing motion, cut into 16 squares. Store blondies in airtight container up to 3 days, or freeze up to 3 months.

Each blondie: about 115 calories, 1g protein, 21g carbohydrate, 3g total fat (1g saturated), 0g fiber, 6mg cholesterol, 94mg sodium

Tin Roof Puffed Rice Treats

These nostalgic cereal treats celebrate the sweet-salty combination featured in the tin roof sundae, a chocolate sundae topped with salted, red-skinned Spanish peanuts that was popular in the early twentieth century.

Active time: 20 minutes plus chilling
Makes: 16 bars

1/2 cup creamy peanut butter
24 large marshmallows
4 cups puffed rice cereal
2/3 cup (4 ounces) semisweet chocolate chips
2 tablespoons roasted, salted Spanish peanuts, chopped

1. Line bottom of 8-inch square baking pan with foil (see page 56); lightly coat with nonstick cooking spray.

2. In microwave-safe 4-quart bowl, combine peanut butter and marshmallows. Cover bowl with vented plastic wrap and cook in microwave on High 1 minute, until melted. With rubber spatula, quickly stir in puffed rice until evenly coated. With hand, evenly pat puffed rice mixture into prepared baking pan.

3. In microwave-safe cup, heat chocolate in microwave on High 35 to 45 seconds, or until soft; stir until smooth. With offset spatula, spread melted chocolate on top of puffed rice mixture. Sprinkle with peanuts; gently press so nuts adhere to chocolate.

4. Refrigerate until chocolate is set, 30 minutes. Lift foil, with pastry, out of pan and place on cutting board; peel foil away from sides. Cut into 4 strips, then cut each strip crosswise into 4 pieces. With small metal spatula, separate treats. Refrigerate bars in airtight container up to 1 week.

Each bar: about 135 calories, 3g protein, 18g carbohydrate, 7g total fat (2g saturated), 1g fiber, 0mg cholesterol, 51mg sodium

TIN ROOF PUFFED RICE TREATS

SHORTBREAD

Whether it's flavored with cardamom and almonds or crystallized ginger and a lemony glaze, this tender-crisp, butter-rich cookie is a perennial favorite. The traditional Scottish Shortbread, which is patted into rounds and cut into wedges, can't be beat.

Scottish Shortbread

The combination of cake flour and all-purpose flour makes a melt-in-your-mouth cookie. The predominant flavor in shortbread is butter, so be sure to use only fresh, sweet butter.

Active time: 20 minutes
Bake time: 40 minutes
Makes: 32 wedges

1¹/2 cups cake flour (not self-rising)
1¹/2 cups all-purpose flour
¹/2 cup sugar
¹/4 teaspoon salt
1¹/2 cups unsalted butter (3 sticks), cut into pieces
   and softened (do not use margarine)

1. Preheat oven to 325°F. In large bowl, combine both flours, sugar, and salt. Knead butter into flour mixture until dough is well blended and holds together. (Or, in food processor with knife blade attached, pulse flours and salt to blend. Add butter and pulse until mixture resembles coarse crumbs.)

2. Divide dough in half. With hand, pat each dough half evenly into bottom of two ungreased 8-inch round cake pans. With tines of fork, prick dough all over to make attractive pattern.

3. Bake 40 minutes, or until golden. Transfer pans to wire racks; immediately run thin knife around edge of pans to loosen shortbread, and cut each round into 16 wedges. Cool completely in pans on wire rack.

4. When cool, with small metal spatula, carefully remove cookies from pans. Store shortbread in airtight container up to 5 days, or freeze up to 3 months.

Each wedge: about 130 calories, 1g protein, 12g carbohydrate, 9g total fat (5g saturated), 0g fiber, 23mg cholesterol, 105mg sodium

---

SHAPELY SHORTBREAD

Shortbread is sometimes formed using a mold that creates raised patterns on its surface. The dough is packed into the mold, which looks like a thick wooden plate with flutings and designs carved deeply into it. Since shortbread is a Scottish specialty, you'll often see these attractive molds decorated with a thistle motif, the national flower.

Lemon-Ginger Shortbread Bars

These citrus-glazed bars are slightly crunchy because they're made with cornmeal.

Active time: 20 minutes plus cooling
Bake time: 30 minutes
Makes: 40 triangles

1 lemon
3/4 cup butter or margarine (1 1/2 sticks), softened
3/4 cup granulated sugar
2 cups all-purpose flour
1/3 cup yellow cornmeal
1/2 cup chopped crystallized ginger
1/4 teaspoon salt
1 large egg
3/4 cup confectioners' sugar

1. Preheat oven to 350°F. Grease 13" by 9" baking pan. Line pan with foil (see page 56); grease foil. From lemon, grate 1/2 teaspoon peel and squeeze 3 tablespoons juice.

2. In large bowl, with mixer on low speed, beat butter, granulated sugar, and lemon peel until blended. Increase speed to high: beat until light and fluffy, about 2 minutes. Reduce speed to low and beat in flour, cornmeal, ginger, salt, and egg just until blended (mixture will be crumbly).

3. Sprinkle dough evenly into prepared pan. With hand, pat firmly into bottom. Bake 30 to 35 minutes, until golden around edges and toothpick inserted in center comes out clean. Cool completely in pan on wire rack.

4. In small bowl, with wire whisk or fork, mix lemon juice and confectioners' sugar until blended. Pour glaze over cooled shortbread and, with small metal spatula, spread in even layer. Allow glaze to set, about 1 hour.

5. When cool, lift foil, with shortbread, out of pan and place on cutting board; peel foil away from sides. Cut lengthwise into 4 strips, then cut each strip crosswise into 5 pieces. Cut each piece diagonally in half. Store bars in airtight container up to 4 days, or freeze up to 3 months.

Each triangle: about 75 calories, 1g protein, 11g carbohydrate, 3g total fat (2g saturated), 0g fiber, 12mg cholesterol, 45mg sodium

Butter-Almond Thins

These buttery bars are bursting with toasty sliced almonds. Ground cardamom adds a warm, spicy-sweet accent.

Active time: 30 minutes
Bake time: 15 minutes
Makes: 108 triangles

3/4 cup butter (1 1/2 sticks), softened (do not use margarine)
1/3 cup granulated sugar
1/2 teaspoon ground cardamom
1/4 teaspoon salt
1 large egg, separated
1 teaspoon almond extract
1 teaspoon vanilla extract
2 cups all-purpose flour
2 cups sliced, blanched almonds
4 tablespoons confectioners' sugar

1. Preheat oven to 375°F. Grease 18" by 12" jelly-roll pan and line with foil (see page 56); grease foil.

2. In large bowl, with mixer on medium speed, beat butter, granulated sugar, cardamom, and salt until creamy. Beat in egg yolk and both extracts until well incorporated. Beat in flour on low just until clumps form.

3. Scatter clumps evenly in prepared pan. With palm and fingertips, press dough into thin, even layer without any gaps.

4. In medium bowl, whisk egg white until frothy; fold in almonds and 2 tablespoons confectioners' sugar. Spread in even layer over dough, pressing gently into dough. With pizza wheel or sharp knife, cut dough into 2-inch strips; cut each strip crosswise to form 2-inch squares. Cut squares diagonally into triangles. Dust tops with remaining 2 tablespoons confectioners' sugar.

5. Bake 15 to 18 minutes or until golden brown. Cool completely in pan on wire rack before lifting foil, with pastries, out of pan. Carefully break cookies into triangles. Store in airtight container up to 3 days, or freeze up to 1 month.

Each triangle: about 45 calories, 1g protein, 4g carbohydrate, 3g total fat (1g saturated), 0g fiber, 7mg cholesterol, 25mg sodium

FRUIT & NUT BARS

From variations on pies to granola bars, these scrumptious treats are all bursting with fruit or nuts. Toasting the nuts is a great way to bring out their flavor.

Cherry Linzer Bars

A reinvention of the classic Viennese pastry, these bars feature a simple pat-in-the-pan crust.

Active time: 45 minutes
Bake time: 35 minutes
Makes: 36 bars

1/2 cup dried tart cherries
2 tablespoons water
1 3/4 cups all-purpose flour
1 teaspoon ground cinnamon
1/2 teaspoon baking powder
1/4 teaspoon salt
1 cup hazelnuts (5 ounces), toasted and skins removed (see page xxiii), cooled
1/2 cup granulated sugar
3/4 cup butter or margarine (1 1/2 sticks), softened
1/2 cup packed light brown sugar
1/2 teaspoon freshly grated lemon peel
1 large egg
1 jar (12 ounces) tart cherry jam
Confectioners' sugar, for garnish (optional)

1. Preheat oven to 350°F. Line 9" by 13" baking pan with foil (see page 56).

2. In small, microwave-safe bowl, combine dried cherries and water; microwave on High 1 minute; set aside. On waxed paper, combine flour, cinnamon, baking powder, and salt; set aside.

3. In food processor with knife blade attached, pulse hazelnuts and granulated sugar until nuts are finely ground. Add butter, brown sugar, and lemon peel; process until creamy. Add egg; pulse until well blended. Add reserved flour mixture; pulse just until mixture comes together to form dough.

4. Reserve 1 1/4 cups dough for top layer; cover and chill. With floured fingers, press remaining dough firmly into bottom of prepared pan. Stir reserved cherries into jam and spread evenly over crust, up to 1/4 inch from edges.

5. With hands, roll reserved dough into 1/4-inch-thick ropes. Arrange ropes diagonally, 1 1/2 inches apart, over jam. Place additional ropes at right angles to the first ones. Position remaining ropes around inside of pan to create a finished edge. Bake 35 minutes or until dough is lightly browned. Cool in pan on wire rack.

6. When cool, lift foil, with pastry, out of pan and place on cutting board. Cut lengthwise into 6 strips, then cut each strip crosswise into 6 bars. Sprinkle with confectioners' sugar just before serving, if you like. Store bars, not yet dusted with confectioners' sugar, in airtight container, with waxed paper between layers, up to 3 days, or freeze up to 3 months.

Each bar: about 135 calories, 2g protein, 19g carbohydrate, 6g total fat (3g saturated), 1g fiber, 15mg cholesterol, 25mg sodium

Apple Crumb Squares

These three-layer bars deliver all the flavor of apple pie, packed into tidy, picnic-perfect portions.

Active time: 45 minutes
Bake time: 1 hour
Makes: 24 bars

CRUMB TOPPING

1 cup all-purpose flour
1 cup pecans or walnuts (4 ounces), coarsely chopped
1/2 cup butter or margarine (1 stick), slightly softened
1/2 cup packed brown sugar
1 tablespoon vanilla extract
1 teaspoon ground cinnamon

CRUST

3 cups all-purpose flour
1/3 cup granulated sugar
1/4 teaspoon salt
3/4 cup cold butter or margarine (1 1/2 sticks)

APPLE FILLING

4 pounds green cooking apples such as Granny Smith, peeled, cored, and cut into 1/2-inch chunks
4 tablespoons butter or margarine
3/4 cup dark seedless raisins or dried currants
1/2 cup packed brown sugar
3/4 teaspoon ground cinnamon
1 tablespoon cornstarch
3 tablespoons fresh lemon juice

1. Prepare crumb topping: In medium bowl, with fingertips, mix all topping ingredients until mixture comes together. Shape into ball; wrap in plastic and refrigerate while preparing crust and filling.

2. Preheat oven to 375°F. Line 15½" by 10½" jelly-roll pan with foil (see page 56); lightly grease foil.

3. Prepare crust: In large bowl, with fork, mix flour, granulated sugar, and salt. With pastry cutter or two knives used scissor-fashion, blend butter in until mixture resembles fine crumbs. With hand, press evenly into bottom of prepared pan. Bake 20 to 24 minutes or until golden brown (crust may crack slightly).

4. Meanwhile, prepare apple filling: In nonstick 12-inch skillet, cook apples, butter, raisins, brown sugar, and cinnamon over medium heat 25 to 30 minutes or until apples are very tender and most liquid has evaporated, stirring occasionally. In cup, mix cornstarch and lemon juice. Stir lemon-juice mixture into apple mixture and cook, stirring, until filling thickens.

5. Spread filling over hot crust. Break topping into chunks and scatter over all. Bake 40 minutes or until topping browns. Cool completely in pan on wire rack.

6. To serve, lift foil, with pastry, out of pan and place on cutting board; peel foil away from sides. Cut lengthwise into 4 strips, then cut each strip crosswise into 6 squares. Refrigerate bars in airtight container up to 1 week, or freeze up to 3 months.

Each bar: about 315 calories, 3g protein, 42g carbohydrate, 16g total fat (8g saturated), 3g fiber, 33mg cholesterol, 155mg sodium

BLUEBERRY CRUMB SQUARES Prepare as directed, but in step 4, prepare blueberry filling instead of apple: In 3-quart saucepan, combine *3 pints fresh blueberries, ½ cup granulated sugar, 3 tablespoons cornstarch,* and *3 tablespoons water;* heat to boiling over medium-high, stirring frequently. Boil 1 minute; remove from heat. Proceed with recipe as instructed. Makes 24 bars.

Each bar: about 260 calories, 3g protein, 34g carbohydrate, 15g total fat (6g saturated), 2g fiber, 25mg cholesterol, 111mg sodium

Fresh Lemon Bars

Our recipe for this timeless classic is straightforward, but its sweet-tart flavor and rich texture are sensational. Whip them up for teatime, bake sales, and potluck suppers.

Active time: 25 minutes
Bake time: 40 minutes
Makes: 32 bars

3/4 cup butter (1 1/2 sticks), softened (do not use margarine)
2 1/4 cups all-purpose flour
2/3 cup plus 1 tablespoon confectioners' sugar
3 to 4 lemons
6 large eggs
2 cups granulated sugar
1 teaspoon baking powder
3/4 teaspoon salt

1. Preheat oven to 350°F. Line 13" by 9" baking pan with foil (see page 56); lightly grease foil.

2. In food processor with knife blade attached, pulse butter, 2 cups flour, and 2/3 cup confectioners' sugar until mixture is moist but crumbly. Dough should hold together when pressed between two fingers. Sprinkle mixture into prepared pan. With fingertips, press dough evenly onto bottom of pan. Bake until lightly browned, 20 to 25 minutes.

3. Meanwhile, from lemons, grate 2 1/2 teaspoons peel and squeeze 2/3 cup juice. In large bowl, with wire whisk, beat eggs. Add lemon peel and juice, granulated sugar, baking powder, salt, and remaining 1/4 cup flour; whisk until blended.

4. Whisk filling again and pour onto hot crust. Bake until filling is just set and golden around edges, 18 to 22 minutes. Transfer pan to wire rack. Sift remaining 1 tablespoon confectioners' sugar over warm filling (see Tip). Cool completely in pan on wire rack.

5. When cool, lift foil, with pastry, out of pan and place on cutting board; carefully peel foil away from sides. Trim edges of bars, if you like. Cut lengthwise into 4 strips, then cut each strip crosswise into 8 pieces. Refrigerate bars in airtight container up to 5 days.

Each bar: about 145 calories, 2g protein, 23g carbohydrate, 5g total fat (3g saturated), 0g fiber, 51mg cholesterol, 126mg sodium

FRESH LIME BARS Prepare as directed, but in step 3, substitute *lime peel* and *lime juice* for lemon. You'll need 5 to 6 large limes.

Each bar: about 145 calories, 2g protein, 23g carbohydrate, 5g total fat (3g saturated), 0g fiber, 51mg cholesterol, 126mg sodium

TIP If you prepare these bars ahead, don't top them with confectioners' sugar and cut them. Instead refrigerate the whole pastry until you are ready to serve, then sprinkle on the sugar just before cutting the bars.

Granola Bars

Bake a pan of these snacks, and you'll never go back to the boxed stuff. They're super easy and fun to make with kids—and far more economical than store-bought granola bars. They're great for breakfast on the go, too!

Active time: 20 minutes
Bake time: 32 minutes
Makes: 18 bars

2 cups old-fashioned oats, uncooked
3/4 cup toasted wheat germ
3/4 cup chopped walnuts (3 ounces)
3/4 cup dried cranberries
2 tablespoons packed light brown sugar
2 teaspoons ground cinnamon
1/2 teaspoon salt
1/2 cup honey
1/2 cup vegetable oil
2 large egg whites

1. Preheat oven to 325°F. Line 13" by 9" pan with foil (see page 56); lightly coat foil with cooking spray.

2. In glass pie plate, spread oats; microwave on High, in 1-minute increments, 4 to 5 minutes or until fragrant and golden, stirring occasionally. Cool to room temperature.

3. In large bowl, combine oats, wheat germ, walnuts, cranberries, brown sugar, cinnamon, and salt. Stir in honey, oil, and egg whites until well mixed. Transfer to prepared pan. Using wet hand, press into even layer.

4. Bake 32 to 35 minutes or until dark golden. Cool completely in pan on wire rack.

5. When cool, lift foil, with bars, out of pan and place on cutting board; peel foil away from sides. Cut lengthwise into 6 strips, then cut each strip crosswise into thirds. Store bars in airtight container up to 1 week, or freeze up to 3 months.

Each bar: about 190 calories, 4g protein, 23g carbohydrate, 10g total fat (1g saturated), 2g fiber, 0mg cholesterol, 70mg sodium

Jam Crumble Bars

The food processor does most of the work here, mixing the dough that serves as both base and topping. Experiment with your favorite jam flavors.

Active time: 15 minutes
Bake time: 40 minutes
Makes: 16 bars

1 1/4 cups all-purpose flour
1/2 cup packed light brown sugar
1/4 teaspoon baking soda
1/4 teaspoon ground cinnamon
1/2 cup cold butter or margarine (1 stick), cut into 8 pieces
1/4 cup pecans (1 ounce), chopped
1/2 cup jam (such as raspberry or blackberry)

1. Preheat oven to 350°F. Line 9-inch square baking pan with foil (see page 56). In food processor with knife blade attached, process flour, brown sugar, baking soda, and cinnamon until blended. Add butter and process until mixture resembles coarse crumbs and, when pressed, holds together. Remove 1/2 cup dough to small bowl and stir in pecans; set aside.

2. Press remaining dough firmly into bottom of prepared pan. Spread with jam up to 1/4 inch from edges. With fingers, crumble reserved nut mixture over jam.

3. Bake 40 to 45 minutes, until browned at edges and on top. Cool completely in pan on wire rack.

4. When cool, lift foil, with pastry, out of pan and place on cutting board; peel foil away from sides. Cut into 4 strips; then cut each strip crosswise into 4 pieces. Store bars in airtight container up to 5 days, or freeze up to 3 months.

Each bar: about 150 calories, 1g protein, 21g carbohydrate, 7g total fat (4g saturated), 0g fiber, 16mg cholesterol, 85mg sodium

Jam Crumble Bars

Caramel Pecan Bars

A tasty trio of pecans, caramel, and chocolate nestles on a sweet, golden pastry crust. For caramel perfection, use a candy thermometer (see box below).

Active time: 1 hour plus chilling
Bake time: 25 minutes
Makes: 48 bars

COOKIE CRUST
3/4 cup butter (1 1/2 sticks), softened
 (do not use margarine)
3/4 cup confectioners' sugar
1 1/2 teaspoons vanilla extract
2 1/4 cups all-purpose flour

CARAMEL PECAN FILLING
1 cup packed brown sugar
1/2 cup honey
1/2 cup butter (1 stick), cut into pieces
 (do not use margarine)
1/3 cup granulated sugar
1/4 cup heavy cream
2 teaspoons vanilla extract
1 1/2 cups pecans (6 ounces), toasted (see page xxiii)
 and coarsely chopped
2 squares (2 ounces) semisweet chocolate, melted

1. Preheat oven to 350°F. Line 13" by 9" baking pan with foil (see page 56); grease foil.

2. Prepare crust: In large bowl, with mixer on medium speed, beat butter, confectioners' sugar, and vanilla until creamy, about 2 minutes. At low speed, gradually beat in flour until mixture resembles fine crumbs. Sprinkle into prepared pan. With hand, firmly pat crumbs onto bottom of pan to form even layer. Bake crust until lightly browned, 25 to 30 minutes.

3. Prepare filling: In 2-quart saucepan, heat brown sugar, honey, butter, granulated sugar, cream, and vanilla to full rolling boil over high heat, stirring frequently. Reduce heat to medium-high; set candy thermometer in place and continue cooking, without stirring, until temperature reaches 248°F, or firm-ball stage (when small amount of mixture dropped into very cold water forms ball that does not flatten upon removal from water).

4. Sprinkle pecans evenly over warm crust. Pour hot caramel over nuts. Cool in pan on wire rack until caramel is room temperature and has formed skin on top, about 1 hour.

5. With fork, drizzle melted chocolate over caramel. Cover and refrigerate until pastry is cold and chocolate is set, at least 1 hour. Lift foil, with pastry, out of pan and place on cutting board; peel foil away from sides. Cut lengthwise into 6 strips, then cut each strip into 8 pieces. Refrigerate bars in airtight container up to 1 week, or freeze up to 3 months.

Each bar: about 140 calories, 1g protein, 16g carbohydrate, 8g total fat (4g saturated), 1g fiber, 15mg cholesterol, 55mg sodium

USING A CANDY THERMOMETER

Measuring the temperature of sugar syrup or caramel accurately with a thermometer ensures the best results.

Attach the thermometer to the side of the saucepan, making sure that the tip doesn't touch the bottom of the pan.

 To dissolve any sugar crystals that form on the side of the pan, swipe a pastry brush that's been dipped into cold water against the sides of the pan.

Flourless Caramel-Almond Brownies

These rich, chewy squares will delight all chocolate lovers, especially those who follow a gluten-free diet!

Active time: 25 minutes plus cooling and setting • Bake time: 25 minutes • Makes: 64 brownies

6 ounces bittersweet chocolate
   (60% to 70% cacao), chopped
2 ounces unsweetened chocolate, chopped
6 tablespoons butter (do not use margarine)
1/2 teaspoon salt
1 1/2 cups sugar
1 teaspoon vanilla extract

2 large eggs
3 tablespoons cornstarch (check label for gluten-free)
1 tablespoon unsweetened cocoa
1 1/2 cups chopped roasted, salted almonds
1/2 cup water
1 tablespoon light corn syrup
1/3 cup heavy cream, warmed

1. Preheat oven to 350°F. Grease 8-inch square baking pan. Line pan with foil (see page 56); grease foil.

2. In 4-quart saucepan, combine both chocolates, 4 tablespoons butter, and 1/4 teaspoon salt. Melt over medium-low 4 minutes or until smooth, stirring. Remove from heat; stir in 3/4 cup sugar and vanilla. Stir in eggs, one at a time, until well blended.

3. Into same pan, sift cornstarch and cocoa; fold to incorporate. Stir vigorously for 1 minute or until batter thickens slightly and begins to pull away from sides of pan. Fold in 1 cup chopped nuts. Spread into prepared baking pan. Bake 25 to 27 minutes or until toothpick inserted 2 inches from edge comes out almost clean. Cool on wire rack.

4. Meanwhile, in 4-quart saucepan, stir remaining 3/4 cup sugar and 1/4 teaspoon salt with water and corn syrup. Cook over medium-high 9 to 12 minutes or until sugar dissolves and mixture is amber, swirling occasionally to get even color. Working quickly, remove from heat and add cream. When bubbles subside, stir in remaining 2 tablespoons butter. Stir in remaining 1/2 cup nuts.

5. Pour caramel over brownie, tilting pan to spread evenly. Let stand 2 hours or until caramel sets.

6. Lift foil, with brownie, out of pan and place on cutting board; peel foil away from sides. Using chef's knife, with gentle sawing motion, cut into 1-inch squares. If brownies are sticky, dip blade in warm water and dry off between cuts. Refrigerate in airtight container, with waxed paper between layers, up to 1 week, or freeze up to 3 months.

Each bite-size brownie: about 75 calories, 1g protein, 8g carbohydrate, 5g total fat (2g saturated), 1g fiber, 11mg cholesterol, 35mg sodium

Cakes

LAYER CAKES & SHEET CAKES

Here's a roundup of old-fashioned favorites. If you're new to cake baking from scratch, start with the Golden Butter Cake recipe below—and always be sure to use the exact pan size called for in a recipe.

Golden Butter Cake

Imagine the buttery flavor of a pound cake, only lighter. This cake is luscious with any frosting, from vanilla or chocolate to the orange butter frosting we recommend below.

Active time: 45 minutes plus cooling

Bake time: 23 minutes

Makes: 16 servings

3 cups cake flour (not self-rising)

1 tablespoon baking powder

1/2 teaspoon salt

1 cup milk

2 teaspoons vanilla extract

2 cups sugar

1 cup butter or margarine (2 sticks), softened

4 large eggs

Orange Butter Frosting (page 333),
   or desired frosting (see Tip)

1. Place one oven rack in upper third of oven and one rack in lower third; preheat oven to 350°F. Grease three 8-inch round cake pans or two 9-inch square cake pans. Line bottoms with waxed paper; grease and flour paper.

2. In medium bowl, stir together flour, baking powder, and salt. In measuring cup, mix milk and vanilla.

3. In large bowl, with mixer on medium-high speed, beat sugar and butter until light and creamy, about 5 minutes. Add eggs, one at a time, beating well after each. Reduce speed to low; add flour mixture alternately with milk mixture, beginning and ending with flour mixture. Beat just until smooth, scraping bowl occasionally with rubber spatula.

4. Divide batter evenly among prepared pans. Stagger pans in oven, placing two on upper rack and one on lower rack so that pans are not directly above one another. Bake 23 to 28 minutes, or until toothpick inserted in center of cake comes out clean. Cool on wire racks 10 minutes. With small knife, loosen layers from sides of pans; invert onto racks. Remove waxed paper; cool completely.

5. Place 1 cake layer on cake plate; spread with ⅔ cup frosting. Top with second layer, spread on ⅔ cup frosting, and place remaining layer on cake. Frost sides and top of cake.

Each serving: about 485 calories, 5g protein, 58g carbohydrate, 26g total fat (16g saturated), 0g fiber, 120mg cholesterol, 430mg sodium

TIP This cake is so buttery, consider skipping the frosting. Instead take a tip from the Brits: Fill the layers with your favorite jam, then dust the top with confectioners' sugar. It's called a Victoria sponge cake after the queen, who often had a slice with cream at afternoon tea.

Yellow Cake

There are few desserts as simple and purely good as a slice of all-American yellow cake with chocolate frosting. It's the classic birthday cake, and this one is so much better than store-bought or a mix.

Active time: 35 minutes plus cooling
Bake time: 30 minutes
Makes: 12 servings

2 cups all-purpose flour
2 teaspoons baking powder
1 teaspoon salt
1/2 cup vegetable shortening, butter, or margarine, softened
1 1/4 cups sugar
3 large eggs
1 teaspoon vanilla extract
1 cup milk
Silky Chocolate Butter Frosting (page 334) or desired frosting

1. Preheat oven to 350°F for round cake or 325°F for square cake. Grease and flour two 8-inch round cake pans, or one 9-inch square metal baking pan.

2. In medium bowl, stir together flour, baking powder, and salt.

3. In large bowl, with mixer on medium speed, beat shortening and sugar until light and fluffy, about 5 minutes. Add eggs, one at a time, beating well after each. Beat in vanilla. Reduce speed to low, add flour mixture alternately with milk, beginning and ending with flour mixture. Beat just until smooth, scraping bowl frequently with rubber spatula.

4. Spoon batter into prepared pans. Bake round layers about 30 minutes, or bake square cake 40 to 45 minutes; toothpick inserted in center of cake should come out clean. Cool in pans on wire racks 10 minutes. With small knife, loosen layers from sides of pans; invert onto wire racks to cool completely.

5. For layer cake, place 1 cake layer, rounded side down, on cake plate; spread with 2/3 cup frosting. Top with second layer, rounded side up. For both round and square cakes, frost sides and top of cake.

Each serving: about 540 calories, 5g protein, 82g carbohydrate, 23g total fat (10g saturated), 1g fiber, 78mg cholesterol, 385mg sodium

TWEED CAKE Prepare cake as instructed, and fold in *4 ounces semisweet chocolate*, grated on coarse side of grater, at end of step 3.

Each serving: about 585 calories, 6g protein, 88g carbohydrate, 25g total fat (11g saturated), 1g fiber, 78mg cholesterol, 385mg sodium

COCONUT CAKE Prepare round cake as instructed in steps 1 through 4, but instead of using chocolate frosting, prepare *Fluffy White Frosting* (page 343). From *1 package (7 ounces) sweetened flaked coconut,* measure out 1 cup and, in bowl, combine with 1 cup frosting. Place first cake layer on plate and spread with coconut-frosting mixture. Cover with second cake layer and frost sides and top with remaining frosting. Sprinkle top and sides of cake with remaining coconut.

Each serving: about 425 calories, 6g protein, 64g carbohydrate, 17g total fat (8g saturated), 2g fiber, 56mg cholesterol, 355mg sodium

FRESH ORANGE CAKE Prepare batter as instructed, but add *1 teaspoon freshly grated orange peel* along with vanilla. Bake in round cake pans and cool as directed. Frost with *Orange Butter Frosting* (page 333).

Each serving: about 495 calories, 5g protein, 77g carbohydrate, 19g total fat (8g saturated), 1g fiber, 77mg cholesterol, 385mg sodium

Banana Layer Cake

This cake's flavor depends on the sweetness of the bananas, so use really ripe ones. If you like, garnish the cake with banana slices, first dipping them in fresh lemon juice to maintain their color.

Active time: 40 minutes plus cooling
Bake time: 30 minutes
Makes: 16 servings

1 cup mashed fully ripe bananas (2 to 3 medium)
1/4 cup buttermilk
1 teaspoon vanilla extract
2 cups cake flour (not self-rising)
1 teaspoon baking powder
1/2 teaspoon baking soda
1/4 teaspoon salt
1/8 teaspoon ground nutmeg
1¼ cups sugar
1/2 cup butter or margarine (1 stick), softened
2 large eggs
Cream Cheese Frosting (page 342)

1. Place one oven rack in upper third of oven and one rack in lower third; preheat oven to 350°F. Grease three 8-inch round cake pans. Line bottoms with waxed paper; grease and flour paper.

2. In small bowl, mix bananas, buttermilk, and vanilla. In medium bowl, stir together flour, baking powder, baking soda, salt, and nutmeg.

3. In large bowl, with mixer on medium speed, beat sugar and butter 5 minutes, or until light and creamy. Add eggs, one at a time, beating well after each. Reduce speed to low; add flour mixture alternately with banana mixture, beginning and ending with flour mixture. Beat just until smooth, scraping bowl occasionally with rubber spatula.

4. Divide batter among prepared pans. Stagger pans in oven, placing two on upper rack and one on lower rack, so that pans are not directly above one another. Bake 30 minutes, or until toothpick inserted in centers of layers comes out clean. Cool in pans on wire racks 10 minutes.

With small knife, loosen layers from sides of pans; invert onto wire racks. Remove waxed paper; cool completely.

5. Place 1 cake layer on cake plate; spread with 1/2 cup frosting. Top with second cake layer, spread on 1/2 cup frosting, and cover with remaining layer. Frost side and top of cake with remaining frosting.

Each serving: about 355 calories, 3g protein, 53g carbohydrate, 15g total fat (9g saturated), 0g fiber, 66mg cholesterol, 250mg sodium

FROSTING A LAYER CAKE

To ice a layer cake like a pro, just follow this advice.

Before you begin, brush off any crumbs and use a serrated knife to trim away crisp edges. If you like, tuck waxed paper strips under the cake to keep the platter clean while you work.

Place the first layer, rounded side down, on a serving platter. Using a narrow offset spatula, spread the top with 1/2 to 1/3 cup frosting. Top with the second layer, rounded side up. Thinly frost the top and sides of the cake—this layer will help hold any crumbs firmly in place.

Finish with a thick layer of frosting, smoothing out the edge where the top and side of the frosting meet by sweeping and swirling the frosting toward the center of the cake.

Lemon Layer Cake

Full of bright citrus flavor, this light and creamy cake is the ideal finale to a spring or summer dinner party. To make it even more spectacular, fill it with our luscious homemade lemon curd.

Active time: 1 hour plus chilling
Bake time: 33 minutes
Makes: 16 servings

3 to 4 lemons
1 Ruby Red grapefruit
2¼ cups cake flour (not self-rising)
1½ cups granulated sugar
2 teaspoons baking powder
½ teaspoon baking soda
½ teaspoon salt
½ cup vegetable oil
5 large eggs, separated
2 large egg whites
½ teaspoon cream of tartar
8 ounces mascarpone cheese
1½ cups heavy whipping cream
1 cup confectioners' sugar
1 teaspoon vanilla extract
⅓ cup sour cream
1 cup lemon curd, store-bought or homemade (page 346)
Edible flowers for garnish (optional)

1. Prepare cake layers: Preheat oven to 325°F. Grease bottoms of three 9-inch round cake pans. Line bottoms of pans with parchment paper; grease parchment. From lemons, finely grate 4 teaspoons peel and squeeze ¼ cup juice. From grapefruit, squeeze ½ cup juice; set aside.

2. In large bowl, with wire whisk, blend flour, 1 cup granulated sugar, baking powder, baking soda, and salt. Make well in center. Add oil, 5 egg yolks, lemon juice, grapefruit juice, and 2 teaspoons lemon peel; whisk into dry ingredients until smooth.

3. In another large bowl, with mixer on high speed, beat all 7 egg whites until foamy. Add cream of tartar and beat until soft peaks form. Gradually sprinkle in remaining ½ cup granulated sugar, 2 tablespoons at a time, and whip until whites just stand in stiff peaks when beaters are lifted. With rubber spatula, gently fold one-third of egg white mixture into yolk mixture to loosen batter, then fold in remaining egg whites.

4. Divide batter among prepared pans. Gently smooth tops. Bake 33 to 35 minutes or until top springs back when lightly touched. Cool cakes completely in pans on wire racks. With knife, carefully loosen cakes from sides of pans. Invert onto wire racks. Carefully peel off parchment and discard. Cake layers can be wrapped tightly in plastic wrap and kept at room temperature up to 1 day.

5. Prepare frosting: In large bowl, with mixer on low speed, beat mascarpone and cream to combine. Gradually beat in confectioners' sugar. Increase speed to medium-low and beat until soft peaks form. Fold in vanilla and remaining 2 teaspoons lemon peel until well blended.

6. Fold sour cream into lemon curd until well blended.

7. Assemble cake: Place 1 cake layer on serving plate, flat side up. Spread with half of curd and top with second cake layer, flat side up. Spread remaining curd on top. Cover with remaining cake layer, flat side up. Frost side and top of cake with frosting. Refrigerate assembled cake at least 1 hour and up to 6 hours to allow flavors to meld and frosting to set. (Cover loosely with plastic wrap after 1 hour.) To serve, let stand at room temperature 15 minutes. Garnish with edible flowers if you like.

Each serving: about 470 calories, 6g protein, 55g carbohydrate, 25g total fat (11g saturated), 0g fiber, 132mg cholesterol, 240mg sodium

Cranberry-Vanilla Cake

This showstopping cake features three delectable layers slathered with a cranberry-apricot filling and all topped with gobs of creamy whipped frosting. To make it extra festive, we finished it with a candied cranberry garnish.

Active time: 50 minutes plus cooling and chilling
Bake time: 40 minutes
Makes: 16 servings

VANILLA CAKE

3 cups cake flour (not self-rising)
1 tablespoon baking powder
1/4 teaspoon salt
1 cup butter or margarine (2 sticks), at room temperature
2 cups sugar
5 large eggs, at room temperature
2 teaspoons vanilla extract
1 1/4 cups low-fat buttermilk

CRANBERRY FILLING

1 bag (12 ounces) fresh or thawed frozen cranberries
1 cup sugar
1/3 cup apricot jam
1/4 teaspoon ground cinnamon

GARNISH AND FROSTING

1/4 cup water
3/4 cup sugar
1 cup fresh or thawed frozen cranberries
Crème Fraîche Whipped Cream Frosting (page 342)

1. Prepare cake: Preheat oven to 350°F. Line bottoms of three 8-inch cake pans with parchment paper. Grease sides of pans and parchment. Into large bowl, sift flour, baking powder, and salt.

2. In large mixer bowl, with mixer on medium-high speed, beat butter and sugar until smooth and fluffy. Beat in eggs, one at a time, until incorporated. Beat in vanilla. Reduce speed to low; alternately add buttermilk and flour mixture in two or three parts, beating well after each addition.

3. Divide batter among pans; smooth tops. Tap pans firmly against counter. Bake 40 to 45 minutes or until toothpick inserted in center of cake comes out clean. Cool in pans on wire rack 10 minutes. Invert cakes onto rack; remove pans and peel off parchment. Cool completely. Cakes may be wrapped in plastic and stored at room temperature up to 1 day.

4. Prepare filling: In 3-quart saucepan, combine cranberries, sugar, jam, and cinnamon. Cook over medium heat 8 to 10 minutes or until most berries burst, stirring often. Transfer to bowl; refrigerate until cold.

5. Prepare garnish: In 1-quart saucepan, combine water and 1/4 cup sugar. Heat to boiling on high. Stir in cranberries. Cool completely, then drain. Place remaining 1/2 cup sugar on plate. Toss berries in sugar to coat. Place on wire rack; let dry 1 hour.

6. To assemble: Place 1 cake layer on cake stand; spread half of filling on top. Repeat with another layer and remaining filling. Top with third layer. Spread frosting all over cake. Garnish with sugared berries. Cake can be covered and refrigerated up to 1 day. Remove from refrigerator 30 minutes before serving.

Each serving: about 590 calories, 6g protein, 85g carbohydrate, 26g total fat (16g saturated), 2g fiber, 137mg cholesterol, 300mg sodium

Carrot Cake

Here's a classic combo: Moist carrot cake with walnuts and raisins and luscious cream cheese icing.

Active time: 40 minutes plus cooling
Bake time: 55 minutes
Makes: 16 servings

2 1/2 cups all-purpose flour
2 teaspoons baking soda
2 teaspoons ground cinnamon
1 teaspoon baking powder
1 teaspoon salt
1/2 teaspoon ground nutmeg
4 large eggs
1 cup granulated sugar
3/4 cup packed light brown sugar
1 cup vegetable oil
1/4 cup milk
1 tablespoon vanilla extract
3 cups lightly packed shredded carrots (about 6 medium)
1 cup walnuts (4 ounces), chopped
3/4 cup dark seedless raisins
Cream Cheese Frosting (page 342)

1. Preheat oven to 350°F. Grease 13" by 9" metal baking pan. Line with waxed paper; grease paper. Dust with flour. In medium bowl, mix flour, baking soda, cinnamon, baking powder, salt, and nutmeg.

2. In large bowl, with mixer on medium-high, beat eggs and both sugars 2 minutes, scraping bowl often with rubber spatula. Beat in oil, milk, and vanilla. Add flour mixture and beat on low until smooth, about 1 minute, scraping bowl often. Fold in carrots, walnuts, and raisins.

3. Pour batter into prepared pan. Bake 55 minutes to 1 hour, until toothpick inserted in center of cake comes out almost clean, with some moist crumbs attached. Cool in pan on wire rack 10 minutes; invert onto rack. Remove waxed paper and cool completely.

4. Place cake on platter and generously frost top.

Each serving: about 550 calories, 6g protein, 7g carbohydrate, 28g total fat (8g saturated), 2g fiber, 77mg cholesterol, 445mg sodium

Double Gingerbread with Lemon Custard Sauce

Gingerbread has been a GH culinary constant since 1886. Over the years, while the essential ingredients—flour, molasses, ginger—have stayed the same, each era tweaked the tradition. Here, our latest take on this spice cake combines ground ginger with fresh for a double dose of sweet heat. The zesty lemon curd, made in minutes, balances the bite.

Active time: 20 minutes
Bake time: 35 minutes
Makes: 9 servings

LEMON CUSTARD SAUCE

2 lemons
1/2 cup sugar
2 teaspoons cornstarch
2 tablespoons cold water
2 large egg yolks
3 tablespoons butter, cut into small pieces
  (do not use margarine)
1/4 cup reduced-fat sour cream

GINGERBREAD

2 cups all-purpose flour
1/2 cup sugar
2 teaspoons ground ginger
1 teaspoon ground cinnamon
1/2 teaspoon baking soda
1/2 teaspoon salt
1 cup light (mild) molasses
1/2 cup butter or margarine (1 stick), cut into 8 pieces
3/4 cup boiling water
1 tablespoon grated peeled fresh ginger
1 large egg

1. Prepare sauce: From lemons, grate 1½ teaspoons peel and squeeze 1/3 cup juice. Set aside separately.

2. In 2-quart saucepan, with wire whisk, combine sugar and cornstarch. Whisk in water and lemon juice until smooth. Whisk in egg yolks. Cook over medium heat, whisking constantly, until mixture boils. Reduce heat to low and simmer 1 minute or until thickened, still whisking constantly.

3. Strain mixture through sieve set over medium bowl. Stir in butter and lemon peel until butter melts. Cool 10 minutes, then cover and refrigerate 20 minutes or until cold. Stir in sour cream. Makes 1 cup lemon sauce.

4. Meanwhile, prepare cake: Preheat oven to 350°F. Grease and flour 9-inch square metal baking pan. In large bowl, with wire whisk, combine flour, sugar, ground ginger, cinnamon, baking soda, and salt.

5. In small heatproof bowl, place molasses and butter. Add boiling water and grated ginger and stir until butter melts. Add molasses mixture and egg to flour mixture; whisk until blended. Pour batter into prepared pan.

6. Bake 35 to 40 minutes or until toothpick inserted in center of gingerbread comes out clean. Cool in pan on wire rack 20 minutes. Cut into squares, drizzle with lemon sauce, and serve warm.

Each serving: about 445 calories, 5g protein, 70g carbohydrate, 18g total fat (10g saturated), 1g fiber, 114mg cholesterol, 375mg sodium

TEST KITCHEN KNOW-HOW

DUSTING A PAN WITH FLOUR

Take this step as added insurance that your cake won't stick.

After you have greased the pan, sprinkle about 1 tablespoon flour into the pan and tilt to coat the bottom and side with the flour; invert the pan and tap out excess flour.

For chocolate cakes that won't be frosted or glazed, substitute unsweetened cocoa for the flour. The cocoa will be invisible on the chocolate cake after baking.

TOP: CARROT CAKE; BOTTOM: DOUBLE GINGERBREAD WITH LEMON CUSTARD SAUCE

Cardamom Buttermilk Cake

Cardamom is often used in Scandinavian baking. This cake has a thin, crunchy pecan crust that beautifully complements the berry-and-cream filling.

Active time: 25 minutes plus cooling
Bake time: 30 minutes
Makes: 12 servings

14 tablespoons butter or margarine, softened
3/4 cup pecans (3 ounces), finely chopped
1 1/4 cups plus 2 tablespoons granulated sugar
1 orange
2 cups all-purpose flour
1 teaspoon baking soda
1/2 teaspoon salt
1/2 teaspoon ground cardamom
1/2 teaspoon ground ginger
1 cup buttermilk
1 1/2 teaspoons vanilla extract
1/2 cup packed light brown sugar
2 large eggs
1/2 cup heavy cream
1/2 pint raspberries (6 ounces)

1. Preheat oven to 350°F. Use 2 tablespoons butter to generously grease two 9-inch round cake pans. In small bowl, stir together pecans and 1/4 cup granulated sugar. Coat prepared pans with pecan mixture. From orange, grate 1/2 teaspoon peel and squeeze 2 tablespoons juice.

2. In bowl, stir together flour, baking soda, salt, cardamom, ginger, and orange peel. In second bowl, mix buttermilk, orange juice, and 1 teaspoon vanilla.

3. In large bowl, with mixer on medium speed, beat remaining 12 tablespoons butter until smooth. Add 1 cup granulated sugar and brown sugar, beating until combined. Reduce speed to low. Add eggs, one at a time, beating well after each. Add flour mixture alternately with buttermilk mixture, beginning and ending with flour mixture. Beat until smooth, scraping bowl occasionally with rubber spatula.

4. Spoon batter into prepared pans. Bake 30 minutes or until toothpick inserted in center of cake comes out clean. Cool in pans on wire racks 10 minutes. With small knife, loosen layers from sides of pans; invert onto racks to cool completely.

5. In medium bowl, combine cream, remaining 2 tablespoons granulated sugar, and remaining 1/2 teaspoon vanilla. With mixer on high speed, beat until stiff peaks form. Fold in raspberries.

6. Place 1 cake layer, nut side down, on cake plate. Spoon whipped-cream mixture over cake. Top with remaining layer, nut side up. Serve immediately, or refrigerate for up to 4 hours.

Each serving: about 420 calories, 5g protein, 52g carbohydrate, 22g total fat (10g saturated), 1g fiber, 81mg cholesterol, 360mg sodium

Applesauce Spice Cake

Served straight from the pan, a square or two of applesauce cake should be quite a hit with the after-school crowd. Not to mention brown-baggers, unexpected guests, and midnight snackers.

Active time: 20 minutes plus cooling
Bake time: 40 minutes
Makes: 9 servings

2 cups all-purpose flour
1 1/2 teaspoons ground cinnamon
1 teaspoon baking powder
1/2 teaspoon baking soda
1/2 teaspoon ground ginger
1/4 teaspoon ground nutmeg
1/2 teaspoon salt
1/2 cup butter or margarine (1 stick), softened
1 cup packed dark brown sugar
1/4 cup granulated sugar
2 large eggs
1 1/4 cups unsweetened applesauce
1/2 cup dark seedless raisins
Confectioners' sugar for sprinkling

1. Preheat oven to 350°F. Grease and flour 9-inch square metal baking pan.

2. In medium bowl, stir together flour, cinnamon, baking powder, baking soda, ginger, nutmeg, and salt.

3. In large bowl, with mixer on low speed, beat butter and both sugars until blended. Increase speed to medium-high; beat 3 minutes until well combined. Add eggs, one at a time, beating well after each. Reduce speed to low. Beat in applesauce (mixture may appear curdled). Beat in flour mixture until smooth, scraping bowl occasionally with rubber spatula. Stir in raisins.

4. Scrape batter into prepared pan and spread evenly. Bake 40 minutes, or until toothpick inserted in center of cake comes out clean. Cool completely in pan on wire rack. Before serving, sprinkle with confectioners' sugar.

Each serving: about 370 calories, 5g protein, 63g carbohydrate, 12g total fat (7g saturated), 2g fiber, 75mg cholesterol, 385mg sodium

Apricot Upside-Down Cake

Instead of the traditional pineapple, this twist on the classic takes advantage of ripe apricots to create a great dessert for any summertime get-together.

Active time: 25 minutes
Bake time: 35 minutes
Makes: 8 servings

1/2 cup packed brown sugar
8 ripe apricots, each cut in half and pitted
1 1/4 cups all-purpose flour
1/2 cup granulated sugar
1/4 cup cornmeal
1 1/4 teaspoons baking powder
1/2 teaspoon salt
1/2 teaspoon baking soda
3/4 cup low-fat buttermilk
2 large eggs
2 teaspoons butter or margarine, melted
2 tablespoons canola oil
1 teaspoon freshly grated lemon peel
1 teaspoon vanilla extract

1. Preheat oven to 350°F. Spray 10-inch cast-iron or ovenproof skillet with nonstick cooking spray. Sprinkle brown sugar evenly over bottom of skillet. Arrange apricot halves, cut side down, over brown sugar.

2. In large bowl, whisk flour, granulated sugar, cornmeal, baking powder, salt, and baking soda until blended. In small bowl, whisk buttermilk, eggs, butter, oil, lemon peel, and vanilla until blended. Add buttermilk mixture to dry ingredients and fold with spatula until just blended. Pour batter over apricots and spread to cover evenly.

3. Bake 35 to 40 minutes, or until toothpick inserted in center of cake comes out clean. Let cool in skillet on wire rack 10 minutes. Run knife around side of skillet. Place platter on top of skillet and carefully invert cake onto platter. Remove skillet. Cool cake about 30 minutes to serve warm.

Each serving: about 290 calories, 5g protein, 49g carbohydrate, 8g total fat (1g saturated), 2g fiber, 62mg cholesterol, 365mg sodium

CHOCOLATE CAKES

Many people think that chocolate cake is more deserving than apple pie of the title America's #1 Dessert. This assortment of rich, fudgy indulgences is sure to sway your vote.

Chocolate Layer Cake

This moist triple-layer cake is layered with swoon-worthy truffle-like frosting.

Active time: 45 minutes plus cooling
Bake time: 22 minutes
Makes: 16 servings

CAKE

2 cups all-purpose flour
1 cup unsweetened cocoa
1 1/2 teaspoons baking soda
1/4 teaspoon salt
3/4 cup butter or margarine (1 1/2 sticks), softened
1 cup packed brown sugar
1 cup granulated sugar
3 large eggs
2 teaspoons vanilla extract
1 1/2 cups low-fat buttermilk

FROSTING

1/3 cup unsweetened cocoa
1/3 cup boiling water
1 cup butter or margarine (2 sticks), softened
2 tablespoons confectioners' sugar
12 ounces semisweet chocolate, melted and cooled

1. Prepare cake: Place one oven rack in upper third of oven and one rack in lower third; preheat oven to 350°F. Grease three 8-inch round cake pans. Line bottoms of pans with waxed paper; grease paper. Dust pans with flour.

2. On another sheet of waxed paper, combine flour, cocoa, baking soda, and salt. In large bowl, with mixer on low speed, beat butter and both sugars until blended. Increase speed to high; beat 5 minutes or until pale and fluffy, occasionally scraping bowl with rubber spatula. Reduce speed to medium-low; add eggs, one at a time, beating well after each. Beat in vanilla until blended. Add flour mixture alternately with buttermilk, beginning and ending with flour mixture; beat just until batter is smooth, occasionally scraping bowl with rubber spatula.

3. Divide batter among prepared pans. Stagger pans in oven, placing two on upper rack and one on lower rack, so that top pans are not directly above bottom one. Bake 22 to 25 minutes or until toothpick inserted in center comes out clean. Cool in pans on wire racks 10 minutes. With small knife, loosen layers from sides of pans; invert onto wire racks. Carefully remove and discard waxed paper; cool completely, about 45 minutes. If you like, wrap layers well and store at room temperature up to one day or freeze up to one month. Bring to room temperature before frosting cake.

4. Meanwhile, prepare frosting: In small bowl, combine cocoa and boiling water, stirring until smooth. In large bowl, with mixer on medium-high speed, beat butter and confectioners' sugar 5 minutes or until fluffy. Reduce speed to medium-low; add melted chocolate, then cocoa mixture, beating until smooth and occasionally scraping bowl with rubber spatula. If frosting is too runny, refrigerate until just stiff enough to spread.

5. Place one cake layer, bottom side up, on serving plate; spread with 1/3 cup frosting. Top with second layer, bottom side up; spread with 1/3 cup frosting. Place remaining layer, bottom side up, on top. Spread remaining frosting over sides and top of cake.

Each serving: about 495 calories, 7g protein, 55g carbohydrate, 30g total fat (18g saturated), 4g fiber, 98mg cholesterol, 415mg sodium

Dark Chocolate–Raspberry Layer Cake

This masterpiece of a cake brings together tangy cream-cheese frosting, fresh raspberries, and three layers of intensely chocolaty cake.

Active time: 1 hour 5 minutes
Bake time: 15 minutes plus cooling
Makes: 12 servings

Unsweetened cocoa, for sprinkling
9 ounces bittersweet chocolate (60% to 70% cacao), chopped
3 ounces unsweetened chocolate, chopped
1 tablespoon vanilla extract
1/4 teaspoon salt
1 1/2 cups granulated sugar
1 cup plus 6 tablespoons butter or margarine (2 3/4 sticks)
8 large eggs, separated
1/2 cup all-purpose flour
1 pint raspberries (12 ounces)
12 ounces cream cheese, softened
1 1/2 cups confectioners' sugar

1. Preheat oven to 350°F. Grease three 9-inch round cake pans. Line bottoms with parchment paper; grease paper. Lightly dust with cocoa, tapping out excess.

2. Fill 4-quart saucepan with *water* to depth of 2 inches. Heat to simmering. In large heatproof bowl, combine both chocolates, vanilla, salt, 1 1/4 cups granulated sugar, and 10 tablespoons butter. Set over simmering water. Gently stir occasionally until chocolates and butter melt. Remove from heat. While stirring, add egg yolks, one at a time, beating well after each. Gently fold in flour just until incorporated.

3. In another large bowl, with mixer on medium-high speed, beat egg whites until frothy. Gradually add remaining 1/4 cup granulated sugar and continue beating until stiff peaks form (see page 235). Gently fold egg whites into chocolate mixture one-third at a time just until incorporated. Divide batter among prepared pans.

4. Bake 15 minutes or until cakes are set and toothpick inserted in centers comes out clean. Cool in pans on wire racks 10 minutes. Invert onto racks; remove pans. Discard parchment paper; cool completely.

5. Place 1/2 cup raspberries in fine-mesh sieve set over small bowl. With wooden spoon, mash raspberries to extract 2 tablespoons juice; discard solids. In large bowl, with mixer on medium speed, beat cream cheese and remaining 12 tablespoons butter until smooth and fluffy. Beat in confectioners' sugar, then raspberry juice, until blended. If frosting is runny, refrigerate 5 minutes to achieve proper consistency. Transfer to piping bag fitted with 1/2-inch plain tip.

6. Place 1 cake layer on cake stand. Decoratively pipe on one-third of frosting. Top with second cake layer. Repeat, piping remaining frosting on final layer. Decorate top of cake with raspberries and serve with any remaining raspberries. Refrigerate up to 1 day. Bring to room temperature before serving.

Each serving: about 670 calories, 10g protein, 57g carbohydrate, 47g total fat (28g saturated), 4g fiber, 211mg cholesterol, 205mg sodium

German's Chocolate Cake

We're not sure what's more delicious: The super-moist chocolate layers or the sweet and gooey coconut and pecan frosting. Happily you get to enjoy an abundance of both in this old-fashioned classic. Contrary to what most people think, this beloved chocolate cake is not a German creation. The correct name is German's, after the man who first created the baking chocolate used for the cake.

Active time: 45 minutes plus cooling
Bake time: 30 minutes
Makes: 16 servings

2 cups all-purpose flour
1 teaspoon baking soda
1/4 teaspoon salt
1 1/4 cups buttermilk
1 teaspoon vanilla extract
3 large eggs, separated
1 1/2 cups sugar
3/4 cup butter or margarine (1 1/2 sticks), softened
4 ounces sweet baking chocolate, melted
Coconut-Pecan Frosting (page 336)

1. Place one oven rack in upper third of oven and one rack in lower third; preheat oven to 350°F. Grease three 8-inch round cake pans. Line bottoms with waxed paper; grease and flour paper.

2. In small bowl, combine flour, baking soda, and salt. In 2-cup measuring cup, mix buttermilk and vanilla.

3. In medium bowl, with mixer on medium-high speed, beat egg whites until frothy. Gradually sprinkle in 3/4 cup sugar, 1 tablespoon at a time, and beat until soft peaks form when beaters are lifted.

4. In large bowl, with mixer on medium speed, beat butter until light and fluffy. Add remaining 3/4 cup sugar and beat until well blended. Reduce speed to medium-low; add egg yolks, one at a time, beating well after each. Beat in melted chocolate.

5. Reduce speed to low; add flour mixture alternately with buttermilk mixture, beginning and ending with flour mixture. Beat until smooth, scraping bowl occasionally. With rubber spatula, fold half of beaten whites into batter; gently fold in remaining whites.

6. Divide batter among prepared pans. Stagger pans in oven, placing two on upper rack and one on lower rack, so that pans are not directly above one another. Bake 30 minutes, or until toothpick inserted in center of cake comes out almost clean. Cool in pans on wire racks 10 minutes. With knife, loosen layers from pans; invert onto racks. Remove waxed paper; cool completely.

7. Place 1 layer on cake plate; spread with 1 cup frosting. Top with second cake layer and another cup of frosting. Top with remaining layer. Frost side and top of cake with remaining frosting.

Each serving: about 505 calories, 5g protein, 53g carbohydrate, 31g total fat (16g saturated), 2g fiber, 140mg cholesterol, 320mg sodium

TIP If you're a serious chocolate lover, in addition to the Coconut-Pecan Frosting, you can whip up a batch of our Chocolate Butter Frosting (page 333), using bittersweet or semisweet chocolate—your call. Generously fill the layers with the coconut frosting, then ice the top and sides of the cake with the chocolate frosting. Garnish with a sprinkling of toasted coconut (see page xxiii) if you like.

Checkerboard Cake

Cookware shops sell special pans for making this cake. However, you can turn out a handsome specimen without them. You will need two pastry bags and three 8-inch round pans.

Active time: 50 minutes plus cooling
Bake time: 20 minutes
Makes: 16 servings

2¼ cups cake flour (not self-rising)
2 teaspoons baking powder
½ teaspoon salt
¾ cup plus 1 tablespoon milk
1½ teaspoons vanilla extract
1½ cups sugar
¾ cup butter or margarine (1½ sticks), softened
3 large eggs
2 ounces semisweet chocolate, melted
1 ounce unsweetened chocolate, melted
Silky Chocolate Butter Frosting (page 334)

1. Place one oven rack in upper third of oven and one rack in lower third; preheat oven to 350°F. Grease three 8-inch round cake pans. Line bottoms with waxed paper; grease paper. Dust pans with flour.

2. In medium bowl, stir together flour, baking powder, and salt. In 1-cup measuring cup, mix ¾ cup milk and vanilla.

3. In large bowl, with mixer on low speed, beat sugar and butter until blended. Increase speed to high; beat 5 minutes, until light and creamy. Reduce speed to medium-low; add eggs, one at a time, beating well after each. Reduce speed to low; add flour mixture in alternation with milk mixture, beginning and ending with flour mixture. Beat just until smooth, scraping bowl occasionally with rubber spatula.

4. Spoon half of batter into medium bowl. Into batter remaining in large bowl, with rubber spatula, stir in both melted chocolates and remaining 1 tablespoon milk.

5. Create checkerboard cake (see photos opposite): Spoon vanilla batter into 1 large pastry bag with ½-inch opening (or use heavy-duty resealable plastic bag with corner cut to make ½-inch opening). Repeat with chocolate batter to fill second large pastry bag with ½-inch opening. Pipe 1½-inch-wide band of chocolate batter around inside edge of two prepared cake pans, then pipe 1½-inch wide band of vanilla batter next to each chocolate band. Pipe enough chocolate batter to fill center of each pan. In third pan, repeat same pattern but reverse colors (start by piping vanilla batter around inside edge of pan).

6. Stagger cake pans on two oven racks, placing two on upper rack and one on lower rack, so that pans are not directly above one another. Bake 20 minutes, or until toothpick inserted in center of cake comes out almost clean. Cool in pans on wire racks 10 minutes. With small knife, loosen layers from sides of pans; invert onto wire racks. Remove waxed paper; cool completely.

7. Place 1 mostly chocolate cake layer on serving plate; spread with ½ cup frosting. Top with mostly vanilla cake layer. Spread with another ½ cup frosting. Top with remaining mostly chocolate layer; spread remaining frosting over side and top of cake.

Each serving: about 455 calories, 4g protein, 51g carbohydrate, 27g total fat (16g saturated), 1g fiber, 98mg cholesterol, 365mg sodium

MAKING A CHECKERBOARD CAKE

The checkerboard effect is created by piping alternating rings of chocolate and vanilla batter into three pans, then stacking the layers. The result: stunning!

To begin, pipe a 1½-inch band of chocolate batter around the edge of one waxed-paper-lined-pan.

Use the second pastry bag, filled with the vanilla batter, to pipe a white ring inside the chocolate ring.

Fill in the center with chocolate batter. Fill a second pan in the same way, then do the third pan in reverse, with vanilla batter at the outer edge and center.

Stack, fill, and frost the cake, alternating mostly chocolate with mostly vanilla layers as directed. When you slice the cake, your fancy checkerboard will be revealed.

Flourless Chocolate Hazelnut Cake

This fudgy flourless cake boasts a creaminess reminiscent of truffles. Toasted hazelnuts folded into the batter add a delectable depth of flavor.

Active time: 30 minutes plus cooling
Bake time: 35 minutes
Makes: 12 servings

1 cup hazelnuts, toasted and skinned (see page xxiii), cooled
1¼ cups sugar
8 ounces semisweet chocolate, chopped
4 tablespoons butter or margarine
5 large eggs
¾ cup heavy cream

1. Preheat oven to 350°F. Lightly grease 9-inch springform pan. Line bottom with waxed or parchment paper; grease paper.

2. In food processor, place ¾ cup nuts and ¼ cup sugar; pulse until finely ground. With chef's knife, roughly chop remaining nuts; set aside separately.

3. In 3-quart saucepan, melt chocolate and butter over medium-low heat, stirring occasionally. Meanwhile, in large bowl, with mixer on medium-high speed, beat eggs and ½ cup sugar 7 minutes or until tripled in volume. With rubber spatula, fold in chocolate mixture, then fold in ground-nut mixture. Pour batter into prepared pan and bake 35 minutes or until top is dry and cracked and toothpick inserted in center comes out slightly wet. Cool in pan on wire rack 10 minutes. Remove side of pan and cool 30 minutes longer on wire rack.

4. Meanwhile, line 9-inch round cake pan with foil. Spread reserved chopped hazelnuts in pan. In 12-inch skillet, spread remaining ½ cup sugar in even layer. Cook over medium-high 3 to 5 minutes or until melted and golden, swirling pan to help sugar cook evenly. (Do not stir.) Immediately drizzle melted sugar over nuts in pan to coat. Cool praline completely in pan.

Top: Flourless Chocolate Hazelnut Cake;
Bottom: Chocolate Truffle Cake

5. Meanwhile, in large bowl, with mixer on medium speed, beat cream until soft peaks form, 3 to 5 minutes.

6. To serve, break cooled praline into 12 large pieces. Cut cake and place slices on plates. Top each slice with dollop of whipped cream and shard of hazelnut praline.

Each serving: about 360 calories, 6g protein, 33g carbohydrate, 25g total fat (11g saturated), 2g fiber, 120mg cholesterol, 75mg sodium

Chocolate Truffle Cake

This devilishly dense flourless chocolate dessert should be baked a day ahead and refrigerated overnight to let it firm up. Adorn the top with hearts, stars, crescent moons, or other shapes made with stencils (see below).

Active time: 1 hour plus chilling
Bake time: 35 minutes
Makes: 20 servings

14 ounces semisweet chocolate
2 ounces unsweetened chocolate
1 cup (2 sticks) butter (do not use margarine)
9 large eggs, separated
1/2 cup granulated sugar
1/4 teaspoon cream of tartar
Confectioners' sugar and/or cocoa for sprinkling

1. Preheat oven to 300°F. Cover bottom of 9-inch springform pan with foil, wrapping foil around to back of metal disk (this will make it easier to remove cake). Replace bottom in pan. Grease and flour foil bottom and side of pan.

2. In heavy 2-quart saucepan, combine both chocolates and butter; melt over very low heat, stirring often, until smooth. Pour chocolate mixture into large bowl.

3. In small bowl, with mixer on high speed, beat egg yolks and granulated sugar until very thick and lemon colored, about 5 minutes. Add egg-yolk mixture to chocolate mixture, stirring well with rubber spatula.

4. In another large bowl, with clean beaters and with mixer on high speed, whip egg whites and cream of tartar until soft peaks form when beaters are lifted.

With rubber spatula or wire whisk, fold beaten egg whites into chocolate mixture, one-third at a time.

5. Pour batter into prepared pan; spread evenly. Bake 35 minutes. (Do not overbake; the cake will firm up while standing and chilling.) Cool cake completely in pan on wire rack. Refrigerate overnight in pan.

6. To remove cake from pan, run hot knife around edge of cake, then lift off side of pan. Invert cake onto cake plate; unwrap foil from back of bottom and lift off bottom of pan. Peel foil from cake.

7. Let cake stand 1 hour at room temperature before serving. Decorate top of cake with sugar and/or cocoa, using fine sieve and stencil, if desired.

Each serving: about 250 calories, 4g protein, 19g carbohydrate, 19g total fat (11g saturated), 2g fiber, 120mg cholesterol, 125mg sodium

TEST KITCHEN KNOW-HOW

SIMPLE CAKE STENCILS

To decorate a cake with stars or other simple shapes, use a stencil.

Cut out your desired shape from a square of lightweight cardboard (a manila file folder works well). Hold the stencil over the top of the cake and sift a heavy layer of unsweetened cocoa, confectioners' sugar, or cinnamon sugar over it. Repeat as needed to make patterns over the whole cake.

Molten Chocolate Cakes

Serve these showstoppers hot from the oven while the centers are still molten. They're the perfect party dessert, because the batter can be made ahead of time, poured into custard cups, and refrigerated for up to 24 hours (or even frozen for up to two weeks). Bake the refrigerated batter for 10 minutes, or the frozen batter—straight from the freezer!—for 16 minutes.

Active time: 20 minutes
Bake time: 8 minutes
Makes: 8 servings

1/2 cup butter or margarine (1 stick)
4 ounces semisweet chocolate, chopped
1/4 cup heavy cream
1/2 teaspoon vanilla extract
1/4 cup all-purpose flour
2 large eggs
2 large egg yolks
1/4 cup sugar
Whipped cream or vanilla ice cream for serving (optional)

1. Preheat oven to 400°F. Grease eight 6-ounce custard cups. Sprinkle with granulated sugar.

2. In 3-quart saucepan, melt butter, chocolate, and cream over low heat, stirring occasionally, until smooth. Remove pan from heat. Whisk in vanilla and flour until blended.

3. In medium bowl, with mixer on high speed, beat eggs, egg yolks, and sugar until thick and lemon-colored, about 10 minutes. Fold egg mixture, one-third at a time, into chocolate mixture.

4. Divide batter among prepared custard cups. Place cups on jelly-roll pan for easier handling and bake 8 to 9 minutes, until edge of each cake is set but center still jiggles. Cool in pan on wire rack 3 minutes. Run small knife around side of each cup to loosen cake and turn out onto individual dessert plate. Serve immediately with whipped cream or ice cream, if desired.

Each serving without whipped cream or ice cream: about 300 calories, 4g protein, 22g carbohydrate, 23g total fat (13g saturated), 1g fiber, 148mg cholesterol, 140mg sodium

Whoopie Pies

Mini chocolate cakes plus marshmallow filling—yum! Everyone gets to enjoy their own little pie.

Active time: 30 minutes plus cooling
Bake: 12 minutes per batch
Makes: 12 whoopie pies

CAKES
2 cups all-purpose flour
1 cup granulated sugar
1/2 cup unsweetened cocoa
1 teaspoon baking soda
6 tablespoons butter or margarine, melted
3/4 cup milk
1 large egg
1 teaspoon vanilla extract
1/4 teaspoon salt

MARSHMALLOW-CREME FILLING
6 tablespoons butter or margarine, slightly softened
1 cup confectioners' sugar
1 jar (7 to 7 1/2 ounces) marshmallow creme
1 teaspoon vanilla extract

1. Preheat oven to 350°F. Grease two large cookie sheets.

2. Prepare cakes: In large bowl, combine flour, sugar, cocoa, and baking soda. Stir in butter, milk, egg, vanilla, and salt until smooth. Drop 12 heaping tablespoons of dough, 2 inches apart, on each prepared cookie sheet. Bake until toothpick inserted in center comes out clean, 12 to 14 minutes, rotating sheets between upper and lower oven racks halfway through. Transfer cookies to wire racks to cool completely.

4. Prepare filling: In large bowl, with mixer on medium speed, beat butter until smooth. Reduce speed to low; beat in sugar, then marshmallow creme and vanilla until smooth.

5. Spread 1 rounded tablespoon filling on flat side of 12 cookies and place 12 cookies on top. Store in airtight container, with waxed paper between layers, up to 3 days, or freeze up to 1 month.

Each pie: about 365 calories, 4g protein, 59g carbohydrate, 14g total fat (8g saturated), 2g fiber, 51mg cholesterol, 290mg sodium

WHOOPIE PIES

GOLDEN BUTTER CUPCAKES (PAGE 104)

CUPCAKES

If you're crazy for cupcakes, then we have the recipes for you. From nut- and raisin-studded carrot cake to filled and glazed Boston creams, these mini cakes are sure to satisfy.

Angel-Food Cupcakes

Light as air, these heavenly cupcakes need only a sprinkling of confectioners' sugar to complete them.

Active time: 35 minutes plus cooling
Bake time: 20 minutes
Makes: 24 cupcakes

1 cup cake flour (not self-rising)
½ cup confectioners' sugar plus additional for sprinkling
1⅔ cups egg whites (from 11 to 13 large eggs)
1½ teaspoons cream of tartar
½ teaspoon salt
1¼ cups granulated sugar
2 teaspoons vanilla extract

1. Preheat oven to 375°F. Line 24 standard muffin-pan cups with paper liners.

2. Onto waxed paper, sift flour with ½ cup confectioners' sugar to combine.

3. In large bowl, with mixer on medium speed, beat egg whites, cream of tartar, and salt until foamy. Increase speed to high; beat until soft peaks form. Sprinkle in granulated sugar, 2 tablespoons at a time, beating until whites stand in stiff, glossy peaks when beaters are lifted (see page 235). Beat in vanilla.

4. Sift flour mixture, one-third at a time, over beaten egg whites; fold in with rubber spatula just until flour mixture is no longer visible.

5. Spoon batter into prepared muffin cups. (Batter will be stiff; it should come almost 2 inches over top of muffin cups.) Bake 20 to 22 minutes or until toothpick inserted in center of cupcakes comes out clean. Immediately remove cupcakes from pans and cool completely on wire rack.

6. When cupcakes are cool, dust with confectioners' sugar.

Each cupcake: about 75 calories, 2g protein, 16g carbohydrate, 0g total fat, 0g fiber, 0mg cholesterol, 75mg sodium

ICING CUPCAKES

Decorating cupcakes is almost as fun as eating them.

To glaze cupcakes, place waxed paper underneath. Use a spoon to drizzle with warm glaze (it's okay if the glaze runs down the sides); let stand to harden.

For piped frosting, spoon buttercream or other dense frosting into a decorating bag fitted with a small decorating tip. Or use a heavy-weight resealable plastic bag instead; simply squeeze the frosting to one corner of the bag and snip diagonally to create small opening. Pipe frosting as desired.

Carrot Cupcakes

These tasty cupcakes feature sweet crushed pineapple and plenty of raisins. We topped ours with a marzipan carrot.

Active time: 35 minutes plus cooling
Bake time: 25 minutes
Makes: 24 cupcakes

2½ cups all-purpose flour
2 teaspoons ground cinnamon
1 teaspoon baking powder
1 teaspoon baking soda
1 teaspoon salt
¼ teaspoon nutmeg
2 large eggs
1 cup granulated sugar
½ cup packed light brown sugar
1 can (8 ounces) crushed pineapple in juice
½ cup vegetable oil
1 tablespoon vanilla extract
2½ cups lightly packed shredded carrots (4 to 5 medium)
⅔ cup dark seedless raisins
Cream Cheese Frosting (page 342)

1. Preheat oven to 350°F. Line 24 standard muffin-pan cups with paper liners.

2. On waxed paper, combine flour, cinnamon, baking powder, baking soda, salt, and nutmeg.

3. In medium bowl, with mixer on medium-high speed, beat eggs and both sugars 2 minutes or until creamy, scraping bowl often with rubber spatula. Beat in pineapple with its juice, oil, and vanilla. On low speed, gradually add flour mixture; beat 1 minute. Fold in carrots and raisins.

4. Spoon batter into prepared muffin cups. Bake 25 to 30 minutes or until toothpick inserted in center of cupcake comes out clean. Immediately remove cupcakes from pans and cool completely on wire rack.

5. When cupcakes are cool, spread generous layer of frosting on top.

Each cupcake: about 270 calories, 2g protein, 42g carbohydrate, 11g total fat (4g saturated), 1g fiber, 38mg cholesterol, 240mg sodium

Banana Cupcakes

Peanut butter frosting is an irresistible complement to rich banana bread cupcakes.

Active time: 35 minutes plus cooling
Bake time: 20 minutes
Makes: 24 cupcakes

2¹/2 cups all-purpose flour
³/4 cup granulated sugar
¹/2 cup packed light brown sugar
1¹/2 teaspoons baking powder
1 teaspoon baking soda
¹/2 teaspoon salt
¹/8 teaspoon ground cinnamon
1¹/3 cups mashed ripe bananas (2 medium)
3 large eggs
²/3 cup low-fat milk (1%)
¹/2 cup butter or margarine (1 stick), softened
1 tablespoon fresh lemon juice
2 teaspoons vanilla extract
Peanut Butter Frosting (page 341)

1. Preheat oven to 350°F. Line 24 standard muffin-pan cups with paper liners.

2. In large bowl, with mixer on low speed (or stand mixer fitted with whisk attachment), mix flour, both sugars, baking powder, baking soda, salt, and cinnamon until combined. Add bananas, eggs, milk, butter, lemon juice, and vanilla, and beat until blended. Increase speed to high; beat 1 to 2 minutes or until creamy, occasionally scraping bowl with rubber spatula.

3. Spoon batter into prepared muffin cups. Bake 20 to 25 minutes or until toothpick inserted in center comes out clean. Immediately remove cupcakes from pans and cool completely on wire rack.

4. When cupcakes are cool, spread generous layer of frosting on top.

Each cupcake: about 170 calories, 4g protein, 30g carbohydrate, 5g total fat (2g saturated), 1g fiber, 38mg cholesterol, 190mg sodium

TOP: CARROT CUPCAKES; BOTTOM: VEGAN DEEP CHOCOLATE CUPCAKES

HEALTHY MAKEOVER

Vegan Deep Chocolate Cupcakes

When shopping for vegan chocolate, be sure to read labels. Some semisweet chocolates contain milk solids.

Active time: 25 minutes
Bake time: 20 minutes
Makes: 12 cupcakes

1¹/2 cups all-purpose flour
³/4 cup granulated sugar
¹/3 cup unsweetened cocoa, sifted
³/4 teaspoon baking soda
¹/2 teaspoon salt
1 cup cold water
¹/3 cup canola oil
1 tablespoon cider vinegar
1¹/2 teaspoons vanilla extract
Silky Chocolate Butter Frosting (page 334; made
   with plain soy milk and vegan stick margarine)

1. Preheat oven to 350°F. Line 12-cup standard muffin pan with paper liners.

2. In large bowl, whisk flour, granulated sugar, cocoa, baking soda, and salt until blended. Add water, oil, vinegar, and vanilla; whisk until batter is smooth.

3. Spoon batter evenly into prepared muffin cups. Bake until toothpick inserted in center of cupcakes comes out clean, 20 to 25 minutes. Transfer cupcakes from pan to wire rack to cool completely.

4. When cupcakes are cool, spread generous layer of frosting on top.

Each cupcake: about 285 calories, 3g protein, 45g carbohydrate, 12g total fat (3g saturated), 2g fiber, 0mg cholesterol, 208mg sodium

Peanut Butter and Jelly Cupcakes

The kids will clamor for these cupcakes inspired by their favorite sandwich. Let them choose which jam to use for the filling.

Active time: 30 minutes plus cooling
Bake time: 23 minutes
Makes: 24 cupcakes

2 cups all-purpose flour
1¹/2 cups sugar
2 teaspoons baking powder
¹/2 teaspoon baking soda
¹/2 teaspoon salt
1 cup whole milk
³/4 cup creamy peanut butter
¹/4 cup vegetable shortening
2 teaspoons vanilla extract
3 large eggs
¹/2 cup jelly, jam, or preserves of choice
Small-Batch Butter Frosting (page 333)

1. Preheat oven to 350°F. Line 24 standard muffin-pan cups with paper liners.

2. In large bowl, with mixer on low speed (or stand mixer fitted with whisk attachment), mix flour, sugar, baking powder, baking soda, and salt until combined. Add milk, peanut butter, shortening, vanilla, and eggs, and beat until blended. Increase speed to high; beat 1 to 2 minutes or until creamy, occasionally scraping bowl with rubber spatula.

3. Spoon half of batter into prepared muffin cups, filling each cup about one-third full. Drop 1 teaspoon jelly in center of each cup; top with remaining batter. Bake 23 to 26 minutes or until toothpick inserted in center of cupcake comes out clean. Immediately remove cupcakes from pans and cool completely on wire rack.

4. When cupcakes are cool, spread generous layer of frosting on top.

Each cupcake: about 180 calories, 4g protein, 25g carbohydrate, 7g total fat (2g saturated), 1g fiber, 28mg cholesterol, 160mg sodium

Golden Butter Cupcakes

Here's a basic birthday cake cupcake. Finish with chocolate frosting as suggested below, or swirl the tops with the birthday boy or girl's icing pick. Vanilla butter frosting and shredded coconut are another favorite.

Active time: 30 minutes plus cooling
Bake time: 20 minutes
Makes: 24 cupcakes

2 cups all-purpose flour
1¹/2 cups sugar
2¹/2 teaspoons baking powder
1 teaspoon salt
³/4 cup butter or margarine (1¹/2 sticks), softened
³/4 cup milk
1¹/2 teaspoons vanilla extract
3 large eggs
Small-Batch Chocolate Butter Frosting (page 333)

1. Preheat oven to 350°F. Line 24 standard muffin-pan cups with paper liners.

2. In large bowl, with mixer on low speed, mix flour, sugar, baking powder, and salt until combined. Add butter, milk, vanilla, and eggs and beat just until blended. Increase speed to high; beat 1 to 2 minutes or until creamy, occasionally scraping bowl with rubber spatula.

3. Spoon batter into muffin cups. Bake cupcakes 20 to 25 minutes or until toothpick inserted in center comes out clean. Immediately remove cupcakes from pans and cool completely on wire rack.

4. When cupcakes are cool, spread generous layer of frosting on top.

Each cupcake: about 355 calories, 4g protein, 37g carbohydrate, 17g total fat (10g saturated), 2g fiber, 60mg cholesterol, 270mg sodium

Boston Cream Cupcakes

Enjoy this classic dessert in miniature form, complete with a pastry cream filling and sweet chocolate glaze.

Active time: 40 minutes plus standing
Makes: 24 cupcakes

4 ounces semisweet chocolate
4 tablespoons butter (do not use margarine)
1 tablespoon light corn syrup
3 to 4 tablespoons whole milk
Golden Butter Cupcakes (at left)
Vanilla Pastry Cream (page 345)

1. In 1-quart saucepan, heat chocolate, butter, corn syrup, and 3 teaspoons milk over medium-low heat until chocolate melts and mixture is smooth, stirring frequently. Stir in remaining 1 tablespoon milk if needed for easy spreading consistency, adding 1 teaspoon at a time. Makes about ¾ cup.

2. With tip of small knife, cut ½-inch-deep slit through bottom of cupcake liner and into cupcake. Spoon pastry cream into small decorating bag fitted with ¼-inch round tip. Place tip inside slit and squeeze in enough pastry cream (about 1 tablespoon) to fill cupcake. With knife, scrape off any excess pastry cream from cupcake bottom. Repeat with remaining cupcakes.

5. Holding cupcake upside down, dip top of each cupcake into chocolate glaze. (If glaze gets too cool to coat cakes, reheat over low heat.) Allow glaze to set 5 minutes before serving, or refrigerate cupcakes in airtight container up to 3 days.

Each cupcake: about 240 calories, 4g protein, 31g carbohydrate, 12g total fat (7g saturated), 1g fiber, 79mg cholesterol, 250mg sodium

---

HEALTHY MAKEOVER

Low-Fat Spice Cupcakes

These cupcakes are super moist, thanks to pumpkin puree and reduced-fat dairy.

Active time: 25 minutes plus cooling
Bake time: 22 minutes
Makes: 24 cupcakes

2½ cups cake flour
2 teaspoon baking soda
1½ teaspoons ground cinnamon
1½ teaspoons ground ginger
1 teaspoon baking powder
½ teaspoon salt
½ teaspoon ground allspice
1¼ cups packed light brown sugar
⅓ cup light corn-oil spread
1 can (15 ounces) pure pumpkin puree
⅔ cup no-cholesterol egg substitute
½ cup low-fat milk (1%)
1 tablespoon vanilla extract

1. Preheat oven to 350°F. Line 24 standard muffin-pan cups with paper liners.

2. On waxed paper, combine flour, baking soda, cinnamon, ginger, baking powder, salt, and allspice. In large bowl, with mixer on low speed, beat sugar and corn-oil spread until well mixed, scraping bowl with rubber spatula often. Increase speed to medium; beat in pumpkin, egg substitute, milk, and vanilla. With mixer on low, beat in flour mixture just until blended.

4. Spoon batter into prepared muffin cups. Bake 22 to 25 minutes or until toothpick inserted in center comes out clean. Remove cupcakes from pans and cool completely on wire rack.

Each cupcake: about 115 calories, 2g protein, 22g carbohydrate, 2g total fat (0g saturated), 1g fiber, 0mg cholesterol, 210mg sodium

RICH CHOCOLATE CUPCAKES

Rich Chocolate Cupcakes

For the chocolate lovers: Moist cocoa-flavored cupcakes swirled with chocolaty buttercream or fluffy white frosting (page 342).

Active time: 25 minutes plus cooling and frosting
Bake time: 22 minutes
Makes: 24 cupcakes

1¹/3 cups all-purpose flour
²/3 cup unsweetened cocoa
1¹/2 teaspoons baking powder
¹/2 teaspoon baking soda
¹/2 teaspoon salt
1 cup milk
1¹/2 teaspoons vanilla extract
1¹/3 cups sugar
10 tablespoons butter or margarine, softened
2 large eggs
Silky Chocolate Butter Frosting (page 334)

1. Preheat oven to 350°F. Line 24 standard muffin-pan cups with fluted paper liners.

2. On waxed paper, combine flour, cocoa, baking powder, baking soda, and salt. In 2-cup liquid measure, mix milk and vanilla; set aside.

3. In large bowl, using handheld mixer or heavy-duty mixer fitted with whisk attachment, beat sugar and butter on low speed, just until blended. Increase speed to high; beat 3 minutes or until mixture is light and creamy. Reduce speed to low; add eggs, one at a time, beating well after each.

4. Add flour mixture in alternation with milk mixture, beginning and ending with flour. Beat batter just until combined, occasionally scraping bowl with rubber spatula.

5. Spoon batter into prepared muffin cups. Bake until toothpick inserted in center of cupcakes comes out clean, 22 to 25 minutes. Immediately remove cupcakes from pans and cool completely on wire rack.

6. When cupcakes are cool, generously frost tops.

Each cupcake: about 210 calories, 7g protein, 18g carbohydrate, 12g total fat (7g saturated), 1g fiber, 36mg cholesterol, 191mg sodium

Black and White Cupcakes

This riff on the popular two-toned cookie tops chocolaty cupcakes with vanilla and chocolate glazes for a black and white effect.

Active time: 35 minutes
Makes: 24 cupcakes

BLACK GLAZE
1 cup confectioners' sugar
¹/2 cup unsweetened cocoa
2 tablespoons light corn syrup
2 to 3 tablespoons warm water

WHITE GLAZE
1¹/4 cup confectioners' sugar
1 tablespoon light corn syrup
4 to 5 teaspoons milk

Rich Chocolate Cupcakes (at left)

1. Prepare black glaze: In medium bowl, with fork, stir together confectioners' sugar, cocoa, and corn syrup. Add warm water, 1 tablespoon at a time, stirring until smooth, spreadable consistency is reached. Makes about ²/3 cup.

3. Prepare white glaze: In small bowl, with fork, stir confectioners' sugar, corn syrup, and 4 teaspoons milk until smooth. Stir in remaining 1 teaspoon milk if needed for easy spreading consistency. Makes about ¹/2 cup.

4. Spread white glaze evenly over half of each cupcake; let set slightly. Spread black glaze evenly over unglazed half; let set completely before serving.

Each cupcake: about 230 calories, 2g protein, 52g carbohydrate, 6g total fat (4g saturated), 1g fiber, 33mg cholesterol, 176mg sodium

POUND, BUNDT & LOAF CAKES

These easy, everyday cakes can all be made in a loaf or Bundt pan. To prevent a cake from sticking to a Bundt pan, make sure all the creases of the fluted sides are well greased.

Pound Cake

Here's a basic recipe plus two variations. Be sure to try the black pepper version—the spice gives the cake a slightly hot kick that's really something special.

Active time: 20 minutes
Bake time: 1 hour
Makes: 12 servings

2 cups cake flour (not self-rising)
1 teaspoon baking powder
1/2 teaspoon salt
1 cup butter or margarine (2 sticks), softened
1 cup sugar
4 large eggs
1 1/2 teaspoons vanilla extract

1. Preheat oven to 325°F. Grease and flour 9" by 5" metal loaf pan.

2. In medium bowl, stir together flour, baking powder, and salt. In large bowl, with mixer on medium speed, beat butter until creamy. Add sugar, and beat 5 minutes, or until light and creamy. Add eggs, one at a time, beating well after each. Beat in vanilla. Reduce speed to low; beat in flour mixture just until combined.

3. Turn batter into prepared pan and spread evenly. Bake 1 hour, or until cake pulls away from sides of pan and toothpick inserted in center of cake comes out clean. Cool in pan on wire rack 10 minutes. With small knife, loosen cake from sides of pan; invert onto wire rack; turn right side up to cool completely.

Each serving: about 300 calories, 4g protein, 32g carbohydrate, 17g total fat (10g saturated), 0g fiber, 112mg cholesterol, 315mg sodium

BLACK PEPPER POUND CAKE Prepare cake as instructed, but add *¾ teaspoon ground black pepper* and *a pinch ground allspice* to flour mixture.

Each serving: about 300 calories, 4g protein, 32g carbohydrate, 17g total fat (10g saturated), 0g fiber, 112mg cholesterol, 315mg sodium

---

HOW POUND CAKE GOT ITS NAME

In the old days, pound cake recipes called for one pound each of butter, sugar, flour, and eggs. It wasn't worth firing up the oven unless you baked several cakes, so pound cake took some effort: The butter and sugar, then the eggs, had to be laboriously creamed until perfectly smooth and fluffy, because the beaten eggs had to serve as leavening (baking soda or powder were not used).

Today, most folks are happy to bake one pound cake at a time, and modern conveniences like electric mixers, baking soda, and baking powder make whipping up a pound cake almost effortless. Still, you do want to cream the butter and sugar until it feels smooth, and not grainy, between your fingers.

Lemon Poppy Seed Pound Cake

This buttery, sugar-glazed cake keeps well and makes a terrific hostess gift.

Active time: 25 minutes
Bake time: 1 hour 20 minutes
Makes: 16 servings

2 cups all-purpose flour
2 tablespoons poppy seeds
1/2 teaspoon baking powder
1/4 teaspoon baking soda
1/4 teaspoon salt
2 large lemons
3/4 cup margarine or butter, softened
1 1/2 cups plus 1/3 cup sugar
4 large eggs
1 teaspoon vanilla extract
1/2 cup sour cream

1. Preheat oven to 325°F. Grease and flour 9" by 5" metal loaf pan. In medium bowl, combine flour, poppy seeds, baking powder, baking soda, and salt. From lemons, grate 1 tablespoon peel and squeeze 3 tablespoons juice.

2. In large bowl, with mixer on low speed, beat butter with 1 1/2 cups sugar until blended. Increase speed to high and beat until mixture is light, about 5 minutes. Add eggs, one at a time, beating well after each. Beat in lemon peel and vanilla. At low speed, alternately add flour mixture and sour cream, beginning and ending with flour mixture. Spoon batter into pan and bake 1 hour 20 minutes or until toothpick inserted in center of cake comes out clean.

3. Cool cake in pan on wire rack 10 minutes. Remove from pan. Mix lemon juice and remaining 1/3 cup sugar; brush over top and sides of warm cake. Cool completely.

Each serving: about 265 calories, 4g protein, 36g carbohydrate, 12g total fat (3g saturated), 0g fiber, 56mg cholesterol, 200mg sodium

TOP: POUND CAKE; BOTTOM: LEMON POPPY SEED CAKE

Chocolate Pound Cake

Unlike some of the more extravagant chocolate creations, this tube cake sneaks up on you with its rich chocolate flavor. Use the large holes on the grater, to create small bits of chocolate.

Active time: 30 minutes plus cooling
Bake time: 1 hour 20 minutes
Makes: 20 servings

3 cups all-purpose flour
1 cup unsweetened cocoa
1/2 teaspoon baking powder
1 1/2 cups butter or margarine (3 sticks), softened
2 3/4 cups sugar
2 teaspoons vanilla extract
5 large eggs
1 1/2 cups milk
2 ounces bittersweet chocolate, coarsely grated

1. Preheat oven to 350°F. Grease and flour 10-inch tube pan with removable bottom. Line outside of pan with foil. In medium bowl, sift flour, cocoa, and baking powder.

2. In large bowl, with mixer on medium speed, beat butter until creamy. Gradually beat in sugar; beat 3 minutes, until fluffy. Beat in vanilla. Add eggs, one at a time, beating well after each. Reduce speed to low; beat in flour mixture alternately with milk, beginning and ending with flour mixture. Stir in grated chocolate.

3. Spoon batter into prepared pan, spreading evenly. Bake 1 hour 20 to 1 hour 25 minutes, until toothpick inserted in center of cake comes out clean. Cool in pan on wire rack 10 minutes. With small knife, loosen cake from side and center of pan. Remove pan side and let cool completely. Run thin knife around bottom of cake to remove pan bottom.

Each serving: about 360 calories, 5g protein, 47g carbohydrate, 18g total fat (10g saturated), 2g fiber, 93mg cholesterol, 180mg sodium

Top: Chocolate Pound Cake; Bottom: Glazed Tangerine Cake

Glazed Tangerine Cake

Reduced-fat cream cheese keeps this cake moist and tangy without loading on the calories. Just before serving, lightly dust the cake with powdered sugar, if you like.

Active time: 25 minutes plus cooling
Bake time: 55 minutes
Makes: 20 servings

3 to 4 tangerines
1 lemon
1 teaspoon vanilla extract
3 cups all-purpose flour
1 teaspoon salt
3/4 teaspoon baking soda
1/2 cup butter or margarine (1 stick), softened
1 package (8 ounces) reduced-fat cream cheese (Neufchâtel), softened
2 cups sugar
4 large eggs
Confectioners' sugar for sprinkling (optional)

1. Preheat oven to 325°F. Coat inside of 12-cup nonstick fluted baking pan (such as Bundt) using nonstick baking spray with flour.

2. From tangerines, grate 2 tablespoons plus 1 teaspoon peel and squeeze 2/3 cup juice. From lemon, grate 1 teaspoon peel and squeeze 2 tablespoons juice. In small bowl, stir lemon peel, 2 tablespoons tangerine peel, and 1/3 cup tangerine juice with vanilla. In another bowl, stir lemon juice and remaining tangerine peel and juice; reserve for glaze.

3. On sheet of waxed paper, combine flour, salt, and baking soda. In large bowl, with mixer on low speed, beat butter and cream cheese with 1¾ cups sugar until blended, scraping bowl frequently with rubber spatula. Increase speed to medium-high and beat until light and creamy, about 2 minutes, occasionally scraping bowl.

4. With mixer on low speed, add eggs, one at a time, beating well after each. Alternately add flour mixture and juice, beginning and ending with flour; beat just until blended, frequently scraping bowl.

5. Pour batter into prepared pan and smooth top with spatula. Bake 55 to 60 minutes or until toothpick inserted in center of cake comes out clean.

6. Prepare glaze: Stir remaining ¼ cup sugar into bowl with reserved peel and juice until sugar dissolves.

7. Cool cake in pan 10 minutes. Gently loosen cake from side of pan; invert onto wire rack set over waxed paper. With skewer, poke 20 holes around top of hot cake; brush with glaze. Sprinkle with confectioners' sugar just before serving, if desired.

Each serving: about 235 calories, 4g protein, 35g carbohydrate, 9g total fat (5g saturated), 1g fiber, 64mg cholesterol, 270mg sodium

Brown Sugar Pound Cake

Dark brown sugar gives this country cake a delicious butterscotch flavor.

Active time 30 minutes
Bake time 50 minutes
Makes: 16 servings

2 cups all-purpose flour
3/4 teaspoon salt
1/2 teaspoon baking powder
1/2 teaspoon baking soda
10 tablespoons butter or margarine, softened
1 cup packed dark brown sugar
1/3 cup granulated sugar
2 large eggs
1 tablespoon vanilla extract
3/4 cup whole milk

1. Preheat oven to 325°F. Coat inside of 10-cup nonstick fluted baking pan (such as Bundt) using nonstick cooking spray with flour.

2. On waxed paper, combine flour, salt, baking powder, and baking soda.

3. In large bowl, with mixer on low speed, beat butter and both sugars until blended, frequently scraping bowl with rubber spatula. Increase speed to medium-high; beat until creamy, about 3 minutes, occasionally scraping bowl.

4. Reduce speed to low; add eggs, one at a time, beating well after each. Beat in vanilla. Alternately add flour mixture and milk, beginning and ending with flour mixture; beat just until smooth.

5. Spread batter evenly into prepared pan. Bake until toothpick inserted in center of cake comes out clean, 50 to 60 minutes.

6. Cool cake in pan 15 minutes. Gently loosen cake from side of pan and invert onto wire rack to cool completely.

Each serving: About 210 calories, 3g protein, 30g carbohydrate, 9g total fat (5g saturated), 0g fiber, 49mg cholesterol, 255mg sodium

Honey Cake

This coffee-and-spice cake is typically enjoyed during the Jewish New Year, when honey is eaten as a symbolic "sweetener" of the coming year. For a traditional garnish, decorate the top with whole blanched almonds before baking.

Active time: 15 minutes
Bake time: 45 minutes
Makes: 2 loaves, 12 servings

3 cups all-purpose flour
2 1/2 teaspoons baking powder
1 teaspoon baking soda
1/2 teaspoon salt
1/2 teaspoon ground cloves
1/4 teaspoon ground allspice
1 cup honey
3/4 cup packed light brown sugar
3/4 cup strong black coffee
1/4 cup vegetable oil
2 tablespoons whiskey
2 teaspoons freshly grated lemon peel
3 large eggs
1 large egg yolk

1. Preheat oven to 325°F. Grease two 8½" by 4½" metal loaf pans.

2. In medium bowl, stir together flour, baking powder, baking soda, salt, cloves, and allspice.

3. In large bowl, with mixer on medium speed, beat honey, brown sugar, coffee, oil, whiskey, and lemon peel until light and creamy. Beat in eggs and egg yolk, one at a time, beating well after each. Reduce speed to low. Beat in flour mixture just until combined.

4. Divide batter between prepared pans. Bake 45 to 55 minutes, until top of loaf springs back when lightly touched and toothpick inserted in center comes out clean (tops may still be a bit sticky). With small knife, loosen loaves from sides of pans; invert onto wire racks, then turn right side up. Cool loaves completely before slicing.

Each serving: about 160 calories, 3g protein, 31g carbohydrate, 4g total fat (1g saturated), 1g fiber, 35mg cholesterol, 165mg sodium

Carrot Cake

A dessert with a vegetable in its name sounds like it should be healthy, but that's not always the case with carrot cake. Our slimmed-down take contains just 210 calories and 5 grams of fat per slice.

Active time: 20 minutes • Bake time: 45 minutes • Makes: 20 servings

CAKE
2¼ cups all-purpose flour
2 teaspoons baking soda
2 teaspoons ground cinnamon
1 teaspoon ground ginger
1 teaspoon baking powder
1 teaspoon salt
2 large eggs
2 large egg whites
1 cup granulated sugar
¾ cup packed dark brown sugar

1 can (8 to 8¼ ounces) crushed pineapple in juice
⅓ cup canola oil
1 tablespoon vanilla extract
1 bag (10 ounces) shredded carrots
½ cup dark seedless raisins

CREAM CHEESE ICING
2 ounces reduced-fat cream cheese
¾ cup confectioners' sugar
½ teaspoon low-fat milk (1%)
¼ teaspoon vanilla extract

1. Preheat oven to 350°F. Coat nonstick 12-cup Bundt pan using nonstick baking spray with flour.

2. Prepare cake: Combine flour, soda, cinnamon, ginger, baking powder, and salt.

3. In large bowl, with mixer on medium speed, beat eggs and egg whites until blended. Add both sugars; beat 2 minutes. On low speed, beat in pineapple with juice, oil, and vanilla. Add flour mixture; beat 1 minute. Stir in carrots and raisins.

4. Pour batter into pan. Bake 45 to 50 minutes or until toothpick inserted in center of cake comes out clean. Cool in pan 10 minutes. Invert cake onto rack; cool completely.

5. Prepare icing: In bowl, stir cream cheese and ¼ cup sugar until smooth. Add milk, vanilla, and ½ cup sugar; stir until smooth. Drizzle over cake.

Each serving: about 210 calories, 3g protein, 40g carbohydrate, 5g total fat (1g saturated), 1g fiber, 23mg cholesterol, 295mg sodium

Amaretto Apricot Cake

A touch of amaretto complements sweet apricots in this moist holiday cake. The cake can be made ahead of time and glazed just before serving. Garnish with raspberries and fresh mint for an extra-special touch.

Active time: 25 minutes plus cooling and standing
Bake time: 1 hour 15 minutes
Makes: 16 servings

2 1/2 cups all-purpose flour
1 teaspoon baking powder
1/4 teaspoon baking soda
1/2 teaspoon salt
1 tube (7 to 8 ounces) almond paste
1 1/2 cups granulated sugar
6 ounces dried apricots (1 3/4 cups)
3/4 cup butter or margarine (1 1/2 sticks), softened
5 large eggs, lightly beaten
2 tablespoons amaretto or 1 teaspoon vanilla extract
8 ounces sour cream, at room temperature
1 cup confectioners' sugar
1 to 2 tablespoons fresh lemon juice
Raspberries for garnish
Fresh mint leaves for garnish

1. Preheat oven to 325°F. Coat inside of 10-cup (10-inch) fluted baking pan (such as Bundt), using baking spray with flour.

2. On large sheet of waxed paper, combine 2 cups flour, baking powder, baking soda, and salt.

3. In food processor with knife blade attached, pulse almond paste and sugar until finely ground. Transfer to large bowl. In same food processor (no need to wipe bowl), pulse apricots and remaining 1/2 cup flour until finely chopped.

4. Add butter to bowl with almond sugar. With mixer on medium-high speed, beat 7 minutes or until pale and fluffy. Add eggs gradually and then add amaretto until incorporated, occasionally scraping bowl with rubber spatula.

5. With mixer on low speed, add flour mixture in alternation with sour cream, beginning and ending with flour mixture, scraping bowl occasionally, until batter is smooth. With rubber spatula, fold in apricot mixture until blended.

6. Transfer batter to prepared pan. Bake 1 hour 15 minutes or until toothpick inserted in center of cake comes out clean. Cool cake in pan on wire rack 15 minutes, then invert onto rack and cool completely. Cake can be kept at room temperature in airtight container up to 3 days or frozen, tightly wrapped in plastic wrap, up to 1 month.

7. To serve, place cake on serving plate. In small bowl, stir confectioners' sugar and 1 tablespoon lemon juice until well mixed. Add more lemon juice if necessary to achieve consistency of honey. Pour over cake to glaze. Garnish with raspberries and mint leaves. Allow glaze to set about 5 minutes before slicing.

Each serving: about 390 calories, 6g protein, 55g carbohydrate, 17g total fat (8g saturated), 2g fiber, 96mg cholesterol, 225mg sodium

Sticky-Toffee Bundt Cake

If you love traditional sticky toffee pudding, then you'll love this cake featuring the same flavors, including a gooey caramel glaze.

Active time: 35 minutes plus cooling and setting
Bake time: 55 minutes
Makes: 16 servings

1 cup chopped pitted dates (5 ounces)
1 cup water
2 teaspoons ground ginger
1 teaspoon baking soda
2 cups all-purpose flour
1 teaspoon baking powder
1/8 teaspoon plus pinch salt
1 cup butter or margarine (2 sticks), at room temperature (see Tip)
1¼ cups packed dark brown sugar
1¼ cups granulated sugar
3 large eggs, at room temperature
2½ teaspoons vanilla extract
1 tablespoon light corn syrup
1/3 cup heavy cream
Red and green grapes for garnish

1. In 2-quart saucepan, combine dates and water. Heat to boiling on high. Remove from heat. Stir in ginger and baking soda. Cool completely.

2. Preheat oven to 350°F. Grease and flour 10-cup Bundt pan. Into large bowl, sift flour, baking powder, and 1/8 teaspoon salt; set aside.

3. In another large bowl, with mixer on medium speed, beat 12 tablespoons butter and 1 cup each brown and granulated sugars until very well combined. Beat in eggs, one at a time, scraping side of bowl occasionally. Beat in 2 teaspoons vanilla extract. Add flour mixture and date mixture in alternation in two or three parts, beating well in between additions, until combined.

4. Pour batter into prepared pan. Bake 55 minutes to 1 hour or until toothpick inserted in center comes out clean. Cool in pan on wire rack 15 minutes. Invert pan onto wire rack. Cool completely. At this point, cooled cake can be wrapped tightly in plastic and stored at room temperature up to 1 day.

5. In 3-quart saucepan, combine corn syrup and remaining 4 tablespoons butter and ¼ cup each brown and granulated sugars. Cook over medium heat 3 minutes or until sugar has dissolved and syrup bubbles, stirring constantly. Stir in cream, remaining ½ teaspoon vanilla extract, and pinch of salt. Cook another 2 minutes, stirring constantly. Let cool 5 minutes.

6. Place sheet of waxed paper under rack where cake is sitting. Pour caramel sauce over top of cooled cake and allow sauce to drip down sides. Let caramel set. Transfer cake to serving plate. Garnish with grapes.

Each serving: about 355 calories, 3g protein, 54g carbohydrate, 14g total fat (9g saturated), 1g fiber, 72mg cholesterol, 265mg sodium

TIP If you use margarine, the glaze will be a little too thin right after you make it; refrigerate it until it thickens before pouring it over the cake.

Dark Christmas Fruitcake

There's a full cup of brandy in this recipe—and for even more of a kick, you can periodically sprinkle the cakes with additional brandy while they age. Unless you have an extremely cool pantry (almost unheard of these days), be sure to store the cakes in the refrigerator.

Active time: 1 hour 30 minutes plus soaking and aging
Bake time: 1 hour 30 minutes
Makes: 12 cakes, 4 servings each

3 cups dried figs, stemmed and chopped
2 cups pitted dates, chopped
2 cups golden raisins
2 cups dark seedless raisins
2 cups dried currants
1¹/2 cups diced candied citron
1 cup diced candied pineapple
1 cup red candied cherries, coarsely chopped
1 cup diced candied orange peel
1 cup brandy
3 cups all-purpose flour
¹/2 teaspoon ground cinnamon
¹/4 teaspoon baking soda
¹/4 teaspoon ground allspice
¹/4 teaspoon ground cloves
2 cups butter or margarine (4 sticks), softened
1 box (16 ounces) dark brown sugar
6 large eggs
¹/3 cup dark molasses
²/3 cup milk
5 cups pecans or walnuts (20 ounces)

1. In large bowl, mix figs, dates, golden raisins, dark raisins, currants, citron, pineapple, cherries, orange peel, and brandy. Cover and let stand 8 hours or overnight, stirring a few times.

2. Preheat oven to 275°F. Grease twelve 5¾" by 3¼" by 2" mini loaf pans. Line bottoms with waxed paper; grease paper.

3. In medium bowl, stir together flour, cinnamon, baking soda, allspice, and cloves.

4. In large bowl, with mixer on low speed, beat butter and brown sugar until blended. Increase speed to medium-high; beat 5 minutes, scraping bowl frequently, until light and creamy. Reduce speed to medium. Add eggs, one at a time, beating well after each. Beat in molasses. Reduce speed to low, and beat in flour mixture alternately with milk, beginning and ending with flour mixture and scraping bowl regularly. Turn batter into larger bowl for easier mixing. Stir in fruit mixture, including any brandy not absorbed by fruit, and nuts.

5. Spoon batter into prepared pans, spreading evenly. Bake cakes 1 hour 30 to 1 hour 35 minutes, until toothpick inserted in center of cake comes out clean, cool in pans on wire racks 15 minutes. With small knife, loosen cakes from sides of pans and invert onto racks. Turn right side up and cool completely. Remove waxed paper. Wrap in plastic and then in foil. Let stand in cool place or refrigerate at least 1 month, and up to 6 months, before serving.

Each serving: about 395 calories, 4g protein, 61g carbohydrate, 17g total fat (6g saturated), 3g fiber, 48mg cholesterol, 125mg sodium

CHIFFON, SPONGE & ANGEL-FOOD CAKES

First devised in the 1940s, chiffon cake was revolutionary in its use of oil rather than butter. Angel-food cake, an earlier creation, is made with egg whites only—so it's fat free. Versatile sponge cake, made with well-beaten whole eggs, can be baked as layers, in a tube pan, or in a rectangular sheet (to be rolled around a filling for a scrumptious cake roll).

Vanilla Chiffon Cake

Made in a tube pan, this tall, handsome cake doesn't need icing. Just dust the top with confectioners' sugar and serve some fresh berries with each slice.

Active time: 20 minutes

Bake time: 1 hour 15 minutes

Makes: 16 servings

2¼ cups cake flour (not self-rising)

1½ cups granulated sugar

1 tablespoon baking powder

1 teaspoon salt

½ cup vegetable oil

5 large eggs, separated

1 tablespoon vanilla extract

¾ cup cool water

2 large egg whites

½ teaspoon cream of tartar

Confectioners' sugar for sprinkling

Fresh berries for serving

1. Preheat oven to 325°F. In large bowl, stir together flour, 1 cup granulated sugar, baking powder, and salt. Make well in center. Add oil, 5 egg yolks, vanilla, and water; whisk into dry ingredients.

2. In another large bowl, with mixer on high speed, beat all 7 egg whites and cream of tartar until soft peaks form when beaters are lifted. Gradually sprinkle in remaining ½ cup granulated sugar, 2 tablespoons at a time, and beat until whites just stand in stiff peaks when beaters are lifted (see page 235). With rubber spatula, gently fold one-third of whites into egg-yolk mixture, then fold in remaining whites.

3. Pour batter into ungreased 9- to 10-inch tube pan. Bake 1 hour 15 minutes, or until top springs back when touched with finger. Invert cake in pan and rest on metal funnel or bottle; cool completely. With small knife, carefully loosen cake from side and center of pan. Transfer to cake plate. Sprinkle with confectioners' sugar. Serve slices with fresh berries alongside.

Each serving: about 220 calories, 4g protein, 32g carbohydrate, 9g total fat (1g saturated), 0g fiber, 66mg cholesterol, 265mg sodium

CITRUS CHIFFON CAKE Prepare batter as instructed, but use *1 tablespoon freshly grated orange peel* and *1 teaspoon freshly grated lemon peel* in place of vanilla. Use *½ cup fresh orange juice* and *¼ cup fresh lemon juice* in place of cool water. Bake cake, cool, and remove from pan as directed. In small bowl, combine *1 cup confectioners' sugar, 1 teaspoon freshly grated lemon peel, ¼ teaspoon vanilla extract*, and about *5 teaspoons orange juice* until smooth. Spoon glaze over cooled cake.

Each serving: about 250 calories, 4g protein, 40g carbohydrate, 9g total fat (1g saturated), 0g fiber, 66mg cholesterol, 265mg sodium

Boston Cream Pie

Why this special New England dessert is called a pie is anyone's guess: it is, in fact, two layers of golden sponge cake, sandwiched with a dense custard filling and slathered with a thick chocolate glaze. One of Boston's greatest hotels, the Parker House, takes credit for this version; a simpler Boston Cream Pie is unglazed and sprinkled with confectioners' sugar instead.

Active time: 35 minutes plus cooling and standing
Bake time: 20 minutes
Makes: 12 servings

1¹/2 cups all-purpose flour
1¹/2 teaspoons baking powder
¹/4 teaspoon salt
3 large eggs
¹/2 cup water
3 tablespoons butter or margarine
1¹/2 teaspoons vanilla extract
1¹/3 cups sugar
Pastry Cream for 9-Inch Tart (page 346)
Chocolate Glaze (page 339)

1. Preheat oven to 350°F. Grease two 8-inch round cake pans. Line with waxed paper; grease and flour.

2. In medium bowl, stir together flour, baking powder, and salt. In large bowl, with mixer on high speed, beat eggs 5 minutes, or until light and tripled in volume.

3. Meanwhile, combine water and butter in small saucepan; heat to boiling. Remove from heat; add vanilla. Gradually beat sugar into eggs, 2 to 8 minutes, until mixture is thick and lemon-colored, and ribbons form when beaters are lifted; scrape bowl occasionally with rubber spatula. In two additions, fold in flour mixture until just blended; pour in water mixture and gently blend.

4. Divide batter between prepared pans. Bake 20 minutes, or until toothpick inserted in center of cake comes out clean. With small knife, loosen layers from sides of pans; invert onto wire rack. Remove waxed paper; cool completely.

5. Place one cake layer, rounded side down, on serving plate; spread with pastry cream. Top with second cake layer, rounded side up. Pour chocolate glaze over top. With small metal spatula, spread glaze evenly to edges allowing it to drip down sides of cake. Let glaze set.

Each serving: about 325 calories, 5g protein, 50g carbohydrate, 12g total fat (7g saturated), 1g fiber, 110mg cholesterol, 210mg sodium

Passover Almond Sponge Cake

During Passover, wheat flour and leavening are forbidden, so this traditional cake is made with matzo meal and is lightened only with beaten eggs.

Active time: 25 minutes
Bake time: 45 minutes
Makes: 16 servings

2 lemons
1¹/2 teaspoons vanilla extract
¹/4 teaspoon almond extract
9 large eggs, separated
1¹/2 cups sugar
³/4 cup slivered almonds (3 ounces), toasted
1¹/3 cups matzo meal
¹/4 teaspoon salt

1. Preheat oven to 350°F. From lemons grate 1½ teaspoons peel; reserve. Squeeze 3 tablespoons lemon juice. In cup, combine lemon juice and both extracts.

2. In large bowl, with mixer on high speed, beat egg whites until soft peaks form when beaters are lifted. Sprinkle in ¾ cup sugar, 2 tablespoons at a time, and whip until sugar dissolves and whites stand in stiff, glossy peaks when beaters are lifted.

3. In food processor with knife blade attached, process almonds and 2 tablespoons matzo meal until finely ground. Add remaining matzo meal and salt, and process to create a flour-like consistency.

4. In another large bowl, with mixer on high speed and using same beaters, beat egg yolks with remaining ¾ cup sugar until mixture is thick and lemon-colored, and ribbons form when beaters are lifted; scrape bowl occasionally with rubber spatula. In three additions, fold in flour mixture until just blended; fold in lemon-juice mixture and peel. In three additions, fold whites into yolk mixture.

5. Pour batter into ungreased 9- to 10-inch tube pan. Bake 45 minutes, or until skewer inserted in center of cake comes out clean. Cool in pan 10 minutes. Invert cake in pan and rest on metal funnel or bottle; cool completely in pan. With small knife, carefully loosen cake from side and center of pan. Remove cake from pan and place on serving plate.

Each serving: about 195 calories, 6g protein, 30g carbohydrate, 6g total fat (1g saturated), 1g fiber, 120mg cholesterol, 70mg sodium

REMOVING A CAKE FROM A TUBE PAN

Here's how to release a chiffon or angel-food cake from its pan with ease.

Cool the cake upside down so that it is suspended above the table. Some pans are made with special feet to stand on, but if yours doesn't have them, slip the tube of the inverted pan onto the neck of a bottle.

Once the cake has cooled, slide a paring knife around the edge of the pan to loosen any parts that might stick. Then turn the cake out onto a plate.

Angel-Food Cake

Unparalleled in its pristine delicacy, angel food is also delightful served with fresh fruit, bright scoops of sorbet, or a divinely decadent chocolate sauce. Or use some of the yolks to make our luscious Custard Sauce (page 351).

Active time: 30 minutes
Bake time: 35 minutes
Makes: 12 servings

1 cup cake flour (not self-rising)
1/2 cup confectioners' sugar
1²/3 cups egg whites (12 to 14 large egg whites)
1¹/2 teaspoons cream of tartar
1/2 teaspoon salt
1¹/4 cups granulated sugar
2 teaspoons vanilla extract
1/2 teaspoon almond extract

1. Preheat oven to 375°F. Sift flour and confectioners' sugar through sieve into medium bowl.

2. In large bowl, with mixer on medium speed, beat egg whites, cream of tartar, and salt until foamy. Increase speed to medium-high; beat until soft peaks form when beaters are lifted. Gradually sprinkle in granulated sugar, 2 tablespoons at a time, and beat until egg whites just stand in stiff peaks when beaters are lifted. Beat in both extracts.

3. Transfer egg-white mixture to larger bowl. Sift flour mixture, one-third at a time, into whites, folding with rubber spatula or wire whisk just until flour mixture is incorporated. Do not overmix.

4. Turn batter into ungreased 9- to 10-inch tube pan. Bake 35 to 40 minutes, until cake springs back when lightly touched. Invert cake in pan and rest on metal funnel or bottle; cool completely in pan. With small knife, carefully loosen cake from side and center of pan; remove cake and place on plate.

Each serving: about 155 calories, 4g protein, 34g carbohydrate, 0g total fat (0g saturated), 0g fiber, 0mg cholesterol, 155mg sodium

CAPPUCCINO ANGEL-FOOD CAKE Prepare batter as instructed, but add *4 teaspoons instant espresso-coffee powder* and *½ teaspoon ground cinnamon* to egg whites before beating; use *1½ teaspoons vanilla extract* and omit almond extract. Bake cake, cool, and remove from pan as directed. In small cup, mix *1 tablespoon confectioners' sugar* with *⅛ teaspoon ground cinnamon*. Sprinkle over cooled cake.

Each serving: about 155 calories, 4g protein, 34g carbohydrate, 0g total fat (0g saturated), 0g fiber, 0mg cholesterol, 155mg sodium

Génoise

Although it has a French name, this light, fine-grained sponge cake originated in Genoa, Italy. The basis for many of the spectacular desserts you'll see in a French pastry, génoise can be iced with any flavor of buttercream, filled with whipped cream and fresh fruit, or glazed and decorated with edible fresh flowers.

Active time: 20 minutes plus cooling
Bake time: 15 minutes
Makes: 16 servingss

6 large eggs, at room temperature
1 cup sugar
1 cup all-purpose flour
1/2 teaspoon salt
2 teaspoons vanilla extract
6 tablespoons butter or margarine, melted and cooled
Flavored Simple Syrup (page 351, see Tip)
Swiss Meringue Buttercream (page 335)

1. Preheat oven to 350°F. Grease and flour three 8-inch round cake pans.

2. In large metal bowl, with wire whisk, mix eggs and sugar. Set bowl on top of large pan filled with *1 inch water* (bottom of bowl should not touch water), and place over medium. Stirring occasionally, heat until egg mixture is lukewarm and sugar has dissolved.

3. With mixer on high speed, beat warm egg mixture about 10 minutes, until mixture is thick and lemon-colored and ribbons form when beaters are lifted; scrape bowl occasionally with rubber spatula. In small bowl, mix flour and salt. In two additions, sift flour mixture over egg mixture and fold in until just blended; fold in vanilla and melted butter.

4. Divide batter among prepared pans. Bake 15 to 20 minutes or until cake is golden and springs back when lightly touched. With small knife, loosen layers from sides of pans; immediately invert onto wire rack to cool.

5. Place 1 cake layer on plate; brush with simple syrup and spread with 1/2 cup frosting. Repeat layering with remaining 2 layers, syrup, and more frosting. Use remaining frosting for side of cake.

Each serving: about 335 calories, 4g protein, 33g carbohydrate, 20g total fat (11g saturated), 0g fiber, 177mg cholesterol, 150mg sodium

LEMON OR ORANGE GÉNOISE Prepare cake as instructed, but add *1 teaspoon freshly grated lemon or orange peel* and *2 tablespoons fresh lemon or orange juice* along with melted butter in step 3.

Each serving: about 335 calories, 4g protein, 33g carbohydrate, 20g total fat (13g saturated), 0g fiber, 177mg cholesterol, 150mg sodium

TIP This cake is made with just a little melted butter, but génoise is typically enhanced after baking by brushing it with a flavored sugar syrup, or by sprinkling it with liqueur.

Chocolate Génoise with Ganache

This may be the ultimate in elegant chocolate cakes— the one that you'd serve with a demitasse of coffee as the finale to a sophisticated dinner party.

Active time: 50 minutes plus cooling
Bake time: 25 minutes
Makes: 20 servings

3/4 cup unsweetened cocoa plus additional for dusting pans
7 large eggs, at room temperature
1 1/4 cups granulated sugar
1 1/2 teaspoons vanilla extract
3/4 cup cake flour (not self-rising)
1/2 teaspoon salt
1/2 cup butter or margarine (1 stick), melted and cooled to lukewarm
Ganache (page 338)
Confectioners' sugar for sprinkling

1. Preheat oven to 350°F. Grease two 9-inch round cake pans. Line bottoms with waxed paper; grease paper. Dust pans with cocoa.

2. In large bowl with mixer on high speed, beat eggs, granulated sugar, and vanilla until mixture has increased in volume about four times and takes on consistency of whipped cream. Depending on your mixer, this will take anywhere from 5 to 25 minutes.

3. Meanwhile, in medium bowl, stir together flour, ¾ cup cocoa, and salt until blended. In four additions, sift flour mixture over egg mixture and gently fold in; fold in melted butter.

4. Divide batter between prepared pans. Bake 25 minutes, or until layers pull away from sides of pan and spring back when lightly touched. Cool in pans on wire racks 10 minutes. With small knife, loosen layers from sides of pans; invert onto wire racks. Remove waxed paper; cool completely.

5. Meanwhile, let ganache stand at room temperature 30 minutes to prepare for use.

6. With serrated knife, cut each cake layer horizontally in half. Place bottom half of 1 layer, cut side up, on cake plate; spread with ⅓ cup ganache. Top with second layer and another ⅓ cup ganache. Repeat layering to make 4 layers cake and 3 layers ganache in all. Sprinkle top of cake with confectioners' sugar. Frost sides with remaining ganache.

Each serving: about 260 calories, 4g protein, 29g carbohydrate, 16g total fat (9g saturated), 2g fiber, 104mg cholesterol, 140mg sodium

MAKE A GÉNOISE CAKE

Patience is required to ensure that this cake comes out airy. The eggs and sugar must be warmed over a double boiler as instructed in recipe, then beaten for as long as 10 minutes.

You'll know that the eggs and sugar have been beaten long enough when the mixture becomes very thick. It should fall in a thick ribbon when the beaters are lifted.

To add dry ingredients, sift half of flour mixture over the beaten egg mixture, and then gently fold it in; repeat with remaining half. Do not stir or beat the batter.

Many génoise recipes require the layers to be halved horizontally. Using a long, serrated knife, carefully cut through the cake with a sawing motion.

Jelly Roll

For a real old-fashioned jelly roll, simply spread the cake with strawberry jam. If the jelly is very stiff, warm it slightly so it will spread without tearing the cake.

Active time: 20 minutes plus cooling
Bake time: 10 minutes
Makes: 10 servings

5 large eggs, separated
½ cup granulated sugar
1 teaspoon vanilla extract
½ cup all-purpose flour
Confectioners' sugar for sprinkling
⅔ cup strawberry jam

1. Preheat oven to 350°F. Grease 15½" by 10½" jelly-roll pan. Line with waxed paper; grease paper.

2. In large bowl, with mixer on high speed, beat egg whites until soft peaks form when beaters are lifted. Gradually sprinkle in ¼ cup granulated sugar, 1 tablespoon at a time, and whip until whites hold stiff peaks when beaters are lifted.

3. In small bowl, with mixer on high speed, beat egg yolks, remaining ¼ cup granulated sugar, and vanilla until very thick and lemon-colored, 5 to 10 minutes; stir in flour. With rubber spatula, gently fold egg-yolk mixture into beaten egg whites.

4. Spread batter in pan. Bake 10 to 15 minutes, until top of cake springs back when lightly touched.

5. Meanwhile, sift confectioners' sugar onto clean kitchen towel. With small knife, loosen edges of cake from sides of pan; invert onto towel. Carefully peel off waxed paper. Trim ¼ inch from edges of cake. Starting from one short side, roll cake and towel together, jelly-roll fashion. Cool completely on wire rack.

6. Unroll cooled cake so that it again lies flat on towel. Spread with jam. Starting from same short side, reroll cake to enclose jam and transfer, seam side down, to platter. Sprinkle with confectioners' sugar.

Each serving: about 160 calories, 4g protein, 30g carbohydrate, 3g total fat (1g saturated), 1g fiber, 106mg cholesterol, 40mg sodium

ROLLING A JELLY-ROLL CAKE

This technique is surprisingly simple to execute, but the results look festive and impressive.

Loosen the cake from the sides of the jelly-roll pan, then flip it out onto a kitchen towel that has been sprinkled with confectioners' sugar. Starting at one short end, roll the still-warm cake up in the towel. Let cool.

Unroll the cooled cake so that it's flat on the towel, then spread with jam of choice or other filling. Reroll the cake to enclose the filling and transfer, seam side down, to a platter.

Chocolate-Raspberry Roll

This raspberry- and mascarpone-filled cake is our contemporary take on the traditional Bûche de Noël. The chocolate-frosted jelly-roll shape looks like a Yule log; slicing it reveals a swirl of delectable raspberry filling.

Active time: 40 minutes plus cooling and chilling
Total time: 15 minutes
Makes: 12 servings

1 tablespoon water
1/3 cup plus 4 tablespoons granulated sugar
1 pint raspberries (12 ounces)
6 ounces bittersweet chocolate, chopped
2 tablespoons butter or margarine
1/4 teaspoon salt
4 tablespoons raspberry liqueur
6 large eggs, separated
3 tablespoons confectioners' sugar
1 cup heavy cream
1/2 cup mascarpone cheese

1. Preheat oven to 350°F. Grease 18" by 12" jelly-roll pan. Line with parchment paper; grease paper.

2. In medium bowl, stir water and 2 tablespoons granulated sugar. Fold in berries. Let stand while preparing cake or refrigerate overnight.

3. Fill 4-quart saucepan with *2 inches water*. Heat to simmering. In large heatproof bowl, combine chocolate, butter, salt, and 2 tablespoons liqueur; set bowl over pan, stirring until smooth. Remove from heat. Stir in egg yolks, one at a time, beating after each.

4. In large mixer bowl, with mixer on medium-high speed, beat egg whites until frothy. Gradually add 1/3 cup granulated sugar; beat until stiff peaks form. Gently fold whites into chocolate, one-third at a time, until incorporated. Spread batter evenly in pan.

5. Bake 15 minutes or until toothpick inserted in center comes out nearly clean. Cool in pan on wire rack 10 minutes. Dust top of cake with 2 tablespoons

confectioners' sugar; place sheet of waxed paper on top of cake. Set cutting board over cake, then flip board and pan together. Remove pan and peel off parchment; cool.

6. In large bowl, with mixer on medium-high speed, beat cream and mascarpone until soft peaks form. Add remaining 2 tablespoons each granulated sugar and liqueur. Beat until stiff; spread over cake, leaving 1/2-inch border.

7. Starting from a long side, roll cake, peeling off paper in process. (Cake may crack slightly during rolling.) Place on platter, cover with plastic wrap, and refrigerate at least 1 hour or up to 1 day.

8. Dust with remaining 1 tablespoon confectioners' sugar. Serve with raspberries.

Each serving: about 305 calories, 6g protein, 26g carbohydrate, 22g total fat (12g saturated), 3g fiber, 139mg cholesterol, 115mg sodium

Caramel Bûche de Noël

We've given this classic holiday dessert a contemporary twist with dulce de leche filling and a decadent milk chocolate frosting.

Active time: 1 hour 10 minutes plus cooling
Bake time: 10 minutes
Makes: 12 servings

CHOCOLATE CAKE

1/3 cup unsweetened cocoa powder (not Dutch-process), plus more for sifting
1/3 cup all-purpose flour
1/2 teaspoon ground cinnamon
1/4 teaspoon salt
1/8 teaspoon baking soda
5 large eggs, separated
3/4 cup sugar
1/4 cup vegetable oil

CARAMEL FILLING

1 teaspoon unflavored gelatin
1 tablespoon cold water
1 cup heavy cream
1/3 cup dulce de leche

MILK CHOCOLATE FROSTING AND DECORATION

6 ounces milk chocolate, finely chopped, plus additional grated chocolate for garnish
1 tablespoon butter or margarine, softened
1/3 cup heavy cream
1/2 teaspoon vanilla extract

1. Prepare cake: Preheat oven to 375°F. Grease 15½" by 10½" jelly-roll pan; line with parchment. Lightly grease parchment.

2. On large sheet of waxed paper, combine cocoa powder, flour, cinnamon, salt, and baking soda.

3. In large bowl, with mixer on high speed, beat egg whites until soft peaks form. Sprinkle in ¼ cup sugar, a tablespoon at a time, beating until whites stand in stiff, glossy peaks when beaters are lifted. Set whites aside.

4. In another large bowl, using same beaters, with mixer on high speed, beat egg yolks and remaining ½ cup sugar 5 minutes or until thick and very pale yellow. With rubber spatula, fold in oil until incorporated. Fold in half of egg whites, then fold in cocoa mixture until no dry streaks remain. Fold in remaining whites just until no white streaks remain.

5. Gently spread batter evenly in prepared pan. Bake 10 to 12 minutes or until top of cake springs back when lightly pressed. Cool cake in pan on wire rack 10 minutes.

6. Move pan from rack to work surface. Sift cocoa onto top of cake. Spread clean lint-free kitchen towel over cake, then place wire rack upside down on top of towel. Invert rack, towel, cake, and pan together. Remove pan, then carefully peel off parchment paper. Starting from a long side, loosely roll up cake with towel inside, jelly-roll fashion. Place roll, seam side down, on wire rack to cool completely, about 1 hour.

7. Prepare caramel filling: In small bowl, sprinkle gelatin over water. Let stand 5 minutes to soften gelatin. Microwave gelatin mixture on High 15 seconds or until just dissolved. Let cool to room temperature. In medium bowl, with mixer on medium speed, whip cream until soft peaks form when beaters are lifted. With mixer running, add gelatin mixture in slow, steady stream. Continue mixing until stiff peaks form. In large bowl, stir dulce de leche and one-third of whipped cream until well combined. Gently fold in remaining cream until combined.

8. Gently unroll cooled cake so it is again lying on towel. With metal spatula, spread filling evenly over cake almost to edges. Starting from same long side, roll cake around filling. (Cake may crack slightly as you roll it.) Wrap cake roll tightly in plastic and refrigerate at least 1 hour and up to 1 day.

9. Prepare frosting: In heatproof medium bowl, combine chocolate and butter. In 1-quart saucepan, heat cream just until boiling. Pour hot cream over chocolate and butter and let stand 1 minute to melt chocolate. With wire whisk, stir chocolate mixture until smooth. Stir in vanilla. Refrigerate frosting 15 minutes, stirring every 5 minutes, until mixture is just stiff enough to spread. Let frosting stand at room temperature.

10. Cut diagonal slice (1½ inches thick) from each end of cake roll and reserve. Transfer log to large serving platter. Reserve ¼ cup frosting; spread remaining frosting all over cake. Place reserved end pieces on side of roll to resemble cut branches, cut sides facing out. Spread reserved frosting over outside of branches, leaving cut sides exposed. With damp paper towel, wipe platter clean. Cake can be covered loosely with plastic wrap and refrigerated up to overnight.

11. When ready to serve, garnish platter with grated chocolate. If cake has been refrigerated, let stand at room temperature 15 to 20 minutes for easier slicing.

Each serving: about 340 calories, 6g protein, 31g carbohydrate, 23g total fat (11g saturated), 1g fiber, 132mg cholesterol, 145mg sodium

---

TEST KITCHEN KNOW-HOW

ROLLING AND DECORATING A BÛCHE DE NOËL

This is a fun holiday project for the whole family.

Roll the cake around the filling and cut both ends off on a diagonal. Set the pieces aside.

Spread chocolate frosting over the roll to coat. Attach the two cut-off diagonal ends to the roll to create branches; frost to finish your Yule log.

CHEESECAKES

You can make quick cheesecakes—which are simply chilled in the refrigerator—and low-fat cheesecakes—by substituting reduced-fat cream cheese as we've done in our healthy makeover recipe. But the fact is, they will never reach the blissful richness of the real thing, made with cream cheese (and sometimes ricotta) and oven-baked.

Berry Cheesecake

Cool, creamy, and topped with mixed summer berries, this cheesecake is the perfect finale to a dinner party. Italian cheesecakes are typically based on ricotta cheese, but we've included cream cheese to create an extra-thick and creamy cake.

Active time: 25 minutes plus standing and chilling
Bake time: 1 hour 8 minutes
Makes: 16 servings

1¹/2 cups graham cracker crumbs

6 tablespoons butter or margarine, melted

1¹/2 cups plus 1 tablespoon granulated sugar

2 lemons

2 packages (8 ounces each) reduced-fat cream cheese (Neufchâtel), softened

1 container (15 ounces) part-skim ricotta cheese

3 tablespoons cornstarch

¹/4 teaspoon salt

2 cups half-and-half

2 teaspoons vanilla extract

1 teaspoon almond extract

4 large eggs, lightly beaten

2¹/2 cups mixed berries (such as blackberries, raspberries, and blueberries)

1 tablespoon confectioners' sugar

1. Preheat oven to 375°F. Wrap outside of 9-inch springform pan with heavy-duty foil to prevent batter from leaking out. Spray pan with nonstick baking spray.

2. In medium bowl, combine crumbs, butter, and 1 tablespoon granulated sugar. Press firmly onto bottom of prepared pan. Bake 8 to 10 minutes or until brown around edge. Cool on wire rack. Reduce oven temperature to 325°F.

3. While crust cools, from lemons, grate 1 tablespoon peel and squeeze ¼ cup juice; set aside.

4. In stand mixer or large bowl, with mixer on high speed, beat both cheeses until smooth. Add cornstarch, remaining 1½ cups granulated sugar, and salt, scraping bowl occasionally with rubber spatula; beat on low until well incorporated. On low speed, beat in half-and-half, both extracts, and lemon peel and juice. Add eggs; beat until just blended. Pour batter onto cooled crust. Bake 1 hour. Turn oven off. Let stand in oven 1 hour.

5. Place cheesecake on wire rack. Run thin knife between edge of cheesecake and pan. Cool in pan on rack 1 hour. Cover; refrigerate at least 6 hours or up to 2 days.

6. To serve, top with berries; sprinkle confectioners' sugar through sieve over berries.

Each serving: about 345 calories, 9g protein, 34g carbohydrate, 20g total fat (11g saturated), 1g fiber, 104mg cholesterol, 260mg sodium

New York–Style Cheesecake

Purists will insist on devouring this cake unadorned, while the more adventurous will enjoy our variations. A garnish of fresh berries always looks festive.

Active time: 20 minutes plus cooling and chilling
Bake time: 55 minutes
Makes: 16 servings

3 packages (8 ounces each) cream cheese, softened
3/4 cup sugar
1 tablespoon all-purpose flour
1 1/2 teaspoons vanilla extract
3 large eggs
1 large egg yolk
1/4 cup milk
Baked Graham-Cracker Crumb Crust (page 143),
    prepared in 8 1/2- or 9-inch springform pan

1. Preheat oven to 300°F.

2. In large bowl, with mixer on medium speed, beat cream cheese and sugar until smooth and fluffy. Beat in flour and vanilla until well combined.

3. Reduce speed to low and add eggs and egg yolk, one at a time, beating well after each. Beat in milk just until blended.

4. Pour batter into cooled crust. Bake 55 to 60 minutes until filling 3 inches from center is still slightly wet and surface is lightly golden and set. Cool completely on wire rack. Refrigerate overnight before serving.

5. To serve, remove side of pan and place cake on plate. Cut with knife dipped in warm water, wiping knife between slices.

Each serving: about 275 calories, 5g protein, 19g carbohydrate, 20g total fat (12g saturated), 1g fiber, 108mg cholesterol, 230mg sodium

APRICOT SWIRL CHEESECAKE In 1-quart saucepan, combine *3/4 cup (5 ounces) dried apricots, 3/4 cup water,* and *2 tablespoons sugar.* Bring to boiling over medium heat. Reduce to simmer, cover, and cook 15 to 20 minutes, until apricots are very soft; puree in food processor. Prepare cheesecake batter as directed in recipe, but omit milk. Spoon batter into prepared crust; spoon apricot mixture on top in several dollops. Using knife, swirl apricot mixture through cheesecake batter, then continue as directed.

Each serving: about 300 calories, 6g protein, 26g carbohydrate, 20g total fat (12g saturated), 1g fiber, 108mg cholesterol, 225mg sodium

GINGER CHEESECAKE Prepare crumb crust as instructed in recipe, but use *9 ounces crushed gingersnaps* instead of graham crackers. Prepare batter as directed, but add *1/3 cup minced crystallized ginger* and *1 teaspoon freshly grated lemon peel.* Continue as directed.

Each serving about 320 calories, 6g protein, 29g carbohydrate, 21g total fat (12g saturated), 0g fiber, 108mg cholesterol, 280mg sodium

AMARETTO CHEESECAKE Prepare crumb crust as instructed in recipe, but omit sugar and use *6 ounces crushed amaretti cookies* instead of graham crackers. Prepare batter as directed, but use only *2 tablespoons milk* and add *2 tablespoons amaretto* (almond-flavored liqueur). Continue as directed.

Each serving: about 280 calories, 5g protein, 20g carbohydrate, 20g total fat (12g saturated), 0g fiber, 110mg cholesterol, 175mg sodium

CHOCOLATE MARBLE CHEESECAKE Prepare Baked Chocolate-Wafer Crumb Crust (page 143) in springform pan as instructed in recipe. Prepare batter as directed, but omit milk. Melt *2 ounces semisweet chocolate.* In small bowl, stir together melted chocolate and 1 cup cheesecake batter. Pour plain cheesecake batter into prepared crust. Spoon chocolate batter over top in several dollops. Using knife, swirl chocolate batter through plain batter. Continue as directed.

Each serving: about 290 calories, 5g protein, 21g carbohydrate, 21g total fat (12g saturated), 1g fiber, 108mg cholesterol, 220mg sodium

Deluxe Cheese Pie

Baked in a graham-cracker crumb crust and filled with a rich cream cheese and sour cream filling, this cheese pie is both easy and irresistible.

Active time: 35 minutes plus cooling and chilling
Bake time: 35 minutes
Makes: 10 servings

1¹/₂ packages (8 ounces each) cream cheese, softened
¹/₂ cup plus 2 tablespoons sugar
2 large eggs
¹/₂ teaspoon vanilla extract
Baked Graham-Cracker Crumb Crust (page 143)
1 container (8 ounces) sour cream

1. Preheat oven to 350°F. In small bowl, with mixer on low speed, beat cream cheese and ½ cup sugar until smooth, scraping bowl with rubber spatula. Add eggs and vanilla; beat just until mixed.

2. Pour cheese filling into cooled piecrust. Bake 30 minutes, or until set. Transfer to wire rack.

3. Mix remaining 2 tablespoons sugar with sour cream. Spread mixture over top of hot pie. Bake 5 minutes, or until set. Cool on wire rack. Refrigerate pie at least 2 hours before serving.

Each serving: about 340 calories, 6g protein, 28g carbohydrate, 24g total fat (14g saturated), 1g fiber, 102mg cholesterol, 265mg sodium

HEALTHY MAKEOVER

Cheesecake

Savor this lightened up version of the Big Apple classic.

Active time: 25 minutes plus standing and cooling
Bake time: 1 hour 15 minutes
Makes: 16 servings

³/₄ cup graham cracker crumbs
2 tablespoons vegetable oil spread, melted
3 packages (24 ounces) reduced-fat cream cheese
1 cup sugar
1 tablespoon cornstarch
1¹/₂ pints fat-free sour cream
1¹/₄ teaspoons vanilla extract
2 large eggs
2 large egg whites

1. Preheat oven to 325°F. In 9-inch springform pan, stir crumbs with spread until moistened. With hand, firmly press mixture onto bottom of pan. Bake crust 15 minutes or until deep golden. Cool 5 minutes on wire rack.

2. In large bowl, with mixer on medium speed, beat cream cheese until smooth. Mix sugar and cornstarch; slowly beat into cream cheese. On low speed, beat in sour cream and vanilla. Add eggs and whites, one at a time, until blended.

3. Pour batter over crust. Bake 1 hour. Edge will be set, but center will still jiggle. Turn oven off; let cake remain in oven 1 hour. Transfer to wire rack. Run thin knife around edge of cake to prevent cracking. Cool in pan 2 hours. Cover and refrigerate 4 hours or overnight. Remove side of pan. Cut with knife dipped in warm water, wiping knife between slices.

Each serving: about 255 calories, 8g protein, 26g carbohydrate, 13g total fat (7g saturated), 0g fiber, 59mg cholesterol, 250mg sodium

Creamy Lemon Ricotta Cheesecake

This is cheesecake all'Italiana—*the filling is made with ricotta. The original recipe is made with a cookie-dough crust, but a vanilla-wafer crust is easier to prepare.*

Active time: 20 minutes plus cooling and chilling
Bake time: 1 hour 25 minutes
Makes: 16 servings

4 large lemons
4 tablespoons butter or margarine
1 cup vanilla-wafer crumbs (about 30 cookies)
1¼ cups sugar
¼ cup cornstarch
2 packages (8 ounces each) cream cheese, softened
1 container (15 ounces) ricotta cheese
4 large eggs
2 cups half-and-half or light cream
2 teaspoons vanilla extract

1. Preheat oven to 375°F. From lemons, grate 4 teaspoons peel and squeeze ⅓ cup juice. In small saucepan, melt butter over low heat; stir in 1 teaspoon lemon peel. Pour butter mixture into 9-inch springform pan. Add wafer crumbs and stir until moistened. With hand, press mixture firmly onto bottom of pan. Bake 10 minutes, or until golden. Cool on wire rack about 30 minutes. Wrap outside of pan with heavy-duty foil.

2. Reduce oven temperature to 325°F. In small bowl, combine sugar and cornstarch until blended. In large bowl, with mixer on medium speed, beat cream cheese and ricotta until smooth, about 5 minutes; slowly beat in sugar mixture. Reduce speed to low; beat in eggs, half-and-half, lemon juice, vanilla, and remaining 3 teaspoons lemon peel just until blended, scraping bowl often with rubber spatula.

3. Pour batter into crust. Bake 1 hour 15 minutes. Turn off oven; let cheesecake remain in oven 1 hour.

Top: Creamy Lemon Ricotta Cheesecake; Bottom: Milk Chocolate Cheesecake

4. Remove cake from oven; discard foil and cool completely in pan on wire rack. Cover and refrigerate until well chilled, at least 6 hours or overnight. To serve, remove side of pan and place cake on plate. Cut with knife dipped in warm water, wiping blade between slices.

Each serving: about 325 calories, 8g protein, 25g carbohydrate, 22g total fat (13g saturated), 0g fiber, 117mg cholesterol, 180mg sodium

Milk Chocolate Cheesecake

How to make the classic cheesecake even creamier?
Add milk chocolate with a dark cookie crust for kicks.

Active time: 25 minutes plus cooling and chilling
Bake time: 50 minutes
Makes: 16 servings

1 package (9 ounces) chocolate wafer cookies
6 tablespoons butter or margarine, melted
2 packages (8 ounces each) cream cheese, softened
1/2 cup plus 2 tablespoons sugar
1/4 teaspoon salt
3 large eggs, lightly beaten
1/4 cup whole milk
2 teaspoons vanilla extract
1 bag (11 1/2 ounces) milk chocolate chips, melted
1 1/2 cups sour cream

1. Preheat oven to 350°F. In food processor with knife blade attached, pulse cookies until fine crumbs form. Add butter to crumbs and pulse several times to combine. Transfer cookie mixture to 9-inch springform pan; press onto bottom and about 2 inches up side of pan to form crust. Bake crust 10 minutes. Cool completely in pan on wire rack.

2. In large bowl, with mixer on medium speed, beat cream cheese, 1/2 cup sugar, and salt 2 minutes or until smooth, occasionally scraping bowl with rubber spatula. Reduce speed to low. Add eggs, milk, and vanilla and beat just until blended, occasionally scraping bowl. Add chocolate and beat until combined.

3. Pour cream-cheese mixture into crust. Bake 45 minutes (cake will still jiggle slightly in center). Meanwhile, in small bowl, stir sour cream and remaining 2 tablespoons sugar until sugar dissolves; set aside.

4. Remove cheesecake from oven. Gently spread sour-cream mixture evenly on top. Return cake to oven and bake 5 minutes longer to set sour cream.

5. Remove cheesecake from oven and cool completely in pan on wire rack. Cover and refrigerate at least 6 hours until well chilled, or up to 3 days. To serve, remove side of pan and place cake on plate. Cut with knife dipped in warm water, wiping blade between slices.

Each serving: about 315 calories, 5g protein, 27g carbohydrate, 22g total fat (12g saturated), 0g fiber, 74mg cholesterol, 755mg sodium

TEST KITCHEN KNOW-HOW

CHILLING AND SERVING CHEESECAKE

For a bakery-perfect cheesecake presentation, follow these steps.

Chill the cake thoroughly, preferably overnight. Tightly wrap it so the filling does not pick up aromas from other foods in the refrigerator.

At serving time, place the springform pan on a platter. Carefully open the clasp and remove the side of the pan. Brush away any crumbs that fall onto the platter. Use a large, sharp knife to slice the cake into wedges, dipping it into warm water and wiping the blade dry before each cut.

Pies & Tarts

PASTRY & PIE DOUGHS

Depending on which type and size pie you're making, you'll want to choose your pastry accordingly. Classic fruit pies work well with a straightforward double-crust pastry. The butter adds great flavor. For single-crust tarts, a sweeter crust or shortbread crust is a good choice.

Pastry for Double-Crust Pie

Every cook should know how to make a from-scratch piecrust. Our foolproof recipe gets its flavor from butter and its flakiness from vegetable shortening. For an extra flaky, tender crust, try the vinegar pastry variation.

Active time: 10 minutes plus chilling
Makes: one-9-inch double crust

$2^{1}/4$ cups all-purpose flour
$^{1}/2$ teaspoon salt
$^{1}/2$ cup cold butter or margarine (1 stick), cut up
$^{1}/4$ cup vegetable shortening
4 to 6 tablespoons ice water

1. In large bowl, mix flour and salt. With pastry blender or two knives used scissor-fashion, cut in butter and shortening until mixture resembles coarse crumbs.

2. Sprinkle in ice water, 1 tablespoon at a time, mixing lightly with fork after each addition, until dough is just moist enough to hold together.

3. Shape dough into 2 disks, one slightly larger than other. Wrap each in plastic and refrigerate 30 minutes or overnight. If chilled overnight, let stand at room temperature 30 minutes before rolling.

4. On lightly floured surface, with floured rolling pin, roll larger disk into 12-inch round. Roll dough gently onto rolling pin; ease into pie plate. Trim edge, leaving 1-inch overhang. Reserve trimmings for decorating pie, if you like. Fill piecrust.

5. Roll remaining disk into 12-inch round. Cut ¾-inch circle out of center and cut 1-inch slits to allow steam to escape during baking; center over filling or make desired pie top (see page 153). Fold overhang under; make desired decorative edge (see page 141). Bake pie as directed in recipe.

FOOD PROCESSOR PASTRY In food processor with knife blade attached, pulse flour and salt to mix. Evenly distribute butter and shortening on top of flour mixture; pulse just until mixture resembles coarse crumbs. With processor running, pour ¼ cup ice water through feed tube. Immediately stop motor and pinch dough; it should be just moist enough to hold together. If not, with fork, stir in up to 2 tablespoons additional ice water. Refrigerate and roll as directed.

ALL-SHORTENING PASTRY Prepare dough as instructed, but omit butter and instead use *¾ cup vegetable shortening* and *1 teaspoon salt.*

VINEGAR PASTRY Prepare dough as instructed, but substitute *1 tablespoon distilled white vinegar* for 1 tablespoon ice water.

WHOLE-WHEAT PASTRY Prepare dough as instructed, but use only *1½ cups all-purpose flour* and add *¾ cup whole-wheat flour.*

Strawberry-Rhubarb Pie (page 159)

Pastry for Single-Crust Pie

This dependable recipe is used for many of the pies in this chapter.

Active time: 10 minutes plus chilling
Makes: one 9-inch crust

1¼ cups all-purpose flour
¼ teaspoon salt
4 tablespoons cold butter or margarine, cut up
2 tablespoons vegetable shortening
3 to 5 tablespoons ice water

1. Prepare dough as for Pastry for Double-Crust Pie (page 138), steps 1 through 4, gathering dough into only 1 disk in step 3. Roll and line pan as instructed in step 4, but do not yet fill pie shell.

2. Make desired decorative edge (see page 141). Refrigerate or freeze 10 to 15 minutes to firm pastry before baking.

3. Fill and bake pie as directed in recipe.

PASTRY FOR DEEP-DISH PIE SHELL Prepare dough as instructed, but use *1½ cups all-purpose flour, ¼ cup vegetable shortening,* and *5 tablespoons cold butter or margarine,* cut up.

Shortbread Crust

Plenty of butter, mixed with confectioners' sugar and cornstarch, gives this crust a melt-in-your-mouth texture. It's the perfect choice for our rich Caramel Walnut Tart (page 171).

Active time: 15 minutes
Bake time: 27 minutes
Makes: one 9-inch crust

¾ cup all-purpose flour
⅓ cup cornstarch
½ cup butter or margarine (1 stick), softened
⅓ cup confectioners' sugar
1 teaspoon vanilla extract

1. Preheat oven to 325°F. In medium bowl, stir together flour and cornstarch. In large bowl, with mixer on medium speed, beat butter and confectioners' sugar until light and fluffy. Beat in vanilla. Reduce speed to low and beat in flour mixture until combined. Scrape dough into 9-inch tart pan with removable bottom.

2. Smooth dough over bottom and up side of pan. Prick all over with fork. Bake 27 to 30 minutes, until lightly golden. Cool on wire rack. Fill as directed in recipe.

Pastry for 11-Inch Tart

When rolling the pastry dough, lift and turn it occasionally to prevent it from sticking.

Active time: 10 minutes plus chilling
Makes: one 11-inch tart

1½ cups all-purpose flour
½ teaspoon salt
½ cup cold butter or margarine (1 stick), cut up
2 tablespoons vegetable shortening
3 to 4 tablespoons ice water

1. Prepare dough as for Pastry for Double-Crust Pie (page 138), steps 1 through 3, gathering dough into only 1 disk in step 3.

2. On lightly floured surface, with floured rolling pin, roll dough into 14-inch round. Fit dough into 11" by 1" round tart pan with removable bottom. Fold overhang in and press against side of tart pan to form ⅛-inch rim above edge of pan. Refrigerate or freeze 10 to 15 minutes to firm pastry before baking.

3. Fill and bake tart as directed in recipe.

PASTRY FOR 9-INCH TART Prepare dough as directed, but reduce to *1 cup all-purpose flour, ¼ teaspoon salt, 6 tablespoons cold butter, 1 tablespoon shortening,* and *2 to 3 tablespoons ice water.* In step 2, roll dough into 11-inch round and fit into 9" by 1" round tart pan with removable bottom. Proceed as directed in recipe.

MAKING DECORATIVE EDGES

These borders add a professional finish to homemade pies and tarts. Chill the dough until it's firm before you begin working with it. For a forked or leaf edge, trim the dough even with the rim of the pie plate. For the others, trim the dough with kitchen shears, leaving a 1-inch overhang. Fold the overhang under, then pinch it to make a stand-up edge. The procedure for double-crust pies is very similar—just trim both the top and bottom crusts together before making a decorative edge.

Forked
With a floured fork, press the dough to the rim of plate. Repeat all around the edge.

Turret
With scissors, make cuts down through the stand-up edge to the rim of the pie plate, spacing the cuts ½ inch apart. Fold the pieces alternately toward the center and the rim.

Crimped
Push one index finger against the outside edge of the rim; with the index finger and thumb of your other hand, pinch to make a flute. Repeat, moving your inner index finger into the impression made by your thumb.

Rope
Press a thumb into the dough edge at an angle, then pinch the dough between the thumb and the knuckle of your index finger. Place your thumb in the groove left by your index finger; pinch as before. Repeat.

Fork-Scallop
Push knuckle of index finger against outer edge of rim; with index finger and thumb of other hand, press to make scallop. Repeat, leaving ¼-inch space between scallops. With floured fork, press edge between each scallop.

Fluted
Push one index finger against the outside edge of the rim; with the index finger and thumb of your other hand, press to make a ruffle. Repeat the pattern around the edge, leaving about ¼-inch of space between ruffles.

Sweet Pastry Crust for 11-Inch Tart

Known as pâte sucrée in France, this cross between a cookie and a pastry shell is the perfect foil for pastry cream and berries.

Active time: 15 minutes plus chilling
Makes: one 11-inch tart shell

1½ cups all-purpose flour
¼ cup sugar
¼ teaspoon salt
10 tablespoons cold butter, cut up (do not use margarine)
1 large egg yolk
¼ cup cold water

1. In large bowl, stir together flour, sugar, and salt. With pastry blender or two knives used scissor-fashion, cut in butter until mixture resembles coarse crumbs. In small bowl, with fork, stir together egg yolk and water. Pour into flour mixture and stir together until dough just forms ball. Shape into disk, wrap, and refrigerate at least 1 hour, or overnight.

2. Place disk between two layers of lightly floured waxed paper. Roll into 14-inch round. If dough becomes too soft to handle, return to refrigerator for 5 minutes.

3. Remove top sheet of waxed paper and invert pastry into 11-inch tart pan with removable bottom, gently pressing dough into bottom and up side of pan. Remove second sheet of waxed paper. If dough cracks, gently press together. Run rolling pin over top of pan to trim excess dough. Refrigerate or freeze 10 to 15 minutes to firm pastry. Prick bottom all over with fork before baking as recipe directs.

SWEET PASTRY CRUST FOR 9-INCH TART Prepare the crust as directed for larger size above, but reduce ingredient amounts to *1¼ cups all-purpose flour, 3 tablespoons sugar, ⅛ teaspoon salt, ½ cup cold butter (1 stick), 1 large egg yolk*, and *2 tablespoons cold water*. Roll dough as instructed in step 2, but make 11-inch round and fit pastry into 9-inch tart pan with removable bottom.

BAKED SWEET PASTRY CRUST Preheat oven to 375°F and prepare 9-inch or 11-inch Sweet Pastry Crust as directed. Line shell with foil and fill foil with pie weights, dry beans, or uncooked rice. Bake 20 minutes. Remove foil and weights and bake 7 to 10 minutes longer, or until golden. If crust puffs up, gently press it to tart pan with back of spoon. Cool in pan on wire rack before filling as directed. Makes one 9- or 11-inch baked tart shell.

TRIMMING A TART CRUST

Tarts pans are shallower than pie plates and typically have fluted edges. Choose a pan with a removable bottom; it'll make it much easier to get the tart out of the pan.

Roll dough into a round that's 2 or 3 inches larger than the circumference of the tart pan. Press the dough gently into the rim of the pan; let the dough hang over the edges.

To trim off the excess dough, simply roll a rolling pin over the edges of the pan; the rim will act as a cutting edge, and the dough will fall away.

Coconut Pastry Crust

Making this toasted coconut crust is as easy as mixing up the ingredients and pressing the dough into the pie plate. Use it in our scrumptious Chocolate Pudding Pie with Coconut Crust (page 173).

Active time: 10 minute
Bake time: 20 minutes
Makes: one 9-inch crust

1 cup all-purpose flour
½ cup sweetened flaked coconut, toasted (see page xxii)
6 tablespoons cold butter or margarine, cut up
2 tablespoons sugar
1 tablespoon cold water

1. Preheat oven to 375°F. Grease 9-inch pie plate. In food processor with knife blade attached, combine flour, coconut, butter, sugar, and water. Pulse until dough just holds together.

2. Press dough evenly into bottom and up side of prepared pie plate, making a small rim. Bake 20 minutes, or until golden. Cover edge loosely with foil to prevent overbrowning if necessary during last 10 minutes of baking. Cool on wire rack. Fill as directed in recipe.

Baked Graham-Cracker Crumb Crust

Here's the quick classic, with two variations. For an almost instant dessert, fill the cooled crust with scoops of ice cream and top with hot fudge or a berry sauce.

Active time: 10 minutes
Bake time: 10 minutes
Makes: one 9-inch crust

1¼ cups graham-cracker crumbs
　　(11 rectangular graham crackers)
4 tablespoons butter or margarine, melted
1 tablespoon sugar

1. Preheat oven to 375°F. In 9-inch pie plate, with fork, mix crumbs, butter, and sugar. With hand, press mixture into bottom and up side of pie plate, making small rim.

2. Bake 10 minutes. Cool on wire rack. Fill as directed in recipe.

BAKED VANILLA-WAFER CRUMB CRUST Prepare as instructed, but substitute *1¼ cups vanilla-wafer cookie crumbs (about 35 cookies)* for the graham-cracker crumbs.

BAKED CHOCOLATE-WAFER CRUMB CRUST Prepare as instructed, but use *1¼ cups chocolate-wafer cookie crumbs (about 24 cookies)* for the graham-cracker crumbs.

MAKING A CRUMB CRUST

This crust can be made in a pie tin, or in a springform pan if you're making a cheesecake.

Press the buttered crumbs evenly and firmly onto the bottom of the pan. Some recipes call for the crumbs to be pressed up the side of the pan as well. Using a measuring cup helps pack crumbs evenly. Or place a piece of plastic wrap over the crumbs and press with your hand.

FRUIT PIES

From rustic crostatas to more elaborate lattice- or streusel-topped creations, these pies and tarts celebrate fresh fruit at its seasonal peak.

Double-Crust Apple Pie

This is double-crust delight: Flaky layers of dough encase a sweet, sticky apple filling.

Active time: 45 minutes plus chilling
Bake time: 1 hour 10 minutes
Makes: 10 servings

PASTRY

2½ cups all-purpose flour
½ teaspoon salt
10 tablespoons cold butter or margarine, cut up
6 tablespoons vegetable shortening
6½ tablespoons ice water

APPLE FILLING AND FINISHING

⅔ cup plus 1 teaspoon sugar
⅓ cup cornstarch
½ teaspoon ground cinnamon
¼ teaspoon ground nutmeg
¼ teaspoon salt
3½ pounds Granny Smith, Golden Delicious, and/or
   Braeburn apples, peeled, cored, and cut into 16 wedges
1 tablespoon fresh lemon juice
2 tablespoons butter or margarine, cut up
1 large egg white, lightly beaten

1. Prepare pastry: In food processor with knife blade attached, blend flour and salt. Add butter and shortening, and pulse until mixture resembles coarse crumbs. Sprinkle in ice water, 1 tablespoon at a time, pulsing after each addition, until large moist crumbs just begin to form.

2. Shape dough into 2 balls, one slightly larger than other. Flatten each into disk; wrap each in plastic and refrigerate 30 minutes or overnight. (If chilled overnight, let stand 30 minutes at room temperature before rolling.)

3. When ready to proceed, preheat oven to 400°F.

4. Prepare apple filling: In large bowl, combine ⅔ cup sugar with cornstarch, cinnamon, nutmeg, and salt. Add apples and lemon juice, and toss to coat evenly.

5. On lightly floured surface, with floured rolling pin, roll larger disk of dough into 12-inch round. Ease dough into 9½-inch deep-dish glass or ceramic pie plate. Gently press dough against bottom and up side of plate without stretching. Trim dough edge, leaving 1-inch overhang; reserve trimmings. Spoon apple mixture into pie crust; dot with butter.

6. Roll remaining dough disk for top crust into 12-inch round. Place round over filling. Trim pastry edge, leaving 1-inch overhang; reserve trimmings. Fold overhang under; bring up over pie-plate rim and pinch to make decorative edge of choice (see page 141). Brush crust with some egg white. Reroll trimmings and use to make apple and/or leaf shapes as described on page 153. Cut short slashes in top crust to allow steam to escape during baking. Brush cutouts with egg white, place on top crust, and sprinkle pie with remaining 1 teaspoon sugar.

7. Place pie on nonstick or foil-lined cookie sheet to catch any overflow during baking. Bake 1 hour 10 minutes or until apples are tender when pierced with knife through slits in crust. To prevent overbrowning, cover pie loosely with tent of foil after 40 minutes. Cool pie on wire rack 3 hours to serve warm. Or cool completely to serve later.

Each serving: about 455 calories, 4g protein, 61g carbohydrate, 23g total fat (11g saturated), 4g fiber, 39mg cholesterol, 330mg sodium

Walnut Crumb Apple Pie

This iconic American dessert is topped with walnut-laden streusel, a delicious time-saving alternative to more elaborate top crusts. Two unexpected additions to the apple filling: fresh thyme and honey.

Active time: 35 minutes
Bake time: 50 minutes
Makes: 12 servings

Pastry for Single-Crust Pie (page 140)

WALNUT CRUMBS

1 1/2 cups walnuts, toasted and chopped

1/2 cup all-purpose flour

1/4 cup sugar

1/4 teaspoon freshly grated nutmeg

1/8 teaspoon salt

3 tablespoons cold unsalted butter or margarine, cut up

APPLE FILLING

4 tablespoons butter or margarine

3 pounds Golden Delicious apples (about 8), peeled, cored, and thinly sliced

1/4 cup sugar

1/8 teaspoon salt

1 lemon

2 tablespoons honey

1 teaspoon chopped fresh thyme leaves

1/4 teaspoon nutmeg, freshly grated

1. Preheat oven to 425°F. Line pie shell with foil; fill with pie weights, dry beans, or uncooked rice. Bake 10 minutes. Remove foil and weights; bake 10 minutes longer, or until golden. If crust puffs up during baking, gently press it to pan with back of spoon. Cool on wire rack. Reduce oven temperature to 375°F.

2. Meanwhile, prepare walnut topping: In medium bowl, toss walnuts, flour, sugar, nutmeg, and salt until well mixed. Add butter and press into mixture with fingertips until small clumps form. (Crumbs can be covered and refrigerated up to 3 days ahead.)

3. Prepare filling: In 12-inch skillet, melt butter on medium. Add sliced apples, sugar, and salt and cook 15 minutes or until tender and juicy, stirring occasionally.

4. While apples cook, finely grate 1/2 teaspoon lemon peel and squeeze 1 tablespoon juice into small bowl. Add honey, thyme, and nutmeg, and mix well. Stir into cooked apples, then pour apple mixture into baked crust, spreading in even layer. Sprinkle walnut crumbs on top in even layer and gently press into apples.

5. Bake 50 minutes to 1 hour or until crumbs are golden brown and apple mixture is bubbling, covering edges of pie crust if browning too quickly. Cool completely on wire rack.

Each serving: about 355 calories, 4g protein, 41g carbohydrate, 21g total fat (9g saturated), 3g fiber, 41mg cholesterol, 65mg sodium

ROLL IT RIGHT

Whether you're using an American- or European-style rolling pin (see page xiv), here's how to roll out a pie or tart crust.

To form a smooth, even round of pastry dough, roll the pin outward from the center of the disk of chilled dough, then give the dough a quarter turn and again roll outward from the center. Keep turning and rolling the dough to maintain an even overall thickness. Don't use the rolling pin to stretch the dough, just to flatten it.

Apple Tarte Tatin

Les demoiselles Tatin were two sisters who ran a restaurant near the French city of Orléans. Their skillet-cooked caramelized-apple tart is now a classic.

Active time: 45 minutes plus chilling
Bake time: 25 minutes
Makes: 10 servings

Pastry for 11-Inch Tart (page 140), prepared only through
    step 1
1 cup sugar
6 tablespoons butter or margarine
1 tablespoon fresh lemon juice
3¾ pounds Golden Delicious apples (about 9),
    peeled, cored, and cut in half

1. Preheat oven to 425°F. Roll dough into 12-inch round, transfer to cookie sheet, and refrigerate until ready to use.

2. In heavy 12-inch skillet with oven-safe handle, heat sugar, butter, and lemon juice over medium-high until mixture boils.

3. Place apples in skillet on their sides, overlapping if necessary. Cook 10 minutes. Carefully turn apples over; cook 8 to 12 minutes longer, until syrup is caramelized and thickened.

4. Place dough on top of apples in skillet; fold edge of dough under to form rim around edge of apples. Cut six ¼-inch-long slits in top to allow steam to escape during baking. Bake 25 minutes, or until crust is golden.

5. To unmold, place large platter over top of skillet. Quickly turn skillet upside down to invert tart onto platter. Cool on wire rack 30 minutes to serve warm, or cool completely to serve later.

Each serving: about 395 calories, 2g protein, 56g carbohydrate, 19g total fat (11g saturated), 3g fiber, 43mg cholesterol, 280mg sodium

PEAR TARTE TATIN Prepare dough and filling as instructed, but substitute *3¾ pounds firm, slightly ripe Bosc pears* (about 7), peeled, cored, and halved lengthwise, for apples.

Each serving: about 405 calories, 3g protein, 58g carbohydrate, 19g total fat (11g saturated), 4g fiber, 43mg cholesterol, 280mg sodium

PEACH TARTE TATIN Prepare dough and filling as instructed, but substitute *3¾ pounds slightly ripe peaches* (about 11), peeled, halved, and pitted, for apples.

Each serving: about 365 calories, 3g protein, 49g carbohydrate, 19g total fat (11g saturated), 3g fiber, 43mg cholesterol, 280mg sodium

Rustic Apricot Crostata

This pretty lattice tart draws inspiration from Italy. In a slight departure from the traditional recipe, for extra flavor, we've replaced some of the flour in the crust with ground toasted almonds.

Active time: 45 minutes plus chilling
Bake time: 40 minutes
Makes: 12 servings

1/2 cup blanched almonds (2 ounces), toasted
    (see page xxiii)
3 tablespoons cornstarch
2 1/2 cups all-purpose flour
1/4 teaspoon salt
1 cup butter (2 sticks), softened (do not use margarine)
1/2 cup plus 2 teaspoons sugar
1 large egg
2 teaspoons vanilla extract
1 cup apricot preserves
1 large egg yolk
1 tablespoon water

1. In food processor with knife blade attached, finely grind toasted almonds with cornstarch. In medium bowl, combine nut mixture, flour, and salt.

2. In large bowl, with mixer on high speed, beat butter and 1/2 cup sugar until creamy. Add whole egg and vanilla; beat until almost combined (mixture will look curdled). With wooden spoon, stir in flour mixture until dough begins to form. With hands, press dough together in bowl. Shape dough into 2 disks, one slightly larger than other. Wrap each in plastic and refrigerate 1 hour 30 minutes to 2 hours.

3. Preheat oven to 375°F. On lightly floured surface, with floured rolling pin, roll larger disk of dough into 13-inch round. Press into bottom and up side of 11-inch tart pan with removable bottom.

4. On lightly floured waxed paper, roll remaining dough into 12-inch round. With pastry wheel or knife, cut dough into twelve 1-inch-wide strips. Refrigerate 15 minutes.

5. Spread preserves over dough in tart pan to within 1/2 inch of edge. Begin simple lattice top by placing 5 dough strips, 1 inch apart, across tart; finish lattice by placing 5 remaining strips placed diagonally across first strips to make diamond pattern (see page 153). Trim ends and reserve trimmings.

6. With hands, roll trimmings and remaining 2 strips of dough into 1/4-inch-thick ropes. Press ropes around edge of tart to create finished rope edge (see page 141).

7. In cup, beat egg yolk with water. Brush mixture over lattice and edge of tart; sprinkle with remaining 2 teaspoons sugar.

8. Bake 40 to 45 minutes, until crust is deep golden. Check tart occasionally during first 30 minutes of baking; if crust puffs up, prick with tip of knife. Cool on wire rack. Remove side of pan to serve.

Each serving: about 390 calories, 5g protein, 50g carbohydrate, 20g total fat (10g saturated), 2g fiber, 77mg cholesterol, 220mg sodium

Pear Pie with a Cookie-Cutter Crust

This pie is easier to prepare than a traditional lattice because it calls for simply cutting out the top crust with cookie cutters—no weaving required!

Active time: 1 hour plus chilling
Bake time: 1 hour 20 minutes
Makes: 12 servings

Pastry for Double-Crust Pie (page 138), dough formed into disks and chilled but not rolled
1 lemon
3 pounds firm but ripe pears (about 6), peeled, cored, and cut into ½-inch chunks
1 cup fresh cranberries, finely chopped
3 tablespoons cornstarch
¼ teaspoon nutmeg
Pinch salt
¾ cup plus 1 tablespoon sugar
1 tablespoon butter or margarine, cut up
1 tablespoon heavy cream or milk

1. Preheat oven to 425°F.

2. On lightly floured surface, with floured rolling pin, roll 1 disk of dough into 12-inch round. Ease dough into 9-inch glass or ceramic pie plate; gently press against bottom and up side of plate without stretching. Trim edge, leaving 1-inch overhang. Fold overhang under. Freeze until firm.

3. Roll remaining disk of dough to ⅛-inch thickness. With 1- to 2-inch cookie or pie cutters, cut out as many shapes as possible. Freeze on waxed paper-lined cookie sheet until firm. Reserve scraps for another use.

4. Into large bowl, finely grate ½ teaspoon lemon peel and squeeze 2 tablespoons juice. Add pears, cranberries, cornstarch, nutmeg, salt, and ¾ cup sugar. Gently fold until well combined. Spread into even layer in prepared pie shell. Dot with butter.

5. Arrange chilled cutouts in lines over filling and in circle over rim, overlapping slightly. With pastry brush, lightly brush cutouts with cream. Sprinkle remaining 1 tablespoon sugar on cutouts.

6. Place pie on jelly-roll pan. Bake 20 minutes.

7. Reduce oven temperature to 350°F. Bake 1 hour to 1 hour 10 minutes longer or until golden brown, covering rim with foil if browning too quickly. Cool on wire rack 4 hours to serve warm, or cool completely.

Each serving: about 335 calories, 3g protein, 51g carbohydrate, 15g total fat (7g saturated), 4g fiber, 25mg cholesterol, 170mg sodium

SPICED PEAR PIE Omit cranberries. Add *1 teaspoon ground cinnamon, ⅛ teaspoon ground cloves,* and *⅛ teaspoon ground allspice* to filling. Proceed as instructed above.

Each serving: about 335 calories, 3g protein, 50g carbohydrate, 14g total fat (7g saturated), 4g fiber, 25mg cholesterol, 170mg sodium

CRUMB-TOP PEAR PIE Omit 1 recipe for pastry and just line pie plate for single crust; omit 1 tablespoon sugar. Omit steps 3 and 5 and instead make crumb topping: In bowl, with fingers, combine *½ cup all-purpose flour, ½ cup packed brown sugar, 4 tablespoons softened butter, ½ teaspoon ground cinnamon;* and *pinch salt* to form large crumbs. Work in *¾ cup pecans*, chopped, until marble-size clumps form. After step 6, sprinkle topping evenly over filling. Continue with step 7 as described.

Each serving: about 375 calories, 3g protein, 57g carbohydrate, 16g total fat (7g saturated), 5g fiber, 23mg cholesterol, 155mg sodium

Peach Pie

If you bake only one fruit pie all summer, this is the one to choose. Make it with a double crust, as suggested below, or with a woven lattice top (opposite).

Active time: 35 minutes
Bake time: 1 hour 5 minutes
Makes: 10 servings

¾ cup sugar
¼ cup cornstarch
Pinch salt
3 pounds ripe peaches, peeled, pitted, and sliced
   (about 7 cups)
1 tablespoon fresh lemon juice
1 tablespoon butter or margarine, cut up
Pastry for Double-Crust Pie (page 138)

1. Preheat oven to 425°F. In large bowl, stir together sugar, cornstarch, and salt. Add peaches and lemon juice; toss gently to combine.

2. Spoon filling into prepared piecrust; dot with butter. Place top crust over filling, cut 1-inch slits to allow steam to escape during baking, and make decorative edge of your choice (see page 141).

3. Place pie on foil-lined cookie sheet to catch any overflow during baking. Bake 20 minutes. Reduce oven temperature to 375°F; bake 45 minutes to 1 hour longer, until filling bubbles in center. If necessary, cover loosely with foil to prevent overbrowning during last 20 minutes of baking. Cool on wire rack 1 hour to serve warm, or cool completely to serve later.

Each serving: about 365 calories, 4g protein, 53g carbohydrate, 16g total fat (8g saturated), 3g fiber, 28 mg cholesterol, 235mg sodium

PLUM PIE Prepare pie as instructed, but substitute *3 pounds tart plums*, pitted and sliced, for peaches and use *1 cup sugar*.

Each serving: about 410 calories, 4g protein, 64g carbohydrate, 17g total fat (8g saturated), 3g fiber, 28mg cholesterol, 235mg sodium

REMOVING SKIN FROM PEACHES

Set aside your paring knife and try this less taxing method instead.

To remove the skins from peaches, submerge whole fruits in boiling water for 15 to 20 seconds. Then, with a slotted spoon, transfer the peaches to a bowl of ice water. When they are cool enough to handle, drain and peel them. The skins should slip right off.

MAKING DECORATIVE PIE TOPS

Peep tops, appliqués, and lattices (both simple and woven) are classic ways to finish a double-crust pie with flair. Our instructions make them all easy to execute.

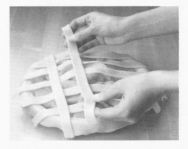

Simple Lattice

When you line the pie plate, trim the bottom-crust dough to leave a 1-inch overhang. Roll the top crust into a 12-inch round and cut it into ½-inch strips. Moisten the edge of the bottom crust with water. Removing every other strip in the rolled round, place the strips about 1 inch apart across the pie and press to seal the edges. Repeat with the remaining strips, placing them at right angles to the first ones. Turn the overhang up over the ends of the strips and pinch to seal.

Woven Lattice

Proceed as instructed in the simple lattice-crust pie described above, but after placing the first layer of strips on the pie, do not seal the ends. Fold every other strip back halfway from the center. Place the longest remaining strip across the center of the pie and reposition the folded strips over it. Now fold back the alternate strips, lay a second cross strip into place, and unfold the strips over it. Repeat to weave all the cross strips into a lattice. Seal the ends and pinch to make a high, fluted edge.

Appliqué

Roll the top crust into a 12-inch round and place it over the filling. Trim the edges, reserving all trimmings, and pinch around the edge of the dough to seal. Roll the trimmings out ⅛ inch thick and use a small knife to cut out freeform shapes, such as an apple, heart, or leaves (you can use the back of the knife to make veins in the leaves, if you like). Brush the shapes with water and place them, wet side down, on top of the pie. Then cut several 1-inch slits as steam vents.

Window

Roll the top crust into a 12-inch round and place it over the filling. Trim the edge, leaving a 1-inch overhang, and pinch to make a high, decorative edge. Cut a 4-inch X in the center of the crust; fold back the points to make a square opening. As well as being decorative, this window will allow steam to escape during baking.

Deep-Dish Peach and Berry Pie

This juicy peach and berry pie is a treat to sink your spoon into. The rustic open shell offers a tempting view of the treasures within.

Active time: 40 minutes plus chilling
Bake time: 35 minutes
Makes: 8 servings

CRUST

1 cup all-purpose flour
1 1/2 teaspoons baking powder
1/4 cup plus 1 tablespoon sugar
3 tablespoons cold butter or margarine,
    cut into 1/2-inch pieces
1/2 cup heavy cream

FRUIT FILLING AND FINISHING

1/2 cup plus 1 tablespoon sugar
1/4 cup cold water
2 tablespoons cornstarch
2 pounds ripe peaches (about 5),
    pitted and cut into 1-inch chunks
1 cup blueberries
1 cup blackberries
1 cup raspberries
1/8 teaspoon ground cinnamon
1 tablespoon heavy cream

1. Prepare crust: In medium bowl, combine flour, baking powder, and 1/4 cup sugar. With pastry blender or two knives used scissor-fashion, cut in butter until mixture resembles fine crumbs. Add cream and stir with fork until dough comes together. Gather dough into ball and place on lightly floured sheet of waxed paper. With floured rolling pin, roll dough to 9-inch round. Slide waxed paper onto cookie sheet and refrigerate dough until ready to use.

2. Preheat oven to 400°F. Line cookie sheet with foil.

3. Prepare filling: In 4-quart saucepan, stir sugar, water, and cornstarch until cornstarch dissolves; stir in peaches. Heat to boiling over medium-high heat, stirring often. Reduce heat to low; simmer 2 minutes, stirring often. Remove from heat; gently stir in all berries. Pour filling into 9 1/2-inch deep-dish pie plate.

4. Immediately, while filling is hot, remove dough from refrigerator and, using waxed paper as handles, invert dough over fruit mixture. Peel off and discard paper. Cut 4-inch X in center of round; fold back points to make square opening. In cup, mix cinnamon and remaining 1 tablespoon sugar. Brush dough with cream; sprinkle with cinnamon sugar.

5. Place pie on foil-lined cookie sheet to catch drips and bake 35 to 40 minutes or until fruit is bubbly in center. If crust is browning too quickly, loosely cover pie with foil after 25 minutes. Cool pie on wire rack.

Each serving: about 310 calories, 3g protein, 51g carbohydrate, 11g total fat (7g saturated), 5g fiber, 35mg cholesterol, 130mg sodium

BUTTER VERSUS SHORTENING

Which fat is best for pastry crust? That depends on who's making the pie or tart.

Many bakers prefer lard, which, because of its high fat content—100 percent—gives a flaky texture and also contributes flavor. Vegetable shortening, which is also 100 percent fat, produces a flaky texture as well, but it has a neutral flavor. Butter, at 80 to 85 percent fat, adds a delicate sweetness, but a less flaky texture.

A good solution is to use a combination of butter and shortening. (If you use margarine, be sure it is stick margarine—at least 80 percent fat—not a soft, whipped, or low-fat version.)

Farm-Stand Cherry Tart

Although sweet cherries are plentiful in season, they're rarely used in baked goods. We say, seize the day and bake this easy, flavorful freeform tart.

Active time: 45 minutes plus chilling
Bake time: 45 minutes
Makes: 8 servings

1¹/2 cups all-purpose flour
¹/3 cup plus 1 tablespoon cornmeal
²/3 cup plus 1 teaspoon sugar
⁵/8 teaspoon salt
¹/2 cup cold butter or margarine (1 stick), cut up
4 to 5 tablespoons ice water
2 tablespoons plus 1 teaspoon cornstarch
1¹/2 pounds dark sweet cherries, pitted
1 large egg white

1. In medium bowl, mix flour, ⅓ cup cornmeal, ⅓ cup sugar, and ½ teaspoon salt. With pastry blender or two knives used scissor-fashion, cut in butter until mixture resembles coarse crumbs. Sprinkle water, 1 tablespoon at a time, into flour mixture, mixing with hands until dough holds together (it will feel dry at first). Shape into disk.

2. Sprinkle large cookie sheet with remaining 1 tablespoon cornmeal. (If you are using jelly-roll pan, invert and use upside down.) Place dampened towel under cookie sheet to prevent slipping. With floured rolling pin, roll dough, directly on cookie sheet, into 13-inch round. With long metal spatula, gently loosen round from cookie sheet.

3. In large bowl, combine ⅓ cup sugar with cornstarch. Sprinkle half of sugar mixture over center of dough round, leaving 2½-inch border all around. Add cherries and any cherry juice to sugar mixture remaining in bowl; toss well. With slotted spoon, spoon cherry mixture over sugared area on dough round; reserve any cherry juice that collects in bowl. Fold dough up around cherries, leaving 4-inch opening in center. Pinch dough to seal cracks.

4. In small cup, mix egg white with remaining ⅛ teaspoon salt. Brush egg-white mixture over dough. Sprinkle dough with remaining 1 teaspoon sugar. Pour cherry-juice mixture through opening in top of tart. Refrigerate until well chilled, about 30 minutes.

5. Preheat oven to 425°F. Bake 45 to 50 minutes, until crust is golden brown and cherry mixture is gently bubbling. If necessary, cover loosely with foil to prevent overbrowning during last 20 minutes of baking.

6. As soon as tart is done, use long metal spatula to loosen it from cookie sheet to prevent sticking. Cool 15 minutes on cookie sheet, then slide tart onto rack to cool completely.

Each serving: about 350 calories, 5g protein, 56g carbohydrate, 13g total fat (7g saturated), 2g fiber, 31mg cholesterol, 310mg sodium

SHAPING AND FILLING THE FARM-STAND CHERRY TART

A generous sprinkling of sugar underneath the cherries and on top of the pastry helps the filling to caramelize and the pastry to brown nicely.

Sprinkle the mixture of granulated sugar and cornstarch onto the middle of the round of dough. Spoon the pitted cherries on top.

Fold up the edges of the dough to make a rounded freeform package, then sprinkle the dough with granulated sugar to help the pastry brown.

EASY PLUM CROSTATA Preheat oven to 400°F and prepare dough as instructed in step 2. Instead of peach filling, in step 3, spread *¾ cup canned almond pastry filling* on crust, leaving 2-inch border. Top with *4 to 5 sliced medium plums*, fold in edges, and bake 30 to 35 minutes or until crust is golden and filling is bubbly. Serves 4.

Each serving: about 275 calories, 5g protein, 32g carbohydrate, 15g total fat (6g saturated), 3g fiber, 15mg cholesterol, 132mg sodium

Apple Galette

This country-style galette is a freeform tart, with the apple slices handsomely arrayed.

Active time: 40 minutes
Bake time: 45 minutes
Makes: 8 servings

Pastry for Single-Crust Pie (page 140), dough prepared
    and chilled but not yet rolled
2 pounds Golden Delicious apples (about 5)
¼ cup sugar
2 tablespoons butter or margarine, cut up
2 tablespoons apricot jam, melted

1. Preheat oven to 425°F. On lightly floured surface, with floured rolling pin, roll dough into 15-inch round. Transfer to ungreased cookie sheet.

2. Peel apples; cut each in half; remove cores. Cut crosswise into ¼-inch-thick slices. Arrange slices in concentric circles on dough, leaving 1½-inch border. Sprinkle with sugar. Dot apple slices with butter. Fold dough up around slices.

3. Place two sheets of foil under cookie sheet; crimp edges to form rim to catch any overflow during baking. Bake 45 minutes, or until apples are tender. Place cookie sheet on wire rack. Brush apples with jam. Cool slightly and serve warm.

Each serving: about 415 calories, 4g protein, 54g carbohydrate, 21g total fat (11g saturated), 3g fiber, 39mg cholesterol, 295mg sodium

Easy Peach Crostata

Similar to the French galette, a crostata is formed by rolling out the dough, arranging the fruit in the center, and folding the edges of the dough over the filling so the fruit is on display. Feel free to use a ready-to-use pie crust.

Active time: 15 minutes
Bake time: 25 minutes
Makes: 4 servings

1 pound peaches, peeled and thinly sliced
3 tablespoons packed brown sugar
1 tablespoon cornstarch
⅛ teaspoon ground ginger
Pinch salt
Pastry for Single-Crust Pie (page 140), formed into disk
    and chilled but not rolled, or 1 ready-to-use pie dough
    for 9-inch pie

1. Preheat oven to 425°F. In large bowl, toss peaches with brown sugar, cornstarch, ginger, and salt.

2. On lightly floured work surface, with floured rolling pin, roll dough into 15-inch round and place on ungreased cookie sheet.

3. Arrange peach mixture on crust, leaving 2-inch border; fold border over filling. Bake 25 to 30 minutes or until crust is golden. Cool slightly and serve warm.

Each serving: about 290 calories, 3g protein, 44g carbohydrate, 13g total fat (6g saturated), 1g fiber, 6mg cholesterol, 297mg sodium

Cherry Pie

Fresh tart cherries (sometimes called pie cherries) are available only for a short time in midsummer. Why not buy extra so you can freeze some? Remove the stems, then spread the cherries on a jelly-roll pan; freeze for 30 minutes or until solid, then transfer to a resealable plastic bag and return to the freezer.

Active time: 1 hour
Bake time: 1 hour 20 minutes
Makes: 10 servings

1 cup sugar
1/4 cup cornstarch
Pinch salt
2 1/4 pounds tart cherries,
    pitted (6 cups)
Pastry for Double-Crust Pie (page 138)
1 tablespoon butter or margarine, cut up

1. Preheat oven to 425°F. In large bowl, stir together sugar, cornstarch, and salt. Add cherries; toss to combine.

2. Spoon filling into prepared piecrust; dot with butter. Before placing top crust on pie, cut center circle 2 inches in diameter. Place crust over filling and cut 1-inch slits to allow steam to escape during baking; make decorative edge of your choice (see page 141).

3. Place pie on nonstick or foil-lined cookie sheet to catch any overflow during baking. Bake 20 minutes. Reduce oven temperature to 375°F; bake 1 hour to 1 hour 10 minutes, until filling bubbles in center. If necessary, cover edges loosely with foil to prevent overbrowning during baking. Cool on wire rack 1 hour to serve warm, or cool completely to serve later.

Each serving: about 385 calories, 4g protein, 58g carbohydrate, 16g total fat (8g saturated), 1g fiber, 28 mg cholesterol, 240 mg sodium

Mince Pie

Mincemeat is a rich, spicy preserve made of assorted chopped fruit, nuts, spices, and brandy or rum. Old-time mincemeats included minced lean beef, but most modern versions do not. Store-bought mincemeat is very dense; the addition of fresh fruit, nuts, and lemon juice to the filling lightens it up.

Active time: 25 minutes
Bake time: 30 minutes
Makes: 10 servings

1 jar (27 to 29 ounces) ready-to-use mincemeat
1 cooking apple, peeled, cored, and finely chopped
1 cup walnuts (4 ounces), coarsely broken
1/2 cup packed brown sugar
2 tablespoons brandy or rum (optional)
1 tablespoon fresh lemon juice
Pastry for Double-Crust Pie (page 138)
1 tablespoon butter or margarine, cut up
Hard Sauce (page 350) or sliced Cheddar cheese

1. Preheat oven to 425°F. In medium bowl, stir mincemeat, apple, walnuts, brown sugar, brandy, if desired, and lemon juice until well mixed.

2. Spoon filling into prepared piecrust; dot with butter. Place top crust over filling, cut 1-inch slits to allow steam to escape during baking, and make decorative edge of your choice (see page 141).

3. Place pie on nonstick or foil-lined cookie sheet. Bake 30 to 40 minutes, until golden. Cool on wire rack 1 hour to serve warm, or cool completely to serve later. Top with hard sauce or Cheddar.

Each serving with hard sauce: about 645 calories, 6g protein, 89g carbohydrate, 30g total fat (11g saturated), 2g fiber, 41mg cholesterol, 490mg sodium

Strawberry-Rhubarb Pie

Because rhubarb (a vegetable masquerading as fruit) is very tart, it's often combined with strawberries, which serve as a sweet complement. It's a match made in heaven. For photo, see page 139.

Active time: 30 minutes
Bake time: 1 hour 35 minutes
Makes: 10 servings

¼ cup cornstarch
1 cup plus 1 tablespoon sugar
1 pint strawberries, hulled, each cut in half if large
1¼ pounds rhubarb, trimmed and cut into ½-inch pieces
    (4 cups)
Pastry for Double-Crust Pie (page 138)
2 tablespoons butter or margarine, cut up

1. Preheat oven to 425°F. In large bowl, mix cornstarch and 1 cup sugar. Add strawberries and rhubarb; toss.

2. Spoon filling into piecrust; dot with butter. Before placing top crust over filling, cut center circle 1 inch in diameter, then set crust on pie. Cut 1-inch slits to allow steam to escape during baking and make decorative edge of your choice (see page 141). Sprinkle with remaining 1 tablespoon sugar.

3. Place pie on nonstick or foil-lined cookie sheet to catch any overflow during baking. Bake 20 minutes. Reduce oven temperature to 375°F; bake 1 hour 15 minutes to 1 hour 25 minutes longer, until filling bubbles in center. Cool on wire rack 1 hour to serve warm, or cool completely to serve later.

Each serving: about 375 calories, 4g protein, 53g carbohydrate, 17g total fat (8g saturated), 2g fiber, 31mg cholesterol, 235mg sodium

---

HEALTHY MAKEOVER

Strawberry-Rhubarb Pie

This is just as tasty as Grandma's—but with one-fifth the calories. Got a spoon? Dig in!

Active time: 15 minutes
Bake time: 45 minutes
Makes: 8 servings

1 small orange
1 pound strawberries, hulled and each cut in half
10 ounces rhubarb, trimmed and sliced
¼ cup granulated sugar
1 tablespoon cornstarch
⅓ cup old-fashioned oats, uncooked
⅓ cup packed dark brown sugar
¼ cup whole-wheat flour
Pinch salt
3 tablespoons butter or margarine, slightly softened

1. Preheat oven to 375°F. From orange, grate peel and divide between two large bowls; squeeze ¼ cup orange juice into small measuring cup.

2. In one large bowl with peel, combine strawberries, rhubarb, and granulated sugar until well mixed. Stir cornstarch into orange juice, then add to fruit mixture. Pour into 9-inch glass or ceramic pie plate and spread filling in layer.

3. In other large bowl with peel, combine oats, brown sugar, flour, and salt. With pastry blender or with fingertips, blend in butter until mixture forms coarse crumbs.

4. Sprinkle oat mixture evenly over strawberry mixture. Bake 45 minutes or until topping is golden brown and fruit is bubbling. Cool pie on wire rack at least 1 hour.

Each serving: about 155 calories, 2g protein, 27g carbohydrate, 5g total fat (3g saturated), 2g fiber, 12mg cholesterol, 70mg sodium

Buttery Blueberry Pie

Warm, bubbling blueberry filling encased in a flaky, buttery piecrust is one summer dessert that's guaranteed to please a crowd.

Active time: 25 minutes plus chilling
Bake time: 1 hour 30 minutes
Makes: 8 servings

2¼ cups all-purpose flour
¼ teaspoon plus pinch salt
13 tablespoons cold butter, cut up (do not use margarine)
6 tablespoons ice water
5 cups blueberries
⅔ cup sugar
3 tablespoons cornstarch
1 tablespoon fresh lemon juice
1 large egg
1 tablespoon heavy cream or milk

1. In food processor, blend flour and ¼ teaspoon salt. Add 12 tablespoons butter and pulse until mixture resembles coarse crumbs. Sprinkle in ice water, 1 tablespoon at a time, pulsing after each, until large clumps begin to form.

2. Shape dough into 2 disks, one slightly larger than other; wrap and refrigerate 30 minutes or overnight.

3. Preheat oven to 400°F. On lightly floured surface, with floured rolling pin, roll larger disk of dough into 12-inch round. Ease dough round into 9-inch pie plate. Gently press against bottom and up side of plate without stretching. Trim dough edge, leaving 1-inch overhang. Fold overhang under.

4. Line pie shell with foil; fill with pie weights, dried beans, or rice. Bake 20 minutes. Remove foil with weights; bake 10 minutes, until golden.

5. Meanwhile, in large bowl, gently toss blueberries, sugar, cornstarch, lemon juice, and pinch salt until well combined. In small bowl, whisk egg and cream.

6. On lightly floured surface, with floured rolling pin, roll remaining disk of dough into 11-inch round.

7. Place warm pie shell on foil-lined jelly-roll pan. Spread blueberry filling evenly in crust; dot with remaining tablespoon butter. Brush egg mixture onto rim of crust. Carefully drape top crust over lightly floured rolling pin and unroll onto top of pie, centering round on filling. Gently press dough to form decorative rim of your choice (see page 141). Brush top crust with egg mixture; cut slits in center to allow steam to escape during baking.

8. Reduce oven temperature to 375°F. Bake 1 hour or until top crust is golden and blueberry mixture bubbles. Cool completely on wire rack.

Each serving: about 440 calories, 5g protein, 60g carbohydrate, 21g total fat (13g saturated), 3g fiber, 75mg cholesterol, 265mg sodium

CHEESE, CUSTARD & CREAM PIES

Call these the crème de la crème of pies—all feature creamy, velvety, silky, or deliciously dense fillings.

Fresh Strawberry Cream Cheese Tart

Strawberries and cream cheese are a match made in heaven, but this easy tart is so versatile it also tastes good topped with raspberries, blueberries, or even grapes. Reduced-fat cream cheese and sour cream keep it light.

Active time: 25 minutes plus chilling and cooling
Bake time: 20 minutes
Makes: 8 servings

1¹/2 cups all-purpose flour
¹/4 teaspoon salt
¹/3 cup plus 3 tablespoons confectioners' sugar
10 tablespoons butter or margarine, chilled and cut into
    ¹/2-inch pieces
1 teaspoon vanilla extract
3 tablespoons ice water
6 ounces reduced-fat cream cheese (Neufchâtel), softened
¹/2 cup reduced-fat sour cream
3 tablespoons chopped crystallized ginger
1¹/2 pounds strawberries, stems and leaves discarded,
    each berry cut lengthwise in half

1. In food processor with knife blade attached, combine flour, salt, and ¹/3 cup sugar; pulse until blended. Add butter and pulse until mixture resembles coarse meal. Add vanilla, then ice water, 1 tablespoon at a time, pulsing until moist clumps form. Gather dough into ball; flatten into disk. Wrap disk in plastic and refrigerate until firm enough to roll, at least 1 hour, or overnight. (If chilled overnight, let dough stand 30 minutes at room temperature before rolling.)

2. Preheat oven to 375°F. On large sheet of parchment paper, with floured rolling pin, roll dough into 12-inch round. Using 11-inch dinner plate as guide, cut 11-inch round from dough; discard trimmings.

3. Transfer round, still on parchment, to large cookie sheet. Press one index finger against outside edge of dough round; with index finger and thumb of other hand, push dough around fingertip toward center to form flute. Repeat around edge to make decorative border. Refrigerate or freeze, on cookie sheet, about 10 minutes to firm dough slightly.

4. Bake 20 to 25 minutes or until golden brown. Cool crust completely on cookie sheet on wire rack, about 20 minutes.

5. When crust is cool, in medium bowl, with spoon, mix cream cheese, sour cream, ginger, and remaining 3 tablespoons sugar until blended. Spread cream cheese mixture evenly on crust. Arrange strawberries, wide ends down, in concentric circles in cream cheese mixture to cover.

Each serving: about 315 calories, 5g protein, 30g carbohydrate, 20g total fat (12g saturated), 2g fiber, 57mg cholesterol, 285mg sodium

Key Lime Pie

The original Key lime pie, which dates back to the 1850s, is filled with a tart citrus custard made with a then-new miracle ingredient: sweetened condensed milk. Canned milk is no novelty to us today, but this recipe lingers deliciously on. If you can't get Key limes—grown in the Florida Keys and not widely available—regular limes will do.

Active time: 20 minutes plus cooling and chilling
Bake time: 15 minutes
Makes: 10 servings

6 to 8 Key limes or 3 to 4 regular limes (see Tip)
1 can (14 ounces) sweetened condensed milk
2 large eggs, separated
Green food coloring (optional)
Baked Graham-Cracker Crumb Crust (page 143)
1/2 cup heavy cream

1. Preheat oven to 375°F. Cut 1 lime in half and cut 1 half into very thin slices; set aside. From remaining limes, grate 2 teaspoons peel and squeeze ½ cup juice. In medium bowl, with wire whisk or fork, combine sweetened condensed milk with lime peel, lime juice, and egg yolks until mixture thickens. Add a few drops green food coloring, if you like.

2. In small bowl, with mixer on high speed, beat egg whites until stiff peaks form when beaters are lifted. With rubber spatula or wire whisk, gently fold egg whites into lime mixture.

3. Pour filling into cooled piecrust; smooth top. Bake 15 to 20 minutes, just until filling is firm. Cool on wire rack, then refrigerate 3 hours, or until well chilled.

4. In small bowl, with mixer on medium speed, beat cream until stiff peaks form. Pipe or spoon whipped cream around edge of filling. Decorate pie with reserved lime slices.

Each serving: about 300 calories, 6g protein, 36g carbohydrate, 15g total fat (8g saturated), 1g fiber, 85 mg cholesterol, 210 mg sodium

TIP For the juiciest limes (and other citrus), look for heavy fruits with fine-grained skins. Warming the lime briefly (under hot tap water or—extremely briefly—in the microwave) will help to maximize the amount of juice you can extract. When grating peel, remove only the colored portion, not the spongy white pith that's under it.

CITRUS EQUIVALENTS

From lemons to tangerines, here's how to calculate approximately how much juice and citrus peel you can expect to get.

1 lemon .... 2 tablespoons juice
2 teaspoons peel

1 lime............................. 1½ tablespoons juice
1 teaspoon peel

1 orange .... ⅓ to ½ cup juice
1 tablespoon peel

1 tangerine .... 2 tablespoons juice
1 teaspoon peel

Note: measurements are an approximation.

Lemon Meringue Pie

Good news for pie lovers: Our luscious recipe for this all-American classic is a cinch to make. Just be sure to spread the meringue all the way out to the edge of the crust—otherwise, it will shrink as it bakes.

Active time: 45 minutes plus cooling and chilling
Bake time: 30 minutes
Makes: 10 servings

Pastry for Single-Crust Pie (page 140)
4 to 5 lemons
1/3 cup cornstarch
1/4 teaspoon plus pinch salt
1 1/2 cups sugar
1 1/2 cups water
3 large eggs, separated
2 tablespoons butter or margarine
1 large egg white
1/4 teaspoon cream of tartar

1. Preheat oven to 425°F. Line pie shell with foil; fill with pie weights, dry beans, or uncooked rice. Bake 10 minutes. Remove foil and weights; bake 10 minutes longer, or until golden. If crust puffs up during baking, press it to pie plate with back of spoon. Cool on wire rack. Reduce oven temperature to 400°F.

2. Meanwhile, from lemons, grate 1 tablespoon peel and squeeze 3/4 cup juice. In 2-quart saucepan, mix cornstarch, 1/4 teaspoon salt, and 1 cup sugar; stir in water. Cook over medium heat, stirring constantly, until mixture thickens and boils. Boil 1 minute, stirring constantly. Remove saucepan from heat.

3. In small bowl, whisk egg yolks. Stir in small amount of hot cornstarch mixture until blended; slowly pour egg-yolk mixture back into hot cornstarch mixture in saucepan, stirring rapidly to prevent curdling. Place saucepan over low heat and cook, stirring constantly, about 4 minutes, until filling is very thick. Remove saucepan from heat; stir in butter until melted. Gradually stir in lemon juice and peel. Pour into cooled piecrust.

4. In small bowl, with mixer on high speed, beat all egg whites, cream of tartar, and pinch of salt until soft peaks form when beaters are lifted. Gradually sprinkle in remaining 1/2 cup sugar, 2 tablespoons at a time, beating until sugar has completely dissolved and egg whites stand in stiff, glossy peaks when beaters are lifted.

5. Spread meringue over filling to edge of crust. Swirl meringue with back of spoon to make attractive top. Bake 10 minutes, or until meringue is golden. Cool pie on wire rack away from drafts. Refrigerate at least 3 hours before serving.

Each serving: about 310 calories, 4g protein, 49g carbohydrate, 11g total fat (5g saturated), 1g fiber, 82mg cholesterol, 225mg sodium

LIME MERINGUE PIE Prepare crust and filling as instructed, but substitute *2 teaspoons freshly grated lime peel* for lemon peel and *1/2 cup fresh lime juice* for lemon juice. Bake and cool as directed.

Each serving: about 305 calories, 4g protein, 48g carbohydrate, 11g total fat (5g saturated), 1g fiber, 82mg cholesterol, 225mg sodium

Banana Cream Pie

Silky vanilla custard, sliced ripe bananas, and a crumb crust made from vanilla wafers form the layers of this heavenly pie. If you're searching for a coconut cream pie recipe, look below—we've given it as a variation.

Active time: 30 minutes plus chilling
Makes: 10 servings

3/4 cup sugar
1/3 cup cornstarch
1/4 teaspoon salt
3 3/4 cups milk
5 large egg yolks
1 3/4 teaspoons vanilla extract
2 tablespoons butter or margarine
Baked Vanilla-Wafer Crumb Crust (page 143)
3 ripe medium bananas
3/4 cup heavy cream

1. In 3-quart saucepan, stir together sugar, cornstarch, and salt; stir in milk until smooth. Cook, stirring constantly, over medium heat, until mixture has thickened and boils; boil 1 minute. In small bowl, beat egg yolks lightly; beat in small amount of hot milk mixture. Slowly pour yolk mixture back into milk mixture, stirring rapidly to prevent lumping. Cook over low heat, stirring constantly, 2 minutes, or until very thick.

2. Remove saucepan from heat and stir in 1½ teaspoons vanilla and butter. Pour half of filling into cooled piecrust. Slice 2 bananas and arrange slices on top of filling; spoon remaining filling over bananas. Place plastic wrap directly on surface of filling. Refrigerate pie at least 4 hours, or overnight.

3. In small chilled bowl, with mixer on medium speed, beat cream and remaining ¼ teaspoon vanilla until stiff peaks form; spread over filling. Slice remaining banana; arrange around edge of pie.

Each serving: about 385 calories, 6g protein, 45g carbohydrate, 21g total fat (12g saturated), 1g fiber, 162mg cholesterol, 275mg sodium

COCONUT CREAM PIE Prepare crust and filling as instructed, but omit bananas. In step 2, fold ¾ cup sweetened flaked coconut into custard before filling piecrust. Refrigerate and top with whipped cream as directed. Sprinkle with ¼ cup sweetened flaked coconut, toasted (see Tip, page xxii).

Each serving: about 390 calories, 6g protein 40g carbohydrate, 23g total fat (14g saturated), 1g fiber, 162mg cholesterol, 295mg sodium

Cream Cheese Fruit Tartlets

These tiny tarts, which look like they came from a French pastry shop, will evoke "oohs" and "aahs" when you bring them to the table.

Active time: 45 minutes plus chilling and cooling
Bake time: 15 minutes
Makes: 24 tartlets

Pastry for 9-Inch Tart (page 140), formed into disk and chilled but not rolled
1 package (8 ounces) cream cheese, softened
3 tablespoons sugar
1 tablespoon milk
¾ teaspoon vanilla extract
2 cups fruit, such as sliced kiwifruit, halved strawberries, and canned mandarin-orange sections
Mint leaves for garnish

1. Preheat oven to 425°F. Divide dough in half. Roll each half into 12-inch rope; cut each rope into twelve 1-inch pieces. Press each piece of dough evenly into bottom and up side of 24 mini muffin cups. Prick each shell several times with toothpick. Bake 15 minutes, or until golden. Cool in pans on wire rack 5 minutes. Remove shells from pans; cool completely on wire rack.

2. Meanwhile, in small bowl, with fork, beat cream cheese, sugar, milk, and vanilla until blended. Refrigerate until ready to serve.

3. Fill each tartlet shell with about 2 teaspoons cream cheese mixture; top with fruit; garnish with mint leaves.

Each tartlet: about 100 calories, 1g protein, 8g carbohydrate, 7g total fat (4g saturated), 1g fiber, 18mg cholesterol, 80mg sodium

Lemon Tart

Lemon Tart

Note that this lovely lemony tart requires a very high rim; the crust should extend above the edge of the pan. To create a raspberry-lemon tart, scatter a pint of fresh raspberries over the top after cooling.

Active time: 20 minutes plus chilling and cooling
Bake time: 52 minutes
Makes: 8 servings

Pastry for 9-Inch Tart (page 140)
4 to 6 lemons
4 large eggs
1 cup granulated sugar
1/3 cup heavy cream
Confectioners' sugar for sprinkling

1. Press dough lining tart pan up sides to form rim 1/4 inch taller than edge of pan. Freeze 15 minutes to discourage puffing during baking.

2. Preheat oven to 425°F. Line tart shell with foil; fill with pie weights, dry beans, or uncooked rice. Bake 15 minutes. Remove foil and weights; bake 7 to 12 minutes longer, until golden. If crust puffs up during baking, gently press it to tart pan with back of spoon. Cool on wire rack. Reduce oven temperature to 350°F.

3. From lemons, grate 1½ teaspoons peel and squeeze 2/3 cup juice. In medium bowl, with wire whisk or fork, beat eggs, granulated sugar, and lemon peel and juice until well combined. Whisk in cream.

4. Carefully pour lemon mixture into cooled tart shell. Place on cookie sheet and bake 30 minutes, or until custard is barely set. Cool completely on wire rack. Just before serving, remove side of pan; sprinkle with confectioners' sugar.

Each serving: about 325 calories, 5g protein, 40g carbohydrate, 17g total fat (9g saturated), 1g fiber, 143mg cholesterol, 195mg sodium

Italian-Style Fresh Berry Tart

You can take this festive dessert a step at a time: Bake the crust in advance, and prepare the filling through the end of step 2. Prepare the whipped cream up to 2 hours before serving time.

Active time: 40 minutes plus chilling
Makes: 12 servings

3 large egg yolks
1/3 cup granulated sugar
2 tablespoons cornstarch
1 cup milk
2 tablespoons butter or margarine
1 teaspoon vanilla extract
1/2 cup heavy cream
Baked Sweet Pastry Crust for 11-Inch Tart (page 142)
2 cups blueberries
2 cups raspberries
2 cups blackberries
Confectioners' sugar for sprinkling

1. In small bowl, with wire whisk, mix egg yolks and granulated sugar until blended. Stir in cornstarch until smooth. In 2-quart saucepan, heat milk to simmering over medium heat. While constantly beating with wire whisk, gradually pour about half of simmering milk into egg-yolk mixture. Return mixture to saucepan and cook, whisking constantly, until pastry cream has thickened and boils; reduce heat and cook, stirring, 1 minute. Remove saucepan from heat: stir in butter and vanilla.

2. Transfer pastry cream to medium bowl; cover surface directly with plastic wrap to prevent skin from forming and refrigerate until cold, at least 2 hours.

3. Meanwhile, in small bowl, with mixer on medium speed, beat cream just until stiff peaks form. Whisk pastry cream until smooth; fold in whipped cream.

4. Spoon cream filling into baked tart shell and spread evenly; top with berries and sprinkle with confectioners' sugar. Remove side of pan to serve.

Each serving: about 285 calories, 4g protein, 29g carbohydrate, 18g total fat (10g saturated), 3g fiber, 95mg cholesterol, 210 mg sodium

Ganache Tart with Salted-Almond Crust

Silky smooth and sprinkled with sea salt, this truffle-like tart gets its richness from deep dark chocolate and heavy cream. Poured warm into a crisp, buttery almond crust, it firms up fast in the fridge.

Active time: 45 minutes plus chilling
Bake time: 25 minutes
Makes: 12 servings

1/2 cup roasted salted almonds
3/4 cup butter (1 1/2 sticks), cut into 12 pieces
    and softened (do not use margarine)
1/2 cup confectioners' sugar
1/4 teaspoon salt
1 large egg yolk
1/2 teaspoon vanilla extract
1 1/4 cups all-purpose flour
1 cup heavy cream
1 pound highest-quality bittersweet chocolate
    (60% to 70% cacao), very finely chopped
Flaky sea salt for sprinkling (optional)

1. Preheat oven to 350°F.

2. In food processor, pulse almonds until finely ground. Transfer to bowl. In same processor (no need to clean), pulse 6 tablespoons butter until creamy. With rubber spatula, scrape bottom and side of processor bowl, then add confectioners' sugar and salt and pulse until smooth. Scraping down bottom and sides of bowl after each addition, add egg yolk and vanilla together and pulse until smooth. Add flour and ground almonds together and pulse until mixture forms fine crumbs. Pour into 11-inch tart pan with removable bottom.

3. With fingers, firmly press crumb mixture into bottom and up side of pan to form even crust. Freeze 10 minutes or until firm.

4. Bake crust 25 minutes or until golden brown. Cool completely on wire rack.

Top: Ganache Tart with Salted-Almond Crust; Bottom: Quick Chocolate Macaroon Tart

5. In 3-quart saucepan, heat cream to bubbling over medium. Remove from heat. Add chocolate and let stand 1 minute. With rubber spatula, stir gently until smooth. Add remaining 6 tablespoons butter, 1 tablespoon at a time, gently stirring until blended after each. Pour mixture into cooled crust. Gently shake tart pan to create smooth, even top.

6. Refrigerate 30 minutes to set, then let stand at room temperature until ready to serve, up to 6 hours. Garnish with sea salt if desired.

Each serving: about 485 calories, 6g protein, 29g carbohydrate, 39g total fat (22g saturated), 3g fiber, 72mg cholesterol, 95mg sodium

Quick Chocolate Macaroon Tart

You need only a few ingredients to make this simple, decadent tart. It's the perfect make-ahead dessert for Passover or Easter.

Active time: 10 minutes plus chilling
Makes: 12 servings

10 ounces coconut macaroon cookies
1 pound semisweet or bittersweet chocolate, finely chopped
1 cup heavy cream
Fresh raspberries and slivered orange peel for garnish

1. Grease a 9-inch tart pan with removable bottom. Press cookies into prepared pan to evenly coat bottom and sides. With fingers, push cookies into fluted edges of pan to create decorative edge.

2. Place chocolate in heatproof bowl. In small saucepan over medium heat, heat cream, stirring frequently, just until boiling. Immediately remove cream from heat and pour over chocolate, stirring until smooth.

3. Pour chocolate mixture into crust and refrigerate for 6 hours or until well chilled. To serve, top with raspberries and slivered orange peel.

Each serving: about 365 calories, 4g protein, 35g carbohydrate, 26g total fat (17g saturated), 4g fiber, 27mg cholesterol, 55mg sodium

Caramel Walnut Tart

The layer of filling in this tart is not very deep, but it is devilishly rich. Follow the instructions for caramelizing the sugar with care.

Active time: 45 minutes plus cooling
Bake time: 53 minutes
Makes: 16 servings

Sweet Pastry Crust for 9-Inch Tart (page 142) or Pastry for 9-Inch Tart (page 140)
1 cup sugar
1/4 teaspoon fresh lemon juice
3/4 cup heavy cream
1 tablespoon butter or margarine
1 large egg
1/2 teaspoon vanilla extract
1 cup walnuts (4 ounces), toasted (see page xxiii)

1. Preheat oven to 375°F. Line tart shell with foil; fill with pie weights, dry beans, or uncooked rice. Bake 15 minutes. Remove foil and weights; bake 8 to 10 minutes longer, until golden brown. Set pan on wire rack to cool. Reduce oven temperature to 350°F.

2. In 2-quart heavy saucepan, stir sugar and lemon juice together to the consistency of wet sand. Cook over low heat, stirring gently, until sugar melts. Increase heat to medium and cook until amber in color. With pastry brush dipped in water, occasionally wash down side of pan to prevent sugar from crystallizing. Remove saucepan from heat. Add cream to pan carefully and gradually, stirring (mixture will bubble and lump up vigorously). Add butter, return pan to heat, and stir until caramel dissolves. Set saucepan aside to cool.

3. In large bowl, whisk egg and vanilla until smooth. Add cooled caramel mixture and whisk until blended.

4. Sprinkle walnuts over cooled shell. Pour caramel mixture on top. Bake 30 to 35 minutes, until bubbly at edges and set but still slightly jiggly in center. Cool on wire rack 10 minutes. Carefully remove side of pan; cool completely.

Each serving: about 245 calories, 3g protein, 24g carbohydrate, 16g total fat (7g saturated), 1g fiber, 59 mg cholesterol, 95mg sodium

Black-Bottom Chocolate Cream Pie

Black-Bottom Chocolate Cream Pie

This pie is seriously decadent—a luscious chocolate custard fills a crust made of crushed chocolate cookies.

Active time: 45 minutes plus chilling
Makes: 12 servings

1/3 cup cornstarch
1/4 teaspoon salt
1 cup plus 2 tablespoons sugar
3 1/2 cups milk
4 large egg yolks
3 ounces unsweetened chocolate,
   finely chopped
2 tablespoons butter or margarine
1 tablespoon dark rum (optional)
Baked Chocolate-Wafer Crumb Crust (page 143)
1 cup heavy cream
Semisweet chocolate curls for garnish (page 352)

1. In heavy 3-quart saucepan, whisk cornstarch, salt, and 1 cup sugar. While whisking, gradually add milk. Cook over medium-high 7 to 8 minutes or until boiling and thickened, whisking constantly. Remove from heat.

2. In large bowl, whisk egg yolks until blended. Whisk in hot milk mixture in steady stream. Return mixture to saucepan and cook over medium 4 to 6 minutes or until mixture boils and thickens, stirring constantly. Remove from heat and add chocolate. Stir until melted, then stir in butter until melted. Stir in rum, if using.

3. Pour mixture into cooled pie crust and spread evenly. Press sheet of plastic wrap directly against surface. Refrigerate at least 4 hours or up to overnight, or until cold and stiff.

4. When ready to serve, beat cream until thickened. While beating, gradually add remaining 2 tablespoons sugar. Beat until soft peaks form. Dollop over pie. Garnish with chocolate curls.

Each serving: about 365 calories, 5g protein, 39g carbohydrate, 22g total fat (13g saturated), 2g fiber, 113mg cholesterol, 185mg sodium

Chocolate Pudding Pie with Coconut Crust

You could cheat by using a packaged pudding mix, but the flavor wouldn't compare to that of the rich and creamy filling we've devised for this pie.

Active time: 20 minutes plus chilling
Bake time: 20 minutes
Makes: 10 servings

3/4 cup sugar
1/3 cup cornstarch
1/2 teaspoon salt
3 3/4 cups milk
5 large egg yolks
3 ounces unsweetened chocolate, melted
2 teaspoons vanilla extract
2 tablespoons butter or margarine
Coconut Pastry Crust (page 143)
1 cup heavy cream
1/4 cup flaked sweetened coconut, toasted
   (see page xxii)

1. In 3-quart saucepan, stir together sugar, cornstarch, and salt; stir in milk until smooth. Cook, stirring constantly over medium heat, until mixture is thickened and boils; boil 1 minute. In small bowl, with wire whisk or fork, beat egg yolks lightly. Beat small amount of hot milk mixture into yolk mixture. Slowly pour yolk mixture back into pan, stirring rapidly to prevent lumping. Cook over low heat 2 minutes, stirring constantly, until very thick, or until instant-read thermometer placed in custard registers 160°F.

2. Remove saucepan from heat and stir in melted chocolate, vanilla, and butter; blend well. Pour filling into cooled piecrust. Place plastic wrap directly on surface of filling. Refrigerate 4 hours, or until filling is set.

3. In chilled bowl, with mixer on medium speed, whip cream until stiff peaks form. Pipe or spoon whipped cream over filling. Sprinkle toasted coconut on top.

Each serving: about 455 calories, 7g protein, 41g carbohydrate, 31g total fat (18g saturated), 2g fiber, 177mg cholesterol, 285mg sodium

Pumpkin Pie with Pecan Brittle

For an anything but ordinary Thanksgiving dessert, crown luxurious slices of custardy deep-dish pumpkin pie with whipped cream and a pecan brittle garnish.

Active time: 25 minutes plus chilling and cooling
Bake time: 1 hour 10 minutes
Makes: 10 servings

PUMPKIN PIE
Pastry for Deep-Dish Pie Shell (page 140)
3/4 cup sugar
3 large eggs
1 can (15 ounces) solid-pack pumpkin
1 cup half-and-half or light cream
1 1/2 teaspoons pumpkin pie spice
1/2 teaspoon salt

GARNISHES
1/2 cup plus 1 tablespoon sugar
2 tablespoons water
2 tablespoons chopped pecans
1/2 cup heavy cream

1. Preheat oven to 425°F. Line prepared pie shell with foil and fill with pie weights, dry beans, or rice. Bake 10 to 12 minutes or until beginning to set. Remove foil with weights and bake 13 to 15 minutes longer or until golden. Cool on wire rack. Reduce oven temperature to 350°F.

2. In large bowl, with wire whisk, mix sugar and eggs until blended. Mix in pumpkin, half-and-half, pumpkin pie spice, and salt until smooth.

3. Pour filling into pie shell. Bake 48 to 50 minutes or until edge is set but center still jiggles slightly. Cool pie completely on wire rack, about 4 hours to serve at room temperature. Or cool slightly, about 1 hour, then cover and refrigerate to serve cold later.

4. Make pecan brittle: Line large cookie sheet with foil. In heavy 2-quart saucepan, heat 1/2 cup sugar and water over medium until boiling. Cook about 5 minutes or until mixture turns golden. With heat-safe spatula, stir in pecans and cook 30 seconds. Working quickly and carefully, pour hot caramel onto prepared cookie sheet and carefully lift and tilt cookie sheet slightly (holding foil in place) to spread caramel into thin, even layer. Let brittle cool completely, about 30 minutes. When cool, peel foil away, and break into 10 pieces to garnish pie.

5. When ready to serve, in medium bowl, with mixer on medium speed, beat cream with remaining 1 tablespoon sugar until soft peaks form. Serve each slice of pie with dollop of sweetened whipped cream, and garnish with pecan brittle.

Each serving: about 385 calories, 6g protein, 45g carbohydrate, 21g total fat (10g saturated), 3g fiber, 97mg cholesterol, 274mg sodium

Grandma's Sweet-Potato Pie

Spiced mashed sweet potato tastes very much like pumpkin, and this pie makes a nice change on the holiday menu.

Active time: 1 hour plus cooling
Bake time: 1 hour
Makes: 10 servings

2 sweet potatoes (1 pound), unpeeled, or 2 cans
　(16 to 17 ounces each) sweet potatoes, drained
1 1/2 cups half-and-half or light cream
3/4 cup packed dark brown sugar
1 teaspoon ground cinnamon
3/4 teaspoon ground ginger
1/4 teaspoon ground nutmeg
1/2 teaspoon salt
3 large eggs
Pastry for Single-Crust Pie (page 140)

1. If using fresh sweet potatoes, in 3-quart saucepan, heat sweet potatoes and enough *water* to cover to boiling over high heat. Reduce heat; cover and simmer 30 minutes, or until fork-tender. Drain. Cool potatoes until easy to handle; peel and cut into chunks.

2. In large bowl, with mixer on low speed, beat fresh or canned sweet potatoes until smooth. Add half-and-half, brown sugar, cinnamon, ginger, nutmeg, salt, and eggs; beat until well blended.

3. Preheat oven to 425°F. Line pie shell with foil; fill with pie weights, dry beans, or uncooked rice. Bake 10 minutes. Remove foil and weights; bake 10 minutes longer, or until golden. If crust puffs up during baking, gently press it to pan with back of spoon. Cool on wire rack. Reduce oven temperature to 350°F.

4. Spoon sweet-potato mixture into cooled piecrust. Bake 40 minutes, or until knife inserted 1 inch from edge comes out clean. Cool on wire rack 1 hour to serve warm, or cool slightly, then refrigerate to serve chilled.

Each serving: about 295 calories, 5g protein, 39g carbohydrate, 13g total fat (7g saturated), 1g fiber, 89mg cholesterol, 265mg sodium

Squash Pie

Butternut squash is close kin to pumpkin, so it's no wonder that it makes a delicious pie.

Active time: 55 minutes plus cooling
Bake time: 1 hour 55 minutes
Makes: 10 servings

1 small butternut squash (2 pounds), peeled and cut into
　2-inch chunks
1/4 cup water
Pastry for 11-Inch Tart (page 140), formed into disk and
　chilled but not rolled
3 large eggs, lightly beaten
3/4 cup packed light brown sugar
6 tablespoons butter or margarine, melted and cooled
1 cup heavy cream
1 teaspoon vanilla extract
1 teaspoon ground cinnamon
3/4 teaspoon ground ginger
1/4 teaspoon ground allspice
1 teaspoon freshly grated orange peel

1. Preheat oven to 425°F. Place squash and water in 13" by 9" glass baking dish; cover with foil. Bake 35 minutes, or until tender. Transfer squash to food processor with knife blade attached. Process squash until smooth (you should have 2 cups puree).

2. Roll dough into 14-inch round and line deep-dish 9-inch pie plate; make decorative edge of your choice (see page 141). Line pie shell with foil; fill with pie weights, dry beans, or uncooked rice. Bake 15 minutes. Remove foil and weights; bake 10 minutes longer, or until golden. Reduce oven temperature to 350°F.

3. In large bowl, combine beaten eggs, brown sugar, and melted butter. Add cream, vanilla, cinnamon, ginger, allspice, orange peel, and squash and whisk until well combined and smooth.

4. Pour filling into cooled piecrust. Bake 55 minutes, or until toothpick inserted 1 inch from edge comes out clean. Cool on wire rack at least 1 hour.

Each serving: about 435 calories, 5g protein, 41g carbohydrate, 29g total fat (17g saturated), 2g fiber, 140mg cholesterol, 320mg sodium

Orange Custard Tart

Fill a vanilla-scented crust with a creamy citrus custard, and you have a beautiful tart that will brighten any holiday party.

Active time: 30 minutes plus chilling and cooling
Bake time: 30 minutes
Makes: 8 servings

VANILLA TART CRUST

1¼ cups all-purpose flour

2 tablespoons sugar

¼ teaspoon salt

½ cup butter (1 stick), chilled and cut up (do not use margarine)

1 large egg yolk

¼ teaspoon vanilla extract

2 to 4 tablespoons ice water

ORANGE CUSTARD FILLING

¾ cup plus 6 tablespoons whole milk

2 large egg yolks

⅓ cup sugar

2 tablespoons cornstarch

2 tablespoons all-purpose flour

1 tablespoon butter (do not use margarine)

⅛ teaspoon salt

1 vanilla bean or ¼ teaspoon vanilla extract

1¼ pounds navel oranges (about 3)

2 tablespoons apple jelly

2 teaspoons triple sec

Red currants for garnish

1. Make crust: In food processor with knife blade attached, pulse flour, sugar, and salt until blended. Add butter. Pulse until mixture resembles coarse meal. Add egg yolk and vanilla; pulse until combined. Add ice water, 1 tablespoon at a time, pulsing, just until mixture holds together when pinched. Gather dough into ball; flatten into disk, wrap disk in plastic, and refrigerate until firm, at least 1 hour or up to 2 days.

2. Preheat oven to 400°F. On lightly floured surface, with floured rolling pin, roll disk into 12-inch round. Gently drape dough over rolling pin to transfer to 9-inch tart pan with removable bottom. Gently press dough onto bottom and side of pan. Run rolling pin along top of tart pan to trim away excess dough. Freeze 30 minutes or until very firm.

3. With fork, pierce dough all over. Line tart shell with foil and fill with pie weights or dry beans. Bake 15 minutes. Reduce oven temperature to 350°F. Remove foil and weights. Bake crust another 15 to 20 minutes or until golden. Cover rim with foil if browning too quickly. Cool in pan on wire rack.

4. While crust cools, make filling: In 2-quart saucepan, heat ¾ cup milk to simmering over medium. In heat-proof medium bowl, whisk together egg yolks, remaining 6 tablespoons milk, and sugar until blended; whisk in cornstarch and flour until smooth. Slowly whisk hot milk into egg mixture. Return to same pan.

5. Cook mixture over medium heat 4 minutes or until very thick, whisking constantly. Remove from heat. Whisk in butter and salt until smooth. With knife, cut vanilla bean lengthwise in half; scrape out seeds and whisk into milk mixture (or whisk in vanilla extract). Transfer mixture to small bowl. Place plastic wrap directly on surface to prevent skin from forming. Refrigerate until cool, about 45 minutes. (Can be kept chilled up to 1 day; remove from refrigerator 30 minutes before using.)

6. With sharp paring knife, cut peel and white pith from oranges. Thinly slice crosswise. Spread pastry cream evenly in cooled tart shell. Arrange orange slices in one layer on pastry cream, overlapping slightly. Can be refrigerated, covered, up to 2 hours.

7. To serve, in 1-quart saucepan, combine jelly and triple sec. Heat over medium until melted, whisking. Cool slightly and brush fruit with jelly. Garnish with currants.

Each serving: about 330 calories, 5g protein, 42g carbohydrate, 16g total fat (10g saturated), 2g fiber, 107mg cholesterol, 240mg sodium

Custard Pie

Fill a flaky crust with silky custard and top that with a sprinkling of nutmeg—heavenly!

Active time: 20 minutes plus cooling
Bake time: 55 minutes
Makes: 8 servings

Pastry for Single-Crust Pie (page 140)
2 cups milk
4 large eggs
1/2 cup sugar
1/4 teaspoon salt
1 teaspoon vanilla extract
Pinch ground nutmeg

1. Preheat oven to 425°F. Line pie shell with foil; fill with pie weights, dry beans, or uncooked rice. Bake 20 minutes. Remove foil and weights; bake 10 minutes, or until golden. Cool on wire rack. Reduce oven temperature to 350°F.

2. Meanwhile, in 2-quart saucepan, heat milk over medium until bubbles form at edge. In medium bowl, whisk eggs, sugar, salt, and vanilla. Slowly pour hot milk into egg mixture, whisking rapidly.

3. Butter a second 9-inch pie plate; set plate in shallow baking pan on oven rack. Pour egg mixture into prepared pie plate; sprinkle with nutmeg. Pour enough *boiling water* into baking pan to come halfway up side of pie plate. Bake 25 minutes, or until knife inserted 1 inch from edge comes out clean. Transfer plate to wire rack to cool.

4. When custard is cool, loosen from side of pie plate with spatula; shake gently to detach bottom. Hold far edge of plate over far edge of baked piecrust; tilt custard gently; as it slips into crust, pull plate back quickly until custard rests in crust. Let filling settle a few minutes before serving.

Each serving: about 290 calories, 7g protein, 32g carbohydrate, 14g total fat (7g saturated), 1g fiber, 132mg cholesterol, 270mg sodium

Chess Pie

Opinions vary about how chess pies—longtime Southern favorites—got their name. Some suspect that it comes from the cabinet (pie chest) where they were stored; others cite it as the reply to "What kind of pie is this?": "Jes' pie." In seventeenth-century England and colonial America, desserts with this texture were called "cheese pies."

Active time: 25 minutes plus cooling
Bake time: 1 hour 5 minutes
Makes: 12 servings

Pastry for 9-Inch Tart (page 140)
5 tablespoons butter or margarine
3 large eggs
1 1/4 cups sugar
1/2 cup milk
2 tablespoons all-purpose flour
2 tablespoons cornmeal
1 teaspoon vanilla extract
1/4 teaspoon salt
1/8 teaspoon ground nutmeg plus additional for sprinkling

1. Preheat oven to 425°F, prick bottom of tart shell all over with fork to prevent puffing during baking; line tart shell with foil and fill with pie weights, dry beans, or uncooked rice. Bake 15 minutes. Remove foil and weights; bake 5 to 10 minutes longer, until golden. If crust puffs up during baking, gently press it to tart pan with back of spoon. Cool on wire rack. Reduce oven temperature to 375°F.

2. In 2-quart saucepan, melt butter over low heat. With whisk or fork, beat in eggs, sugar, milk, flour, cornmeal, vanilla, salt, and 1/8 teaspoon nutmeg until blended.

3. Pour egg mixture into cooled tart shell; sprinkle with additional nutmeg. Bake 45 minutes, or until knife inserted 1 inch from edge comes out clean. Cool on wire rack. Serve at room temperature, or refrigerate to serve chilled. Remove side of pan to serve.

Each serving: about 255 calories, 3g protein, 32g carbohydrate, 13g total fat (7g saturated), 1g fiber, 83mg cholesterol, 225mg sodium

Aunt Alice's Ricotta Pie

This simple ricotta pie is reminiscent of cannoli filling. Serve dusted with confectioners' sugar or topped with fruit.

Active time: 15 minutes plus chilling and cooling
Bake time: 1 hour
Makes: 10 servings

CRUST

1¼ cups all-purpose flour
⅓ cup sugar
¼ teaspoon salt
6 tablespoons cold butter, cut up (do not use margarine)
1 large egg yolk
2 tablespoons ice water
1 teaspoon vanilla extract

RICOTTA FILLING

4 ounces reduced-fat cream cheese (Neufchâtel)
⅓ cup sugar
⅛ teaspoon ground cinnamon
1 container (15 ounces) part-skim ricotta cheese
3 large egg whites

Confectioners' sugar for sprinkling (optional)
Fresh raspberries for serving (optional)

1. Prepare crust: In food processor, combine flour, sugar, and salt; pulse to blend. Add butter and pulse until mixture resembles coarse crumbs. In cup, with fork, mix egg yolk, water, and vanilla. Drizzle egg mixture over flour mixture; pulse until dough begins to form small clumps that leave side of bowl. Shape into a ball.

2. Spray 9-inch glass pie plate with nonstick cooking spray. Roll dough between two sheets of floured waxed paper into 12-inch round. Remove top sheet of paper and invert round into pie plate. Remove second sheet of waxed paper. Gently press dough against bottom and side of pie plate; trim dough even with rim. Pinch dough to form ¼-inch-high edge. With floured fork, press dough to rim of plate all around. Cover and refrigerate 30 minutes, until firm.

3. Preheat oven to 400°F. Line pie shell with foil, covering edge as well; fill with pie weights, dry beans, or rice. Bake pie shell 20 minutes or until set but not browned. Remove foil with weights. Reduce oven temperature to 350°F. Bake 5 to 8 minutes longer or until lightly browned. Cool on wire rack.

4. Meanwhile, prepare ricotta filling: In same processor, mix cream cheese, sugar, and cinnamon until blended. Add ricotta and egg whites; pulse just until mixed, scraping side of processor once. Pour filling into pie shell. Cover edge of crust with foil.

5. Bake pie 35 to 40 minutes or until set at edge but jiggly in center. Cool on wire rack. Cover and refrigerate 4 hours or overnight. Sprinkle with confectioners' sugar or serve with raspberries if desired.

Each serving: about 270 calories, 9g protein, 27g carbohydrate, 14g total fat (9g saturated), 0g fiber, 63mg cholesterol, 240mg sodium

NUT PIES

Among the richest of all desserts are nut pies, packed with pecans, hazelnuts, pine nuts, almonds, or walnuts. Serve slender slices, accompanied by mugs of hot coffee or tall glasses of ice-cold milk.

Brown Sugar Pecan Pie

Pecans drenched with brown sugar and maple or corn syrup are the sweet and sticky filling for this perfect pecan pie.

Active time: 35 minutes
Bake time: 1 hour
Makes: 12 servings

Pastry for Single-Crust Pie (page 140), trimmings
    reserved for decoration if desired (see Tip)
1 cup packed dark brown sugar
²/₃ cup pure maple syrup or corn syrup
3 large eggs
3 tablespoons butter or margarine, melted
1 tablespoon bourbon or 1 teaspoon vanilla extract
¹/₄ teaspoon salt
2 cups pecan halves (8 ounces), toasted (see page xxiii)

1. Preheat oven to 375°F.

2. Line prepared pie shell with foil or parchment, and fill with pie weights, dried beans, or uncooked rice. Blind-bake 12 to 14 minutes or until beginning to set. Remove foil with weights and bake 13 to 15 minutes longer or until golden.

3. Meanwhile, in large bowl, with wire whisk, mix sugar, syrup, eggs, butter, bourbon, and salt until well blended.

4. Place hot pie shell in jelly-roll pan to catch drips during baking. Spread pecans in even layer in pie shell, then pour sugar mixture over them.

5. Bake 35 minutes or until filling is golden brown, puffed, and set around edge, but center still jiggles slightly. Cool completely on wire rack.

Each serving: about 395 calories, 5g protein, 43g carbohydrate, 24g total fat (7g saturated), 2g fiber, 73mg cholesterol, 180mg sodium

TIP We decorated our pie with cutouts arranged around the edge. To do this, once you've eased the rolled dough round into the pie plate, trim the edge, keeping the overhang intact. Transfer this piece to your work surface and, using a ¾-inch decorative cookie cutter, cut 40 shapes, rerolling if necessary. Refrigerate the shapes along with the pie shell. In step 4, before filling the blind-baked shell, gently brush around the rim with 1 lightly beaten egg white. Gently and carefully press the cut shapes around the rim and proceed as directed.

Warm Banana-Pecan Tart

If you love banana cream pie but would like to serve something a bit more elegant, make this tart. A layer of sliced bananas is topped with pecan pastry cream and a sprinkling of sugar, then broiled until the sugar caramelizes slightly. You can bake the crust and prepare the pecan cream a day ahead of time. Assemble the tart just before serving.

Active time: 45 minutes plus chilling
Bake time: 30 minutes
Makes: 12 servings

1/2 cup pecans (2 ounces), toasted (see page xxiii)
1/2 cup plus 1 tablespoon sugar
3 large egg yolks
1 tablespoon cornstarch
3/4 cup half-and-half or light cream
2 tablespoons butter or margarine
1 teaspoon vanilla extract
Pastry for 11-Inch Tart (see page 140)
2 pounds ripe medium bananas (about 5),
   thinly sliced on diagonal

1. In food processor with knife blade attached, combine pecans with ¼ cup sugar; pulse until nuts are very finely ground.

2. In small bowl, with wire whisk, mix egg yolks, cornstarch, and ¼ cup sugar until blended. In 2-quart saucepan, heat half-and-half to simmering over medium. While constantly beating with wire whisk, gradually pour about half of simmering cream into bowl with egg-yolk mixture. Reduce heat to low. Return egg-yolk mixture to saucepan and cook 4 to 5 minutes, stirring constantly, until thickened (do not boil). Stir in toasted pecan mixture, butter, and vanilla. Transfer toasted pecan cream to medium bowl; cover surface directly with plastic wrap, and refrigerate at least 30 minutes.

3. Preheat oven to 425°F. Line tart shell with foil; fill with pie weights, dry beans, or uncooked rice. Bake 20 minutes. Remove foil and weights and bake 10 minutes longer, or until golden. If crust puffs up during baking,

gently press it to tart pan with back of spoon. Transfer pan to wire rack. Place oven rack at position closest to heat source and preheat broiler.

4. Arrange banana slices, overlapping slightly, in tart shell. Spoon toasted pecan cream on top of bananas and sprinkle with remaining 1 tablespoon sugar. Cover edge of crust with foil to prevent overbrowning. Broil tart until top is lightly caramelized, 1 to 2 minutes. Cool slightly on wire rack. Remove side of pan and serve warm.

Each serving: about 310 calories, 4g protein, 35g carbohydrate, 18g total fat (8g saturated), 1g fiber, 85mg cholesterol, 205mg sodium

NUTTY AND SWEET

Nuts can make or break a pie, so take care when selecting and storing them. Because nuts contain a lot of fat, if improperly stored, they can become rancid quickly. Rancid nuts will have an unpleasant, stale flavor and odor. They may also seem soft and limp rather than crisp; some of their nutritional benefits will be lost as well.

For freshness, buy whole, not chopped, nuts in packages or from bulk bins at a grocery store with a high turnover rate. Keep them in a tightly sealed container (use a resealable plastic freezer bag after opening the original container) and store them in the freezer. There's no need to thaw nuts before chopping them or using them in baking.

Chocolate Walnut Tart

Imagine an ultra-rich, walnut-fudge brownie baked in a shortbread crust. Sound good? Here's the recipe. All you have to decide is whether to serve it warm or cool— and if you'd like to add a big spoonful of whipped cream or ice cream.

Active time: 45 minutes
Bake time: 30 minutes
Makes: 12 servings

1/2 cup butter or margarine (1 stick)
3 ounces unsweetened chocolate
1/2 cup granulated sugar
1/2 cup packed light brown sugar
2 large eggs
3/4 cup all-purpose flour
1 teaspoon vanilla extract
1/8 teaspoon salt
3/4 cup walnuts (3 ounces), coarsely chopped
Shortbread Crust (page 140)

1. Preheat oven to 325°F. In 3-quart saucepan, melt butter and chocolate over low heat, stirring occasionally. Remove from heat and stir in both sugars. Add eggs, one at a time, stirring well after each. Stir in flour, vanilla, salt, and nuts until blended. Pour into cooled baked tart crust.

2. Bake 30 minutes, or until top is just set. Cool on wire rack 1 hour to serve warm, or cool completely to serve later.

Each serving: about 385 calories, 5g protein, 39g carbohydrate, 25g total fat (13g saturated), 2g fiber, 77mg cholesterol, 195 mg sodium

Almond Tartlets

A platter of tiny tarts, filled with sweet almond or hazelnut cream, is a real show-stopper.

Active time: 1 hour plus chilling
Bake time: 15 minutes
Makes: 36 tartlets

1 cup blanched almonds (4 ounces), toasted
    (see page xxiii)
1 cup confectioners' sugar plus additional for sprinkling
1 large egg
3 tablespoons butter or margarine, softened
1 teaspoon vanilla extract
Pastry for Single-Crust Pie (page 140), formed into disk
    and chilled but not rolled

1. Preheat oven to 400°F. In food processor with knife blade attached, pulse almonds with 1 cup confectioners' sugar until nuts are very finely ground. Add egg, butter, and vanilla; process until smooth.

2. On lightly floured surface, roll dough paper-thin (thinner than 1/16 inch thick). With 2½ inch round cutter, cut out 36 pastry rounds (if necessary, reroll scraps). Fit each round into cup of mini muffin pan or 1¾-inch tartlet mold.

3. Spoon almond mixture into each tartlet shell, filling to within ¼ inch of rim. Bake 15 minutes, or until golden. Remove tartlets from pans; cool completely on wire racks. Sift confectioners' sugar over tartlets.

Each tartlet: about 85 calories, 2g protein, 8g carbohydrate, 5g total fat (2g saturated), 1g fiber, 12mg cholesterol, 40mg sodium

HAZELNUT TARTLETS Prepare tartlets as instructed above, but substitute *1 cup hazelnuts (5 ounces)*, toasted and skinned (see page xxiii), for almonds. Bake and cool as directed.

Each tartlet: about 80 calories, 1g protein, 8g carbohydrate, 5g total fat (2g saturated), 1g fiber, 12mg cholesterol, 40mg sodium

Cherry Hazelnut Linzer Tart

Here, sour cherry preserves step in for the more traditional raspberry filling in a subtle twist on a classic holiday dessert. For a playful touch, we've decorated the top of the tart with stand-up Christmas tree cookies made from the tart dough.

Active time: 30 minutes plus chilling and cooling
Bake time: 35 minutes
Makes: 12 servings

2/3 cup hazelnuts, toasted and skinned (see page xxiii), cooled
1 1/4 cups all-purpose flour
1/4 teaspoon baking powder
1/4 teaspoon salt
1/2 cup butter (1 stick), softened (do not use margarine)
1/2 cup granulated sugar
1/4 teaspoon ground cinnamon
1/4 teaspoon ground cloves
1 large egg, separated
1 teaspoon vanilla extract
1 cup sour cherry preserves
3 tablespoons confectioners' sugar

1. Preheat oven to 375°F. In food processor with knife blade attached, pulse nuts, flour, baking powder, and salt until finely ground.

2. In large bowl, with mixer on medium-high speed, beat butter, sugar, cinnamon, and cloves 3 minutes or until pale and fluffy. Set aside 1 tablespoon egg white. With mixer on medium, beat remaining egg white and yolk into butter mixture, then add vanilla and beat until blended, occasionally scraping bowl.

3. With mixer on low speed, gradually add nut mixture. Beat 2 minutes or until blended. Transfer two-thirds of dough to 9-inch tart pan with removable bottom; transfer remaining dough to pastry bag fitted with 1/3-inch plain round tip. Press dough evenly into bottom and up side of pan. Freeze 20 minutes.

4. Brush reserved egg white on bottom crust. Spread preserves evenly over tart. Pipe dough from pastry bag in straight lines, 1 inch apart, across top. Pipe additional straight lines, 1 inch apart, diagonally over first lines to form diamond-lattice pattern. Bake 35 minutes or until browned.

5. Meanwhile, line cookie sheet with parchment. Transfer remaining dough from pastry bag onto sheet of waxed paper; cover with second sheet. Roll to 1/8-inch thickness. Freeze 5 minutes. With 2" by 1" tree cookie cutter, cut out as many cookies as possible; transfer to cookie sheet. Bake 7 to 9 minutes or until golden brown.

6. Cool cookies and tart in pan completely on wire racks. Remove side of pan. Dust cookies and tart with confectioners' sugar. Insert cookies upright into tart.

Each serving: about 265 calories, 3g protein, 38g carbohydrate, 12g total fat (5g saturated), 1g fiber, 38mg cholesterol, 120mg sodium

SAVORY PIES & TARTS

Don't restrict your pastry-making skill to sweets. Use your expertise in creating tender flaky crusts to produce an international array of savory tarts, pies, quiches, and turnovers.

Tomato and Goat Cheese Quiche

This flavorful tomato and goat cheese quiche makes for a no-fuss brunch. The crust comes together in a jiffy, courtesy of the food processor.

Active time: 25 minutes plus chilling

Bake time: 1 hour 5 minutes

Makes: 6 main-dish servings

1¼ cups all-purpose flour

1 teaspoon sugar

½ teaspoon salt

½ cup butter or margarine (1 stick), cut up

2 to 3 tablespoons ice water

2 tablespoons extra-virgin olive oil

12 ounces green onions or trimmed shallots, finely chopped (1¾ cups)

⅛ teaspoon cayenne (ground red) pepper

5 large eggs

1¾ cups whole milk

4 ounces goat cheese, crumbled (1 cup)

¾ cup chopped, seeded plum tomatoes

Chopped fresh parsley for garnish

1. In food processor, with knife blade attached, blend flour, sugar, and ¼ teaspoon salt. Add butter; pulse until mixture resembles coarse crumbs. Sprinkle in ice water, 1 tablespoon at a time, pulsing after each addition, until large moist crumbs just begin to form.

2. Shape dough into disk; wrap in plastic. Refrigerate at least 30 minutes, or overnight. (If overnight, remove from refrigerator 30 minutes before rolling.)

3. Preheat oven to 375°F. On lightly floured surface, with floured rolling pin, roll dough into 13-inch round. Ease dough round into deep 10-inch (2-quart) quiche plate; gently press against bottom and up side of plate without stretching. Trim edges of dough. Freeze 15 minutes.

4. Line quiche shell with foil and fill with pie weights, dry beans, or uncooked rice. Bake 25 to 30 minutes or until dry to touch. Remove foil and weights; bake 10 to 15 minutes longer or until golden brown. Place crust on jelly-roll pan.

5. Meanwhile, in 12-inch skillet, heat oil on medium. Add onions, cayenne, and ⅛ teaspoon salt. Remove from heat.

6. In large bowl, whisk eggs until blended. Whisk in milk until smooth. Stir in goat cheese, tomatoes, cooked onions, and remaining ⅛ teaspoon salt. Carefully pour mixture into hot crust.

7. Bake 30 to 35 minutes or until edges are set and center jiggles slightly. Let cool on wire rack until warm or room temperature. Garnish with parsley.

Each serving: about 440 calories, 15g protein, 28g carbohydrate, 31g total fat (16g saturated), 2g fiber, 212mg cholesterol, 495mg sodium

Quiche Lorraine

This creamy custard tart, which took the states by storm in the 1960s, has settled into its rightful place as a favorite American adoptee. For the most authentic flavor, use a good French Gruyère.

Active time: 20 minutes plus cooling
Bake time: 1 hour 10 minutes
Makes: 8 main-dish servings

Pastry for Single-Crust Pie (page 140)
4 slices bacon, chopped
2 cups half-and-half or light cream
4 large eggs
1/2 teaspoon salt
1/8 teaspoon ground black pepper
Pinch nutmeg
4 ounces Gruyère or Swiss cheese, coarsely shredded
   (1 cup)

1. Preheat oven to 425°F. Line prepared pie shell with foil; fill with pie weights, dry beans, or uncooked rice. Bake 10 minutes. Remove foil and weights; bake 5 minutes longer, or until lightly golden. If crust puffs up during baking, gently press it to pie plate with back of spoon. Transfer to wire rack to cool. Reduce oven temperature to 350°F.

2. In 2-quart saucepan, cook bacon over medium-low heat about 5 minutes, until brown. With slotted spoon, transfer bacon to paper towels to drain.

3. In medium bowl, with wire whisk or fork, mix half-and-half, eggs, salt, pepper, and nutmeg until well blended.

4. Sprinkle bacon and cheese over cooled piecrust. Pour half-and-half mixture over bacon and cheese. Place sheet of foil underneath pie plate; crimp foil edges to form rim to catch any overflow during baking. Bake 55 minutes to 1 hour, or until knife inserted in center comes out clean. Cool on wire rack at least 15 minutes before serving. Serve hot or at room temperature.

Each serving: about 350 calories, 12g protein, 19g carbohydrate, 25g total fat (13g saturated), 1g fiber, 162mg cholesterol, 430mg sodium

Ricotta and Tomato Pie

This is a summer dish, for one simple reason: The tomato slices that cover the ricotta filling must be truly ripe, red, and tasty. If peak-of-the-season tomatoes are not available, serve it plain or turn it into a ricotta pizza by topping it with our Pizza Sauce (page 280).

Active time: 35 minutes plus cooling
Bake time: 1 hour 5 minutes
Makes: 8 first-course servings

Pastry for Single-Crust Pie (page 140), prepared with high
   fluted decorative edge
1 container (15 ounces) ricotta cheese
3/4 cup grated Pecorino-Romano cheese
1/2 teaspoon ground black pepper
3 large eggs, lightly beaten
2 ripe medium tomatoes, cored and thinly sliced
1/4 cup fresh basil, shredded

1. Preheat oven to 425° F. Line pie shell with foil; fill with pie weights, dry beans, or uncooked rice. Bake 15 minutes. Remove foil and weights; bake 7 to 10 minutes longer, until golden. If crust puffs up during baking, gently press it to pie plate with back of spoon. Cool on wire rack 15 minutes. Reduce oven temperature to 350°F.

2. While crust is cooling, prepare filling: In medium bowl, whisk together ricotta, Pecorino, and pepper. Add eggs and whisk to combine.

3. Pour filling into cooled piecrust. With paper towel, pat tomatoes dry; arrange tomato slices on top of cheese mixture, overlapping if necessary. Sprinkle basil over top. Bake 40 minutes, or until set and lightly puffed. Cool on wire rack 30 minutes before serving. Serve warm or at room temperature.

Each serving: about 315 calories, 14g protein, 20g carbohydrate, 20g total fat (11g saturated), 1g fiber, 130mg cholesterol, 290mg sodium

Asparagus Tart

An elegant addition to any brunch table, this spring tart showcases tender asparagus encased in a savory, quiche-like custard with a biscuit crust. To increase the herb appeal, try adding a few leaves of chopped fresh basil to the egg mixture before baking.

Active time: 25 minutes plus cooling
Bake time: 35 minutes
Makes: 8 main-dish servings

1³/₈ teaspoons salt
1³/₄ cups all-purpose flour
1 teaspoon baking powder
¹/₄ teaspoon ground black pepper
6 tablespoons cold butter or margarine, cut up
6 to 8 tablespoons ice water
1 pound thin asparagus, ends trimmed
3 large eggs
1¹/₃ cups milk
1 teaspoon Dijon mustard
2 teaspoons freshly grated lemon peel

1. Preheat oven to 425°F. In covered 10-inch skillet, heat about *1 inch water* and 1 teaspoon salt to boiling over high heat. Spray removable bottom of 11-inch tart pan with nonstick cooking spray.

2. In food processor with knife blade attached, combine flour, baking powder, ¹/₈ teaspoon salt, and pepper; pulse until blended. Add butter and pulse until mixture resembles coarse meal. Add ice water, 1 tablespoon at a time, pulsing until moist clumps form. Gather dough into ball; flatten into a disk. On lightly floured surface, with floured rolling pin, roll dough into 13-inch round. Gently ease dough into prepared tart pan. Fold in overhang to make double layer of pastry around side of pan; press dough against side to reinforce edge. (Dough can be covered and refrigerated up to 4 hours before baking.) Place tart pan on cookie sheet; bake 15 minutes. Cool slightly on wire rack.

3. Meanwhile, add asparagus to boiling water in skillet and cook 5 minutes. Drain asparagus and rinse under cold running water; drain well. In medium bowl, with wire whisk or fork, mix eggs, milk, Dijon, and remaining ¹/₄ teaspoon salt until well blended.

4. Cut ends from asparagus so that spears are about 5 inches long, reserving ends for another use. Arrange asparagus spears in spoke fashion in baked tart shell with tips pointing outward. Sprinkle lemon peel evenly over asparagus. Carefully pour egg mixture over all.

5. Bake tart, on cookie sheet, 20 to 25 minutes or until tart puffs and custard jiggles only slightly in center. Cool on wire rack 15 minutes to serve warm or cool completely to serve at room temperature. Remove side of pan before serving.

Each serving: about 245 calories, 8g protein, 24g carbohydrate, 13g total fat (7g saturated), 1g fiber, 110mg cholesterol, 340mg sodium

Spicy Empanadas

Beloved in many Latin American countries, empanadas are turnovers filled with meat, vegetables, or both. Sliced into smaller servings, they make wonderful party fare.

Active time: 1 hour plus chilling
Bake time: 30 minutes
Makes: 6 empanadas

PASTRY

2¹/2 cups all-purpose flour

¹/2 cup yellow cornmeal

1 teaspoon salt

¹/4 teaspoon cayenne (ground red) pepper

1 cup cold butter (2 sticks), cut up

1 container (8 ounces) sour cream

FILLING

8 ounces boneless pork loin, trimmed

2 tablespoons olive oil

8 ounces lean ground beef

1 onion, chopped (1 cup)

1 small green pepper, finely chopped (³/4 cup)

1 small red pepper, finely chopped (³/4 cup)

4 large garlic cloves, finely chopped

2 pickled jalapeño chiles, finely chopped

¹/3 cup pimiento-stuffed green olives, chopped

¹/3 cup dried currants

1 teaspoon ground cumin

³/4 teaspoon salt

¹/4 teaspoon ground black pepper

¹/4 teaspoon ground cinnamon

¹/4 teaspoon cayenne (ground red) pepper

2 ripe medium tomatoes, chopped (1¹/2 cups)

1 large egg, lightly beaten

1. Prepare pastry: In a food processor with knife blade attached, combine flour, cornmeal, salt, and cayenne. Add butter and process until mixture resembles fine crumbs. Add sour cream and pulse until dough begins to hold together. Turn dough out onto surface, gather together, and divide in half. Press each half into disk. Wrap and refrigerate at least 2 hours or up to 2 days.

2. Prepare filling: Finely chop pork. In 12-inch skillet, heat 1 tablespoon oil over high heat. Add pork and beef. Cook 5 minutes, until meat is browned and any liquid has evaporated. Transfer to plate.

3. Add remaining 1 tablespoon oil, onion, and green and red peppers to skillet; cook over medium-high heat 5 minutes, or until vegetables have softened. Add garlic, jalapeños, olives, currants, cumin, salt, pepper, cinnamon, and cayenne. Cook over medium heat 5 minutes. Add meat and tomatoes. Heat to a simmer, partially cover, and cook 10 minutes, until flavors are blended. Turn filling into large bowl, cover loosely, and refrigerate until cold.

4. On floured surface, with floured rolling pin, roll 1 disk dough into 24" by 8" rectangle. Cut crosswise into six 8" by 4" rectangles. Place ¹/3 cup filling on one end of each rectangle, about ¹/2 inch from end and sides. Brush edges with beaten egg. Fold pastry over to cover filling. Press edges together and press with floured fork to seal. Transfer to large cookie sheet; refrigerate. Repeat with remaining dough and filling.

5. Preheat oven to 400°F. Brush tops of empanadas with beaten egg. Bake 30 minutes, rotating sheets between upper and lower oven racks halfway through, until browned. Transfer to wire rack to cool. Serve warm or at room temperature.

Each empanada: about 435 calories, 13g protein, 34g carbohydrate, 28g total fat (14g saturated), 2g fiber, 93 mg cholesterol, 665 mg sodium

Sweet Onion Tart

Our adaptation of an Alsatian onion tart is topped with onions that have been slowly simmered in butter until they're soft, golden, and sweet.

Active time: 1 hour plus chilling and cooling
Bake time: 55 minutes
Makes: 32 appetizer servings

3 cups all-purpose flour
2 teaspoons salt
¹/2 cup vegetable shortening
¹/2 cup (1 stick) plus 3 tablespoons cold butter or margarine
7 to 8 tablespoons cold water
2 pounds sweet onions, thinly sliced
2¹/2 cups milk
5 large eggs
³/4 cup freshly grated Parmesan cheese
2 teaspoons chopped fresh thyme or ¹/2 teaspoon dried thyme
1 tablespoon chopped fresh parsley
¹/2 teaspoon coarsely ground black pepper

1. In large bowl, with fork, stir together flour and 1 teaspoon salt. With pastry blender or two knives used scissor-fashion, cut in shortening and ¹/2 cup butter until mixture resembles coarse crumbs. Sprinkle cold water, 1 tablespoon at a time, into flour mixture, mixing lightly with fork after each addition, until mixture is just moist enough to hold together. With hands, shape dough into ball.

2. On lightly floured surface, with floured rolling pin, roll dough into rectangle about 18" by 13". Gently fold rectangle into fourths and carefully center in ungreased 15¹/2" by 10¹/2" jelly-roll pan; unfold. Lightly press dough into bottom and up sides of pan. Trim dough, leaving ¹/2-inch overhang. Fold overhang under and pinch to form decorative edge level with rim of pan (see page 141). Wrap and refrigerate tart shell about 30 minutes.

3. Meanwhile, in deep 12-inch skillet, melt remaining 3 tablespoons butter over medium-high heat Add onions and cook, stirring frequently, about 25 minutes, until golden. Remove from heat.

4. Preheat oven to 425°F. Line tart shell with foil; fill with pie weights, dry beans, or uncooked rice. Bake 20 minutes. Remove foil and weights; bake 10 minutes longer, or until golden. Transfer to wire rack to cool. Reduce oven temperature to 400°F.

5. In large bowl, whisk together milk, eggs, Parmesan, thyme, parsley, pepper, and remaining 1 teaspoon salt until blended.

6. Spread cooked onions evenly over baked tart shell. Pour egg mixture over onions. Bake 25 minutes, or until egg mixture is set and tart is nicely browned. Serve hot. Or cool on wire rack; then wrap and refrigerate to serve cold later.

Each serving: about 155 calories, 4g protein, 13g carbohydrate, 9g total fat (4g saturated), 1g fiber, 48mg cholesterol, 250mg sodium

Summery Vegetable Tart

This savory freeform tart is slathered with basil cream cheese and filled with zucchini, peppers, and squash. We've called for our pastry for a single-crust pie, but if you prefer, swap in store-bought roll-out pie dough. It makes this tart a cinch to pull together.

Active time: 25 minutes
Bake time: 30 minutes
Makes: 4 main-dish servings

Pastry for Single-Crust Pie (page 140), formed into disk
   and chilled but not rolled
1 tablespoon plus 1 teaspoon extra-virgin olive oil
1 clove garlic, crushed with press
1 small red onion, finely chopped
1 large red pepper, finely chopped
¼ teaspoon salt
¼ teaspoon ground black pepper
4 ounces cream cheese, softened
¼ cup fresh basil leaves, finely chopped, plus additional
   for garnish
1 small zucchini (4 ounces), trimmed
1 small yellow squash (4 ounces), trimmed

1. Preheat oven to 425°F.

2. On lightly floured work surface, with floured rolling pin, roll dough into 15-inch round. Lay pastry flat on large jelly-roll pan.

3. In 12-inch skillet, heat 1 tablespoon oil over medium-high heat. Add garlic and cook 30 seconds, stirring. Add onion, red pepper, and ⅛ teaspoon each salt and black pepper. Cook 4 minutes or until vegetables are softened and browned, stirring frequently. Remove from heat and let cool to room temperature. Onion-pepper mixture can be refrigerated, in airtight container, up to overnight.

4. While onion-pepper mixture cools, in small bowl, combine cream cheese, chopped basil, and remaining ⅛ teaspoon each salt and black pepper; stir with fork until well mixed. With vegetable peeler, peel zucchini and squash lengthwise into thin ribbons (see Tip). You'll use these to create your vegetable lattice.

5. Spread cream cheese mixture in even layer on piecrust, leaving 1-inch border. Spread onion-pepper mixture over cream cheese. Decoratively arrange zucchini and squash ribbons on top. To create lattice, place yellow squash strips in row about 2 inches apart on pie. Repeat with an equal number of zucchini strips placed at right angles to yellow squash strips. (You can weave zucchini strips under and over yellow squash strips, if you like; see page 153). Fold border of dough over vegetables. Brush remaining 1 teaspoon oil over zucchini and squash.

6. Bake 30 to 35 minutes or until browned. Serve tart warm or at room temperature.

Each serving: about 395 calories, 5g protein, 34g carbohydrate, 29g total fat (12g saturated), 2g fiber, 37mg cholesterol, 520mg sodium

TIP Shave off pretty zucchini and squash ribbons using a vegetable peeler. If the vegetables have a lot of seeds, rotate them 90 degrees each time you hit the seeds, then start peeling on a different side. Discard the core of seeds.

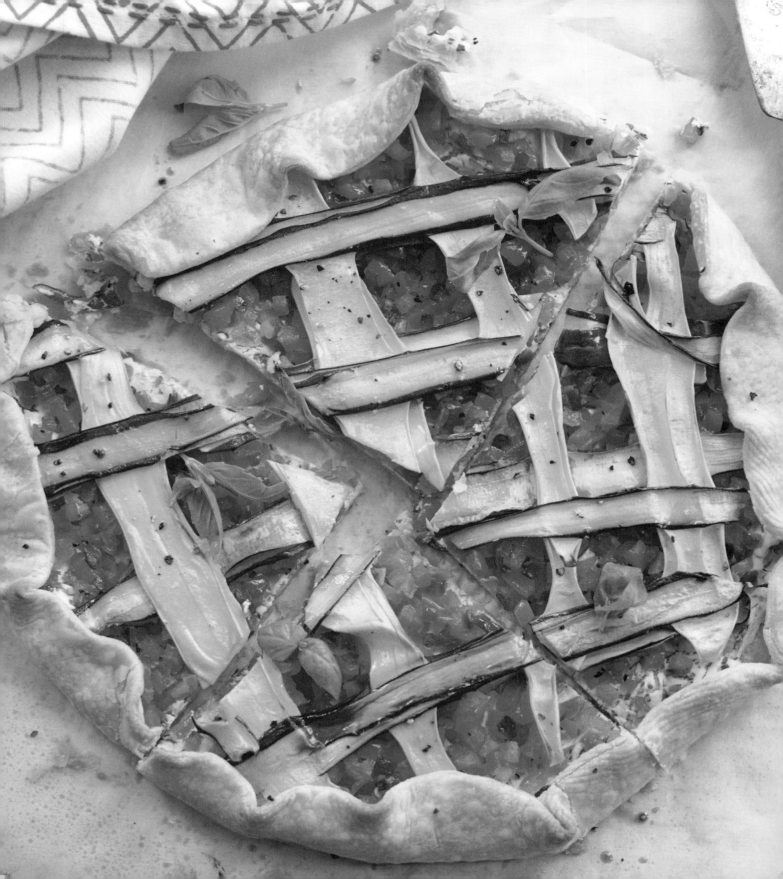

Cobblers, Custards & Baked Desserts

COBBLERS, CRISPS & CRUMBLES

Seasonal fruits are the inspiration for these country-style desserts. Bake them with the specified fruits or experiment with the best that your local orchard or berry patch has to offer. You can even use frozen, unsweetened fruits in these desserts.

Deep-Dish Apple Cobbler
This deep-dish dessert bubbles with homespun charm and flavor.

Active time: 30 minutes
Bake time: 35 minutes
Makes: 12 servings

COBBLER CRUST
1 cup all-purpose flour
1¹/2 teaspoons baking powder
¹/4 cup sugar
3 tablespoons cold butter or margarine, cut into
    ¹/2-inch pieces
¹/2 cup heavy cream

APPLE FILLING
1 lemon
2¹/2 pounds Granny Smith, Golden Delicious, and/or Gala
    apples, peeled, cored, and cut into ¹/2-inch-thick wedges
¹/3 cup sugar
2 tablespoons cornstarch
¹/8 teaspoon salt

FINISHING
¹/8 teaspoon ground cinnamon
1 tablespoon sugar
1 tablespoon heavy cream

1. Prepare cobbler crust: In medium bowl, combine flour, baking powder, and sugar. With pastry blender or using two knives scissors-fashion, cut in butter until mixture resembles fine crumbs. Add cream and stir with fork until dough comes together.

2. Gather dough into ball and place on lightly floured sheet of waxed paper. With floured rolling pin, roll dough into 9-inch round. Slide waxed paper onto cookie sheet and refrigerate dough until ready to use.

3. Preheat oven to 400°F. Prepare apple filling: From lemon, grate ¹/2 teaspoon peel and squeeze 1 tablespoon juice. In large bowl, toss lemon peel and juice with apples, sugar, cornstarch, and salt. Transfer apple mixture to 9¹/2-inch deep-dish glass or ceramic pie plate. Cover with waxed paper and cook in microwave oven on High 8 minutes or until apples are fork-tender, stirring well halfway through cooking.

4. Immediately, while filling is hot, remove dough round from refrigerator and, leaving waxed paper attached to serve as handles, invert dough over apple mixture. Peel off paper. Cut 4-inch X in center of round; fold back points to make square opening.

5. To finish pie assembly, in cup, mix cinnamon and sugar. Brush dough with heavy cream; sprinkle with cinnamon sugar.

6. Bake cobbler 35 to 40 minutes or until filling is bubbling in center. If crust is browning too quickly, loosely cover with foil after 25 minutes. Cool on wire rack.

Each serving: about 195 calories, 2g protein, 32g carbohydrate, 8g total fat (5g saturated), 2g fiber, 24mg cholesterol, 110mg sodium

Apple Brown Betty

Brown Betty is an old-fashioned American dessert that combines fruit with buttery bread crumbs. You can use any flavorful variety of apples you like—Granny Smiths are just a suggestion. You could also use a combination of thinly sliced apples and pears.

Active time: 35 minutes
Bake time: 50 minutes
Makes: 8 servings

8 slices firm white bread, torn into 1/2-inch pieces
1/2 cup butter or margarine (1 stick), melted
1 teaspoon ground cinnamon
2 1/2 pounds Granny Smith apples (about 6), peeled, cored, and thinly sliced
2/3 cup packed light brown sugar
2 tablespoons fresh lemon juice
1 teaspoon vanilla extract
1/4 teaspoon ground nutmeg

1. Preheat oven to 400°F. In 15½" by 10½" jelly-roll pan, bake bread pieces, stirring occasionally, 12 to 15 minutes, until very lightly toasted. Grease shallow 2-quart glass or ceramic baking dish.

2. In medium bowl, combine melted butter and ½ teaspoon cinnamon. Add toasted bread; toss gently until evenly moistened.

3. In large bowl, combine apples, brown sugar, lemon juice, vanilla, nutmeg, and remaining ½ teaspoon cinnamon; toss to coat.

4. Place ½ cup bread pieces in prepared dish. Top with half of apple mixture, then 1 cup bread pieces. Add remaining apple mixture, then sprinkle remaining bread pieces on top, leaving 1-inch border all around edge.

5. Cover dish with foil and bake 40 minutes. Remove foil and bake 10 minutes longer, or until apples are tender and bread on top is brown. Cool on wire rack 10 minutes before serving warm.

Each serving: about 325 calories, 3g protein, 51g carbohydrate, 13g total fat (8g saturated), 3g fiber, 31mg cholesterol, 275mg sodium

BANANA BROWN BETTY Prepare as instructed, but use *6 ripe medium bananas*, sliced ¼ inch thick (about 4 cups), instead of apples and ½ *teaspoon ground ginger* instead of nutmeg. Increase butter to *6 tablespoons melted butter.*

Each serving: about 410 calories, 3g protein, 53g carbohydrate, 22g total fat (13g saturated), 2g fiber, 55mg cholesterol, 365 mg sodium

Rhubarb-Strawberry Cobbler

We've included blueberry and peach variations below, but this basic cobbler works beautifully with just about any fruit filling you can dream up. How about nectarine-blackberry, raspberry-peach, apple-cranberry, or fresh apricot? If your fruit is particularly tart, you may want to add an extra tablespoon or two of sugar.

Active time: 25 minutes
Bake time: 20 minutes
Makes: 8 servings

FILLING

1¼ pounds rhubarb, cut into 1-inch chunks (4 cups)
½ cup sugar
1 tablespoon cornstarch
¼ cup cold water
1 pint strawberries, hulled and quartered

BISCUITS

1½ cups all-purpose flour
¼ cup plus 1 teaspoon sugar
1½ teaspoons baking powder
½ teaspoon baking soda
¼ teaspoon salt
¼ teaspoon ground cinnamon
¼ teaspoon ground nutmeg
4 tablespoons cold butter or margarine, cut up
¾ cup plus 1 tablespoon heavy cream

1. Prepare filling: In 3-quart saucepan, heat rhubarb and sugar to boiling over high heat, stirring constantly. Reduce heat to medium-low and simmer until rhubarb is tender, about 8 minutes.

2. In cup, blend cornstarch and water until smooth. Stir cornstarch mixture and strawberries into rhubarb mixture; continue cooking 2 minutes, or until mixture boils. Remove saucepan from heat.

3. Preheat oven to 400°F.

4. Prepare biscuits: In bowl, stir together flour, ¼ cup sugar, baking powder, baking soda, salt, cinnamon, and nutmeg. With pastry blender or two knives used scissor-fashion, cut in butter until mixture resembles coarse crumbs. Add ¾ cup cream, stirring just until mixture forms soft dough that pulls away from side of bowl.

5. Turn dough onto lightly floured surface; knead 6 to 8 times to blend thoroughly. With floured rolling pin, roll dough into 10½" by 6½" rectangle, ½ inch thick. Cut dough lengthwise in half, then cut half crosswise into 4 pieces. Brush biscuits with remaining 1 tablespoon cream and sprinkle with remaining 1 teaspoon sugar.

6. Reheat filling until hot. Pour into 11" by 7" glass or ceramic baking dish or shallow 2-quart casserole. Place biscuits on top of filling. Place sheet of foil under baking dish; crimp edges to form rim to catch any overflow during baking. Bake 20 to 25 minutes, until biscuits are lightly browned and filling is bubbly. Cool on wire rack 30 minutes; serve warm.

Each serving: about 330 calories, 4g protein, 46g carbohydrate, 15g total fat (9g saturated), 2g fiber, 49mg cholesterol, 315mg sodium

BLUEBERRY COBBLER Prepare cobbler as described, but use blueberry filling instead: In 3-quart saucepan, stir together *½ cup sugar* and *2 tablespoons cornstarch*. Stir in *1 tablespoon fresh lemon juice*, *¼ cup water*, and *6 cups fresh blueberries*. Heat to boiling over medium-high heat, stirring frequently.

Each serving: about 370 calories, 4g protein, 56g carbohydrate, 15g total fat (9g saturated), 3g fiber, 49mg cholesterol, 315mg sodium

PEACH COBBLER Prepare cobbler as described, but use peach filling instead: In 3-quart saucepan, stir together *½ cup sugar* and *3 tablespoons cornstarch*. Stir in *1 tablespoon fresh lemon juice* and *3 pounds (about 8 large) ripe peaches*, peeled, pitted, and thickly sliced. Heat to boiling over medium-high heat, stirring.

Each serving: about 365 calories, 4g protein, 56g carbohydrate, 15g total fat (9g saturated), 3g fiber, 49mg cholesterol, 310mg sodium

Plum Kuchen

A kuchen is a simple cake made from a sweet dough topped with baked or whole fruits. Plum kuchen is the most popular: Small, egg-shaped European prune plums are especially suitable for this German recipe.

Active time: 20 minutes
Bake time: 30 minutes
Makes: 10 servings

5 large plums or 16 prune plums, pitted
1/2 cup sugar
1 cup all-purpose flour
7 tablespoons butter or margarine, softened
1/4 cup milk
1 large egg
1 1/2 teaspoons baking powder
1/4 teaspoon salt
1/4 teaspoon ground cinnamon
Pinch ground nutmeg
1/3 cup apricot jam or currant jelly
1 tablespoon boiling water

1. Preheat oven to 400°F. Grease 11" by 7" glass or ceramic baking dish. Cut large plums into 8 wedges each or cut prune plums in half.

2. In large bowl, combine 1/4 cup sugar, flour, 4 tablespoons butter, milk, egg, baking powder, and salt. With mixer on low speed, beat, scraping bowl frequently with rubber spatula, until mixture leaves sides of bowl and clings to beaters, about 2 minutes.

3. Spread dough evenly in prepared dish. Arrange plums, skin side up, in slightly overlapping rows on dough.

4. In small saucepan, melt remaining 3 tablespoons butter over medium heat. Stir in remaining 1/4 cup sugar, cinnamon, and nutmeg; spoon over plums. Bake 30 to 35 minutes, until plums are tender.

5. In small bowl, with fork, stir together jam and water until smooth. Brush glaze over hot fruit. Cool kuchen on wire rack 10 minutes before serving warm.

Each serving: about 220 calories, 3g protein, 32g carbohydrate, 10g total fat (5g saturated), 1g fiber, 44mg cholesterol, 225mg sodium

BLUEBERRY KUCHEN Prepare kuchen as instructed, but substitute *1 pint blueberries* for plums.

Each serving: about 215 calories, 2g protein, 31g carbohydrate, 9g total fat (5g saturated), 1g fiber, 44mg cholesterol, 230mg sodium

SWEET CHERRY KUCHEN Prepare kuchen as instructed, but substitute *1 pound sweet cherries*, pitted, for plums.

Each serving: about 225 calories, 3g protein, 34g carbohydrate, 10g total, fat (5g saturated), 1g fiber, 44mg cholesterol, 225mg sodium

APPLE KUCHEN Prepare kuchen as instructed, but substitute *1½ pounds Golden Delicious apples (about 3)*, peeled, cored, and thinly sliced, for plums.

Each serving: about 230 calories, 2g protein, 35g carbohydrate, 9g total fat (5g saturated), 2g fiber, 44mg cholesterol, 225mg sodium

Cherry-Almond Clafouti

Clafouti is a French country specialty that's rather like a thick, fruit-studded pancake.

Active time: 20 minutes
Bake time: 40 minutes
Makes: 12 servings

1 pound dark sweet cherries, pitted (see Tip)
2 cups half-and-half or light cream
1/3 cup granulated sugar
2 tablespoons amaretto (almond-flavored liqueur)
4 large eggs
2/3 cup all-purpose flour
Confectioners' sugar for sprinkling

1. Preheat oven to 350°F. Grease 10" by 1½" round ceramic baking dish.

2. Place cherries in prepared dish. In medium bowl, with wire whisk or fork, beat half-and-half, granulated sugar, amaretto, and eggs until well blended. Whisk in flour, a little at a time, until smooth.

3. Pour egg mixture over cherries in prepared dish. Bake 40 to 45 minutes, until custard is set and knife inserted 1 inch from edge comes out clean (center will still jiggle). Sprinkle with confectioners' sugar. Serve hot.

Each serving: about 155 calories, 4g protein, 20g carbohydrate, 7g total fat (4g saturated), 1g fiber, 86mg cholesterol, 40mg sodium

TIP If you don't own a cherry pitter, you can use a paring knife: Slice a cherry in half, avoiding the pit, then dig out the pit with the tip of the knife. Or, if you want to keep the cherries intact, you can use a straightened out paper clip: Stick the sharp tip of the paper clip into the stem end until you hit the pit, then rotate the tip around the pit to remove it.

Cherry and Nectarine Crisp

Juicy cherries and nectarines make an unexpectedly delicious filling in this easy summer dessert.

Active time: 30 minutes
Bake time: 40 minutes
Makes: 8 servings

3 pounds nectarines, cut into wedges
1½ pounds (3 cups) cherries, pitted
1/4 cup granulated sugar
3 tablespoons cornstarch
1 tablespoon fresh lemon juice
1 tablespoon brandy (optional)
3/4 cup packed brown sugar
3/4 cup old-fashioned oats, uncooked
1/3 cup all-purpose flour
1/2 cup roasted salted almonds, chopped
1/4 teaspoon freshly grated nutmeg
1/8 teaspoon salt
1/2 cup cold butter or margarine, cut up

1. Preheat oven to 375°F. Grease 3-quart shallow ceramic baking dish.

2. In large bowl, toss nectarines, cherries, granulated sugar, cornstarch, lemon juice, and brandy, if using, until well mixed. Spread in even layer in prepared dish.

3. In medium bowl, combine brown sugar, oats, flour, almonds, nutmeg, and salt. Add butter. With pastry blender or fingertips, combine butter and dry ingredients until pea-size clumps form. Sprinkle over fruit mixture.

4. Bake 40 to 45 minutes or until golden brown on top. Serve warm.

Each serving: about 430 calories, 6g protein, 69g carbohydrate, 17g total fat (8g saturated), 6g fiber, 31mg cholesterol, 175mg sodium

BUMBLEBERRY CRISP

Bumbleberry Crisp

A mix—or bumble!—of apples and colorful, juicy berries forms the base for this sweet, saucy, crunchy dessert. You can substitute raw almonds or pecans for the hazelnuts if you prefer; they're equally yummy.

Active time: 15 minutes
Bake time: 45 minutes
Makes: 6 servings

1 cup hazelnuts, toasted and skinned (see page xxiii), chopped
1 cup all-purpose flour
6 tablespoons butter or margarine, cut up
1/3 cup packed brown sugar
1/4 teaspoon ground cinnamon
1/4 teaspoon salt
2 Golden Delicious apples, peeled, cored, and chopped
1 pound strawberries, hulled and sliced (about 3 cups)
1 container (6 ounces) blueberries
1 container (6 ounces) raspberries
3/4 cup granulated sugar
1/4 cup cornstarch
3 tablespoons fresh lemon juice
Vanilla ice cream for serving (optional)

1. Preheat oven to 375°F. Grease 2-quart baking dish.

2. In medium bowl, place hazelnuts, flour, butter, brown sugar, cinnamon, and salt. With hands, mix until ingredients are combined and small clumps form.

3. In large bowl, combine apples, all berries, granulated sugar, cornstarch, and lemon juice; transfer to prepared dish. Sprinkle with nut mixture. Bake 45 minutes or until bubbly and golden. Serve warm, with ice cream if desired.

Each serving: about 560 calories, 7g protein, 81g carbohydrate, 26g total fat (8g saturated), 7g fiber, 31mg cholesterol, 205mg sodium

---

HEALTHY MAKEOVER

Peach and Blueberry Crumble

Oatmeal and hazelnuts contribute fiber, while the juicy fruit is antioxidant rich. And, with just a smidgeon of butter and canola oil, this dessert is low in saturated fat, too.

Active time: 20 minutes
Bake time: 30 minutes
Makes: 8 servings

2 1/2 pounds ripe peaches, peeled (see page 152), pitted, and sliced
1 pint blueberries (12 ounces)
1/2 cup packed light brown sugar
1/3 cup all-purpose flour
1 cup old-fashioned oats, uncooked
1 teaspoon ground cinnamon
1 tablespoon butter or margarine, cut up
2 tablespoons canola oil
1/4 cup hazelnuts, toasted and skinned (see page xxiii), chopped

1. In shallow 2-quart ceramic or glass baking dish, toss peaches, blueberries, 1/4 cup brown sugar, and 1 tablespoon flour until evenly coated. Spread mixture in even layer in prepared dish.

2. In medium bowl, mix oats, cinnamon, remaining flour, and remaining 1/4 cup brown sugar. Add butter and oil. With fingertips, blend until mixture resembles coarse crumbs. Mix in hazelnuts. Sprinkle topping over fruit.

3. Bake crumble 30 to 35 minutes or until fruit is bubbly at edges and topping is browned. Cover loosely with foil after 25 minutes if top browns too quickly. Cool slightly on wire rack and serve warm, or serve at room temperature.

Each serving: about 270 calories, 4g protein, 45g carbohydrate, 10g total fat (1g saturated), 5g fiber, 0mg cholesterol, 45mg sodium

FRUIT SHORTCAKES

To many of us, fruit + cake + cream = ambrosia. The fruits—and they must be at their ripe, sweet peak—are shortcake's raison d'être, and whipped cream elevates it to a sublime status. Baking-powder biscuits or butter cake form the base.

Classic Strawberry Shortcake

This recipe is for biscuit partisans; the variations will keep you happy for many seasons to come. You can bake the biscuit in an 8-inch pan for one large shortcake, or cut the dough into small rounds for individual servings. For truly superb shortcake, assemble and serve the dessert while the biscuits are still warm.

Active time: 25 minutes
Bake time: 20 minutes
Makes: 10 servings

2 cups all-purpose flour
6 tablespoons plus 1/3 cup sugar
2 teaspoons baking powder
1/4 teaspoon salt
1/3 cup cold butter or margarine, cut up
2/3 cup milk
6 cups strawberries
1 cup heavy cream

1. Preheat oven to 425°F. Grease 8-inch round cake pan.

2. In medium bowl, stir together flour, 3 tablespoons sugar, baking powder, and salt. With pastry blender or two knives used scissor-fashion, cut in butter until mixture resembles coarse crumbs. Drizzle in milk and stir just until mixture forms soft dough that leaves side of bowl.

3. On lightly floured surface, knead dough about ten times, just to mix. Pat dough evenly into prepared pan and sprinkle top with 1 tablespoon sugar. Bake 20 to 22 minutes, until dough is lightly golden.

4. Meanwhile, set aside 4 whole strawberries for garnish; hull and halve or quarter remaining strawberries. In medium bowl, mix cut-up strawberries with 1/3 cup sugar until sugar has dissolved.

5. Invert shortcake onto work surface. With long serrated knife, carefully split hot shortcake horizontally. In bowl, with mixer on medium speed, beat cream just until soft peaks form. Beat in remaining 2 tablespoons sugar.

6. Place bottom half of shortcake, cut side up, on cake plate; top with half of strawberry mixture and half of whipped cream. Place cake top, cut side down, on strawberry mixture. Spoon remaining strawberry mixture on top and then spoon whipped cream on top of strawberries. Garnish with reserved whole strawberries and serve immediately.

Each serving: about 325 calories, 4g protein, 42g carbohydrate, 16g total fat (10g saturated), 3g fiber, 51mg cholesterol, 235mg sodium

INDIVIDUAL SHORTCAKES Prepare dough as described opposite. In step 3, after kneading, pat dough 1 inch thick. With 2½-inch floured cutter, cut 8 biscuits. Transfer to cookie sheet and bake 15 to 20 minutes, or until bottoms are golden brown. Split biscuits horizontally, place bottom halves on dessert plates, and top evenly with fruit mixture and whipped cream. Replace tops and serve immediately. Makes 8 servings.

Each serving: about 410 calories, 5g protein, 53g carbohydrate, 21g total fat (12g saturated), 4g fiber, 64mg cholesterol, 295mg sodium

PECAN SHORTCAKES Prepare Individual Shortcakes as described above, but add *1 cup pecans*, toasted (see page xxiii) and coarsely chopped, to flour and butter mixture in step 2. Makes 8 servings.

Each serving: about 500 calories, 6g protein, 55g carbohydrate, 30g total fat (13g saturated), 5g fiber, 64mg cholesterol, 295mg sodium

BROWN SUGAR-PEAR SHORTCAKES Prepare Individual Shortcakes as described above. Instead of making strawberry filling, in 12-inch nonstick skillet, melt *4 tablespoons butter* over medium-high heat. *Add 2¼ pounds ripe Bose pears* (about 6), peeled, cored, and cut lengthwise into ¾-inch wedges. Cook, uncovered, stirring gently and frequently, 10 to 15 minutes, until pears are browned and tender. Stir in *¼ cup packed light brown sugar*, *¼ teaspoon ground cinnamon*, *2 strips (2½" by ½" each) lemon peel*, and *¼ cup water*. Cook 1 minute; discard peels. Spoon mixture onto bottom of each shortcake. Top each with whipped cream and biscuit top. Serve immediately.

Each serving: about 525 calories, 5g protein, 70g carbohydrate, 26g total fat (16g saturated), 3g fiber, 80mg cholesterol, 355mg sodium

TART CHERRY SHORTCAKES Prepare Individual Shortcakes as described at left. Instead of making strawberry filling, in 3-quart saucepan, stir *⅔ cup sugar* with *1 tablespoon cornstarch* until evenly blended. Working over bowl to catch juices, with cherry pitter or paring knife, remove pits from *1 quart tart cherries*. Stir cherries and any juice into sugar mixture. Heat to boiling over medium-high heat, stirring, and cook until mixture has thickened. Reduce heat and simmer, stirring, 1 minute. Spoon warm cherry mixture onto bottom of each shortcake. Top each with whipped cream and biscuit top. Serve immediately.

Each serving: about 470 calories, 5g protein, 69g carbohydrate, 20g total fat (12g saturated), 1g fiber, 64mg cholesterol, 295mg sodium

BLUEBERRY-PEACH SHORTCAKES Prepare Individual Shortcakes as described at left. Instead of making strawberry filling, in 3-quart nonreactive saucepan, stir together *2 tablespoons fresh lemon juice* and *1 tablespoon cornstarch*. Add *1½ pints blueberries* and *⅔ cup sugar* and bring to boiling over medium heat. Boil 1 minute. Remove saucepan from heat and stir in *6 medium peaches*, peeled, pitted, and each sliced into 8 wedges. Spoon warm fruit mixture onto bottom of each shortcake. Top each with whipped cream and biscuit top. Serve immediately.

Each serving: about 520 calories, 6g protein, 82g carbohydrate, 20g total fat (12g saturated), 4g fiber, 64mg cholesterol, 295mg sodium

Strawberry Shortcakes

Sun-kissed berries star in this luscious dessert. It has less sugar than traditional versions, so the fruit's sweetness stands out, fiber-rich oats give the cakes a bolder flavor, and you can dollop on the low-fat-sour-cream-and-yogurt filling sans guilt.

Active time: 30 minutes • Bake time: 16 minutes • Makes: 8 servings

3/4 cup old-fashioned oats, uncooked
11/4 cups all-purpose flour
11/2 teaspoons baking powder
1/2 teaspoon baking soda
1/4 teaspoon salt
7 tablespoons plus 1/2 teaspoon sugar
2 tablespoons cold butter or margarine, cut up

3/4 cup low-fat buttermilk
2 large egg whites
2 pounds strawberries, hulled, cut in half
1/4 teaspoon freshly grated lemon peel
1 cup plain fat-free Greek yogurt
1/2 cup reduced-fat sour cream
1 teaspoon vanilla extract

1. Preheat oven to 425°F. Line cookie sheet with parchment paper or foil.

2. In food processor with knife blade attached, pulse oats until coarsely ground. Add flour, baking powder, baking soda, salt, and 3 tablespoons sugar. Pulse until combined. Add butter; pulse until mixture resembles cornmeal. Add buttermilk and 1 egg white; pulse just until dry ingredients are evenly moistened.

3. With 1/4-cup measuring cup, scoop mixture into mounds on prepared sheet, 2 inches apart.

4. In small bowl, lightly beat remaining egg white. Brush on top of mounds, then sprinkle with 1/2 teaspoon sugar.

5. Bake 16 minutes or until shortcakes are golden brown. Cool completely on sheet on wire rack. (Shortcakes can be kept, tightly wrapped, at room temperature up to overnight. Refresh before serving in toaster oven or 375°F oven for 5 minutes.)

6. Meanwhile, in large bowl, combine strawberries, lemon peel, and 1 tablespoon sugar. Let stand. Can be refrigerated, covered, up to overnight.

7. In medium bowl, stir yogurt, sour cream, vanilla, and remaining 3 tablespoons sugar. Can be refrigerated, covered, up to overnight.

8. Split open shortcakes. Divide strawberries and filling among shortcakes. Serve immediately.

Each serving: About 255 calories, 8g protein, 43g carbohydrate, 6g total fat (2g saturated), 3g fiber, 9mg cholesterol, 335mg sodium

Banana Shortcakes

Ripe bananas star in this perfect winter-season choice. Since the bananas brown in a rich rum-butterscotch sauce (think bananas Foster minus the flambé), we cut the cake's sweetness with two tangy tweaks—buttermilk in the batter and sour cream in the topping. You could substitute one medium pineapple, cubed, for the bananas.

Active time: 25 minutes
Bake time: 12 minutes
Makes: 8 servings

SHORTCAKES

1/2 cup old-fashioned oats, uncooked
1/3 cup pecans, toasted and cooled (see page xxiii)
1 1/2 cups all-purpose flour
1/4 cup packed dark brown sugar
2 teaspoons baking powder
1/2 teaspoon salt
1/4 teaspoon baking soda
3/4 cup low-fat buttermilk
3 tablespoons canola oil
1 large egg

CREAM FILLING

1/2 cup cold heavy cream
1/2 cup reduced-fat sour cream
1 tablespoon confectioners' sugar

BANANA FILLING

2 tablespoons butter or margarine
6 firm, ripe bananas, each cut lengthwise in half, then crosswise into 1-inch chunks
1/3 cup packed brown sugar
2 tablespoons dark rum

1. Prepare shortcakes: Preheat oven to 425°F. Spray large cookie sheet with nonstick cooking spray. In food processor with knife blade attached, pulse oats and pecans until finely ground.

2. In large bowl, with wire whisk, combine oat mixture, flour, brown sugar, baking powder, salt, and baking soda. Break up any lumps of brown sugar with fingers.

3. In small bowl, with wire whisk, mix buttermilk, oil, and egg until blended. Add buttermilk mixture to flour mixture and stir just until blended.

4. Spoon by 1/3 cups onto prepared cookie sheet, making 8 mounds placed 3 inches apart. Bake 12 minutes or until firm when pressed. Transfer shortcakes to wire rack.

5. Prepare cream filling: In medium bowl, with mixer on high speed, beat heavy cream, sour cream, and confectioners' sugar until thickened. Cover and refrigerate until ready to serve. Makes 1¼ cups.

6. Prepare bananas: In 12-inch skillet, melt butter over medium-high heat. Add bananas; cook 1 minute or until bananas begin to brown, stirring gently. Remove skillet from heat; stir in brown sugar and rum. Return skillet to heat; cook 1 minute or until mixture begins to simmer.

7. To serve, split shortcakes. Place 1 bottom half on each dessert plate. Top with bananas and cream; replace shortcake tops. Serve immediately.

Each serving: about 445 calories, 7g protein, 62g carbohydrate, 20g total fat (7g saturated), 4g fiber, 54mg cholesterol, 370mg sodium

BAKED PUDDINGS

Bread pudding, Indian pudding, and sticky toffee pudding are just a few of the dense, satisfying recipes we share here. These long-standing favorites are all easy to make and perfect do-ahead family or company desserts. Puddings are wonderful served warm, especially when topped with a dollop of whipped cream or a scoop of ice cream.

Bread-and-Butter Pudding

This old-fashioned favorite is simply flavored with cinnamon and vanilla.

Active time: 10 minutes plus standing
Bake time: 50 minutes
Makes: 8 servings

³/₄ teaspoon ground cinnamon
8 tablespoons sugar
4 tablespoons butter or margarine, softened
12 slices firm white bread
3 cups milk
1¹/₂ teaspoons vanilla extract
4 large eggs
Whipped cream (optional)

1. Preheat oven to 325°F. Grease 8-inch-square baking dish. In cup, combine cinnamon and 1 tablespoon sugar. Spread butter on bread slices. Arrange 4 bread slices in single layer in prepared dish, overlapping slightly if necessary; sprinkle lightly with cinnamon sugar. Repeat to make two more layers.

2. In medium bowl, with wire whisk or fork, beat milk, remaining 7 tablespoons sugar, vanilla, and eggs until well combined. Pour egg mixture over bread slices. Let stand 20 minutes, occasionally pressing bread into egg mixture.

3. Bake 50 to 60 minutes, until knife inserted in center of pudding comes out clean. Cool on wire rack 15 minutes. Serve pudding warm, or cover and refrigerate to serve cold later. Top with whipped cream if desired.

Each serving: about 315 calories, 10g protein, 38g carbohydrate, 13g total fat (7g saturated), 1g fiber, 135mg cholesterol, 365mg sodium

BREAD-AND-BUTTER PUDDING WITH DRIED FRUIT Chop *³/₄ cup mixed dried fruit* (such as apricots, prunes, and pears). Follow instructions for bread pudding above, but in step 1, when making first layer, sprinkle half of dried fruit on top of cinnamon sugar. Repeat for second bread layer. Top with remaining bread and cinnamon sugar. Bake as directed.

Each serving: about 350 calories, 10g protein, 48g carbohydrate, 13g total fat (7g saturated), 2g fiber, 135mg cholesterol, 365mg sodium

BREAD-AND-BUTTER PUDDING WITH BERRIES In bowl, combine *1 cup hulled and sliced strawberries, ½ cup blueberries, ½ cup raspberries,* and *1 tablespoon sugar.* Follow instructions for bread pudding above, but in step 1, when making first layer, sprinkle half of berry mixture on top of cinnamon sugar. Repeat for second bread layer. Top with remaining bread and cinnamon sugar. Bake as directed.

Each serving: about 335 calories, 10g protein, 43g carbohydrate, 13g total fat (7g saturated), 2g fiber, 135mg cholesterol, 365mg sodium

Spiced Chocolate Bread Pudding

Adding a little cinnamon and cayenne to custardy chocolate bread pudding gives this dessert a pleasantly surprising kick.

Active time: 30 minutes plus chilling
Bake time: 45 minutes
Makes: 16 servings

1 loaf (12 ounces) egg bread, such as challah
3 cups whole milk
1¼ cups sugar
½ teaspoon ground cinnamon
Pinch cayenne (ground red) pepper
Pinch salt
½ cup heavy cream
4 ounces unsweetened chocolate, chopped
7 large eggs
1 cup (6 ounces) semisweet chocolate chips or chunks
Vanilla ice cream or dulce de leche for serving (optional)

1. Grease shallow 3-quart baking dish.

2. Cut bread into ¾-inch-thick slices. Toast lightly until golden brown. Cool completely, then cut each slice in half diagonally.

3. In 3-quart saucepan, whisk milk, sugar, cinnamon, cayenne, salt, and cream to blend. Heat over medium until bubbles form around edge. Add unsweetened chocolate and whisk until melted. In large bowl, whisk eggs until blended. Continue whisking while adding hot chocolate mixture in slow, steady stream.

4. In prepared dish, decoratively arrange slices of toast in overlapping layers to cover dish evenly. Scatter chocolate chips over slices of toast, then pour chocolate mixture evenly over all. If toast slices are not coated with chocolate mixture, gently press down to coat with mixture. Cover with plastic wrap. Refrigerate at least 1 hour or up to 1 day.

5. Preheat oven to 350°F. Uncover bread pudding and bake 45 minutes to 1 hour or until knife inserted in center comes out clean. Let cool on wire rack at least 15 minutes.

6. Cut bread pudding into squares. Serve with ice cream or drizzle with dulce de leche if desired.

Each serving: about 295 calories, 8g protein, 38g carbohydrate, 15g total fat (8g saturated), 2g fiber, 107mg cholesterol, 155mg sodium

Sticky Toffee Pudding

In England, any sort of dessert is "pudding" (as in "what's for pudding?"). This is a very British pudding indeed, with a gooey butterscotch topping.

Active time: 20 minutes plus standing
Bake time: 30 minutes
Makes: 12 servings

1 cup chopped pitted dates
1 teaspoon baking soda
1¹/2 cups boiling water
10 tablespoons butter or margarine, softened
1 cup granulated sugar
1 large egg
1 teaspoon vanilla extract
1 teaspoon baking powder
2 cups all-purpose flour
1 cup packed brown sugar
¹/4 cup heavy cream

1. Preheat oven to 350°F. Grease 13" by 9" broiler-safe baking pan. In medium bowl, combine dates, baking soda, and boiling water; let stand 15 minutes.

2. In large bowl, with mixer on medium speed, beat 6 tablespoons butter until creamy. Beat in granulated sugar. Add egg and vanilla; beat until blended. Reduce speed to low and add baking powder and flour, beating to combine. Add date mixture and beat until evenly combined (batter will be very thin).

3. Pour batter into prepared pan. Bake 30 minutes, or until pudding is golden and toothpick inserted in center of pudding comes out clean.

4. Meanwhile, in 2-quart saucepan, heat brown sugar, cream, and remaining 4 tablespoons butter to boiling over medium heat; boil 1 minute.

5. Position rack at closest position to broiler and preheat broiler. Spread brown-sugar mixture evenly over top of hot pudding and broil until bubbly, about 30 seconds. Cool in pan on wire rack 15 minutes. Serve warm.

Each serving: about 360 calories, 3g protein, 62g carbohydrate, 12g total fat (7g saturated), 1g fiber, 50mg cholesterol, 260mg sodium

New Orleans Bread Pudding

Bourbon, French bread, and pecan-praline sauce are the key Louisianan features in this slightly tipsy pudding.

Active time: 20 minutes plus standing and cooling
Bake time: 45 minutes
Makes: 8 servings

¹/2 cup dark seedless raisins
2 tablespoons bourbon
¹/3 cup granulated sugar
¹/8 teaspoon ground nutmeg
¹/8 teaspoon ground cinnamon
3 large eggs
2 teaspoons vanilla extract
1 pint half-and-half or light cream
3 cups day-old French bread cubes (¹/2 inch)
¹/4 cup packed dark brown sugar
2 tablespoons butter or margarine
1 tablespoon corn syrup
¹/3 cup pecans, toasted (see page xxiii) and chopped

1. In small bowl, combine raisins and bourbon; let stand 15 minutes. Meanwhile, grease 8-inch-square glass or ceramic baking dish.

2. In large bowl, stir together granulated sugar, nutmeg, and cinnamon until blended. Whisk in eggs and vanilla until combined. Set aside 1 tablespoon half-and-half. Add remaining half-and-half to egg mixture and whisk until well blended. Stir in bread cubes. Let stand 15 minutes, stirring occasionally. Stir in raisin mixture.

3. Preheat oven to 325°F. Pour bread mixture into prepared dish. Bake 45 to 50 minutes, until knife inserted near center of pudding comes out clean. Cool on wire rack 30 minutes.

4. In 1-quart saucepan, heat reserved 1 tablespoon half-and-half, brown sugar, butter, and corn syrup to boiling over medium heat. Reduce heat and simmer 2 minutes, stirring occasionally. Remove saucepan from heat and stir in pecans. Serve pudding drizzled with praline sauce.

Each serving: about 300 calories, 6g protein, 36g carbohydrate, 16g total fat (7g saturated), 1g fiber, 110mg cholesterol, 175mg sodium

STICKY TOFFEE PUDDING

Persimmon-Date Pudding

Puddings like this go way back in the South and the Midwest, where persimmons grow in the wild. Fortunately for the rest of us, Asian persimmons are now widely available. The fruit must be fully ripe—soft to the point of mushiness—or the flavor will not be sweet.

Active time: 25 minutes
Bake time: 50 minutes
Makes: 8 servings

1 cup all-purpose flour
1 cup sugar
2 teaspoons baking soda
1½ teaspoons baking powder
¼ teaspoon ground cinnamon
⅛ teaspoon ground ginger
Pinch ground cloves
1 cup walnuts, coarsely chopped (4 ounces)
½ cup chopped pitted dates
½ cup dark seedless raisins
½ teaspoon freshly grated orange peel
1 cup persimmon pulp, from 1 to 2 large, ripe hachiya
    persimmons
½ cup milk
2 tablespoons butter or margarine, melted
1 teaspoon vanilla extract
Hard Sauce (page 350) or whipped cream

1. Preheat oven to 325°F. Grease 8-inch square glass or ceramic baking dish.

2. In large bowl, stir together flour, sugar, baking soda, baking powder, cinnamon, ginger, and cloves. Stir in walnuts, dates, raisins, and orange peel. Stir in persimmon pulp, milk, melted butter, and vanilla until well combined. Spoon batter evenly into prepared dish.

3. Bake 50 to 60 minutes, until toothpick inserted in center of pudding comes out clean. Serve warm with hard sauce or whipped cream.

Each serving: about 375 calories, 5g protein, 63g carbohydrate, 14g total fat (3g saturated), 2g fiber, 10mg cholesterol, 445mg sodium

Nantucket Indian Pudding

Native Americans introduced European settlers to cornmeal, which the newcomers subsequently referred to as "Indian meal." That's how this New England specialty got its name.

Active time: 30 minutes
Bake time: 2 hours
Makes: 8 servings

⅔ cups cornmeal
4 cups milk
½ cup light (mild) molasses
4 tablespoons butter or margarine, cut up
¼ cup sugar
1 teaspoon ground ginger
1 teaspoon ground cinnamon
½ teaspoon salt
¼ teaspoon ground nutmeg
Whipped cream or vanilla ice cream (optional)

1. Preheat oven to 350°F. Heat kettle of *water* to boiling; remove from heat. Grease shallow 1½-quart glass or ceramic baking dish.

2. In small bowl, combine cornmeal and 1 cup milk. In 4-quart saucepan, heat remaining 3 cups milk to boiling over high heat. Stir in cornmeal mixture; heat to boiling. Reduce heat and simmer, stirring often to prevent lumps, 20 minutes (mixture will be very thick). Remove saucepan from heat; stir in molasses, butter, sugar, ginger, cinnamon, salt, and nutmeg until well combined.

3. Spread batter evenly into prepared dish. Cover with foil and place dish in 13" by 9" roasting pan; place on oven rack. Carefully pour water from kettle into roasting pan to come halfway up sides of baking dish. Bake 1 hour. Remove foil and bake pudding 1 hour longer, or until lightly browned and just set.

4. Carefully remove baking dish from water and cool on wire rack 30 minutes. Serve pudding warm with whipped cream or vanilla ice cream, if desired.

Each serving: about 255 calories, 5g protein, 35g carbohydrate, 11g total fat (6g saturated), 1g fiber, 33mg cholesterol, 270mg sodium

Meyer Lemon Pudding Cakes

Half custard, half cake, these sweet-tart desserts are chiffon light. If you can't locate thin-skinned Meyer lemons, regular lemons will do.

Active time: 25 minutes
Bake time: 30 minutes
Makes: 8 cakes

⅓ cup plus ¼ cup sugar, plus additional for ramekins
¼ cup all-purpose flour
¼ teaspoon salt
2 Meyer lemons
3 large eggs, separated
2 tablespoons butter or margarine, melted and cooled
1 cup whole milk
1 pint raspberries for garnish
Fresh mint sprigs for garnish

1. Preheat oven to 350°F. Grease eight 4- to 5-ounce ramekins; sprinkle with sugar to coat bottoms and sides. Shake out any excess. Heat kettle of *water* to boiling; remove from heat.

2. On sheet of waxed paper, with fork, combine flour, ⅓ cup sugar, and salt. From lemons, grate 1½ tablespoons peel and squeeze ½ cup juice. In large bowl, with wire whisk, beat egg yolks and lemon peel and juice. Whisk in butter and milk. Gradually whisk in flour mixture.

3. In another large bowl, with mixer on medium speed, beat egg whites until foamy. Gradually beat in remaining ¼ cup sugar until soft peaks form when beaters are lifted, 2 to 3 minutes.

4. Add one-third beaten whites to yolk mixture and, with rubber spatula, stir gently until incorporated. Gently fold in remaining whites until just incorporated. With ladle, divide batter among prepared ramekins.

5. Arrange ramekins 1 inch apart in large (17" by 13") roasting pan and place pan on oven rack. Fill pan with enough water from kettle to come halfway up sides of ramekins. Bake 30 to 35 minutes or until cakes are golden brown and tops have risen ½ inch above rims.

6. Cool cakes in pan on wire rack 5 minutes. With sturdy metal spatula, carefully remove ramekins from pan of water and transfer to wire rack to cool 15 minutes longer.

7. Run thin knife around edge of each ramekin. Place small serving plate on top of ramekin and invert plate and ramekin together to unmold puddings. Garnish each with raspberries and mint sprig; serve warm.

Each serving: about 170 calories, 4g protein, 25g carbohydrate, 6g total fat (3g saturated), 3g fiber, 92mg cholesterol, 145mg sodium

Chocolate Bread Pudding

For this decadent pudding, cubes of bread are steeped in chocolate custard and then layered with ribbons of melted semisweet chocolate.

Active time: 25 minutes
Bake time: 50 minutes
Makes: 8 servings

8 slices stale firm white bread
3 tablespoons plus 1/3 cup sugar
8 squares (8 ounces) semisweet chocolate, melted
3 cups milk
3 large eggs
1 1/2 teaspoons vanilla extract

1. Grease 8-inch square baking dish. Cut bread into 1-inch squares. Scatter one-third of bread in prepared dish in single layer; sprinkle with 1 tablespoon sugar and drizzle with 2 tablespoons melted chocolate. Repeat to make second layer. Top with remaining bread.

2. In 2-quart saucepan, heat milk to boiling over medium-high heat. Meanwhile, in medium bowl, with wire whisk, combine eggs and 1/3 cup sugar. While whisking, slowly pour hot milk into egg mixture. Add remaining melted chocolate and vanilla; stir to combine.

3. Pour egg mixture over bread. Refrigerate, gently stirring mixture occasionally, 3 hours, or until bread is soaked with chocolate mixture.

4. Preheat oven to 325°F. Heat kettle of *water* to boiling; remove from heat.

5. Sprinkle pudding with remaining 1 tablespoon sugar. Place dish in 13" by 9" roasting pan; place on oven rack. Carefully pour water from kettle into roasting pan to come halfway up sides of dish. Bake 50 minutes, or until knife inserted in center of pudding comes out dean. Transfer dish from roasting pan to wire rack to cool 15 minutes. Serve pudding warm, or cover and refrigerate to serve cold later.

Each serving: about 355 calories, 9g protein, 49g carbohydrate, 15g total fat (8g saturated), 2g fiber, 93mg cholesterol, 225mg sodium

Brownie Pudding Cake

This is one of those culinary miracles: You fill a pan with batter, pour what seems like a lot of boiling water over it, and it comes out of the oven—quite astonishingly—as a light cake with a warm, custardy layer of pudding underneath.

Active time: 20 minutes
Bake time: 30 minutes
Makes: 8 servings

2 teaspoons instant coffee granules or powder
2 tablespoons plus 1 3/4 cups boiling water
1 cup all-purpose flour
1/2 cup granulated sugar
2 teaspoons baking powder
1/4 teaspoon salt
3/4 cup unsweetened cocoa
1/2 cup milk
4 tablespoons butter or margarine, melted
1 teaspoon vanilla extract
1/2 cup packed light brown sugar
Whipped cream or vanilla ice cream (optional)

1. Preheat oven to 350°F. In cup, dissolve instant coffee in 2 tablespoons boiling water.

2. In medium bowl, stir together flour, granulated sugar, baking powder, salt, and 1/2 cup cocoa. In 2-cup measuring cup, combine milk, melted butter, vanilla, and coffee mixture. With spoon, stir milk mixture into flour mixture until just blended. Pour batter into ungreased 8-inch square glass or ceramic baking dish.

3. In small bowl, combine brown sugar and remaining 1/4 cup cocoa; sprinkle over batter. Carefully pour remaining 1 3/4 cups boiling water over batter; do not stir.

4. Bake 30 minutes. Cool on wire rack 10 minutes. Serve immediately or pudding will be absorbed by cake. Serve with whipped cream or ice cream if desired.

Each serving: about 240 calories, 4g protein, 43g carbohydrate, 7g total fat (5g saturated), 3g fiber, 18mg cholesterol, 265mg sodium

CUSTARD DESSERTS

These smooth and irresistibly creamy desserts make elegant dinner-party fare. All require chilling time, making them ideal make-ahead desserts. Egg-rich mixtures must be protected from direct heat, so bake these delicate custards in a bain-marie, or hot-water bath. For tips, see page 217.

Crème Brûlée

A thin covering of brown sugar is scattered over the surface of the cooled custard, and then it is broiled in the ramekins. A shatteringly crisp, totally irresistible top layer results.

Active time: 20 minutes plus chilling

Bake time: 35 minutes

Makes: 10 servings

1/2 vanilla bean (cut lengthwise), or 2 teaspoons vanilla extract

1 1/2 cups heavy cream

1 1/2 cups half-and-half or light cream

8 large egg yolks

2/3 cup granulated sugar

1/3 to 1/2 cup packed brown sugar

1. Preheat oven to 325°F. Heat kettle of *water* to boiling; remove from heat.

2. With knife, scrape seeds from vanilla bean into 3-quart saucepan. Add vanilla bean pod, cream, and half-and-half and cook over medium heat until tiny bubbles form around edge of pan. Remove cream mixture from heat. With slotted spoon, remove vanilla bean pod from saucepan.

3. Meanwhile, in large bowl, with wire whisk or fork, mix egg yolks with granulated sugar until blended. Slowly stir in warm cream mixture until well combined. Pour mixture into ten 4- to 5-ounce broiler-safe ramekins or custard cups, or one 2½-quart shallow broiler-safe casserole.

4. Place ramekins or casserole in 17" by 11½" roasting pan; place on oven rack. Carefully pour water from kettle into roasting pan to come halfway up sides of ramekins or casserole (see "Baking in a Bain-Marie," page 217.) Bake 35 to 40 minutes, or just until set (mixture will still be slightly soft in center). Remove ramekins or casserole from roasting pan; cool to room temperature on wire rack. Cover and refrigerate at least 2 hours, until well chilled.

5. Up to 4 hours before serving, set oven rack in closest position to broiler and preheat broiler. Place brown sugar in small sieve; with spoon, press sugar through sieve to cover top of chilled custard.

6. Place ramekins or casserole in jelly-roll pan for easier handling. Broil custard 3 to 4 minutes, just until sugar melts and forms a shiny, crisp crust. Refrigerate until ready to serve. Serve within 4 hours, or brown sugar topping will lose its crispness.

Each serving: about 305 calories, 4g protein, 25g carbohydrate, 21g total fat (12g saturated), 0g fiber, 232mg cholesterol, 40mg sodium

Simple Vanilla Crème Brûlée

For ease, in this variation on the classic, we prepare the custard in the microwave rather than on the stovetop.

Active time: 12 minutes plus chilling
Bake time: 30 minutes
Makes: 6 servings

1 cup light cream or half-and-half
1 cup heavy cream
1½ teaspoons vanilla extract
5 large egg yolks
⅓ cup granulated sugar
2 tablespoons packed dark brown sugar

1. Preheat oven to 325°F. Heat kettle of *water* to boiling; remove from heat.

2. In microwave-safe 2-cup liquid measuring cup, heat both creams in microwave on Medium (50% power) 5 minutes. Stir in vanilla.

3. Meanwhile, in 4-cup liquid measuring cup, whisk egg yolks and granulated sugar until well blended. Slowly whisk in warm cream until combined; with spoon, skim off foam.

4. Place 6 broiler-safe 4-ounce ramekins or custard cups in 13" by 9" metal baking pan. Pour cream mixture into ramekins, filling almost to tops. Place pan on oven rack and carefully pour in water from kettle to come halfway up sides of cups (see "Baking in a Bain-Marie," opposite.) Bake custards 30 minutes or until custard is just set but center still jiggles slightly. Remove ramekins from water and place on wire rack to cool. Cover and refrigerate until custards are well chilled, at least 4 hours or overnight.

5. Up to 1 hour before serving, position rack as close as possible to heat source and preheat broiler. Place brown sugar in coarse sieve; with spoon, press through sieve to evenly cover tops of chilled custards. Place ramekins in jelly-roll pan for easier handling. Broil custards 2 to 3 minutes or just until brown sugar melts. Immediately refrigerate for 1 hour to cool custards and allow sugar to form crust.

Each serving: about 365 calories, 4g protein, 18g carbohydrate, 31g total fat (18g saturated), 0g fiber, 276mg cholesterol, 35mg sodium

Crème Caramel

To get that luscious caramel on top of the custard, you'll first pour the hot caramel into the custard dishes; while it sets and firms up, prepare the custard and pour it on top. Be sure the custards chill for at least 4 hours so the caramel has time to soften and become a sauce. When you're ready to serve, turn out the custards onto desserts plates—the rich caramel will cascade over the tops and down the sides.

Active time: 15 minutes plus chilling
Bake time: 50 minutes
Makes: 6 servings

¼ cup plus ⅓ cup sugar
4 large eggs
2 cups milk
1½ teaspoons vanilla extract
¼ teaspoon salt

1. Preheat oven 325°F. Heat kettle of *water* to boiling; remove from heat.

2. In small saucepan, heat ¼ cup sugar over medium heat, swirling pan occasionally, until sugar is melted and amber in color. Immediately pour into six 6-ounce custard cups.

3. In large bowl, with wire whisk or fork, mix eggs and remaining ⅓ cup sugar until well blended. Whisk in milk, vanilla, and salt until well combined. Pour mixture into prepared custard cups. Place custard cups in 13" by 9" roasting pan; place on oven rack. Carefully pour water from kettle into pan to come halfway up sides of cups (see "Baking in a Bain-Marie," right).

Bake 50 to 55 minutes, until knife inserted in center of custard comes out clean. Transfer cups to wire rack to cool. Cover and refrigerate at least 4 hours or overnight, until chilled.

4. To unmold, run small metal spatula around side of each custard cup; invert cup onto dessert plate, allowing caramel syrup to drip from cup onto custard.

Each serving: about 180 calories, 7g protein, 24g carbohydrate, 6g total fat (3g saturated), 0g fiber, 153mg cholesterol, 175mg sodium

TIP This is sometimes called *crème renversée* because it's "reversed" or inverted onto plates for serving.

BAKING IN A BAIN-MARIE

A bain-marie (hot-water bath) is the best way to ensure that delicate custards cook evenly.

Set the dish containing the custard in a roasting pan, then pull the oven rack out and place the pan on it. Carefully pour hot (not boiling) water from a teakettle into the pan until the water reaches half the height of the cups. Push the rack carefully back into the oven and bake. (This method can be used for cheesecakes and other egg-based dishes too.)

Mocha Pots de Crème

*Rich and spiked with the intense flavor of espresso,
these little chocolate pots are a creamy delight.
Traditionally, pôts de crème are made in graceful
little porcelain cups; some even have lids like tiny
teapots. Here we've used ramekins, but glass custard
cups would work as well.*

Active time: 30 minutes plus chilling
Bake time: 25 minutes
Makes: 8 servings

POTS DE CRÈME

4 squares (4 ounces) bittersweet chocolate,
   finely chopped
3 large egg yolks
2 large eggs
1/4 cup packed dark brown sugar
Pinch salt
1 3/4 cups whole milk
1/2 cup heavy cream
1/4 cup brewed espresso
1 teaspoon vanilla extract

TOPPING

1/4 teaspoon instant espresso powder
1 teaspoon vanilla extract
1/2 cup heavy cream
1 tablespoon granulated sugar

1. Preheat oven to 325°F. Heat kettle of *water* to boiling; remove from heat.

2. To make pots de crème: Place chocolate in small heatproof bowl. In large bowl, whisk egg yolks, whole eggs, brown sugar, and salt until blended. In 3-quart saucepan, heat milk and cream over medium until bubbling. Pour enough milk mixture over chocolate to cover; let stand. Slowly whisk remaining hot milk mixture into egg mixture. Gently whisk chocolate mixture until smooth; pour into milk-egg mixture, while whisking, until smooth. Whisk in brewed espresso and vanilla. Skim off and discard any bubbles or foam on surface.

3. Place eight 4-ounce ramekins in roasting pan and fill with equal amounts custard mixture. Place pan on oven rack.

4. Pour enough water from kettle into roasting pan to come halfway up sides of ramekins. Cover pan loosely with foil. Bake custards 25 to 30 minutes, until knife inserted halfway between edge and center of custard comes out clean.

5. Remove foil and set pan on wire rack until ramekins are cool enough to touch; transfer ramekins to wire rack to cool completely. Cover with plastic wrap; refrigerate 3 hours, or up to 3 days.

6. When ready to serve, in small bowl, stir espresso powder into vanilla until dissolved. In large bowl, beat cream until thickened. Add granulated sugar and beat until soft peaks form. Fold in vanilla mixture. Dollop on top of custards and serve.

Each serving: about 290 calories, 6g protein, 17g carbohydrate, 22g total fat (13g saturated), 1g fiber, 162mg cholesterol, 80mg sodium

Pumpkin Crème Caramel

Pumpkin purists will welcome this sweet, creamy alternative to pumpkin pie at the holiday table.

Active time: 15 minutes plus chilling
Bake time: 45 minutes
Makes: 12 servings

¼ cup water
1¼ cups sugar
1 can (14 ounces) coconut milk (not cream of coconut), well shaken
¾ cup heavy cream
1 cup solid-pack pumpkin
6 large eggs
2 teaspoons vanilla extract
⅛ teaspoon salt
2 tablespoons dark or coconut rum (optional)
Freshly whipped cream for serving
Toasted, shredded coconut for garnish (see page xxii)
Freshly grated nutmeg for garnish

1. Preheat oven to 350°F. Heat kettle of *water* to boiling; remove from heat.

2. In 1-quart saucepan, heat water and ¾ cup sugar to boiling over medium-high, stirring to dissolve sugar. Continue to cook, without stirring, 5 to 9 minutes or until caramel is just amber in color. Pour caramel into 9-inch-round, 2-inch-deep ceramic dish, swirling to evenly coat bottom of dish.

3. In 2-quart saucepan, heat coconut milk, cream, and remaining ½ cup sugar just to boiling over medium-high, stirring to dissolve sugar.

4. Meanwhile, in large bowl, with wire whisk, mix pumpkin, eggs, vanilla, salt, and rum, if using, until blended.

5. Gradually whisk hot milk mixture into pumpkin mixture until blended. Pour pumpkin mixture through sieve into 8-cup glass measuring cup, then into caramel-coated dish. Place dish in roasting pan; set on oven rack. Pour water from kettle into roasting pan to come three-quarters up side of custard dish (see "Baking in a Bain-Marie," page 217.) Bake 45 to 55 minutes or until knife comes out clean when inserted 1 inch from edge of custard (center will still jiggle slightly).

6. Carefully remove custard from water. Allow crème caramel to cool 1 hour in dish on wire rack. Cover and refrigerate crème caramel overnight or up to 2 days. To unmold, run small spatula around side of pan; invert crème caramel onto serving plate, allowing caramel syrup to drip down over surface. Finish each serving with dollop of whipped cream, and sprinkle with coconut and nutmeg.

Each serving: about 240 calories, 5g protein, 24g carbohydrate, 15g total fat (11g saturated), 1g fiber, 126mg cholesterol, 70mg sodium

SOUFFLÉS

These high-rise creations must be served as soon as they come out of the oven, or they'll deflate. Plan to have your guests (or lucky family) sitting at the table when the timer goes off. If you put a sweet soufflé in the oven when you serve the entrée, your dessert should be ready at just the right moment for serving.

Classic Cheese Soufflé

The flavor of this classic soufflé can be varied by using different cheeses. Well-aged Cheddar adds a bold, sharp note, while nutty-sweet Gruyère is more subtle (and more traditionally French). Stirring some of the hot cheese sauce into the egg yolks before adding the slightly warmed yolks to the sauce helps keep the eggs from curdling.

Active time: 25 minutes
Bake time: 55 minutes
Makes: 6 main-dish servings

4 tablespoons butter or margarine
¼ cup all-purpose flour
¼ teaspoon salt
⅛ teaspoon cayenne (ground red) pepper
1½ cups milk
8 ounces sharp Cheddar cheese, shredded (2 cups)
5 large eggs, separated
2 tablespoons plain dried bread crumbs or freshly
    grated Parmesan cheese
1 large egg white

1. In 3-quart saucepan, melt butter over low heat. Stir in flour, salt, and cayenne until blended; cook, stirring, 1 minute. Gradually stir in milk; cook, stirring constantly, until mixture boils and thickens. Stir in Cheddar; cook, stirring, just until cheese melts. Remove saucepan from heat.

2. In small bowl, with wire whisk or fork, beat egg yolks slightly; stir in small amount hot cheese sauce. Gradually pour egg-yolk mixture into cheese sauce, stirring rapidly to prevent curdling. Cool slightly.

3. Preheat oven to 325°F. Grease 2-quart soufflé dish; sprinkle with bread crumbs or Parmesan.

4. In large bowl, with mixer on high speed, beat all egg whites until stiff peaks form when beaters are lifted. With rubber spatula, gently fold one-third of whites into cheese mixture. Fold cheese mixture gently back into remaining whites.

5. Pour mixture into prepared soufflé dish. With back of spoon, about 1 inch from edge of dish, make 1-inch-deep indentation to form circle in soufflé mixture. Bake 55 to 60 minutes, until knife inserted under "top hat" comes out clean. Serve immediately.

Each serving: about 355 calories, 18g protein, 9g carbohydrate, 27g total fat (15g saturated), 0g fiber, 246mg cholesterol, 520mg sodium

GRUYÈRE-SPINACH SOUFFLÉ Prepare cheese soufflé as described opposite, but substitute *pinch ground nutmeg* for cayenne and *8 ounces shredded Gruyère cheese (2 cups)*, for Cheddar. Stir *1 package (10 ounces) frozen chopped spinach*, thawed and squeezed dry, into cheese mixture before folding in egg whites. Bake as directed.

Each serving: about 370 calories, 21g protein, 11g carbohydrate, 27g total fat (15g saturated), 1g fiber, 248mg cholesterol, 445mg sodium

Tomato Soufflé

This rosy soufflé is really a summer recipe—don't bother making it unless fresh flavorful, vine-ripened tomatoes are available. It is always impressive, whether served as the main dish for a light supper or as a side dish with simply cooked chicken or fish.

Active time: 45 minutes
Bake time: 45 minutes
Makes: 8 side-dish or 4 main-dish servings

1 tablespoon vegetable oil
1 onion, chopped
2 pounds ripe tomatoes, peeled and finely chopped, juices reserved (see Tip)
1/2 teaspoon sugar
1/4 teaspoon ground black pepper
1 1/4 teaspoons salt
4 tablespoons butter or margarine
1/4 cup all-purpose flour
1 1/4 cups milk
1 tablespoon plain dried bread crumbs
6 large eggs, separated
2 tablespoons freshly grated Parmesan cheese

1. In 12-inch skillet, heat oil over medium heat. Add onion and cook, stirring, 10 minutes, or until tender. Add tomatoes with their juice, sugar, pepper, and 1/2 teaspoon salt. Increase heat to high and cook, stirring, 15 minutes, or until all juices have evaporated.

2. Meanwhile, in 2-quart saucepan, melt butter over low heat. Stir in flour and remaining 3/4 teaspoon salt until blended; cook, stirring, 1 minute. Gradually stir in milk and cook, stirring constantly, until mixture boils and thickens. Remove saucepan from heat, stir in tomato mixture until blended.

3. Preheat oven to 325°F. Grease 2-quart soufflé dish, then sprinkle evenly with bread crumbs.

4. In large bowl, with wire whisk or fork, beat egg yolks slightly; stir in small amount hot tomato mixture. Gradually pour egg-yolk mixture into tomato mixture, stirring rapidly to prevent curdling. Pour mixture back into bowl.

5. In clean large bowl, with mixer on high speed, beat egg whites until stiff peaks form when beaters are lifted. With rubber spatula, gently fold beaten egg whites, one-third at a time, into tomato mixture just until blended.

6. Pour mixture into prepared soufflé dish. Sprinkle with Parmesan. With back of spoon, about 1 inch from edge of dish, make 1-inch-deep indentation to form circle in soufflé mixture. Bake 45 minutes, or until soufflé is puffy and brown and knife inserted under "top hat" comes out clean. Serve immediately.

Each side-dish serving: about 205 calories, 8g protein, 13g carbohydrate, 14g total fat, (6g saturated), 2g fiber, 181mg cholesterol, 530 mg sodium

TIP To peel tomatoes, bring pot of water to a boil. With paring knife, cut small X in base of each tomato. Drop tomatoes into boiling water and let boil for about 30 seconds, then remove with slotted spoon to colander to drain. When tomatoes are cool enough to handle, peels should lift off with ease. Chop as instructed.

Cheddar Grits Soufflé

This savory soufflé turns the Southern diner staple—cheese and grits—into an elegant side that's perfect for brunch or a holiday meal.

Active time: 30 minutes plus cooling
Bake time: 45 minutes
Makes: 8 side-dish servings

6½ ounces extra-sharp Cheddar cheese,
    shredded (2½ cups)
2 cups water
2 tablespoons butter or margarine
½ teaspoon salt
2½ cups whole milk
1 cup quick-cooking grits
¼ teaspoon freshly grated nutmeg
⅛ teaspoon cayenne (ground red) pepper
3 large eggs, separated
3 large egg whites

1. Preheat oven to 375°F. Grease 3-quart soufflé dish and sprinkle 2 tablespoons shredded Cheddar onto sides.

2. In 4-quart saucepan, heat water, butter, salt, and 1½ cups milk to boiling over medium-high. Whisk in grits. Cover, reduce heat to low, and simmer 5 minutes or until thick. Whisk well, then whisk in nutmeg, cayenne, remaining 1 cup milk, and remaining Cheddar. Whisk in egg yolks; transfer to bowl and cool to room temperature.

3. In large bowl, with mixer on medium-high speed, beat all egg whites until stiff peaks form. Add one-third whites to grits mixture; beat until blended. Fold in remaining whites. Transfer to soufflé dish.

4. Bake 45 to 50 minutes or until puffed and golden brown on top and knife inserted into center comes out clean.

Each serving: about 280 calories, 13g protein, 20g carbohydrate, 17g total fat (8g saturated), 1g fiber, 111mg cholesterol, 415mg sodium

Ham and Pepper Jack Soufflé

Ham and pepper Jack cheese partner up in this savory soufflé. Add a mixed green salad and brunch is served.

Active time: 20 minutes
Bake time: 50 minutes
Makes: 6 main-dish servings

4 tablespoons butter or margarine
¼ cup all-purpose flour
1½ cups reduced-fat milk (2%), warmed
6 ounces pepper Jack cheese, shredded (1½ cups)
4 large eggs, separated
3 ounces smoked ham, chopped
1 can (4½ ounces) chopped mild green chiles, drained
1 large egg white

1. Preheat oven to 325°F. Grease 2-quart soufflé dish.

2. In heavy 2-quart saucepan, melt butter over low heat. Add flour and cook 1 minute, stirring. With wire whisk, gradually mix in milk. Cook over medium heat until sauce thickens and boils, stirring constantly. Reduce heat to low and simmer 3 minutes, stirring frequently. Stir in pepper Jack and cook just until cheese melts and sauce is smooth, stirring. Remove saucepan from heat.

3. In medium bowl, with whisk, lightly beat egg yolks; gradually whisk in hot cheese sauce. Stir in ham and green chiles.

4. In large bowl, with mixer on high speed, beat all egg whites until stiff peaks form when beaters are lifted. With rubber spatula, gently fold one-third of beaten egg whites into cheese mixture. Fold in remaining whites just until blended.

5. Pour mixture into prepared soufflé dish. Bake about 50 minutes or until soufflé is puffed and golden-brown and knife inserted 1 inch from edge comes out clean. Serve immediately.

Each serving: about 295 calories, 17g protein, 9g carbohydrate, 22g total fat (9g saturated), 1g fiber, 183mg cholesterol, 595mg sodium

HAM AND PEPPER JACK SOUFFLÉ

Chocolate Soufflés

Make eight individual desserts or one delectably tall, dark, and handsome soufflé.

Active time: 20 minutes
Bake time: 20 minutes
Makes: 8 servings

1¼ cups plus 2 tablespoons granulated sugar
¼ cup all-purpose flour
1 teaspoon instant espresso-coffee powder
1 cup milk
3 tablespoons butter or margarine, softened
5 squares (5 ounces) unsweetened chocolate,
   coarsely chopped
4 large eggs, separated
2 teaspoons vanilla extract
2 large egg whites
¼ teaspoon salt
Confectioners' sugar for sprinkling

1. In 3-quart saucepan, combine 1¼ cups granulated sugar, flour, and espresso powder; gradually stir in milk until blended. Cook over medium heat, stirring constantly, until mixture thickens and boils; boil, stirring, 1 minute. Remove saucepan from heat.

2. Stir in butter and chocolate until smooth. With wire whisk, beat in egg yolks until well blended. Stir in vanilla. Cool to lukewarm, stirring mixture occasionally.

3. Preheat oven to 350°F. Grease eight 6-ounce ramekins, or custard cups, or one 2-quart soufflé dish; sprinkle with remaining 2 tablespoons granulated sugar. If using ramekins, place in jelly-roll pan for easier handling.

4. In large bowl, with mixer on high speed, beat all egg whites and salt until stiff peaks form when beaters are lifted. With rubber spatula, gently fold one-third of beaten whites into chocolate mixture. Fold chocolate mixture gently back into remaining whites.

5. Pour into ramekins or soufflé dish. Bake ramekins 20 to 25 minutes (centers will still be glossy). If using 2-quart soufflé dish, bake 25 to 30 minutes. Sprinkle with confectioners' sugar and serve immediately.

Each serving: about 365 calories, 7g protein, 45g carbohydrate, 20g total fat (10g saturated), 3g fiber, 122mg cholesterol, 180mg sodium

Banana Rum Soufflé

For this dessert, it's best to use fully ripe bananas (the ones with skins that are thoroughly dotted with brown freckles). To speed up ripening, you can put them in a bag along with an apple.

Active time: 15 minutes
Bake time: 55 minutes
Makes: 8 servings

2 medium-large bananas
4 tablespoons butter or margarine
$1/3$ cup all-purpose flour
$1/8$ teaspoon salt
1 cup milk
$1/4$ cup packed brown sugar
4 large eggs, separated
$1/4$ cup dark rum
2 tablespoons plus $1/4$ cup granulated sugar
2 large egg whites
Confectioners' sugar for sprinkling

1. In blender or food processor with knife blade attached, puree bananas until smooth; measure out 1 cup and reserve any remainder for another use.

2. In 2-quart saucepan, melt butter over low heat. Stir in flour and salt until blended; gradually stir in milk. Cook, stirring constantly, until mixture boils and thickens; cook 1 minute. Remove saucepan from heat.

3. With wire whisk, beat brown sugar into milk mixture. Beat in egg yolks until well blended. Stir in pureed bananas and rum. Cool to lukewarm, stirring mixture occasionally.

4. Preheat oven to 350°F. Grease 2½-quart soufflé dish, then sprinkle with 2 tablespoons granulated sugar.

5. In large bowl, with mixer on high speed, beat all egg whites until soft peaks form. Sprinkle in remaining ¼ cup granulated sugar, 1 tablespoon at a time, and beat until whites hold stiff peaks when beaters are lifted. With rubber spatula, gently fold one-third of beaten egg whites into banana mixture. Fold banana mixture gently into remaining whites.

6. Pour mixture into prepared soufflé dish. With back of spoon, about 1 inch from edge of dish, make 1-inch-deep indentation to form circle in soufflé mixture. Bake 55 to 60 minutes, until soufflé is puffy and brown and knife inserted into center comes out clean. Sprinkle with confectioners' sugar and serve immediately.

Each serving: about 225 calories, 6g protein, 29g carbohydrate, 10g total fat (5g saturated), 1g fiber, 126mg cholesterol, 160mg sodium

---

SOUFFLÉ SECRETS

If you've never made a soufflé before, you may want to try one for private consumption before attempting it for company.

SOME POINTERS:

- Beat the egg whites until they are stiff but not dry. Then fold them into the soufflé base quickly but gently, so as not to deflate the beaten whites.

- Be sure to use a straight-sided dish for maximum height, and—this is perhaps the most important thing—get the soufflé to the table quickly, before it starts to shrink!

- To serve, insert two serving forks, back-to-back, into the center and gently divide the soufflé into portions, then scoop out the portions with a large spoon.

Orange Liqueur Soufflé

Grand Marnier and Cointreau are the most famous names in orange liqueur; you can also use any brand of curaçao or triple sec.

Active time: 20 minutes
Bake time: 30 minutes
Makes: 8 servings

4 tablespoons butter or margarine
1/3 cup all-purpose flour
1/8 teaspoon salt
1 1/2 cups milk
1/2 cup plus 2 tablespoons granulated sugar
4 large eggs, separated
1/3 cup orange liqueur
1 tablespoon freshly grated orange peel
2 large egg whites
Confectioners' sugar for sprinkling
Whipped cream (optional)

1. In 2-quart saucepan, melt butter over low heat. Stir in flour and salt until blended; gradually stir in milk. Cook, stirring constantly, until mixture thickens and boils; boil 1 minute. Remove saucepan from heat.

2. With wire whisk, beat 1/2 cup granulated sugar into milk mixture. Beat in egg yolks until well blended. Cool to lukewarm, stirring occasionally. Stir in orange liqueur and orange peel.

3. Preheat oven to 375°F. Grease 2-quart soufflé dish with butter, then sprinkle with remaining 2 tablespoons granulated sugar.

4. In large bowl, with mixer on high speed, beat all egg whites until stiff peaks form when beaters are lifted. With rubber spatula, gently fold one-third of whites into egg-yolk mixture; fold egg-yolk mixture gently back into remaining whites.

5. Pour mixture into prepared soufflé dish. With back of spoon, about 1 inch from edge of dish, make 1-inch-deep indentation to form circle in soufflé mixture. Bake 30 to 35 minutes, until soufflé is puffy and brown and knife inserted into center comes out clean.

6. Sprinkle with confectioners' sugar and serve immediately, with whipped cream alongside, if you like.

Each serving: about 220 calories, 6g protein, 26g carbohydrate, 10g total fat (5g saturated), 0g fiber, 128mg cholesterol, 160mg sodium

LEMON SOUFFLÉ Prepare soufflé as instructed, but in step 1, use just *1 cup milk*. In step 2, use just *1/3 cup granulated sugar*; after egg yolk mixture is well blended and cooled, stir in *1 tablespoon lemon peel* and *1/3 cup juice* (from 2 large lemons). In step 4, beat egg whites to soft peaks, then gradually sprinkle in *1/3 cup granulated sugar* and continue beating until stiff peaks form. Proceed as directed in recipe, baking soufflé 35 to 40 minutes.

Each serving: about 215 calories, 6g protein, 27g carbohydrate, 33g total fat (5g saturated), 0g fiber, 126mg cholesterol, 155mg sodium

MERINGUES

The desserts in this section are all made with meringue that has been slowly baked until crisp. The oven temperatures are notably low; you could say that the meringues are really dried rather than baked—and for that reason, they're best made when the humidity is very low.

Meringue Shells

If you love pies and tarts but want to avoid the extra fat that comes with pie dough, these meringue shells may be your salvation.

Active time: 15 minutes plus drying
Bake time: 2 hours
Makes: 6 meringue shells

3 large egg whites
1/8 teaspoon cream of tartar
3/4 cup sugar
1/2 teaspoon vanilla extract

1. Preheat oven to 200°F. Line large cookie sheet with foil or parchment paper.

2. In medium bowl, with mixer on high speed, beat egg whites and cream of tartar until soft peaks begin to form when beaters are lifted. Gradually sprinkle in sugar, 2 tablespoons at a time, beating well after each addition, until sugar dissolves and egg whites stand in stiff, glossy peaks when beaters are lifted (see page 235). Beat in vanilla.

3. Onto prepared cookie sheet, spoon meringue into 6 equal mounds, 4 inches apart. With back of tablespoon, spread each mound into 4-inch round. Make well in center of each meringue round to form a nest (see page 233).

4. Bake 2 hours, or until meringues are crisp but not brown. Turn oven off; leave meringues in oven 1 hour or overnight to dry. If not leaving overnight, cool completely on cookie sheet on wire rack. Store shells in airtight container for up to 1 month.

Each shell: about 105 calories, 2g protein, 25g carbohydrate, 0g total fat (0g saturated), 0g fiber, 0mg cholesterol, 30mg sodium

ANGEL PIE Line 9-inch pie plate with foil. Generously grease and flour foil. Prepare meringue as directed in step 1 of Meringue Shells. Spoon mixture into prepared plate and, with rubber spatula, spread evenly up sides of pan. Bake 1 hour, or until dry and set. Turn off oven; leave shell to dry in oven 1 hour 30 minutes or overnight. To serve, lift shell out of pan and carefully remove foil. Place shell on plate and fill with *Lemon Curd Cream* (page 346) or softened ice cream. Makes 8 servings.

Each serving with lemon cream: about 205 calories, 2g protein, 29g carbohydrate, 9g total fat (5g saturated), 0g fiber, 70mg cholesterol, 80mg sodium

---

ANGEL PIE

Not just a sweet talker's endearment, angel pie is also a boon to the fat conscious. The meringue crust is, of course, fat-free, and if the filling is not too rich, you can serve up a fabulous low-fat dessert.

One possibility is juicy fresh berries—puree some of the fruit, then stir the whole berries into it and spoon the mixture into the meringue shell; top with dollops of vanilla yogurt. Or try a new take on an ice-cream cake: Fill the shell with scoops of tropical sorbets, like mango, lime, and passion fruit, then cover and freeze.

MINIATURE MERINGUE SHELLS Proceed as described opposite, but line 2 large cookie sheets with foil or parchment paper. In step 3, drop meringue by rounded teaspoons, 2 inches apart, on prepared cookie sheets. Spread each mound into 1½-inch round. With back of teaspoon, make well in center of each meringue to form nest. Follow step 4 as instructed, but bake meringues for only 1 hour. Makes 20 miniature meringue shells.

Each shell: about 30 calories, 1g protein, 8g carbohydrate, 0g total fat (0g saturated), 0g fiber, 0mg cholesterol, 10mg sodium

MERINGUE SHELLS WITH LEMON FILLING AND STRAWBERRIES Prepare Meringue Shells. In medium bowl, toss *1 pint strawberries*, hulled and quartered, with *1 tablespoon strawberry preserves*. Spoon *2 tablespoons Lemon Curd Cream* (page 346) into cooled shells. Top with strawberry mixture. Garnish with *fresh mint leaves*. Makes 6 servings.

Each serving: about 275 calories, 3g protein, 42g carbohydrate, 11g total fat (6g saturated), 1g fiber, 93mg cholesterol, 105mg sodium

STRAWBERRIES AND CREAM MERINGUE SHELLS Prepare Miniature Meringue Shells. Wash and hull *20 strawberries*. In small bowl with mixer on medium speed, beat *½ cup heavy cream* and *2 teaspoons sugar* until soft peaks form; stir in *1 to 2 teaspoons orange liqueur*. Spoon flavored cream into cooled shells. Top each with 1 strawberry. Makes 20 servings.

Each serving: about 55 calories, 1g protein, 9g carbohydrate, 2g total fat (1g saturated), 0g fiber, 8mg cholesterol, 10mg sodium

MAKING MERINGUE SHELLS

Although the outcome looks fancy, meringues are simply a beaten mixture of egg whites and sugar. Never make meringue on a humid or rainy day; it will absorb the moisture in the air and end up soggy.

Depending on the recipe, sugar is added to the egg whites after they've been beaten until foamy, or when they've reached the soft-peak stage. Add it gradually, a tablespoon or two at a time.

To make a perfect round, use a toothpick to trace a circle onto a sheet of aluminum foil (a plate makes a good pattern). Spoon the meringue onto the foil, then spread it to the size of the circle.

After baking and cooling the meringue completely, carefully peel off the foil. Fill meringue shell as instructed in recipe.

Grapefruit Meringue Nests with Mixed Berries

Grapefruit adds citrus appeal to these edible meringue serving vessels.

Active time: 25 minutes plus drying
Bake time: 2 hours
Makes: 8 servings

MERINGUE NESTS

3 large egg whites
1/8 teaspoon cream of tartar
1/2 cup sugar
1 teaspoon freshly grated Ruby Red grapefruit peel

BERRY FILLING

1 container (6 ounce) blueberries
1 container (6 ounce) raspberries
2 pounds strawberries, hulled and cut in half
1/4 cup sugar
1/4 cup fresh Ruby Red grapefruit juice

1. Prepare meringue nests: Preheat oven to 200°F. Line large cookie sheet with parchment paper or silicone baking mat. In large bowl, with mixer on high speed, beat egg whites and cream of tartar until soft peaks form. Sprinkle in sugar, 2 tablespoons at a time, beating until sugar dissolves and meringue stands in stiff, glossy peaks when beaters are lifted (see page 235). With large rubber spatula, gently fold grapefruit peel into meringue until well combined.

2. Divide mixture into 8 even mounds on prepared sheet, spacing about 2 inches apart. Pressing back of spoon into center of each meringue, spread mounds into 3-inch nests. Bake 2 hours or until firm. Turn off oven; leave meringues to dry in oven 1 hour or overnight. When meringues are dry, carefully remove from parchment. (Meringues can be stored in tightly sealed container at room temperature up to 2 weeks.)

3. Prepare berries: In large bowl, combine blueberries, raspberries, and half of strawberries. In 12-inch skillet, combine sugar and grapefruit juice. Heat to boiling on medium, stirring occasionally. Boil 2 minutes or until sugar dissolves and mixture is clear pink. Add remaining strawberries and cook 1 to 3 minutes or until berries release juices and have softened slightly. Pour mixture over uncooked berries. Stir gently until well combined.

4. Place meringue nests on serving plates. Divide berries among nests and drizzle juices from fruit over all. Serve immediately.

Each serving: about 130 calories, 2g protein, 30g carbohydrate, 1g total fat, 4g fiber, 0mg cholesterol, 25mg sodium

FORMING A MERINGUE NEST

For a pretty presentation, form your meringue so you can nestle fruit or another filling in it.

Spoon the meringue mixture onto a sheet of foil and spread it to the edges of the circle. Then push meringue from the center of the round toward the outer edge to build a rim.

Berry and Lemon Pavlova

Bake the meringue shell up to two days ahead, and this dessert assembles fast. Just spoon in whipped cream and ready-made lemon curd, then top with berries. Done!

Active time: 15 minutes plus drying
Bake time: 2 hours
Makes: 6 servings

²/₃ cup sugar
1 tablespoon cornstarch
4 large egg whites
¹/₄ teaspoon salt
1 teaspoon distilled white vinegar
1 teaspoon vanilla extract
¹/₂ teaspoon almond extract
³/₄ cup heavy cream
1 cup prepared lemon curd
1 tablespoon honey
1 tablespoon water
1 container (12 ounces) blueberries
1 container (6 ounce) blackberries

1. Preheat oven to 225°F. Onto sheet of parchment paper, trace 9-inch circle. Turn over; use to line cookie sheet.

2. In small bowl, whisk together sugar and cornstarch. With mixer on medium speed, beat egg whites and salt until soft peaks form. Add sugar mixture to whites 1 tablespoon at a time, beating well between additions. Add vinegar and both extracts; beat until stiff peaks form (see opposite).

3. Transfer whites to parchment circle and spread to form nest with sides higher than center (see page 233). Bake 2 hours. Turn off oven; let stand in oven to dry at least 3 hours or up to overnight.

4. To serve, remove meringue from parchment and set on serving plate. Beat cream on medium-high speed until stiff peaks form. Spread over meringue. Dollop top with curd; spread evenly. In large bowl, microwave honey and water on High 20 seconds. Stir in berries until well coated. Spoon over curd. Serve immediately.

Each serving: about 420 calories, 4g protein, 66g carbohydrate, 14g total fat (8g saturated), 2g fiber, 81mg cholesterol, 175mg sodium

Chocolate-Hazelnut Meringue Puff

What could be more delectable than a feather-light chocolate and hazelnut meringue ring filled with cocoa, whipped cream, and fresh raspberries?

Active time: 40 minutes plus drying and cooling
Bake time: 2 hours
Makes: 10 servings

1 tablespoon cornstarch
3/4 cup plus 3 tablespoons sugar
4 large egg whites
1/4 teaspoon salt
1 teaspoon white vinegar
1 teaspoon vanilla extract
3 tablespoons plus 1/4 cup unsweetened cocoa
1 cup hazelnuts (5 ounces), toasted and skinned
    (see page xxiii), chopped
1 cup heavy cream
1 container (6 ounces) raspberries

1. Preheat oven to 250°F. Line cookie sheet with foil. Grease foil; dust with flour. Using 9-inch round cake pan as guide, with toothpick, outline circle on foil.

2. In small bowl, combine cornstarch and 3/4 cup sugar. In large bowl, with mixer on medium speed, beat egg whites and salt until foamy. Beat in cornstarch mixture, 1 tablespoon at a time, until mixture completely dissolves. Increase speed to high; beat until whites stand in stiff, glossy peaks when beaters are lifted (see box). Beat in vinegar and vanilla. Sift 3 tablespoons cocoa over meringue; sprinkle with hazelnuts. With rubber spatula, fold cocoa and hazelnuts into meringue just until well blended.

3. Spoon meringue into circle on foil; spread to edge of circle, forming nest with 2-inch-high edge (see page 233).

4. Bake meringue 2 hours. Turn off oven; leave meringue in oven 2 hours to dry. Move to wire rack to cool completely.

5. When ready to serve, in medium bowl, with mixer on medium speed, beat cream with remaining 1/4 cup cocoa and 3 tablespoons sugar until soft peaks form. Transfer meringue to plate; fill center with whipped cream mixture and sprinkle with raspberries.

Each serving: about 260 calories, 5g protein, 25g carbohydrate, 18g total fat (6g saturated), 3g fiber, 33mg cholesterol, 90mg sodium

BEATING EGG WHITES

The secret to feather-light soufflés is properly beaten egg whites.

To get the fullest volume, start with room-temperature egg whites and chill your mixing bowl and beaters. For "stiff glossy peaks," beat the whites until they form peaks that hold their shape when the beaters are lifted but are still moist. Overbeaten whites turn lumpy and watery; there is no way to salvage them. Begin again with new egg whites.

Savory & Sweet Breads

CORN BREADS

Most corn quick breads are dense and almost cakelike. The cornmeal contributes a slightly sweet, rich flavor. Use yellow or white cornmeal, as you like. Try to get stone-ground meal, which adds interesting texture to the bread.

Golden Corn Bread
You probably have the ingredients for this basic corn bread in your kitchen. Try variations flavored with bacon or peppery cheese, or bake the batter as muffins.

Active time: 10 minutes
Bake time: 20 minutes
Makes: 9 servings

1 cup all-purpose flour
3/4 cup cornmeal
3 tablespoons sugar
1 tablespoon baking powder
3/4 teaspoon salt
1 large egg
2/3 cup milk
4 tablespoons butter or margarine, melted

1. Preheat oven to 425°F. Grease 8-inch square metal baking pan. In medium bowl, stir together flour, cornmeal, sugar, baking powder, and salt. In small bowl with fork, beat egg, milk, and melted butter until blended. Add egg mixture to flour mixture; stir just until flour is moistened (batter will be lumpy).

2. Spread batter evenly in prepared pan. Bake 20 to 25 minutes, until bread is golden and toothpick inserted in center comes out clean. Cut corn bread into squares; serve warm.

Each serving: about 180 calories, 4g protein, 25g carbohydrate, 7g total fat (4g saturated), 1g fiber, 40mg cholesterol, 425mg sodium

GOLDEN CORN BREAD WITH BACON AND PEPPER Prepare flour mixture as instructed. In 10-inch skillet, cook *5 slices bacon* over medium heat until browned. Drain bacon on paper towel. Pour *¼ cup bacon fat* into measuring cup (if necessary, add enough *vegetable oil* to equal ¼ cup). Crumble bacon; stir crumbled bacon and *½ teaspoon ground black pepper* into flour mixture. Use bacon fat in place of melted butter.

Each serving: about 195 calories, 5g protein, 25g carbohydrate, 8g total fat (3g saturated), 1g fiber, 33mg cholesterol, 460mg sodium

GOLDEN CORN BREAD WITH PEPPER JACK Prepare corn bread as instructed, stir in *4 ounces Monterey Jack cheese with jalapeños,* shredded (1 cup), and *¾ teaspoon mild to medium chili powder* into flour mixture in step 1. Use only *3 tablespoons melted butter.*

Each serving: about 220 calories, 7g protein, 26g carbohydrate, 10g total fat (5g saturated), 1g fiber, 50mg cholesterol, 825mg sodium

GOLDEN CORN MUFFINS Grease 12 standard muffin-pan cups. Prepare corn bread as instructed, but use *1 cup milk.* Spoon batter into prepared muffin cups, filling each two-thirds full. Bake about 20 minutes, or until muffins are golden and toothpick inserted in center comes out clean. Immediately remove muffins from pans; serve warm. Makes 1 dozen muffins.

Each muffin: about 145 calories, 3g protein, 19g carbohydrate, 6g total fat (3g saturated), 1g fiber, 31mg cholesterol, 320mg sodium

Double Corn Bread

Frozen corn enhances the texture and flavor of this hearty corn bread; jalapeño chiles add some zip.

Active time: 20 minutes
Bake time: 22 minutess
Makes: 24 servings

1¹/2 cups all-purpose flour
1¹/2 cups yellow cornmeal
¹/4 cup sugar
4 teaspoons baking powder
¹/2 teaspoon baking soda
1 teaspoon salt
2¹/2 cups buttermilk
3 large eggs
1 package (10 ounces) frozen corn, thawed
6 tablespoons butter or margarine, melted
2 jalapeño chiles, seeds and membranes discarded, finely chopped

1. Preheat oven to 450°F. Grease 13" by 9" metal baking pan.

2. In large bowl, combine flour, cornmeal, sugar, baking powder, baking soda, and salt. In medium bowl, with wire whisk or fork, beat buttermilk and eggs until blended.

3. Add corn, melted butter, and jalapeños to buttermilk mixture; then add to flour mixture. Stir until ingredients are just mixed.

4. Pour batter into prepared pan. Bake 22 to 25 minutes or until corn bread is golden at edges and toothpick inserted in center comes out clean. Cut lengthwise into 4 strips, then cut each strip crosswise into 6 pieces. Serve warm.

Each serving: about 125 calories, 4g protein, 19g carbohydrate, 4g total fat (2g saturated), 1g fiber, 36mg cholesterol, 255mg sodium

TIP You can bake and freeze the cornbread, tightly wrapped, up to 1 month ahead. When you're ready to serve it, thaw it first, then reheat it, covered, at 450°F for 15 minutes.

CORNMEAL: AN AMERICAN TRADITION

Cornmeal may not be as versatile as wheat flour, but over the centuries, inventive American cooks have devised a wide variety of corn breads.

One of the earliest was ashcake, or hoecake, which was baked right in the coals of the cooking fire. Other old-time favorites include corn dodgers—a sort of free-form drop biscuit made with bacon drippings, corn pone (thick, sturdy corn cakes baked on a griddle), hush puppies, which are spoonfuls of corn batter that are deep-fried, like fritters, and elegant, airy spoon bread (see opposite).

Buttermilk Corn Bread

Buttermilk or clabbered (soured) milk appears as an ingredient in many Southern corn bread recipes, and we've take the Northern liberty of adding a bit of sugar.

Active time:10 minutes
Bake time: 15 minutes
Makes: 9 servings

2 large eggs
1/3 cup butter or margarine, melted and cooled
1 1/2 cups buttermilk
1 1/3 cups cornmeal
2/3 cup all-purpose flour
1 tablespoon sugar (optional)
2 teaspoons baking powder
1/2 teaspoon baking soda
1/2 teaspoon salt

1. Preheat oven to 400°F. Grease 9-inch cast-iron skillet or square metal baking pan. In medium bowl, with wire whisk or fork, mix eggs, melted butter, and buttermilk until blended. In large bowl, stir together cornmeal, flour, sugar, baking powder, baking soda, and salt.

2. Stir buttermilk mixture into flour mixture just until flour is moistened.

3. Spread batter evenly in prepared pan. Bake 15 to 20 minutes, until toothpick inserted in center of bread comes out clean. Serve warm, or cool in pan on wire rack to serve later.

Each serving: about 210 calories, 5g protein, 27g carbohydrate, 9g total fat (5g saturated), 1g fiber, 67mg cholesterol, 435mg sodium

Spoon Bread

A Southern standby since Colonial times, this is more like a soufflé than a bread. Rather than cutting it into slices, bring the spoon bread to the table in its baking dish and spoon it out—steaming hot—as a dinner side dish.

Active time: 15 minutes
Bake time: 40 minutes
Makes: 8 servings

3 cups milk
1/2 teaspoon salt
1/4 teaspoon ground black pepper
1 cup cornmeal
4 tablespoons butter or margarine, cut up
3 large eggs, separated

1. Preheat oven to 400°F. Grease shallow 1½-quart ceramic or glass baking dish.

2. In 4-quart saucepan, heat milk, salt, and pepper to boiling. Remove saucepan from heat; with wire whisk or fork, mix in cornmeal. Whisk in butter until melted. Let stand 5 minutes.

3. Whisk egg yolks, one at a time, into cornmeal mixture. In small bowl, with mixer on medium speed, beat egg whites until soft peaks form when beaters are lifted. Fold half of whites into cornmeal mixture; fold in remaining whites.

4. Pour batter into prepared baking dish and spread evenly with rubber spatula. Bake 40 minutes, or until set. Serve immediately.

Each serving: about 205 calories, 7g protein, 18g carbohydrate, 11g total fat (6g saturated), 1g fiber, 108mg cholesterol, 270mg sodium

BISCUITS & SCONES

The old Southern saying is that biscuit baking requires "a good heart and a light hand," and the same goes for scones. Don't stir the dough too long or too hard or knead it too vigorously (it's a far gentler process than kneading yeast dough).

Baking Powder Biscuits

There's nothing like a fresh, hot biscuit, dripping with butter or doused with gravy.

Active time: 10 minutes
Bake time: 12 minutes
Makes: 18 high biscuits or 36 thin biscuits

2 cups all-purpose flour
1 tablespoon baking powder
1/2 teaspoon salt
1/4 cup cold vegetable shortening
3/4 cup milk

1. Preheat oven to 450°F. In large bowl, stir together flour, baking powder, and salt. With pastry blender or two knives used scissor-fashion, cut in shortening until mixture resembles coarse crumbs. Gradually add in milk, stirring just until mixture forms soft dough that leaves side of bowl.

2. Turn dough out onto lightly floured work surface; knead six to eight times, just until smooth. With floured rolling pin, roll dough 1/2 inch thick for high, fluffy biscuits or 1/4 inch thick for thin, crusty ones.

3. With floured 2-inch biscuit cutter, cut out as many biscuits as possible from rolled dough. With wide metal spatula, place biscuits on ungreased large cookie sheet, 1 inch apart for crusty biscuits, or nearly touching for soft-sided ones.

4. Press trimmings together; reroll and cut. Bake 12 to 15 minutes, until biscuits are golden. Serve warm.

Each high biscuit: about 85 calories, 2g protein, 12g carbohydrate, 3g total fat (1g saturated), 1g fiber, 1mg cholesterol, 150mg sodium

Each thin biscuit: about 40 calories, 1g protein, 6g carbohydrate, 2g total fat (0g saturated), 0g fiber, 1mg cholesterol, 75mg sodium

BUTTERMILK BISCUITS Prepare dough as instructed, but use *2½ teaspoons baking powder* and add *½ teaspoon baking soda* to flour mixture. Substitute *¾ cup buttermilk* for milk.

Each high biscuit: about 85 calories, 2g protein, 12g carbohydrate, 3g total fat (1g saturated), 1g fiber, 0mg cholesterol, 180mg sodium

BACON-GREEN ONION BISCUITS Prepare dough as instructed, but in step 1, use *3 tablespoons cold vegetable shortening* plus *1 tablespoon chilled bacon drippings*. Stir 3 *slices bacon*, cooked and crumbled, and *2 tablespoons chopped green onion* into flour mixture.

Each high biscuit: about 90 calories, 2g protein, 12g carbohydrate, 4g total fat (1g saturated), 1g fiber, 3mg cholesterol, 170mg sodium

CHEDDAR-JALAPEÑO BISCUITS Prepare dough as instructed, but cut *4 ounces Cheddar cheese*, shredded (1 cup), into flour mixture with shortening; stir in *3 tablespoons pickled jalapeño chiles*, drained and chopped, along with milk.

Each high biscuit: about 110 calories, 3g protein, 12g carbohydrate, 5g total fat (2g saturated), 1g fiber, 8mg cholesterol, 210mg sodium

DROP BISCUITS Prepare dough as instructed, but use *1 cup milk*; stir dough just until blended. Drop dough by heaping tablespoons, 1 inch apart, on ungreased cookie sheet. Bake as directed. Makes about 20 biscuits.

Each biscuit: about 75 calories, 2g protein, 5g carbohydrate, 3g total fat (1g saturated), 1g fiber, 2mg cholesterol, 135mg sodium

MIXING AND SHAPING BISCUITS

When you cut out biscuits, be sure to press the cutter straight down. If you twist it, the biscuits may rise unevenly. In lieu of a biscuit cutter, you can use a jelly jar or drinking glass.

With a pastry blender (or two knives used scissor-fashion), "chop" the shortening or butter into the dry ingredients just until the mixture becomes crumblike.

On a lightly floured work surface, pat or roll the dough out into a round. The less you work the dough at this point, the more tender the finished biscuits will be.

Use a 2-inch cutter to cut out the biscuits. If you don't have one, cut the dough with the rim of a drinking glass that's roughly the right size.

Angel Biscuits

Made with yeast, baking powder, and baking soda, these triple-leavened biscuits are feather light.

Active time: 15 minutes plus rising
Bake time: 17 minutes
Makes: 24 biscuits

1/4 cup warm water (105°F to 115°F)
1 package active dry yeast
1 teaspoon sugar
3 cups all-purpose flour
1 1/2 teaspoons baking powder
1/2 teaspoon baking soda
1/4 teaspoon salt
4 tablespoons cold butter or margarine, cut up
2 tablespoons vegetable shortening
1 cup plus 2 tablespoons buttermilk

1. In small bowl, combine warm water, yeast, and sugar; stir to dissolve. Let stand 5 minutes, or until foamy.

2. In large bowl, stir flour, baking powder and soda, and salt. With pastry blender or two knives used scissor-fashion, cut in butter and shortening until mixture resembles coarse crumbs. Make well in center and pour in buttermilk and yeast mixture. Stir until well combined.

3. Turn dough out onto lightly floured work surface and knead several times until smooth and elastic. Place in greased bowl, turning dough over to grease top. Cover bowl and let stand in warm place until doubled, 1 hour.

4. Punch dough down, then cover and let stand 10 minutes. On lightly floured work surface, with floured hands, pat dough out to ¾ inch thick. With 2-inch round biscuit cutters, cut out biscuits; place 2 inches apart on two large ungreased cookie sheets. Reroll trimmings to cut as many biscuits as possible. Cover and let rise until almost doubled, about 30 minutes.

5. Preheat oven to 400°F. Bake biscuits 17 to 20 minutes, rotating sheets between upper and lower oven racks halfway through. Serve warm.

Each biscuit: about 95 calories, 2g protein, 14g carbohydrate, 3g total fat (2g saturated), 1g fiber, 6mg cholesterol, 110mg sodium

Fancy Sesame Biscuits

Sesame seeds lend unexpected crunch and flavor to these classic buttermilk biscuits.

Active time: 15 minutes
Bake time: 14 minutes
Makes: 16 biscuits

3 cups self-rising flour
6 tablespoons cold butter, cut up (do not use margarine)
1/2 teaspoon salt
1 1/2 cups low-fat buttermilk
1 large egg, lightly beaten
1/4 cup sesame seeds

1. Preheat oven to 450°F. In large bowl, combine flour, butter, and salt. With pastry blender or two knives used scissor-fashion, cut butter into flour until mixture resembles coarse crumbs. Stir in buttermilk; with rubber spatula, mix until dough just comes together.

3. Transfer dough onto floured work surface. Fold and gently knead just until no longer sticky. Pat into 7-inch square. Cut crosswise into 4 strips, then lengthwise to form 16 cubes. Lightly brush tops with egg.

4. Place sesame seeds in shallow dish. Working one at a time, press each biscuit, egg-brushed side down, into seeds. Place biscuit, seed side up, on large cookie sheet.

Repeat with remaining biscuits, spacing 1 inch apart. Bake 14 to 16 minutes or until golden. Biscuits can be made up to 2 weeks ahead and frozen. To reheat, bake in 400°F oven for 13 to 14 minutes.

Each serving: about 155 calories, 5g protein, 22g carbohydrate, 6g total fat (3g saturated), 1g fiber, 24mg cholesterol, 450mg sodium

Cornmeal Biscuits

For the tastiest biscuits, choose stone-ground cornmeal. Yellow and white cornmeal are quite similar, and interchangeable in recipes.

Active time: 10 minutes
Bake time: 17 minutes
Makes: 12 biscuits

1 1/4 cups all-purpose flour
3/4 cup cornmeal
2 tablespoons sugar
2 teaspoons baking powder
1/2 teaspoon baking soda
1/4 teaspoon salt
6 tablespoons cold butter or margarine, cut up
3/4 cup buttermilk
1 large egg

1. Preheat oven to 375°F. In large bowl, stir together flour, cornmeal, sugar, baking powder, baking soda, and salt. With pastry blender or two knives used scissor-fashion, cut in butter until mixture resembles coarse crumbs.

2. In medium bowl, whisk buttermilk and egg; stir into flour mixture just until dough holds together.

3. Turn dough out onto lightly floured work surface and, with floured rolling pin, roll dough ¾ inch thick. With 2-inch biscuit cutters, cut out biscuits. Place, 1 inch apart, on ungreased large cookie sheet. Press trimmings together, reroll, and cut as above.

4. Bake 17 to 18 minutes, until biscuits are golden and cooked through. Cool briefly and serve warm.

Each biscuit: about 155 calories, 3g protein, 21g carbohydrate, 7g total fat (4g saturated), 1g fiber, 34mg cholesterol, 260mg sodium

Simple Scones

Once a humble afternoon-tea staple, these rich British tea breads have been transformed in recent years to include a wide variety of sweet and savory mix-ins.

Active time: 15 minutes
Bake time: 22 minutes
Makes: 8 scones

2 cups all-purpose flour
2 tablespoons plus 2 teaspoons sugar
2¹/2 teaspoons baking powder
¹/4 teaspoon salt
¹/2 cup cold butter or margarine (1 stick), cut up
²/3 cup milk
1 large egg, separated

1. Preheat oven to 375°F. In large bowl, stir together flour, 2 tablespoons sugar, baking powder, and salt. With pastry blender or two knives used scissor-fashion, cut in butter until mixture resembles coarse crumbs.

2. In small cup, with fork, mix milk and egg yolk. Make well in center of flour mixture, pour in milk mixture, and stir just until combined.

3. Transfer dough to ungreased large cookie sheet. With floured hands, shape into 7½-inch round. With floured knife, score round into 8 wedges, cutting about halfway through. Brush scones with egg white and sprinkle remaining 2 teaspoons sugar on top.

4. Bake 22 to 25 minutes, until golden brown and just cooked through. Separate scones and serve warm, or transfer to wire rack to cool.

Each scone: about 255 calories, 5g protein, 29g carbohydrate, 13g total fat (8g saturated), 1g fiber, 60mg cholesterol, 360mg sodium

BUTTERMILK SCONES Prepare scones as instructed, but use *2 teaspoons baking powder.* Add *½ teaspoon baking soda* and use *²/3 cup buttermilk* in place of milk.

Each scone: about 250 calories, 5g protein, 30g carbohydrate, 13g total fat (8g saturated), 1g fiber, 58mg cholesterol, 420mg sodium

DRIED FRUIT SCONES Prepare scones as instructed, but add *¾ cup dried fruit* (such as raisins or coarsely chopped apricots, cherries, dates, or figs) along with milk mixture.

Each scone: about 290 calories, 5g protein, 39g carbohydrate, 13g total fat (8g saturated), 2g fiber, 60mg cholesterol, 360mg sodium

ORANGE SCONES Prepare scones as instructed, but add *1 teaspoon freshly grated orange peel* to flour mixture.

Each scone: about 255 calories, 5g protein, 29g carbohydrate, 13g total fat (8g saturated), 1g fiber, 60mg cholesterol, 360mg sodium

CHOCOLATE CHIP SCONES Prepare scones as instructed, but add *¾ cup semisweet chocolate chips* to flour mixture.

Each scone: about 330 calories, 5g protein, 40g carbohydrate, 17g total fat (10g saturated), 1g fiber, 61mg cholesterol, 360mg sodium

JAM-FILLED SCONES Prepare dough as instructed; divide in half. On ungreased large cookie sheet, shape 1 dough half into 7½-inch round. Spread with ¼ *cup jam of your choice*, leaving ½-inch border. On lightly floured work surface, with lightly floured hands, shape remaining dough half into 7½-inch round; place on top of jam. When scoring dough into wedges, do not cut through to jam. Bake as directed.

Each scone: about 285 calories, 5g protein, 37g carbohydrate, 13g total fat (8g saturated), 1g fiber, 60mg cholesterol, 365mg sodium

TRADITIONAL CURRANT SCONES Prepare scones as instructed, but stir *1 cup dried currants* into flour mixture before adding milk mixture. Pat out into 9" by 5" by ¾" rectangle. Brush with egg white and sugar as directed in step 3. With 2-inch round biscuit cutter, cut 14 rounds. Bake, 2 inches apart, on ungreased large cookie sheet 18 minutes, or until just baked through. Makes 14 scones.

Each scone: about 175 calories, 3g protein, 24g carbohydrate, 7g total fat (4g saturated), 1g fiber, 35mg cholesterol, 205mg sodium

---

BRITISH TEA BREADS

The British tradition of afternoon tea is enhanced by the multiplicity of breads and buns that appear alongside the steaming kettle. Oven-baked scones and griddle scones, cooked on the stovetop, are two favorites. Then there are crumpets (similar to what we call English muffins) and pikelets (miniature crumpets); currant-studded bath buns and cinnamon-raisin-filled Chelsea buns. Snow-white Irish soda bread and Welsh *bara brith* (bursting with dried fruit) cakes and biscuits follow, for those with any appetite remaining.

Blueberry Hill Scones

Blueberries are sturdy enough to stir right into this dough, but if you'd like to use more fragile fruits such as raspberries or blackberries, don't mix them in. Instead, gently press the berries into the top of the dough.

Active time: 15 minutes
Bake time: 22 minutes
Makes: 12 scones

2 cups all-purpose flour
¼ cup packed brown sugar
1 tablespoon baking powder
¼ teaspoon salt
4 tablespoons cold butter or margarine, cut up
1 cup blueberries, picked over
⅔ cup heavy cream
1 large egg
½ teaspoon freshly grated lemon peel

1. Preheat oven to 375°F. In large bowl, stir together flour, brown sugar, baking powder, and salt. With pastry blender or two knives used scissor-fashion, cut in butter until mixture resembles coarse crumbs. Add blueberries and toss to mix.

2. In small bowl, with fork, mix cream, egg, and lemon peel until blended. Slowly pour into flour mixture, stirring with rubber spatula just until soft dough forms.

3. With lightly floured hand, knead dough in bowl three or four times, just until it holds together; do not overmix. Divide dough in half. On lightly floured work surface, shape each half into 6-inch round. With floured knife, cut each round into 6 wedges. With wide metal spatula, place wedges, 1 inch apart, on ungreased large cookie sheet.

4. Bake 22 to 25 minutes, until golden brown. Serve scones warm, or transfer to wire rack to cool.

Each scone: about 190 calories, 3g protein, 24g carbohydrate, 9g total fat (6g saturated), 1g fiber, 46mg cholesterol, 220mg sodium

Oatmeal Scones

Hearty and just slightly sweet, these nutritious scones are delicious with jam or marmalade for breakfast, or with a slice of sharp Cheddar and a dab of chutney at any time of day.

Active time: 20 minutes

Bake time: 20 minutes

Makes: 8 scones

1 cup old-fashioned or quick-cooking oats, uncooked
1/2 cup pecans (2 ounces)
1 3/4 cups all-purpose flour
3 tablespoons sugar
2 teaspoons baking powder
1/2 teaspoon baking soda
1/4 teaspoon salt
6 tablespoons cold butter or margarine, cut up
2/3 cup buttermilk
1 large egg, separated
2 teaspoons water

1. Preheat oven to 400°F. On two separate jelly-roll pans, toast oats and pecans 5 to 7 minutes, until lightly browned, stirring nuts occasionally; set aside to cool. Coarsely chop pecans. Grease large cookie sheet; dust with flour.

2. In large bowl, stir together flour, 2 tablespoons sugar, baking powder, baking soda, salt, and oats. With pastry blender or two knives used scissor-fashion, cut in butter until mixture resembles coarse crumbs. Stir in pecans.

3. In small bowl, with fork, mix buttermilk and egg yolk. Make well in center of flour mixture, pour in buttermilk mixture, and stir until combined. Lightly knead in bowl until dough just holds together.

4. Transfer dough to prepared cookie sheet. Shape into 7½-inch round. With floured knife, score round into 8 wedges, cutting about halfway through. In small bowl, stir together egg white and water. Brush over top of round. Sprinkle with remaining 1 tablespoon sugar.

5. Bake 20 to 25 minutes, until toothpick inserted in center of round comes out clean. Separate scones and serve warm, or transfer to wire rack to cool.

Each scone: about 305 calories, 7g protein, 36g carbohydrate, 15g total fat (6g saturated), 2g fiber, 51mg cholesterol, 390mg sodium

Cream Scones

Destined for the afternoon tea table, these are the most elegant members of scone society. In berry season, melt a pat of sweet butter on a split, still-warm cream scone, then cover it with thinly sliced sugared strawberries.

Active time: 10 minutes

Bake time: 20 minutes

Makes: 8 scones

2 cups all-purpose flour
2 teaspoons baking powder
1/2 teaspoon salt
1/4 cup plus 1½ teaspoons sugar
4 tablespoons cold butter or margarine, cut up
1 large egg
2/3 cup plus 1½ teaspoons heavy or whipping cream

1. Preheat oven to 400°F. In large bowl, stir together flour, baking powder, salt, and 1/4 cup sugar. With pastry blender or two knives used scissor-fashion, cut in butter until mixture resembles coarse crumbs.

2. Stir egg and 2/3 cup cream into flour mixture just until dough holds together.

3. Transfer dough to ungreased large cookie sheet. With lightly floured hands, shape dough into 8-inch round. Brush remaining 1½ teaspoons cream over dough and sprinkle with remaining 1½ teaspoons sugar. With floured knife, score round into 8 wedges, cutting about halfway through.

4. Bake 20 minutes, or until golden. Separate scones and serve warm, or transfer to wire rack to cool.

Each scone: about 275 calories, 5g protein, 33g carbohydrate, 14g total fat (9g saturated), 1g fiber, 71mg cholesterol, 340mg sodium

SHAPING AND FINISHING SCONES

The scone, a Scottish quick bread, is traditionally served in wedges with a pot of tea. Oatmeal Scones are shown here.

After patting the dough into a round, score it with a sharp knife into wedges, without cutting all the way through the dough. The wedges can be easily broken apart after the scones are baked and cooled.

After scoring the dough, brush it with egg whites, heavy cream, or oil for a glossy finish if you like. You can also sprinkle with sugar to add some sparkle if desired.

Olive-Rosemary Scones

A British tradition meets the flavors of Italy with fabulous results. These rich, crumbly scones are redolent of rosemary, and there are bits of tangy olives in every bite. Serve the scones warm, alongside a bowl of minestrone or tomato soup. Or make scone sandwiches with smoked Provolone and strips of roasted pepper.

Active time: 10 minutes
Bake time: 20 minutes
Makes: 12 scones

3 cups all-purpose flour
4 tablespoons cold butter or margarine, cut up
1 tablespoon sugar
1 tablespoon baking powder
2 teaspoons chopped fresh rosemary or $1/4$ teaspoon dried rosemary, crumbled
1 teaspoon baking soda
$1/2$ teaspoon salt
$1/4$ cup plus 1 tablespoon olive oil
1 cup milk
1 large egg
$1/2$ cup Kalamata olives, pitted and coarsely chopped

1. Preheat oven to 425°F. Grease large cookie sheet. In food processor with knife blade attached, pulse flour, butter, sugar, baking powder, rosemary, baking soda, salt, and ¼ cup oil until mixture resembles coarse crumbs.

2. In small bowl, with fork, mix milk and egg. Pour mixture through feed tube and pulse just until dough forms.

3. Turn dough out onto lightly floured work surface. With floured hands, press olives into dough. Place dough on prepared cookie sheet and pat into 10-inch round. With floured knife, score round into 12 wedges, cutting about halfway through. Brush tops with remaining 1 tablespoon oil.

4. Bake 20 to 25 minutes, until golden. Separate scones and serve warm, or transfer to wire rack to cool.

Each scone: about 245 calories, 5g protein, 28g carbohydrate, 13g total fat (4g saturated), 1g fiber, 31mg cholesterol, 480mg sodium

MUFFINS & POPOVERS

Breakfast favorites and satisfying snacks, muffins are the quickest of quick breads, and they freeze very well (wrap them individually). The muffin's close cousin, the popover, looks like an overgrown muffin and is almost completely hollow. It's an airy pouf that gets its loft from eggs.

Basic Muffins

Here's a simple batter that can be transformed into a multitude of variations through the addition of yummy mix-ins, including berries, jam, and lemon peel.

Active time: 10 minutes
Bake time: 20 minutes
Makes: 12 muffins

2¹/₂ cups all-purpose flour
¹/₂ cup sugar
1 tablespoon baking powder
¹/₂ teaspoon salt
1 large egg
1 cup milk
¹/₂ cup butter or margarine (1 stick), melted
1 teaspoon vanilla extract

1. Preheat oven to 400°F. Grease 12 standard muffin-pan cups or line with paper baking liners. In large bowl, stir together flour, sugar, baking powder, and salt. In medium bowl, with wire whisk or fork, mix egg, milk, melted butter, and vanilla; stir egg mixture into flour mixture just until flour is moistened (batter will be lumpy).

2. Spoon batter into prepared muffin cups. Bake 20 to 25 minutes, until toothpick inserted in center of muffin comes out clean. Immediately remove muffins from pan. Serve warm, or cool on wire rack to serve later.

Each muffin: about 225 calories, 4g protein, 30g carbohydrate, 10g total fat (6g saturated), 1g fiber, 41mg cholesterol, 310mg sodium

BLUEBERRY OR RASPBERRY MUFFINS Prepare muffins as instructed, but gently fold in *1 cup blueberries or raspberries* into batter at end of step 1.

Each muffin: about 230 calories, 4g protein, 31g carbohydrate, 10g total fat (6g saturated), 1g fiber, 41mg cholesterol, 315mg sodium

LEMON MUFFINS Prepare batter as instructed, but add *1½ teaspoons freshly grated lemon peel* to egg mixture. Bake as directed. Meanwhile, combine *¼ cup confectioners' sugar* and *1 tablespoons fresh lemon juice*; brush glaze on muffins while they are hot.

Each muffin: About 235 calories, 4g protein, 32g carbohydrate, 10g total fat (6g saturated), 1g fiber, 41mg cholesterol, 310mg sodium

LEMON POPPY SEED MUFFINS Prepare Lemon Muffins as instructed, but fold *¼ cup poppy seeds* into batter along with lemon peel.

Each muffin: about 250 calories, 4g protein, 33g carbohydrate, 11g total fat (6g saturated), 1g fiber, 41mg cholesterol, 315mg sodium

CRANBERRY-ORANGE MUFFINS Prepare muffins as instructed, but add *½ teaspoon freshly grated orange peel* to flour mixture. After adding liquid ingredients, fold in *1½ cups chopped cranberries*. Before baking, sprinkle muffins with *2 tablespoons sugar*.

Each muffin: about 240 calories, 4g protein, 33g carbohydrate, 10g total fat (6g saturated), 1g fiber, 41mg cholesterol, 310mg sodium

JAM-FILLED MUFFINS Prepare muffins as instructed. In step 2, fill each muffin cup one-third full, then drop *1 rounded teaspoon strawberry or raspberry preserves* in center of each cup before topping with remaining batter.

Each muffin: about 250 calories, 4g protein, 36g carbohydrate, 10g total fat (6g saturated), 1g fiber, 41mg cholesterol, 315mg sodium

BROWN SUGAR STREUSEL MUFFINS Prepare muffin batter as instructed, but substitute *⅓ cup packed dark brown sugar* for granulated sugar. Add streusel topping: Combine *⅔ cup pecans*, chopped; *¼ cup packed dark brown sugar*; and *½ teaspoon ground cinnamon*. Sprinkle mixture on top of muffins after spooning batter into muffin cups. Bake as directed, but cover loosely with foil after 20 minutes to prevent overbrowning.

Each muffin: about 275 calories, 4g protein, 33g carbohydrate, 14g total fat (6g saturated), 1g fiber, 41mg cholesterol, 315mg sodium

MAKING MUFFINS

Muffins are a snap to prepare: Mix the batter by hand, spoon it into the muffin cups or liners, and bake.

Combine the dry ingredients in a bowl and stir until they are well mixed, then add the liquid ingredients all at once.

Stir the wet ingredients into the dry ingredients just until the flour mixture is moistened. The batter will be slightly lumpy; do not overmix.

Spoon the batter into the prepared muffin cups, two-thirds full or as recipe instructs. Immediately remove the muffins from the pan after baking: Run a small knife around the inside of the muffin-pan cups, then turn the pan on its side and rap it on the counter to remove the muffins. Let cool.

Bran Muffins

Muffins made with bran cereal do not have a heavy health-foody flavor. Add raisins or prunes if you like.

Active time: 10 minutes
Bake time: 20 minutes
Makes: 12 muffins

1 cup milk
1 large egg, lightly beaten
¼ cup vegetable oil
¼ cup light (mild) molasses
1 cup whole bran cereal (such as All-Bran)
1 cup all-purpose flour
¼ cup sugar
1 tablespoon baking powder
½ teaspoon salt

1. Preheat oven to 400°F. Grease 12 standard muffin-pan cups or line with paper baking liners. In medium bowl, with wire whisk, mix milk, egg, oil, molasses, and cereal until blended; let stand 10 minutes.

2. Meanwhile, in large bowl, stir together flour, sugar, baking powder, and salt. Stir egg mixture into flour mixture just until flour is moistened (batter will be lumpy).

3. Spoon batter into prepared muffin cups. Bake 20 to 25 minutes, until muffins are golden and toothpick inserted in center comes out almost clean. Immediately remove muffins from pan. Serve warm, or cool on rack to serve later.

Each muffin: about 155 calories, 3g protein, 22g carbohydrate, 7g total fat (1g saturated), 2g fiber, 21mg cholesterol, 285mg sodium

Pumpkin Muffins

Perfect for the autumn breakfast table or in the Thanksgiving bread basket. Mix in 1 cup raisins or chopped nuts if you like. Pop extras into a zip-seal plastic bag and freeze up to 1 month.

Active time: 15 minutes
Bake time: 25 minutes
Makes: 24 muffins

3½ cups all-purpose flour
1 tablespoon baking powder
2 teaspoons pumpkin-pie spice
1 teaspoon baking soda
1 teaspoon salt
3 large eggs
1 can (16 ounces) solid-pack pumpkin
¾ cup butter or margarine (1½ sticks), melted
⅔ cup plus 2 tablespoons packed brown sugar
⅔ cup honey
⅔ cup milk
1 teaspoon ground cinnamon

1. Preheat oven to 400°F. Grease 24 standard muffin-pan cups or line with paper baking liners. In large bowl, stir together flour, baking powder, pumpkin-pie spice, baking soda, and salt.

2. In medium bowl, with wire whisk or fork, mix eggs, pumpkin, melted butter, ⅔ cup brown sugar, honey, and milk. Stir egg mixture into flour mixture just until flour is moistened (batter will be lumpy).

3. Spoon batter into prepared muffin cups. In small bowl, combine remaining 2 tablespoons brown sugar and cinnamon; sprinkle over muffins. Bake 25 to 30 minutes, rotating pans between upper and lower oven racks halfway through. When muffins are done, tops will be browned and toothpick inserted in center of muffin will come out clean. Immediately remove muffins from pan. Serve warm, or cool on wire rack to serve later.

Each muffin: about 205 calories, 3g protein, 31g carbohydrate, 8g total fat (4g saturated), 1g fiber, 43mg cholesterol, 285mg sodium

Apple Streusel Muffins

For these, the muffin cups are completely filled with batter, so the tops of the muffins will run together. Cut them apart with a sharp knife before turning them out.

Active time: 25 minutes
Bake time: 25 minutes
Makes: 12 muffins

1/3 cup packed light brown sugar
3 tablespoons plus 1/2 cup butter or margarine
2 2/3 cups all-purpose flour
1 1/2 teaspoons ground cinnamon
1/2 cup granulated sugar
2 teaspoons baking powder
1/2 teaspoon baking soda
1/2 teaspoon salt
1 cup buttermilk
1 large egg
1 large Granny Smith apple (see Tip), peeled, cored, and finely chopped (1 heaping cup)

1. In medium bowl, with pastry blender or fingertips, mix brown sugar, 3 tablespoons butter, cut into pieces, 1/3 cup flour, and 1 teaspoon cinnamon until mixture resembles coarse crumbs. Set aside.

2. Preheat oven to 400°F. Grease 12 standard muffin-pan cups or line with paper baking liners. Melt remaining 1/2 cup butter.

3. In large bowl, stir together remaining 2 cups flour and 1/2 teaspoon cinnamon, as well as granulated sugar, baking powder, baking soda, and salt. In medium bowl, with wire whisk or fork, mix buttermilk, egg, and melted butter until blended. Stir in apple. Stir egg mixture into flour mixture just until flour is moistened.

4. Spoon batter into prepared muffin cups (cups will be full). Sprinkle streusel over muffins, pressing lightly into batter. Bake 25 minutes, or until toothpick inserted in center of muffin comes out clean. Cool in pan 10 minutes. Cut through tops to separate, then transfer muffins to wire rack to cool. Serve warm, or cool on wire rack to serve later.

Each muffin: about 270 calories, 4g protein, 36g carbohydrate, 12g total fat (7g saturated), 1g fiber, 47mg cholesterol, 365mg sodium

TIP Instead of apples, you could swap in 2 ripe medium pears. Peel, core, and finely chop them just before adding them to the batter.

Oatmeal Muffins

A sweet and crunchy blend of chopped walnuts, toasted oats, and brown sugar crowns these fruit-filled muffins.

Active time: 20 minutes
Bake time: 20 minutes
Makes: 12 muffins

1¼ cups old-fashioned or quick-cooking oats, uncooked
¼ cup walnuts (1 ounce)
1½ cups all-purpose flour
½ cup granulated sugar
2 teaspoons baking powder
½ teaspoon baking soda
¼ teaspoon salt
1 cup buttermilk
⅓ cup butter or margarine, melted
1 large egg
1 teaspoon vanilla extract
½ cup dried cranberries or raisins
¼ cup packed light brown sugar

1. Preheat oven to 400°F. Grease 12 standard muffin-pan cups or line with paper baking liners. Spread oats on jelly-roll pan and spread walnuts on smaller baking pan and toast both at same time, 5 to 7 minutes, until lightly browned, stirring nuts once or twice. Cool. Coarsely chop walnuts.

2. In large bowl, stir together flour, granulated sugar, baking powder, baking soda, salt, and 1 cup oats. In small bowl, with wire whisk or fork, mix buttermilk, melted butter, egg, and vanilla. Stir buttermilk mixture into flour mixture until flour is moistened (batter will be lumpy). Fold in cranberries.

3. Spoon batter into prepared muffin cups. In small bowl, stir together brown sugar, walnuts, and remaining ¼ cup oats; sprinkle over muffins. Bake 20 to 25 minutes, until toothpick inserted in center of muffin comes out clean. Immediately remove muffins from pan. Serve warm, or cool on wire rack to serve later.

Each muffin: about 230 calories, 4g protein, 34g carbohydrate, 9g total fat (2g saturated), 2g fiber, 18mg cholesterol, 260mg sodium

---

HEALTHY MAKEOVER

Whole-Grain Blueberry Muffins

Deliciously dense, these muffins are made with a combination of flours and oats. Blueberries, almonds, and orange add antioxidants.

Active time: 20 minutes
Bake time: 22 minutes
Makes: 12 muffins

1 cup old-fashioned oats, uncooked
1 cup whole-wheat flour
½ cup all-purpose flour
2 teaspoons baking powder
½ teaspoon baking soda
½ teaspoon salt
¼ cup plus 1 tablespoon packed brown sugar
1 cup low-fat buttermilk
¼ cup fresh orange juice
2 tablespoons canola oil
1 large egg
1 teaspoon vanilla extract
2 cups blueberries
¼ cup natural almonds, chopped

1. Preheat oven to 400°F. Line standard 12-cup muffin pan with paper baking liners.

2. Grind oats in blender. In bowl, whisk oats, flours, baking powder, baking soda, salt, and ¼ cup sugar. In small bowl, whisk buttermilk, juice, oil, egg, and vanilla. Stir into flour mixture; fold in blueberries.

3. Combine almonds and 1 tablespoon sugar. Spoon batter into muffin cups; sprinkle with almond sugar. Bake 22 minutes or until toothpick inserted in center comes out clean. Cool in pan on wire rack 5 minutes.

Each serving: about 170 calories, 5g protein, 28g carbohydrate, 5g total fat (1g saturated), 3g fiber, 16mg cholesterol, 270mg sodium

Whole-Grain Blueberry Muffins

Morning Glory Muffins

Here is the ultimate breakfast muffin—a carrot-cake-like batter with coconut, sunflower seeds, and raisins. Toasting the coconut and sunflower seeds is key.

Active time: 20 minutes
Bake time: 25 minutes
Makes: 12 muffins

1/2 cup sweetened flaked coconut

1/4 cup hulled sunflower seeds

2 cups all-purpose flour

2 teaspoons baking powder

1/2 teaspoon baking soda

1/2 teaspoon salt

1/2 teaspoon ground cinnamon

1/2 cup plain low-fat yogurt

1/2 cup packed light brown sugar

1/4 cup vegetable oil

1 large egg

1 1/2 cups shredded carrots (2 to 3 carrots; see Tip)

1/2 cup dark seedless raisins

1. Preheat oven to 375°F. Grease 12 standard muffin-pan cups or line with paper baking liners. On jelly-roll pan, toast coconut and sunflower seeds 7 minutes, stirring occasionally, or until coconut is golden. Cool.

2. In large bowl, stir together flour, baking powder, baking soda, salt, and cinnamon. In small bowl, with wire whisk or fork, mix yogurt, brown sugar, oil, and egg. Stir egg mixture into flour mixture just until flour is moistened. Stir in carrots, raisins, coconut, and sunflower seeds until combined.

3. Spoon batter into prepared muffin cups. Bake 25 minutes, or until toothpick inserted in center of muffin comes out clean. Immediately remove muffins from pan. Serve warm, or cool on wire rack to serve later.

Each muffin: about 240 calories, 5g protein, 36g carbohydrate, 9g total fat (4g saturated), 2g fiber, 32mg cholesterol, 260mg sodium

TIP To quickly shred carrots, cut them into large chunks and shred them in a food processor. Or purchase already-shredded carrots at the grocery store.

Applesauce Muffins

Sprinkling a bit of cinnamon sugar on top of these muffins before baking gives them a crunchy crust. Serve them with a pot of coffee for breakfast. They're delicious spread with soft cream cheese.

Active time: 15 minutes
Bake time: 25 minutes
Makes: 12 muffins

2 cups all-purpose flour
2 teaspoons baking powder
1/2 teaspoon salt
1 1/2 teaspoons ground cinnamon
1 large egg
1 cup unsweetened applesauce
1/2 cup plus 2 tablespoons packed brown sugar
1/3 cup butter or margarine, melted
1/2 teaspoon vanilla extract
1 cup dark seedless raisins

1. Preheat oven to 400°F. Grease 12 standard muffin-pan cups or line with paper baking liners. In large bowl, stir together flour, baking powder, salt, and ½ teaspoon cinnamon.

2. In medium bowl, with wire whisk or fork, mix egg, applesauce, ½ cup brown sugar, melted butter, and vanilla, stirring until well combined. Stir egg mixture into flour mixture just until flour is moistened (batter will be lumpy). Stir in raisins.

3. Spoon batter into prepared muffin cups. In small cup, combine remaining 2 tablespoons sugar and remaining 1 teaspoon cinnamon; sprinkle over muffins. Bake 25 to 30 minutes, until muffins are browned and toothpick inserted in center comes out clean. Immediately remove muffins from pan. Serve warm, or cool on wire rack to serve later.

Each muffin: about 225 calories, 3g protein, 39g carbohydrate, 7g total fat (4g saturated), 2g fiber, 31mg cholesterol, 240mg sodium

---

HEALTHY MAKEOVER

Lemon-Yogurt Muffins

In these fresh-flavored muffins, nonfat yogurt takes the place of butter and egg yolks. The yogurt's tartness is a pleasing complement to the muffins' lemony zing—and of course it keeps the fat in check.

Active time: 10 minutes
Bake time: 20 minutes
Makes: 12 muffins

2 cups all-purpose flour
1/2 cup plus 1 tablespoon sugar
2 teaspoons baking powder
1/2 teaspoon baking soda
1/2 teaspoon salt
2 large egg whites
1 container (8 ounces) nonfat plain yogurt
2 tablespoons vegetable oil
2 teaspoons freshly grated lemon peel
1 teaspoon vanilla extract

1. Preheat oven to 400°F. Grease 12 standard muffin-pan cups or line with paper baking liners. In large bowl, stir together flour, ½ cup sugar, baking powder, baking soda, and salt.

2. In medium bowl with wire whisk or fork, mix egg whites, yogurt, oil, lemon peel, and vanilla. Stir yogurt mixture into flour mixture just until flour is moistened (batter will be lumpy).

3. Spoon batter into prepared muffin cups. Sprinkle remaining 1 tablespoon sugar over muffins. Bake 20 to 25 minutes, or until toothpick inserted in center of muffin comes out clean. Immediately remove muffins from pan. Serve warm, or cool on wire rack to serve later.

Each muffin: about 155 calories, 4g protein, 27g carbohydrate, 4g total fat (1g saturated), 1g fiber, 0mg cholesterol, 255mg sodium

Popovers

Popovers are made from just five ingredients—eggs, milk, butter, flour, and salt—but the batter puffs into astonishingly high domes. Theories of popover perfection vary. Some recipes start the batter in a cold oven, while others specify that both oven and pans be hot before pouring in the batter. We find the latter method to work perfectly. Special popover pans are available, but custard cups or muffins tins work just as well.

Active time: 10 minutes
Bake time: 1 hour
Makes: 8 medium or 12 small popovers

3 large eggs
1 cup milk
3 tablespoons butter or margarine, melted
1 cup all-purpose flour
1/2 teaspoon salt

1. Preheat oven to 375°F. Grease eight 6-ounce custard cups or 12 standard muffin-pan cups well with melted butter or vegetable oil. Set custard cups on jelly-roll pan for easier handling.

2. In medium bowl, with mixer on low speed, beat eggs until frothy; beat in milk and melted butter until blended. Gradually beat in flour and salt until well combined. Alternatively, combine all ingredients in blender and blend until smooth.

3. Pour about ⅓ cup batter into each custard cup, or fill muffin cups half full. Bake 50 minutes, then quickly cut small slit in top of each popover to let out steam; bake 10 minutes longer. (Don't open oven during first 50 minutes of baking time or popovers may fall.) Immediately remove popovers from cups, loosening with spatula if necessary. Serve hot.

Each medium popover: about 160 calories, 5g protein, 14g carbohydrate, 9g total fat (5g saturated), 1g fiber, 101mg cholesterol, 250mg sodium

Each small popover: about 105 calories, 3g protein, 9g carbohydrate, 6g total fat (3g saturated), 1g fiber, 67mg cholesterol, 165mg sodium

PARMESAN POPOVERS Prepare popovers as instructed, but use *only ¼ teaspoon salt*. Add *½ cup freshly grated Parmesan cheese* and *⅛ teaspoon coarsely ground black pepper* to batter.

Each medium popover: about 185 calories, 8g protein, 14g carbohydrate, 11g total fat (6g saturated), 1g fiber, 106mg cholesterol, 290mg sodium

Each small popover: about 125 calories, 5g protein, 9g carbohydrate, 7g total fat (4g saturated), 1g fiber, 70mg cholesterol, 190mg sodium

LOW-FAT POPOVERS Prepare popovers as instructed, but use *1 whole large egg* and *3 large egg whites* in place of the 3 whole eggs; use *1 tablespoon melted butter* and *1 cup low-fat milk (1%)* in place of the whole milk.

Each medium popover: about 115 calories, 5g protein, 14g carbohydrate, 4g total fat (2g saturated), 1g fiber, 37mg cholesterol, 225mg sodium

Each small popover: about 80 calories, 3g protein, 9g carbohydrate, 3g total fat (2g saturated), 1g fiber, 25mg cholesterol, 150mg sodium

GIANT POPOVERS Grease six 8-ounce deep ceramic custard cups well; place on jelly-roll pan. Proceed as instructed, but use *6 eggs, 2 cups milk, 6 tablespoons melted butter or margarine, 2 cups all-purpose flour,* and *1 teaspoon salt.* Bake 1 hour before cutting slits in top, then bake 10 minutes longer, as directed. Makes 6 large popovers.

Each giant popover: about 410 calories, 13g protein, 36g carbohydrate, 23g total fat (13g saturated), 1g fiber, 265mg cholesterol, 650mg sodium

TEA BREADS & COFFEE CAKES

Sweet fruit and nut loaves, country-style soda bread, and buttery streusel-topped cakes are perfect with morning coffee or for an afternoon snack. Baked in foil loaf pans, tea breads make gracious holiday or housewarming gifts. Many of these breads and cakes freeze well, and loaf-shaped tea breads are excellent for toasting.

Sour Cream Tea Bread

This light, fine-textured cake (or any of the five variations that follow) may be baked in four 5¾" by 3¼" mini loaf pans for 40 minutes, or until the bread tests done with a toothpick.

Active time: 25 minutes
Bake time: 1 hour 5 minutes
Makes: 1 loaf, 16 servings

2¹/2 cups all-purpose flour
1¹/2 teaspoons baking powder
¹/2 teaspoon baking soda
¹/2 teaspoon salt
¹/2 cup butter or margarine (1 stick), softened
1¹/4 cups sugar
2 large eggs
1 container (8 ounces) sour cream
1 teaspoon vanilla extract

1. Preheat oven to 350°F. Grease 9" by 5" metal loaf pan; dust with flour. In medium bowl, stir together flour, baking powder, baking soda, and salt. In large bowl, with mixer on low speed, beat butter until smooth. Add sugar and beat until creamy.

2. Reduce speed to low and add eggs, one at a time, beating after each addition until well blended, scraping bowl occasionally with rubber spatula. Add flour mixture alternately with sour cream, beginning and ending with flour mixture. Beat in vanilla.

3. Spoon batter into prepared loaf pan. Bake 1 hour 5 minutes, or until toothpick inserted in center of loaf comes out clean. Cool loaf in pan on wire rack 10 minutes: remove loaf from pan and cool completely on rack before slicing.

Each serving: about 225 calories, 3g protein, 31g carbohydrate, 10g total fat (6g saturated), 1g fiber, 48mg cholesterol, 230mg sodium

ROSEMARY AND GOLDEN RAISIN TEA BREAD Prepare bread as instructed, but omit vanilla. Combine *1½ teaspoons finely chopped dried rosemary* with *½ teaspoon vegetable oil* and stir into batter after adding eggs. Fold in *¾ cup golden raisins* before spooning into pan.

Each serving: about 245 calories, 4g protein, 37g carbohydrate, 10g total fat (6g saturated), 1g fiber, 48mg cholesterol, 235mg sodium

APRICOT- OR CHERRY-ALMOND TEA BREAD Prepare bread as instructed, but add *½ teaspoon almond extract* with vanilla. Fold *1 cup dried apricots or dried tart cherries*, coarsely chopped, into batter before spooning into pan, then sprinkle *¼ cup sliced almonds (1 ounce)* on top of batter. Bake as directed, covering loaf with foil after 45 minutes of baking to prevent overbrowning.

Each serving apricot-almond bread: about 255 calories, 4g protein, 37g carbohydrate, 11g total fat (6g saturated), 1g fiber, 48mg cholesterol, 235mg sodium

Each serving cherry-almond bread: about 255 calories, 4g protein, 38g carbohydrate, 11g total fat (6g saturated), 1g fiber, 48mg cholesterol, 230mg sodium

BLUEBERRY STREUSEL TEA BREAD Prepare bread as instructed, but fold in *1½ cups blueberries* before spooning into pan. In small bowl, combine *¼ cup all-purpose flour, ¼ cup packed light brown sugar, 2 tablespoons chopped pecans, ⅛ teaspoon ground cinnamon, 2 tablespoons softened butter or margarine*; mix with fingertips until blended. Sprinkle streusel over batter. Bake 1 hour 15 to 1 hour 25 minutes.

Each serving: about 270 calories, 4g protein, 38g carbohydrate, 12g total fat (7g saturated), 1g fiber, 52mg cholesterol, 250mg sodium

GINGER TEA BREAD Prepare bread as instructed, but add *1 teaspoon ground ginger* to flour mixture. Fold in *½ cup crystallized ginger*, coarsely chopped, before spooning into pan.

Each serving: about 250 calories, 3g protein, 38g carbohydrate, 10g total fat (6g saturated), 1g fiber, 48mg cholesterol, 240mg sodium

CHOCOLATE CHIP TEA BREAD Prepare bread as instructed, but fold *1 cup mini chocolate chips* into batter before spooning into pan.

Each slice: about 275 calories, 4g protein, 38g carbohydrate, 13g total fat (8g saturated), 1g fiber, 48mg cholesterol, 235mg sodium

Perfect Banana Bread

Really ripe bananas (fully golden and covered with brown "freckles") are a must for a naturally sweet bread. If you have green bananas, leave them in a plastic bag at room temperature for a few days to hasten the process. Once ripe, the bananas can be frozen for future baking. If you like nuts in your banana bread, feel free to add 1 cup coarsely chopped walnuts or pecans to the batter.

Active time: 20 minutes
Bake time: 1 hour
Makes: 1 loaf, 16 servings

2 cups all-purpose flour
3/4 teaspoon baking soda
1/2 teaspoon salt
2 cups mashed very ripe bananas (4 medium)
1 teaspoon vanilla extract
1/2 cup butter or margarine (1 stick), softened
1/2 cup granulated sugar
1/2 cup brown sugar
2 large eggs

1. Preheat oven to 325°F. Evenly grease 8½" by 4½" metal loaf pan. In medium bowl, with wire whisk, stir together flour, baking soda, and salt. In small bowl, stir together bananas and vanilla until blended.

2. In large bowl, with mixer on medium speed, beat butter and both sugars until light and fluffy. Beat in eggs, one at a time. Reduce speed to low; alternately add flour mixture and banana mixture, beginning and ending with flour mixture and occasionally scraping bowl with rubber spatula. Beat batter just until blended.

3. Pour batter into prepared pan. Bake until toothpick inserted in center comes out clean, about 1 hour. Cool loaf in pan on wire rack 10 minutes; remove from pan and cool completely on rack before slicing.

Each serving: about 200 calories, 3g protein, 32g carbohdyrate, 7g total fat (4g saturated), 1g fiber, 43mg cholesterol, 205mg sodium

Zucchini Cheese Loaf

The addition of Cheddar and Parmesan create an irresistible savory loaf. The generous amount of black pepper gives the bread a spicy bite, but you can reduce it or leave it out, if you prefer.

Active time: 15 minutes
Bake time: 55 minutes
Makes: 1 loaf, 12 slices

2¹/₂ cups all-purpose flour
4 teaspoons baking powder
1 tablespoon sugar
1¹/₂ teaspoons salt
¹/₂ teaspoon ground black pepper
4 ounces sharp Cheddar cheese, shredded (1 cup)
¹/₂ cup freshly grated Parmesan cheese
2 cups coarsely shredded zucchini (1 medium)
3 green onions, finely chopped
2 large eggs
³/₄ cup milk
¹/₃ cup olive oil

1. Preheat oven to 350°F. Grease 9" by 5" metal loaf pan. In large bowl, stir together flour, baking powder, sugar, salt, and pepper.

2. In small bowl, combine ¼ cup Cheddar and 2 tablespoons Parmesan; set aside. Stir remaining ¾ cup Cheddar and 6 tablespoons Parmesan into flour mixture. Add zucchini and green onions. In medium bowl with a fork, beat eggs; stir in milk and oil. Add egg mixture to flour mixture, stirring just until dry ingredients are moistened (batter will be very thick).

3. Scrape batter into prepared loaf pan and spread evenly; sprinkle with reserved cheese mixture. Bake 55 to 60 minutes, until toothpick inserted in center of loaf comes out clean. Cool loaf in pan on wire rack 5 minutes. Remove from pan and cool completely on rack.

Each slice: about 240 calories, 9g protein, 23g carbohydrate, 12g total fat (4g saturated), 1g fiber, 51mg cholesterol, 610mg sodium

Orange Cranberry Bread

An obvious choice for Thanksgiving, this orange-scented bread is packed with fresh cranberries. You may want to make several loaves—one to serve with dinner, and one or more extras for the holiday breakfasts that follow.

Active time: 20 minutes
Bake time: 55 minutes
Makes: 1 loaf, 12 servings

1 large orange
2¹/₂ cups all-purpose flour
1 cup sugar
2 teaspoons baking powder
¹/₂ teaspoon baking soda
¹/₂ teaspoon salt
2 large eggs
4 tablespoons butter or margarine, melted
2 cups cranberries, coarsely chopped
³/₄ cup walnuts (3 ounces), chopped (optional)

1. Preheat oven to 375°F. Grease 9" by 5" metal loaf pan. From orange, grate 1 teaspoon peel and squeeze ¹/₂ cup juice. Set aside.

2. In large bowl, stir together flour, sugar, baking powder, baking soda, and salt. In small bowl, with whisk or fork, beat eggs, melted butter, and orange peel and juice. Add egg mixture to flour mixture; stir just until batter is mixed (batter will be stiff). Fold in cranberries and, if using, walnuts.

3. Pour batter into prepared loaf pan. Bake 55 to 60 minutes, until toothpick inserted in center of bread comes out clean. Cool loaf in pan on wire rack 10 minutes; remove from pan and cool completely on rack before slicing.

Each serving: about 225 calories, 4g protein, 40g carbohydrate, 5g total fat (3g saturated), 2g fiber, 46mg cholesterol, 280mg sodium

ORANGE CRANBERRY BREAD

Easy Christmas Stollen

Traditionally, this holiday sweetbread is leavened with yeast; our quick alternative is made with baking powder. It's of course perfect for breakfast on Christmas morning, but why not bake multiple loaves? They'll make delightful holiday gifts, wrapped in cellophane and tied with a big bow.

Active time: 25 minutes
Bake time: 1 hour
Makes: 1 loaf, 12 servings

2¼ cups all-purpose flour
½ cup granulated sugar
1½ teaspoons baking powder
¼ teaspoon salt
8 tablespoons cold butter or margarine (1 stick)
1 cup ricotta cheese
½ cup candied lemon peel or coarsely chopped red candied cherries
½ cup dried tart cherries or dark seedless raisins
⅓ cup slivered blanched almonds or chopped pecans, toasted (see page xxiii)
1 teaspoon vanilla extract
½ teaspoon freshly grated lemon peel
1 large egg
1 large egg yolk
Confectioners' sugar for sprinkling (optional)

1. Preheat oven to 325°F. Grease large cookie sheet. In large bowl, stir together flour, granulated sugar, baking powder, and salt. With pastry blender or two knives used scissor-fashion, cut in 6 tablespoons butter until mixture resembles fine crumbs. With spoon, stir in ricotta until moistened. Stir in candied peel, raisins, almonds, vanilla, lemon peel, egg, and egg yolk until well combined.

2. Turn dough out onto lightly floured work surface; gently knead two or three times to blend. With floured rolling pin, roll dough into 10" by 8" oval. Fold lengthwise almost in half, letting bottom dough extend about 1 inch beyond edge of top dough.

3. Place stollen on prepared cookie sheet. Bake 1 hour, or until toothpick inserted in center of bread comes out clean. Transfer from cookie sheet to wire rack. Melt remaining 2 tablespoons butter and brush over stollen. Cool completely on wire rack. Sprinkle with confectioners' sugar, if you like, before slicing.

Each serving: about 300 calories, 7g protein, 38g carbohydrate, 14g total fat (7g saturated), 1g fiber, 67mg cholesterol, 210mg sodium

---

STOLLEN: A HOLIDAY CLASSIC

Germany's traditional Christmas loaf, this rich sweetbread is dotted with dried and candied fruit and nuts and often topped with confectioners' sugar or a sugary icing. A ribbon of marzipan through the middle of the loaf is optional, as is macerating the dried fruits in rum or brandy for added flavor. With stollen, there's no fancy shaping required. Just roll the dough into an oval and fold it in half; the dough is thick and easy to work with.

The first stollens appeared as early as the fifteenth century in Dresden, Germany. In 1730, King Augustus II asked the Baker's Guild of Dresden to bake a giant stollen for a farewell dinner; the resulting loaf was said to feed over 24,000 guests. To commemorate this event, every December, Dresden holds a Stollenfest. A two-ton stollen is paraded through the market square, then sliced and sold to the public; the proceeds support local charities.

Although there is a basic recipe for making traditional Dresden *Christollen*, every home seems to have its own secret recipe, passed down from one generation to the next. Commercially, the official Dresden Stollen is produced by only 150 master bakers and distinguished by a special seal depicting King Augustus II.

Traditional Irish Soda Bread

Don't save this recipe for St. Patrick's Day. Enjoy it any day with butter, jam, or honey.

Active time: 15 minutes
Bake time: 1 hour
Makes: 1 loaf, 12 servings

4 cups all-purpose flour
1/4 cup sugar
1 tablespoon baking powder
1¹/2 teaspoons salt
1 teaspoon baking soda
6 tablespoons butter or margarine
1¹/2 cups buttermilk

1. Preheat oven to 350°F. Grease large cookie sheet. In large bowl, stir together flour, sugar, baking powder, salt, and baking soda. With pastry blender or two knives used scissor-fashion, cut in butter until mixture resembles coarse crumbs. Stir in buttermilk just until flour is moistened (dough will be sticky).

2. Turn dough out onto well-floured work surface. With floured hands, knead 8 to 10 times until combined. (Do not overmix, or bread will be tough.) Shape into ball; place on prepared cookie sheet.

3. Sprinkle ball lightly with flour. In center, cut 4-inch cross about ¼ inch deep. Bake 1 hour, or until toothpick inserted in center of loaf comes out clean. Remove loaf from cookie sheet and cool completely on wire rack.

Each serving: about 235 calories, 5g protein, 38g carbohydrate, 7g total fat (4g saturated), 1g fiber, 17mg cholesterol, 610mg sodium

SODA BREAD WITH CURRANTS AND CARAWAY SEEDS

Prepare bread as instructed, but add *1½ cups dried currants* and *2 teaspoons caraway seeds* along with the buttermilk.

Each slice: about 300 calories, 6g protein, 52g carbohydrate, 7g total fat (4g saturated), 2g fiber, 17mg cholesterol, 610mg sodium

Top: Easy Christmas Stollen; Bottom: Traditional Irish Soda Bread

Classic Crumb Cake

Moist yellow cake with a buttery cinnamon-sugar topping is guaranteed to please. This recipe makes two cakes: one to eat immediately, one to freeze for another day. Wrap tightly in foil, then place in a freezerweight zip-seal bag; freeze for up to 1 month.

Active time: 40 minutes
Bake time: 40 minutes
Makes: 2 coffee cakes, 10 servings each

CRUMB TOPPING

2 cups all-purpose flour
1/2 cup granulated sugar
1/2 cup packed light brown sugar
1 1/2 teaspoons ground cinnamon
1 cup butter or margarine (2 sticks), softened

CAKE

2 1/4 cups all-purpose flour
2 1/4 teaspoons baking powder
1/2 teaspoon salt
1 1/4 cups granulated sugar
1/2 cup butter or margarine (1 stick), softened
3 large eggs
3/4 cup milk
2 teaspoons vanilla extract

1. Prepare topping: In medium bowl, mix flour, both sugars, and cinnamon until well blended. With fingertips, work in butter until mixture resembles coarse crumbs.

2. Prepare cake: Preheat oven to 350°F. Grease two 9-inch round cake pans; dust with flour. In medium bowl, stir together flour, baking powder, and salt.

Top: CLASSIC CRUMB CAKE; Bottom: BANANA CRUMB CAKE

3. In large bowl, with mixer on low speed, beat granulated sugar and butter until blended, scraping bowl often with rubber spatula. Increase speed to medium; beat about 2 minutes, until well mixed, scraping bowl occasionally. Reduce speed to low; add eggs, one at a time, beating well after each.

4. In cup, combine milk and vanilla. With mixer on low speed, add flour mixture alternately with milk mixture, beginning and ending with flour mixture, scraping bowl occasionally, until batter is smooth.

5. Pour batter into prepared pans. With hand, press crumb topping into large chunks; sprinkle evenly over batter. Bake 40 to 45 minutes, until toothpick inserted in center of cake comes out clean. Cool cakes in pans on wire racks 15 minutes. With small metal spatula, loosen each cake from side of pan. Turn out onto plate; remove pan. Immediately invert cakes onto wire racks to cool completely, with crumb topping up.

Each serving: about 330 calories, 4g protein, 45g carbohydrate, 16g total fat (9g saturated), 1g fiber, 70mg cholesterol, 270mg sodium

Banana Crumb Cake

Brunch always calls for something sweet, like this crumb cake with notes of honey, cinnamon, and toasted coconut.

Active time: 15 minutes

Bake time: 50 minutes

Makes: 12 servings

COCONUT-PECAN TOPPING

1/2 cup pecans, toasted (see page xxiii) and chopped

1/4 cup unsweetened shredded coconut, toasted (see page xxii)

1/4 cup all-purpose flour

1/4 cup packed dark brown sugar

1/4 teaspoon ground cinnamon

2 tablespoons butter or margarine

BANANA CAKE

1 1/2 cups all-purpose flour

1 teaspoon baking powder

1/2 teaspoon baking soda

1/4 teaspoon salt

1/8 teaspoon ground cinnamon

4 tablespoons butter or margarine, at room temperature

1/2 cup packed dark brown sugar

3 tablespoons pure honey

2 large eggs, lightly beaten

1 cup mashed very ripe bananas (about 3 medium)

1 teaspoon vanilla extract

1. Prepare topping: In medium bowl, combine pecans, coconut, flour, brown sugar, and cinnamon. With pastry blender or two knives used scissor-fashion, cut in butter until mixture resembles coarse crumbs, with a few pea-size chunks remaining.

2. Prepare cake: Preheat oven to 350°F. Grease 9-inch springform pan; line bottom with parchment and grease parchment. On sheet of waxed paper, mix flour, baking powder, baking soda, salt, and cinnamon until well blended. In large bowl, with mixer on medium speed, beat butter, sugar, and honey until light and creamy, about 5 minutes, scraping bowl occasionally. Gradually add eggs, one at a time, beating after each. On low speed, add half of flour mixture, then mashed bananas, and vanilla. Add remaining flour mixture and beat just until smooth.

3. Spoon batter into prepared pan and spread evenly. Sprinkle with crumb topping. Bake 50 to 55 minutes, until toothpick inserted in center comes out clean. Cool in pan on wire rack 10 minutes. With small metal spatula, loosen cake from side of pan and remove. Cool completely. (Cake can be wrapped tightly in plastic and kept at room temperature up to 1 day.)

Each serving: about 255 calories, 4g protein, 37g carbohydrate, 11g total fat (5g saturated), 51mg cholesterol, 205mg sodium

Sour Cream Coffee Cake

This is a real tried-and-true American classic that your grandmother may well have served to her friends. Baked in a tube pan, the cake has a layer of walnuts and cinnamon sugar in the middle and a topping of the same spicy-sweet mixture. In the variations, this is replaced with a cinnamon-chocolate layer or a ribbon of raspberry jam and walnuts.

Active time: 30 minutes
Bake time: 1 hour 20 minutes
Makes: 1 coffee cake, 16 servings

2/3 cup plus 1¾ cups sugar
2/3 cup walnuts, finely chopped
1 teaspoon ground cinnamon
3¾ cups all-purpose flour
2 teaspoons baking powder
1 teaspoon baking soda
¾ teaspoon salt
1/2 cup butter or margarine (1 stick), softened
3 large eggs
1 container (16 ounces) sour cream
2 teaspoons vanilla extract

1. Preheat oven to 350°F. Grease 9- to 10-inch tube pan with removable bottom; dust with flour. In small bowl, mix 2/3 cup sugar, walnuts, and cinnamon. In medium bowl, stir together flour, baking powder, baking soda, and salt.

2. In large bowl, with mixer on low speed, beat remaining 1¾ cups sugar and butter until blended, scraping bowl with rubber spatula. Increase speed to high; beat until creamy, about 2 minutes, scraping bowl occasionally. Reduce speed to low; add eggs, one at a time, beating well after each.

3. With mixer on low speed, add flour mixture alternately with sour cream, beginning and ending with flour mixture, scraping bowl occasionally, until batter is smooth. Beat in vanilla.

4. Spoon one-third of batter into prepared tube pan. Sprinkle ½ cup nut mixture evenly over batter, then spread half of remaining batter on top. Sprinkle with ½ cup more nut mixture; layer with remaining batter, then remaining nut mixture.

5. Bake cake 1 hour 20 minutes, or until toothpick inserted in center comes out clean. Cool cake in pan on wire rack 10 minutes. With small metal spatula, loosen cake from side of pan and lift cake from pan bottom. Invert cake onto plate; remove bottom of pan. Immediately invert cake onto wire rack, with nut mixture on top, to cool completely before slicing.

Each serving: about 390 calories, 6g protein, 55g carbohydrate, 17g total fat (8g saturated), 1g fiber, 68mg cholesterol, 335mg sodium

CHOCOLATE-CHERRY COFFEE CAKE Prepare batter as instructed, but omit nut mixture in step 1. Stir *2/3 cup dried tart cherries* into batter after adding vanilla in step 3. In small bowl, mix *½ cup semisweet mini chocolate chips, 1 tablespoon unsweetened cocoa, 2 teaspoons ground cinnamon,* and *1/3 cup sugar.* Spoon one-third of batter into prepared pan; sprinkle with half of chocolate mixture. Top with half of remaining batter; sprinkle with remaining chocolate mixture. Spread remaining batter on top. Bake as directed. To serve, sprinkle with *confectioners' sugar.*

Each serving: about 380 calories, 5g protein, 58g carbohydrate, 15g total fat (9g saturated), 1g fiber, 68mg cholesterol, 335mg sodium

RASPBERRY-WALNUT SOUR CREAM COFFEE CAKE Prepare batter as instructed, but omit nut mixture in step 1. Spoon three-fourths of batter into prepared pan. Spread *½ cup seedless red raspberry jam* over batter, spread remaining batter over jam. Sprinkle *½ cup walnuts,* toasted (see page xxiii) and chopped, over top of batter. Bake as directed.

Each serving: about 370 calories, 6g protein, 53g carbohydrate, 16g total fat (8g saturated), 1g fiber, 68mg cholesterol, 340mg sodium

Fruit-Streusel Coffee Cake

Here's a coffee-time treat to suit every season. You can cover the buttery cake with just about any fruit you please, from summer's berries and stone fruits to autumn's pears and apples. Or try an unexpected midwinter treat—frozen rhubarb.

Active time: 25 minutes
Bake time: 50 minutes
Makes: 1 coffee cake, 15 servings

STREUSEL TOPPING

3/4 cup all-purpose flour
1/2 cup packed light brown sugar
1 teaspoon ground cinnamon
4 tablespoons butter or margarine, chilled and cut up

CAKE

2 1/4 cups all-purpose flour
1 1/2 teaspoons baking powder
1/2 teaspoon baking soda
1/2 teaspoon salt
1 1/2 cups granulated sugar
3/4 cup butter or margarine (1 1/2 sticks), softened
3 large eggs
1 cup milk
1 teaspoon vanilla extract
1 1/4 pounds ripe pears, apples, or peaches, peeled and thinly sliced (see Tip)

1. Prepare streusel topping: In medium bowl, with fingertips, stir together flour, brown sugar, cinnamon, and butter until mixture resembles coarse crumbs.

2. Prepare cake: Preheat oven to 350°F. Grease 13" by 9" metal baking pan; dust with flour. In medium bowl, stir together flour, baking powder, baking soda, and salt.

3. In large bowl, with mixer on low speed, beat sugar and butter until blended, scraping bowl often with rubber spatula. Increase speed to high; beat until creamy, about 2 minutes, scraping bowl occasionally. Reduce speed to low; add eggs, one at a time, beating well after each addition.

4. In cup, combine milk and vanilla. With mixer on low speed, add flour mixture alternately with milk mixture, beginning and ending with flour mixture, scraping bowl occasionally, until batter is smooth.

5. With metal spatula, spread batter evenly in prepared pan. Arrange fruit slices, overlapping slightly, on top. Sprinkle streusel topping over fruit.

6. Bake cake 50 to 55 minutes, until toothpick inserted in center comes out clean. Cool cake in pan on wire rack 10 minutes to serve warm. Or cool completely in pan.

Each serving: about 355 calories, 5g protein, 53g carbohydrate, 14g total fat (8g saturated), 2g fiber, 78mg cholesterol, 315mg sodium

TIP To substitute a different fruit, just make sure you use an equal weight. Thin-skinned stone fruits like nectarines or plums don't need to be peeled; just pit and thinly slice them (you need about 3 cups' worth). To use fresh or frozen rhubarb, cut the stalks into 1-inch pieces (you need about 4 cups). Fresh blueberries also work well; you need about 1 pint.

SWEET YEAST BREADS & BUNS

These holiday and special-occasion breads are well worth the time and effort required. Some of the recipes, like Challah, are only mildly sweet. Others, like the Overnight Sticky Buns and Baba au Rhum, which is soaked in a rum syrup, are unabashedly rich and sweet.

Panettone

Tall, domed loaves of panettone are often given as Christmas gifts. Commercially made versions of this festive bread are widely available, but they're not nearly as good as homemade. Beat the dough by hand or use a heavy-duty stand mixer.

Active time: 35 minutes plus rising
Bake time: 30 minutes
Makes: 2 loaves, 8 servings each

1/2 cup milk, heated to lukewarm (105°F to 115°F)
1 package active-dry yeast
3 1/4 cups all-purpose flour
1/2 cup butter or margarine (1 stick), softened
1/2 cup sugar
1 tablespoon freshly grated orange peel
1 1/2 teaspoons vanilla extract
1/2 teaspoon salt
3 large eggs
1/2 cup golden raisins
1/3 cup chopped candied lemon peel

1. In medium bowl, combine warm milk, yeast, and 1/2 cup flour. Cover bowl and let stand 45 minutes. (Mixture will bubble and rise.)

2. In bowl of heavy-duty stand mixer, with mixer on medium speed, beat butter, sugar, orange peel, vanilla, and salt until light and fluffy. Alternately, beat in eggs and remaining 2 3/4 cups flour until well combined. Beat in yeast mixture. Stir in raisins and candied lemon peel.

3. Place dough in greased large bowl, turning dough over to grease top. Cover bowl and let rise in warm, draft-free place until doubled, about 2 hours.

4. Meanwhile, brush insides of two clean 11 1/2-ounce coffee cans with vegetable shortening. Punch down dough and divide between cans. Cover cans and let rise in warm place until dough has doubled in volume and has risen almost to top of cans, 1 hour 15 minutes to 2 hours.

5. Preheat oven to 350°F. Bake breads 30 to 35 minutes, until surface is golden brown and skewer inserted in center of each loaf comes out clean. Remove from cans to cool on wire rack. To serve, cut into wedges.

Each serving: about 225 calories, 4g protein, 33g carbohydrate, 9g total fat (4g saturated), 1g fiber, 56mg cholesterol, 150mg sodium

---

THE STORY OF BABA

It's a rather complicated tale that begins with a polish king (Stanislas) in exile in France. The king found the traditional sweet yeast breads too dry for his taste and came up with the idea of soaking them in rum. As refined by his pastry chef, the recipe became a brioche dough baked in a cylindrical mold (or molds, for individual servings). After baking, the baba was drenched in a sweet rum syrup, just as in our recipe.

Baba au Rhum

It's kin to Kugelhopf (page 272) and to the Polish yeast cake called babka, but with a special finish. Baba au Rhum is soaked with a rum syrup after baking.

Active time: 25 minutes plus rising
Bake time: 25 minutes
Makes: 12 servings

CAKE

2/3 cup milk, heated to lukewarm (105°F to 115°F)
1 teaspoon active dry yeast
1 teaspoon plus 1 tablespoon sugar
2 cups all-purpose flour
1 teaspoon salt
3 large eggs
6 tablespoons butter or margarine, melted and cooled

SYRUP

1¹/2 cups water
1 cup sugar
6 strips (3" by ¹/2" each) orange peel
¹/2 cup dark rum
1 teaspoon vanilla extract

1. Prepare cake: In large bowl, combine warm milk, yeast, and 1 teaspoon sugar; stir to dissolve. Let stand 5 minutes, or until foamy. Stir in flour, salt, and eggs until well combined. Cover and let rise in warm, draft-free place until doubled, about 1 hour. With wooden spoon, mix in melted butter, stirring about 5 minutes, until batter is thick, smooth, and elastic.

2. Grease and flour 9- to 10-inch tube pan. Spoon batter into pan, cover, and let rise in warm place until doubled, about 45 minutes.

3. Preheat oven to 375°F. Bake cake 25 minutes, or until surface is golden brown and toothpick inserted in center of cake comes out clean. Cool in pan on wire rack 5 minutes; remove from pan and set on wire rack.

4. Prepare syrup: In 3-quart saucepan, stir together water, sugar, and orange peel over medium heat. Heat to boiling; boil 1 minute. Remove and discard orange peel. Stir in rum and vanilla.

5. Transfer warm cake to deep-dish pie plate. With skewer or toothpick, prick cake several times. Spoon 1½ cups warm syrup over cake. Continue spooning syrup over top. Let stand 20 minutes before serving warm or at room temperature. Pass remaining syrup with cake.

Each serving: about 250 calories, 4g protein, 36g carbohydrate, 8g total fat (4g saturated), 1g fiber, 71mg cholesterol, 275mg sodium

TEST KITCHEN KNOW-HOW

KNEADING DOUGH

Although not all yeast breads and buns require kneading, it's a gratifying hands-on activity. Here's how to get the best results.

Use the heel of one hand to push the dough away from you. The dough may be soft at first, but will firm up as you continue to knead it.

After each kneading stroke, fold the dough over and give it a quarter turn. Start the next kneading stroke on top of the folded-over portion of the dough—and repeat until the dough is smooth and elastic.

Kugelhopf

Cousin to both brioche and panettone (pages 277 and 270), this rich, sweet bread is made with eggs and butter, studded with raisins, crusted with almonds, and flavored with liquor. You can purchase a traditional Kugelhopf mold (a deep, fluted pan with a tube in the middle) at a kitchen supply store or online, but a Bundt or tube pan will do the job.

Active time: 25 minutes plus rising
Bake time: 35 minutes
Makes: 1 loaf, 16 servings

1 package active dry yeast
3/4 cup milk, heated to lukewarm (105°F to 115°F)
4 cups all-purpose flour
1 cup golden or dark seedless raisins
2 tablespoons rum, bourbon, or brandy
2/3 cup granulated sugar
4 large eggs
1 1/4 teaspoons salt
3/4 cup butter or margarine (1 1/2 sticks), softened (see Tip)
1/2 cup sliced blanched almonds (2 ounces)
Confectioner' sugar for sprinkling (optional)

1. In large bowl, combine yeast, warm milk, and 1 cup flour. Whisk until smooth. Cover bowl with plastic wrap and let sponge rise in warm place 1 hour.

2. In saucepan, combine raisins and liquor. Bring to boiling over high heat. Cover and cool.

3. Add 1 cup flour, granulated sugar, eggs, and salt to sponge. Beat well with wooden spoon until smooth. Gradually stir in 1 1/2 cups flour, beating vigorously with wooden spoon. Add remaining 1/2 cup flour and butter, and beat well with wooden spoon, pulling and stretching dough until butter is blended in. Stir in raisins with any liquid. Cover bowl with plastic wrap and let rise in warm, draft-free place until almost doubled, about 1 hour 30 minutes.

4. Stir down dough. Generously butter 9-inch (12-cup) fluted Kugelhopf mold or Bundt pan. Sprinkle bottom and sides with almonds, covering evenly. Spoon dough into prepared pan, smoothing top. Cover pan with greased plastic wrap. Let rise in warm place until dough is doubled and comes up to 1/2 inch from top of pan, about 1 hour 30 minutes.

5. Preheat oven to 375°F. Bake 35 minutes, covering top loosely with foil after about 30 minutes to prevent overbrowning. Cool in pan on wire rack 3 minutes. Turn out onto rack. Let cool completely. Before slicing, sprinkle confectioners' sugar lightly on top if desired.

Each serving: about 300 calories, 6g protein, 41g carbohydrate, 13g total fat (7g saturated), 2g fiber, 80mg cholesterol, 300mg sodium

TIP The butter is beaten into the already-mixed dough. Be sure it's nice and soft, or it will be difficult to work in.

Greek Christmas Bread

Fragrant with anise, this rich holiday bread is baked as two round loaves topped with decorative crosses. The bread is delicious warm—a wonderful treat for Christmas morning.

Active time: 35 minutes plus rising
Bake time: 40 minutes per batch
Makes: 2 loaves, 12 servings each

3/4 cup warm water (105°F to 115°F)
2 packages active dry yeast
1 teaspoon plus 1 cup sugar
1 1/4 cups milk, heated to lukewarm (105°F to 115°F)
1 cup butter or margarine (2 sticks), softened
1 1/2 teaspoons salt
1 teaspoon anise seeds, crushed
3 large eggs
About 7 1/2 cups all-purpose flour
1 1/2 cups dark seedless raisins
2 tablespoons sliced blanched almonds

1. In large bowl, combine warm water, yeast, and 1 teaspoon sugar; stir to dissolve. Let stand 5 minutes, or until foamy. Add remaining 1 cup sugar, warm milk, butter, salt, anise, 2 eggs, and 3 cups flour. Beat well with wooden spoon. Stir in raisins. Gradually stir in enough remaining flour (about 4 cups) to make soft dough.

2. Turn dough onto lightly floured work surface and knead about 10 minutes, until smooth and elastic, working in just enough of remaining 1/2 cup flour to keep dough from sticking. Shape dough into ball; place in greased large bowl, turning dough over to grease top. Cover bowl and let rise in warm, draft-free place until doubled, about 1 hour 30 minutes.

4. Grease two large cookie sheets. Punch down dough. Remove about 1/2 cup dough and set aside. Divide remaining dough into 2 pieces; cover and refrigerate 1 piece. Place remaining large piece on lightly floured work surface and shape into smooth ball. Place in center of one prepared cookie sheet and press into 8-inch round. Cut small reserved piece of dough into quarters. With hands, roll each quarter into 10-inch-long rope. With knife, cut

2-inch-long split in each end of all 4 ropes. Cover 2 ropes and place in refrigerator. Arrange remaining 2 ropes on shaped loaf to form cross; curl ends. Cover loaf loosely with greased plastic wrap and let rise in warm place until doubled, 45 to 60 minutes.

5. After 45 minutes, remove dough ball and ropes from refrigerator and repeat step 4 to form second loaf.

6. Preheat oven to 350°F. In small cup, with fork, beat remaining egg. Brush first loaf with beaten egg; sprinkle with half of sliced almonds. Bake 40 to 45 minutes, until bottom sounds hollow when lightly tapped, covering loaf loosely with foil to prevent overbrowning after 30 minutes. Transfer loaf to wire rack to cool before slicing. When second loaf has risen, repeat same process to bake.

Each serving: about 295 calories, 6g protein, 47g carbohydrate, 10g total fat (5g saturated), 2g fiber, 49mg cholesterol, 240mg sodium

DECORATING GREEK CHRISTMAS BREAD

A crisscross of dough on top of each loaf creates the Easter emblem.

To create the decorative curls at the ends of the cross, split each end of the dough ropes to a depth of 2 inches, then curl the split tips outward. Brush an egg wash on the top of the loaf for a shiny finish and to help the sliced almonds adhere.

Challah

Served on the Jewish Sabbath, holidays, and for everyday consumption, challah is a traditional bread that's rich with eggs and has a light, airy texture. Though it can be shaped in many ways, the braided loaf is the most classic form.

Active time: 30 minutes plus rising
Bake time: 30 minutes
Makes: 1 loaf, 12 servings

¾ cup warm water (105°F to 115°F)
1 package active dry yeast
1 teaspoon plus ¼ cup sugar
3 large eggs, lightly beaten
¼ cup vegetable oil
1 teaspoon salt
About 4¼ cups all-purpose flour, or about 3½ cups bread flour

1. In large bowl, combine warm water, yeast, and 1 teaspoon sugar; stir to dissolve. Let stand 5 minutes, or until foamy. Measure 1 tablespoon beaten egg into small cup; cover and refrigerate. Add remaining eggs, remaining ¼ cup sugar, oil, salt, and 2 cups flour to yeast mixture. Beat well with wooden spoon. Stir in about 1¾ cups all-purpose flour or 1¼ cups bread flour to make soft dough.

2. Turn dough onto lightly floured work surface and knead about 8 minutes, until smooth and elastic, working in only as much of remaining flour as necessary to keep dough from sticking.

3. Shape dough into ball; place in greased large bowl, turning dough over to grease top. Cover and let dough rise in warm, draft-free place until doubled, about 1 hour. Punch down dough. Grease large cookie sheet.

4. Form braided loaf (see photos at right): Turn dough onto lightly floured work surface and cut into 2 pieces, making one twice as large as other. Cut larger piece of dough into thirds; with hands, roll each piece into 13-inch-long rope. Place ropes side by side on cookie sheet and braid, pinching ends to seal. Place on prepared cookie sheet.

5. Cut remaining piece of dough into thirds; roll each piece into thin, 14-inch-long rope. Place ropes side by side and braid; pinch ends to seal. Place small braid on top of large braid and tuck ends under loaf, stretching top braid if necessary; pinch ends to seal. Cover loosely with greased plastic wrap and let rise in warm place until doubled, about 45 minutes.

6. Preheat oven to 375°F. Brush reserved beaten egg over top and sides of loaf. Bake 30 to 35 minutes, covering loaf loosely with foil to prevent overbrowning after 20 minutes if necessary, until bottom sounds hollow when lightly tapped with fingers. Transfer to wire rack to cool.

Each slice: about 250 calories, 6g protein, 40g carbohydrate, 7g total fat (1g saturated), 1g fiber, 53mg cholesterol, 210mg sodium

SHAPING CHALLAH

You can form challah into any shape you like, but a braided loaf is traditional.

To make a double-braided challah, start by forming two-thirds of the dough into three ropes and braiding them together. Pinch the ends to seal them.

Divide the remaining dough into three pieces and roll them into ropes. Braid these and pinch the ends together, then place the small braid on top of the large one and tuck the ends under.

Overnight Sticky Buns

These delectable breakfast treats rise slowly overnight in the refrigerator—all you have to do in the morning is bake and serve.

Active time: 1 hour plus rising and chilling
Bake time: 30 minutes
Makes: 20 buns

DOUGH

¼ cup warm water (105°F to 115°F)
1 package active dry yeast
1 teaspoon plus ¼ cup granulated sugar
¾ cup milk
4 tablespoons butter or margarine, softened
1 teaspoon salt
3 large egg yolks
About 4 cups all-purpose flour

FILLING AND TOPPING

½ cup plus ⅔ cup packed dark brown sugar
¼ cup dried currants
1 tablespoon ground cinnamon
7 tablespoons butter or margarine
2 tablespoons light corn syrup
2 tablespoons honey
1¼ cups pecans (5 ounces), coarsely chopped

1. Prepare dough: In cup, combine warm water, yeast, and 1 teaspoon granulated sugar; stir to dissolve. Let stand 5 minutes, or until foamy.

2. In large bowl, with mixer on low speed, blend yeast mixture with milk, butter, salt, egg yolks, 3 cups flour, and remaining ¼ cup granulated sugar until blended. With wooden spoon, stir in ¾ cup flour.

3. Turn dough out onto lightly floured work surface and knead about 5 minutes, until smooth and elastic, working in only as much of remaining ¼ cup flour as necessary to keep dough from sticking. Shape dough into ball; place in greased large bowl, turning dough over to grease top. Cover bowl and let dough rise in warm, draft-free place about 1 hour.

4. Meanwhile, prepare filling: In small bowl, combine ½ cup brown sugar, currants, and cinnamon. Set aside.

5. Prepare topping: In 1-quart saucepan, heat remaining ⅔ cup brown sugar, 3 tablespoons butter, corn syrup, and honey over low heat, stirring occasionally, until butter has melted. Grease 13" by 9" metal baking pan; pour brown-sugar mixture into pan and sprinkle evenly with pecans; set aside.

6. Punch down dough. Turn dough onto lightly floured work surface; cover and let rest 15 minutes. Melt remaining 4 tablespoons butter. With floured rolling pin, roll dough into 18" by 12" rectangle. Brush dough with melted butter and sprinkle with currant mixture.

7. Starting at one long side, roll up dough jelly-roll fashion; place, seam side down, on work surface. Cut crosswise into 20 slices. Place slices, cut side down, on topping in baking pan, making 4 rows of 5 slices each. Cover pan and refrigerate at least 12 hours or up to 20 hours.

8. Preheat oven to 375°F. Bake buns 30 minutes, or until golden. Remove pan from oven. Immediately place serving tray or jelly-roll pan over top of baking pan and invert buns onto tray; remove baking pan. Let buns cool slightly to serve warm, or cool completely to serve later.

Each bun: about 290 calories, 4g protein, 42g carbohydrate, 12g total fat (5g saturated), 1g fiber, 50mg cholesterol, 195mg sodium

CINNAMON BUNS Prepare dough and shape buns as instructed, but omit pecan topping. Bake as directed. Invert baked buns onto cookie sheet; remove baking pan and transfer buns right side up to wire rack. In small bowl, mix *1 cup confectioners' sugar* with *5 teaspoons water* until smooth; drizzle icing over hot buns.

Each bun: about 215 calories, 4g protein, 36g carbohydrate, 6g total fat (3g saturated), 1g fiber, 46mg cholesterol, 170mg sodium

TIP If you have any leftover sticky buns, wrap them in foil and freeze up to 1 month. Reheat the still-wrapped buns in a preheated 350°F oven for 15 to 20 minutes.

Individual Brioches

You need a heavy-duty stand mixer and individual brioche molds to make this rich French classic. It's an overnight recipe—all you need to do before serving is bake the breads for 17 minutes. So knock 'em dead with brioche at brunch!

Active time: 45 minutes plus rising
Bake: 17 minutes
Makes: 24 individual brioches

³/4 cup milk, heated to lukewarm (105°F to 115°F)
1 package active dry yeast
1 teaspoon plus ¹/4 cup sugar
4 cups bread or all-purpose flour
1 teaspoon salt
7 large eggs
1 cup butter (2 sticks), softened and cut into 4 pieces (do not use margarine)
1 tablespoon water

1. In large bowl of heavy-duty mixer, combine warm milk, yeast, and 1 teaspoon sugar; stir to dissolve. Let stand 5 minutes, or until foamy.

2. Stir in 1 cup flour, remaining ¼ cup sugar, and salt until blended. With mixer on low speed, beat in 1 egg. Beat in ¾ cup flour and then 1 egg, and repeat, alternately beating in flour and egg, until remaining 2¼ cups flour and total of 6 eggs have been well incorporated. Gradually beat in butter until smooth.

3. Place dough in lightly buttered bowl and turn to coat surface of dough with butter. Cover loosely with plastic wrap and let rise in warm, draft-free place until doubled, about 2 hours 30 minutes.

4. Refrigerate bowl, still covered, overnight. Punch down dough. Divide dough in half. Roll each half into 16-inch-long rope and cut into 12 equal pieces. Roll each piece into tight ball.

5. Lightly butter twenty-four ½-cup fluted individual brioche molds. Place 1 ball in front of you and, with side of hand, press almost but not quite through one-third of ball to form attached large and small balls. With fingers, push smaller ball of dough inside larger one, pressing all around so that small ball is deeply set into large ball. Place ball, larger section down, in each prepared mold. Repeat with remaining dough. Cover molds with lightly greased plastic wrap and let rise in warm place until doubled, about 45 minutes.

6. Preheat oven to 400°F. In cup, beat remaining egg with water until combined. Brush tops of brioches with egg wash, being careful not to let egg drip down sides of mold, as this could inhibit rising. Place molds on two large cookie sheets for easier handling. Bake 17 to 20 minutes, rotating sheets between upper and lower oven racks halfway through, until golden brown. Remove brioches from molds and cool on wire rack.

Each brioche: about 190 calories, 5g protein, 19g carbohydrate, 10g total fat (6g saturated), 1g fiber, 84g cholesterol, 200mg sodium

PIZZA, CALZONES & FOCACCIA

Pizza toppings are so scrumptious, it's easy to forget that the crust is a simple-to-prepare flatbread. When stretched thin, pizza dough bakes up crisp, but if formed into a thick layer, it rises into an airy bread—focaccia, which can be made with or without toppings. Stromboli and calzones are savory stuffed breads made from pizza dough.

Basic Pizza Dough

This recipe makes enough dough for two pizzas. You can try a couple of the topping variations that follow (each is designed to top one pizza).

Active time: 15 minutes plus rising
Bake time: 15 minutes
Makes: about 1½ pounds dough, enough dough for 2 pizzas, 4 main-dish servings each

1¼ cups warm water (105°F to 115°F)
1 package active dry yeast
1 teaspoon sugar
2 tablespoons olive oil
2 teaspoons salt
About 4 cups bread flour or 4½ cups all-purpose flour
Cornmeal for sprinkling on pan

1. In large bowl, combine ¼ cup warm water, yeast, and sugar; stir to dissolve. Let stand 5 minutes, or until foamy. With wooden spoon, stir in remaining 1 cup warm water, oil, and salt; gradually add 1½ cups bread flour or 2 cups all-purpose flour until smooth. Gradually add 2 cups additional flour, stirring until dough comes away from sides of bowl.

2. Turn dough out onto lightly floured work surface and knead 10 minutes, working in only as much of remaining ½ cup flour as necessary to keep dough from sticking. Shape dough into ball; place in greased large bowl, turning dough over to grease top. Cover bowl and let rise in warm, draft-free place until doubled, 1 hour.

3. Punch down dough (see Tip). Turn out onto lightly floured work surface and cut in half; cover and let rest 15 minutes.

4. Preheat oven to 450°F. Sprinkle two large cookie sheets with cornmeal. Shape each dough half into ball and place on prepared cookie sheet. With floured rolling pin, roll dough into 14" by 10" rectangle, folding edge in to make 1-inch rim. Repeat with second half of dough.

5. Sprinkle each crust with topping of choice (see page 280 for ideas).

6. Let rest 20 minutes. Bake 15 to 20 minutes, until crust is golden and topping is heated through. Serve hot.

Each serving: about 280 calories, 7g protein, 51g carbohydrate, 5g total fat (1g saturated), 2g fiber, 0mg cholesterol, 585mg sodium

TIP If not using pizza dough right away, place in greased large bowl, cover loosely with greased plastic wrap, and refrigerate up to 24 hours until ready to use. Or cut the dough in half, tightly wrap one ball in plastic and freeze for another meal—it'll keep up to six months.

WHOLE-WHEAT PIZZA DOUGH Prepare dough as instructed, using 2 cups all-purpose flour in step 1. Add *1 tablespoon dark molasses* along with oil and use *2½ cups whole-wheat flour* instead of remaining all-purpose flour.

Each serving: about 270 calories, 8g protein, 50g carbohydrate, 5g total fat (1g saturated), 6g fiber, 0mg cholesterol, 585mg sodium

SICILIAN PIZZA Prepare and bake Basic Pizza Dough (page 278) or Whole-Wheat Pizza Dough (above) as instructed. For step 5, sprinkle 1 dough round with *2 tablespoons freshly grated Parmesan cheese*, spread with *1 cup Pizza Sauce (see box)*, and sprinkle with *1 cup shredded mozzarella*. Makes 1 pizza, 4 main-dish servings.

Each serving: about 400 calories, 14g protein, 56g carbohydrate, 13g total fat (5g saturated), 2g fiber, 25mg cholesterol, 900mg sodium

PIZZA CARBONARA Prepare and bake Basic Pizza Dough (page 278) or Whole-Wheat Pizza Dough (above) as instructed. While dough rises during step 2, in skillet, cook *6 slices bacon* over medium-high heat 5 minutes, or until brown. Transfer to paper towels to drain, reserving 1 tablespoon fat in skillet. Stir *2 tablespoons flour*, *¼ teaspoon salt*, and *¼ teaspoon ground black pepper* into pan. Cook 30 seconds; do not brown. Whisk in *1½ cups warmed milk* and heat to boiling over medium-high heat. Reduce heat to low and simmer 3 minutes. Remove saucepan from heat and stir in *¼ cup freshly grated Parmesan cheese* and *2 tablespoons chopped parsley*. In step 5, spoon sauce over 1 dough round; crumble bacon on top. Makes 1 pizza, 4 main-dish servings.

Each serving: about 450 calories, 15g protein, 59g carbohydrate, 16g total fat (6g saturated), 2g fiber, 27mg cholesterol, 1,035mg sodium

PIZZA PUTTANESCA Prepare and bake Basic Pizza Dough (page 278) or Whole-Wheat Pizza Dough (above) as instructed. While dough rises during step 2, in 12-inch skillet, heat *1 tablespoon olive oil* over medium-high heat. Stir in *2 minced garlic cloves*, *4 minced anchovy fillets*, and *⅛ teaspoon crushed red pepper*. Cook, stirring often, 1 minute, until garlic is pale golden. Add *1½ pounds coarsely chopped plum tomatoes* and *⅛ teaspoon ground black pepper*. Simmer 4 minutes. Remove from heat; stir in *¼ cup pitted Kalamata or pimiento-stuffed olives*, chopped, and *1 tablespoon capers*, chopped. In step 5, sprinkle *5 tablespoons freshly grated Parmesan cheese* over 1 dough round. Spread with sauce. Makes 1 pizza, 4 main-dish servings.

Each serving: about 400 calories, 11g protein, 61g carbohydrate, 14g total fat (2g saturated), 4g fiber, 5mg cholesterol, 1,065mg sodium.

Pizza Sauce

You can find jars of pizza sauce at the super-market, but it's so easy to make your own. If you're a garlic lover, add as much as you like.

Active time: 5 minutes
Cook time: 20 minutes
Makes: about 3 cups (enough for 1 pizza)

1 tablespoon olive oil
1 large garlic clove or more to taste, finely chopped
1 can (28 ounces) tomatoes in thick puree, chopped
1/4 teaspoon salt

In 2-quart saucepan, heat oil over medium-high heat. Stir in garlic and cook, stirring often, 30 seconds, or until golden. Add tomatoes with puree and salt; heat to boiling over high heat. Reduce heat and simmer, uncovered, 10 minutes.

Each 1/4 cup sauce: about 30 calories, 1g protein, 4g carbohydrate, 1g total fat (0g saturated), 1g fiber, 0mg cholesterol, 155mg sodium

SHAPING A PIZZA CRUST

Make our basic homemade pizza dough recipe (page 278), then follow these easy instructions for rolling and shaping it.

Pizza doesn't have to be round: You can make it rectangular to fit the cookie sheet, or even go freeform. With a lightly floured rolling pin, roll out the dough on a cornmeal-dusted baking sheet.

Turn the outer inch or so of the dough inward all around to form a rim; this will help contain the toppings. Spoon pizza sauce on the dough and sprinkle with toppings as desired, or try one of the variations (opposite). Bake as instructed.

Stromboli

Any combination of thinly sliced deli meats or cheeses can be used to fill this rolled pizza "sandwich." Stromboli can be served as an appetizer, snack, or light meal.

Active time: 30 minutes plus rising
Bake time: 30 minutes
Makes: 16 appetizer servings

Basic Pizza Dough (page 278), prepared through step 2
¼ pound thinly sliced salami
¼ pound thinly sliced Provolone cheese
¼ pound thinly sliced smoked baked ham or prosciutto
¼ cup freshly grated Parmesan cheese
¼ cup black olives, pitted and finely chopped
¼ cup green olives, pitted and finely chopped
1 large egg

1. Preheat oven to 375°F. Grease large cookie sheet

2. Punch down dough. On lightly floured work surface, with floured rolling pin, roll dough into 16" by 12" rectangle. Arrange salami slices on dough up to ½ inch from edges, overlapping slightly if necessary. Repeat with Provolone and ham. Sprinkle with Parmesan and both olives. Roll up dough, from a long side, jelly-roll style. Pinch seam and ends to seal and tuck ends under slightly. Place loaf, seam side down, diagonally on prepared cookie sheet. Cover with oiled plastic wrap and let rest 15 minutes.

3. In small cup, with fork, beat egg. With serrated knife or single-edge razor blade, cut 5 long diagonal slashes, each about 1½ inches deep, in top of loaf. Brush loaf with beaten egg, but do not brush slashes.

4. Bake stromboli 30 to 35 minutes, until browned. With wide metal spatula, loosen bottom of loaf and slide onto wire rack. Let cool slightly before slicing; serve warm or at room temperature.

Each serving: about 225 calories, 9g protein, 26g carbohydrate, 9g total fat (3g saturated), 1g fiber, 28mg cholesterol, 690mg sodium

Focaccia

Whether plain, herbed, or embellished with a topping, focaccia is the ideal accompaniment for an Italian meal; it also makes irresistible sandwiches when filled with meats, cheeses, or grilled vegetables.

Active time: 25 minutes plus rising
Bake time: 18 minutes
Makes: 12 servings

1½ cups warm water (105°F to 115°F)
1 package active dry yeast
1 teaspoon sugar
3¾ cups all-purpose flour or 3½ cups bread flour
5 tablespoons extra-virgin olive oil
1½ teaspoons table salt
1 teaspoon kosher salt or coarse sea salt

1. In large bowl, combine ½ cup warm water, yeast, and sugar; stir to dissolve. Let stand 5 minutes, or until foamy. Add remaining 1 cup warm water, flour, 2 tablespoons oil, and table salt: stir to combine.

2. Turn dough out onto lightly floured work surface and knead 7 minutes, or until smooth and elastic (dough will be soft: do not add more flour). Shape dough into ball; place in greased large bowl, turning over to coat. Cover bowl and let stand in warm, draft-free place until doubled, about 1 hour.

3. Lightly oil 15½" by 10½" jelly-roll pan. Punch down dough and pat into prepared pan. Cover and let rise in warm place until doubled, about 45 minutes.

4. With fingertips, make deep indentations, 1 inch apart, over entire surface of dough, almost to bottom of pan. Drizzle with remaining 3 tablespoons oil; sprinkle with kosher salt. Cover loosely and let rise in warm place until doubled, about 45 minutes.

5. Place oven rack in lowest position and preheat oven to 450°F. Bake focaccia 18 minutes, or until bottom is crusty and top is lightly browned. With wide metal spatula, transfer focaccia from pan to wire rack to cool.

Each serving: about 205 calories, 4g protein, 31g carbohydrate, 7g total fat (1g saturated), 1g fiber, 0mg cholesterol, 415mg sodium

RED PEPPER FOCACCIA Prepare focaccia as instructed, but omit kosher salt. While dough is rising in step 2, in 12-inch skillet, heat *1 tablespoon olive oil* over medium heat. Add *4 red peppers*, sliced, and *¼ teaspoon salt* and cook, stirring frequently, 20 minutes, or until tender. Cool to room temperature. Spoon peppers over dough in step 4, just after making indentations. Continue as directed.

Each serving: about 220 calories, 5g protein, 32g carbohydrate, 8g total fat (1g saturated), 2g fiber, 0mg cholesterol, 340mg sodium

SUN-DRIED TOMATO AND OLIVE FOCACCIA Prepare focaccia as instructed, but use only *½ teaspoon kosher salt*. Pit *½ cup Gaeta olives* and coarsely chop olives together with *¼ cup oil-packed dried tomatoes*, drained. Sprinkle mixture over dough just before baking.

Each serving: about 235 calories, 5g protein, 33g carbohydrate, 10g total fat (1g saturated), 2g fiber, 0mg cholesterol, 570mg sodium

ONION FOCACCIA Prepare focaccia as instructed, but omit kosher salt. While dough is rising in step 2, in 12-inch skillet, heat *2 teaspoons olive oil* over medium heat. Add *2 large onions (about 1 pound each)*, halved and sliced; *1 teaspoon sugar*; and *½ teaspoon salt*. Cook, stirring frequently, 20 minutes, or until golden brown. Cool to room temperature. Spoon onions over dough in step 4, just after making indentations. Continue as directed.

Each serving: about 225 calories, 5g protein, 34g carbohydrate, 8g total fat (1g saturated), 2g fiber, 0mg cholesterol, 390mg sodium

HERB FOCACCIA Prepare focaccia as instructed, but just before baking, sprinkle dough with either *2 tablespoons chopped fresh sage* or *1 tablespoon chopped fresh rosemary.*

Each serving: about 205 calories, 4g protein, 31g carbohydrate, 7g total fat (1g saturated), 1g fiber, 0mg cholesterol, 415mg sodium

Asparagus-Fontina Pizzettes with Bacon

These mini pizzas are each topped with a baked egg (and crispy bacon), making them an irresistible alternative to a breakfast sandwich. Pair them with a green salad and serve them for brunch or as a light dinner.

Active time: 35 minutes
Bake time: 17 minutes
Makes: 6 servings

8 ounces asparagus, trimmed
6 ounces shiitake mushrooms, stems discarded, thinly
  sliced
¼ cup olive oil
2 garlic cloves, crushed with press
¼ teaspoon salt, plus more to taste
Basic Pizza Dough (page 278), prepared through step 2
5 slices bacon
6 ounces Fontina cheese, shredded (1½ cups)
6 large eggs
Ground black pepper to taste

1. Arrange oven racks in top and bottom thirds of oven. Preheat oven to 475°F. Lightly grease two 18" by 12" jelly-roll pans.

2. Slice asparagus at angle into 2-inch pieces. Transfer to large bowl, along with mushrooms, oil, garlic, and ¼ teaspoon salt; toss until well coated.

3. Divide dough into 6 balls. On lightly floured work surface, with floured rolling pin, roll and press 1 dough ball into 6-inch round; place on prepared pan. Repeat with remaining dough.

4. Evenly divide asparagus mixture among rounds, creating well in center of each. Bake 10 minutes or until edges are golden brown, rotating pans between upper and lower oven racks halfway through.

5. Meanwhile, place bacon on paper-towel-lined plate. Cover with two sheets paper towel. Microwave on High 4 to 6 minutes or until beginning to crisp. Cool bacon slightly; tear into small pieces.

6. Sprinkle pizzettes with bacon and Fontina. Bake 1 to 2 minutes or until cheese melts. Carefully crack eggs directly onto centers of pizzettes. Bake 6 to 8 minutes or until whites are opaque and set, again rotating positions of pans halfway through. Sprinkle with pepper and salt; serve warm.

Each serving: about 585 calories, 27g protein, 57g carbohydrate, 28g total fat (9g saturated), 1g fiber, 226mg cholesterol, 1,130mg sodium

Sausage Calzones

A pizza-parlor specialty, these half-moon turnovers are stuffed with a "three-cheese-plus" filling—the plus is either sausage as in the main recipe or spinach as in the variation. Served hot from the oven, with a salad alongside, calzones make an excellent supper.

Active time: 45 minutes plus rising
Bake time: 30 minutes
Makes: 6 calzones

Basic Pizza Dough (page 278), prepared through step 3
8 ounces sweet or hot Italian sausage links, casings
  removed
1 small onion, finely chopped
1 garlic clove, finely chopped
1 container (15 ounces) part-skim ricotta cheese
2 ounces part-skim mozzarella cheese,
  shredded (½ cup)
⅓ cup freshly grated Parmesan cheese
⅛ teaspoon ground black pepper
Cornmeal for sprinkling on pan
1 tablespoon olive oil

1. While pizza dough is resting for 15 minutes, in 10-inch skillet, cook sausage, onion, and garlic over medium heat, stirring to break up sausage, about 8 minutes, or until browned. With slotted spoon, transfer sausage mixture to large bowl. Stir in ricotta, mozzarella, Parmesan, and pepper until blended.

2. Place oven rack in lowest position and preheat oven to 450°F. Sprinkle large cookie sheet with cornmeal.

3. Divide each dough half into thirds to make 6 equal pieces. On lightly floured work surface, with floured rolling pin, roll each piece of dough into 6-inch round. Spoon about ⅔ cup filling onto half of each round, leaving ½-inch border. Fold uncovered half over filling and pinch edges together firmly. With back of fork, press edges to seal. Brush with oil.

4. Bake calzones 30 to 35 minutes, until golden. Transfer to wire rack and let calzones cool 5 minutes before serving.

Each serving: about 670 calories, 28g protein, 77g carbohydrate, 27g total fat (10g saturated), 3g fiber, 57mg cholesterol, 1,280mg sodium

SPINACH-CHEESE CALZONES Prepare calzones as instructed, but omit sausage in step 1 and cook onion and garlic with 1 tablespoon olive oil. Instead of sausage, cook *1 package (10 ounces) frozen chopped spinach* as label directs; squeeze dry. Add spinach to skillet and cook, stirring, 5 minutes, until heated through. In addition to cheeses and black pepper, in step 2, add *¼ teaspoon salt and pinch ground nutmeg*.

Each serving: about 590 calories, 24g protein, 79g carbohydrate, 20g total fat (7g saturated), 4g fiber, 32mg cholesterol, 1,145mg sodium

TOP: ASPARAGUS-FONTINA PIZZETTES WITH BACON; BOTTOM: SAUSAGE CALZONES

Pissaladière

This version of a Provençal onion pizza is baked in a rectangular pan and cut into squares, which make great appetizers. You can prepare the dough in advance, let it rise once, then freeze it, well wrapped, for up to 3 months.

Active time: 45 minutes plus rising
Bake time: 25 minutes
Makes: 32 appetizer servings

1 cup warm water (105°F to 115°F)
1 package active dry yeast
3 cups all-purpose flour
1³/4 teaspoons salt
2 tablespoons olive oil
2 pounds large yellow onions, cut into ¹/2-inch pieces
1 can (2 ounces) anchovy fillets, rinsed, drained, and coarsely chopped
¹/3 cup pitted and halved Kalamata or Gaeta olives

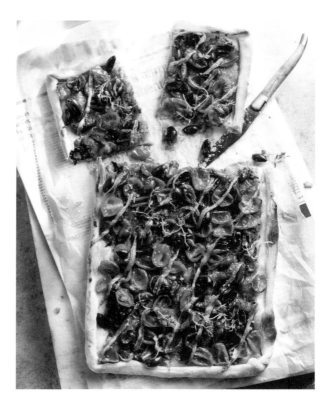

1. In cup, combine ¼ cup warm water and yeast; stir to dissolve. Let stand about 5 minutes, or until foamy.

2. In large bowl, stir together flour and 1½ teaspoons salt. Stir in yeast mixture, remaining ¾ cup warm water, and 1 tablespoon oil.

3. Turn dough out onto lightly floured work surface and knead about 8 minutes, until smooth and elastic. Shape dough into ball and place in greased large bowl, turning over to grease top. Cover bowl and let rise in warm, draft-free place until doubled, about 45 minutes.

4. Meanwhile, in 12-inch skillet, heat remaining 1 tablespoon oil over low heat. Add onions and remaining ¼ teaspoon salt and cook, stirring frequently, about 30 minutes, or until onions are soft. Cool to room temperature.

5. Oil 15½" by 10½" jelly-roll pan. Punch down dough and pat evenly into prepared pan. Cover loosely and let rise until almost doubled, 30 minutes.

6. Place oven rack in lowest position and preheat oven to 425°F. With fingertips, make indentations, 1 inch apart, over surface of dough. Add anchovies to onion mixture and spread mixture on top. Place olives at 2-inch intervals on onion mixture. Bake pizza 25 minutes, or until crust is golden. Cut into 2-inch squares. Cool in pan on wire rack.

Each serving: about 70 calories, 2g protein, 12g carbohydrate, 2g total fat (0g saturated), 1g fiber, 1mg cholesterol, 205mg sodium

CRACKERS, PRETZELS & BREADSTICKS

You can buy crackers at the supermarket, of course. But they're easy to make at home—and sure to impress guests at your next party. And pretzels, breadsticks, and rolls are fun to shape into rings, twists, sticks, knots, and even crescents. Top them with seeds, coarse salt, and a shiny glaze, and watch them bake up golden brown.

Soft Pretzels

Like the big pretzels sold by street vendors, these are best when eaten hot, with mustard for dipping. Try mixing the coarse salt with sesame or poppy seeds.

Active time: 30 minutes plus rising

Bake time: 16 minutes

Makes: 12 pretzels

2 cups warm water (105°F to 115°F)

1 package active dry yeast

1 teaspoon sugar

About 4 cups all-purpose flour

1 teaspoon table salt

2 tablespoons baking soda

1 tablespoon kosher or coarse or sea salt

1. In a bowl, combine 1½ cups warm water, yeast, and sugar; stir to dissolve. Let stand 5 minutes, or until foamy. Add 2 cups flour and table salt. Beat well with wooden spoon. Gradually stir in 1½ cups flour to make soft dough.

2. Turn dough onto floured work surface and knead 6 minutes, until smooth and elastic, working in only as much of remaining ½ cup flour as necessary to keep dough from sticking.

3. Shape dough into ball; place in greased large bowl, turning dough over to grease top. Cover bowl and let rise in warm, draft-free place until doubled, about 30 minutes.

4. Preheat oven to 400°F. Grease two large cookie sheets. Punch down dough and cut into 12 pieces.

5. Shape pretzels: Roll each piece into 24-inch-long rope. Shape ropes into loop-shaped pretzels (to make ahead, see Tip).

6. In small bowl, whisk remaining ½ cup warm water and baking soda until soda has dissolved.

7. Dip pretzels in baking-soda mixture and place 1½ inches apart, on prepared cookie sheets. Sprinkle lightly with kosher salt. Bake pretzels 16 to 18 minutes, until browned, rotating sheets between upper and lower oven racks halfway through. Transfer to wire racks to cool. Serve warm or at room temperature.

Each pretzel: about 165 calories, 5g protein, 33g carbohydrate, 1g total fat (0g saturated), 1g fiber, 0mg cholesterol, 1,190mg sodium

SOFT PRETZEL STICKS Prepare dough as instructed above through step 4. On lightly floured work surface, with hands, roll each piece into 8-inch-long rope. Dip ropes into baking-soda mixture as instructed in step 6; place sticks 2 inches apart on greased cookie sheets. Sprinkle with coarse salt and bake as directed.

Each pretzel stick: about 170 calories, 5g protein, 33g carbohydrate, 1g total fat (0g saturated), 1g fiber, 0mg cholesterol, 945mg sodium

TIP You can freeze unbaked pretzels or pretzel sticks on a cookie sheet, covered tightly with foil. Then just thaw them and proceed with step 6.

Romano Cheese Flatbread Crisps

No dip is necessary when you serve up these peppery, cheese-topped strips.

Active time: 45 minutes
Bake time: 15 minutes per batch
Makes: 36 crisps

2¼ cups all-purpose flour
1½ teaspoons baking powder
1 teaspoon salt
1 teaspoon coarsely ground black pepper
¾ cup water
1 tablespoon olive or vegetable oil
½ cup freshly grated Pecorino-Romano cheese

1. In medium bowl, stir together flour, baking powder, salt, and pepper. Add water, stirring until dough comes together. With hand, knead dough in bowl until smooth, about 2 minutes. Divide dough in half; cover half of dough.

2. Preheat oven to 350°F. On floured work surface, with floured rolling pin, roll dough half into paper-thin rectangle, about 20" by 12" (edges may be ragged). With pizza wheel or sharp knife, cut dough lengthwise in half to form two 20" by 6" rectangles. Cut rectangles crosswise into 2-inch-wide strips.

3. Place strips ½ inch apart on two ungreased large cookie sheets; let rest 10 minutes. With pastry brush, brush strips lightly, using half of oil; sprinkle with half of grated cheese. Bake 15 to 18 minutes, until lightly browned, rotating sheets between upper and lower oven racks halfway through. With wide metal spatula, immediately transfer crisps to wire racks to cool.

4. Repeat with remaining dough, oil, and cheese.

Each crisp: about 40 calories, 1g protein, 6g carbohydrate, 1g total fat (0g saturated), 0g fiber, 1mg cholesterol, 100mg sodium

Spicy Cornmeal Cheddar Wafers

The food processor mixes the dough for these irresistibly savory crackers, which are zesty with Cheddar, Parmesan, and Dijon mustard. Be careful when transferring the wafers to and from the cooling rack, as they are quite fragile.

Active time: 25 minutes plus chilling
Bake time: 18 minutes per batch
Makes: 48 wafers

1 cup all-purpose flour
¼ cup cornmeal
¼ cup freshly grated Parmesan or
    Pecorino-Romano cheese
½ teaspoon coarsely ground black pepper
½ teaspoon baking powder
¼ teaspoon cayenne (ground red) pepper
½ cup butter (1 stick), cut into 8 pieces, softened
1 tablespoon Dijon mustard
8 ounces sharp Cheddar cheese, shredded (2 cups)

1. In food processor with knife blade attached, combine flour, cornmeal, Parmesan, pepper, baking powder, and cayenne; process until blended. Add butter and process until mixture resembles fine meal. Add mustard and Cheddar and process until mixture is blended and begins to hold together.

2. Turn dough out onto lightly floured work surface and knead to blend. With hands, shape into 10-inch-long log. Wrap in waxed paper and refrigerate at least 4 hours, or overnight.

3. Preheat oven to 350°F. With serrated knife, cut log into scant ¼-inch-thick slices. Place slices 1½ inches apart on two ungreased large cookie sheets. Bake 18 minutes, or until lightly browned and crisp, rotating sheets between upper and lower oven racks halfway through. While wafers are still hot, with wide metal spatula, carefully transfer to wire rack to cool completely.

Each wafer: about 50 calories, 2g protein, 3g carbohydrate, 4g total fat (2g saturated), 0g fiber, 11mg cholesterol, 70mg sodium

Crisp Breadsticks

We sprinkle these golden-brown breadsticks with caraway, sesame, or poppy seeds. Try our Parmesan and rosemary-fennel variations too.

Active time: 15 minutes plus rising
Bake time: 20 minutes per batch
Makes: 64 breadsticks

2 packages quick-rise yeast
2¹/2 teaspoons salt
About 4³/4 cups all-purpose flour
1¹/3 cups very warm water (120°F to 130°F)
¹/2 cup olive oil
3 tablespoons caraway seeds, sesame seeds, or poppy seeds

1. In large bowl, combine yeast, salt, and 2 cups flour. With wooden spoon, stir in warm water; beat vigorously 1 minute. Stir in oil. Gradually stir in 2¼ cups flour. If using caraway seeds, stir in now.

2. Turn dough onto floured work surface and knead about 8 minutes, until smooth and elastic, working in only as much of remaining ½ cup flour as necessary to keep dough from sticking. Cover dough loosely; let rest 10 minutes.

3. Preheat oven to 375°F. Grease two large cookie sheets. Cut dough in half. Keeping remaining dough covered, cut 1 dough half into 32 pieces. Shape each piece into 12-inch-long rope. Place ropes, about 1 inch apart, on prepared cookie sheets. If using sesame or poppy seeds, sprinkle half of seeds on top of breadsticks.

4. Bake breadsticks 20 minutes, or until golden on surface and crisp throughout, rotating cookie sheets between upper and lower oven racks halfway through. Transfer to wire racks to cool.

5. Repeat with remaining dough and seeds.

Each breadstick: about 50 calories, 1g protein, 7g carbohydrate, 2g total fat (0g saturated), 1g fiber, 0mg cholesterol, 90mg sodium

TIP You can make these up to 2 weeks ahead of time. Store them in an airtight container at room temperature.

PARMESAN BREADSTICKS Prepare breadsticks as instructed, but omit seeds. Prepare *2½ cups freshly grated Parmesan cheese*. After forming sticks in step 3, roll each rope in 1 slightly rounded teaspoon cheese.

Each breadstick: about 70 calories, 3g protein, 7g carbohydrate, 3g total fat (1g saturated), 1g fiber, 3mg cholesterol, 160mg sodium

ROSEMARY-FENNEL BREADSTICKS Prepare breadsticks as instructed, but instead of using caraway seeds, in step 1, stir *2 teaspoons fennel seeds*, crushed; *1 teaspoon dried rosemary leaves*, crumbled; and *½ teaspoon coarsely ground black pepper* into dough.

Each breadstick: about 50 calories, 1g protein, 7g carbohydrate, 2g total fat (0g saturated), 1g fiber, 0mg cholesterol, 90mg sodium

Soft Breadsticks

The perfect companions for a salad or bowl of soup, these puffy breadsticks can be topped with sesame, poppy, caraway, or fennel seeds, or simply sprinkled with coarse salt.

Active time: 15 minutes plus rising
Bake time: 15 minutes per batch
Makes: 32 breadsticks

1 cup warm water (105°F to 115°F)
1 package active dry yeast
1 teaspoon sugar
2 tablespoons olive oil
1½ teaspoons salt
About 3¼ cups all-purpose flour
1 large egg
1 tablespoon water
3 tablespoons sesame seeds, poppy seeds, caraway seeds, or fennel seeds, or 1 tablespoon coarse salt

1. In large bowl, combine ¼ cup warm water, yeast, and sugar; stir to dissolve. Let stand 5 minutes, or until foamy. With wooden spoon, stir in remaining ¾ cup water, oil, salt, and 3 cups flour until combined.

2. Turn dough out onto lightly floured work surface and knead 10 minutes, until smooth and elastic, working in only as much of remaining ¼ cup flour as necessary to keep dough from sticking.

3. Shape dough into ball; place in greased large bowl, turning dough to grease top. Cover bowl and let rise in warm, draft-free place until doubled, about 45 minutes.

4. In bowl, stir together egg and water.

5. Preheat oven to 400°F. Grease two large cookie sheets. Punch down dough and turn out onto lightly floured work surface; divide into 32 pieces and cover with slightly damp clean kitchen towel. Remove piece of dough from under towel and roll into 10" by ¼" rope; place on prepared cookie sheet. Repeat for remaining dough pieces, placing ropes about 2 inches apart on sheets. With pastry brush, brush each rope with egg mixture; sprinkle with seeds or salt.

6. Bake breadsticks 15 to 20 minutes, until golden brown, rotating sheets between upper and lower oven racks halfway through. With wide metal spatula, transfer breadsticks to wire racks to cool.

Each breadstick: about 65 calories, 2g protein, 10g carbohydrate, 2g total fat (0g saturated), 1g fiber, 7mg cholesterol, 110mg sodium

Dinner Rolls

Homemade rolls, hot from the oven, make any dinner special. We offer instructions for shaping this basic dough three different ways.

Active time: 30 minutes plus rising
Bake time: 10 minutes
Makes: 24 rolls

½ cup warm water (105°F to 115°F)
2 packages active dry yeast
1 teaspoon plus ⅓ cup sugar
¾ cup milk, heated to lukewarm (105°F to 115°F)
4 tablespoons butter or margarine, softened
About 3¾ cups all-purpose flour
1½ teaspoons salt
2 large eggs
1 egg yolk
1 tablespoon water

1. In large bowl, combine warm water, yeast, and 1 teaspoon sugar; stir to dissolve. Let stand 5 minutes, until foamy.

2. With wooden spoon, or mixer on low speed, beat in warm milk, butter, ½ cup flour, remaining ⅓ cup sugar, salt, and whole eggs to make thick batter; continue beating 2 minutes, scraping bowl often. Gradually stir in 3 cups flour to make soft dough.

3. Turn dough out onto lightly floured work surface and knead about 10 minutes, until smooth and elastic, working in only as much of remaining ¼ cup flour as necessary to keep dough from sticking. Shape dough into ball; place in greased large bowl, turning dough over to grease top. Cover bowl and let rise in warm, draft-free place until doubled, about 1 hour.

4. Punch down dough. Turn out onto lightly floured work surface; cover and let rest 15 minutes.

5. Grease baking pan or pans required for desired type of roll (see below); shape rolls.

6. Cover and let rise in warm place, until doubled, about 30 minutes.

7. Preheat oven to 400°F. Whisk together egg yolk and water. Brush rolls with egg-yolk wash. Bake 10 to 12 minutes, rotating sheets between upper and lower oven racks halfway through. When done, rolls will be golden and bottoms will sound hollow when lightly tapped with fingers. Transfer to wire racks. Serve warm or let cool to serve later.

BASIC DINNER ROLLS Prepare dough as instructed through step 4. Grease two large cookie sheets. Cut dough into 24 equal pieces. Shape each piece into 2-inch ball; with floured hands, roll each ball 4 inches long, tapering ends slightly. Place rolls, 2 inches apart, on prepared cookie sheets. With serrated knife or single-edge razor blade, make slash lengthwise through center of each roll. Continue as directed in step 6. Makes 24 rolls.

Each roll: about 120 calories, 3g protein, 19g carbohydrate, 4g total fat (2g saturated), 1g fiber, 33mg cholesterol, 175mg sodium

CLOVERLEAF ROLLS Prepare dough as instructed through step 4. Grease 24 standard muffin-pan cups. Divide dough in half. Cut 1 half into 36 equal pieces; shape each piece into ball. Place 3 balls together in prepared muffin-pan cup. Repeat with all remaining dough to make 24 rolls. Continue as directed in step 6. Makes 24 rolls.

Each roll: about 130 calories, 3g protein, 19g carbohydrate, 4g total fat (2g saturated), 1g fiber, 33mg cholesterol, 75mg sodium

CRESCENT ROLLS Prepare dough as instructed through step 4. Grease two large cookie sheets. Melt *2 tablespoons butter or margarine*. Divide dough in half. Roll 1 half into 9-inch circle. With serrated knife, cut circle into 8 wedges; brush wedges with half of melted butter. Starting at wide base, roll up each wedge toward point. Curve ends toward each other and place, point side up, on one prepared cookie sheet. Repeat with remaining dough and butter and place on second sheet. Continue as directed in step 6. Makes 16 rolls.

Each roll: about 195 calories, 5g protein, 28g carbohydrate, 7g total fat (3g saturated), 1g fiber, 53mg cholesterol, 275mg sodium

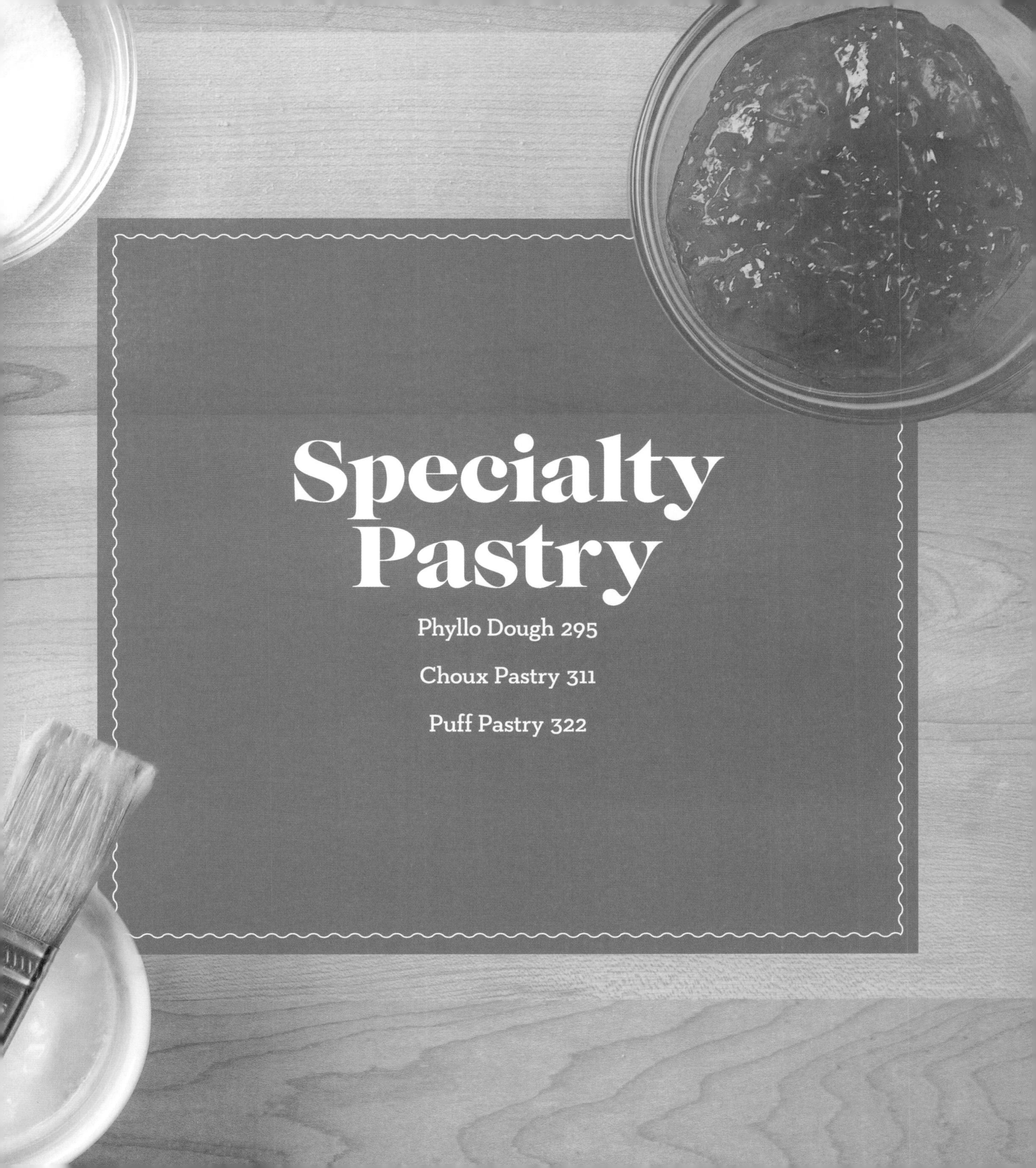

Specialty Pastry

Phyllo Dough 295

Choux Pastry 311

Puff Pastry 322

PHYLLO DOUGH

These paper-thin leaves of pastry—a Greek and Middle-Eastern specialty—can be purchased readymade, refrigerated, or frozen. If you buy it frozen, thaw the sealed package for several hours, then remove only as many leaves as you need. Wrap the remainder in plastic wrap, and refreeze for another time.

Baklava

Packaged phyllo makes this deservedly famous Greek pastry easy to prepare at home. Just layer the sheets of phyllo with the sweet, cinnamony walnut filling, bake, and then soak the whole pan of pastry with warm honey. Food of the gods!

Active time: 30 minutes
Bake time: 1 hour 25 minutes
Makes: 24 servings

4 cups walnuts (about 16 ounces), finely chopped
1/2 cup sugar
1 teaspoon ground cinnamon
16 sheets (14" by 9" each) fresh or thawed frozen phyllo
3/4 cup butter or margarine (1 1/2 sticks), melted
1 cup honey

1. Preheat oven to 300°F. Grease 13" by 9" glass or ceramic baking dish. In large bowl, combine walnuts, sugar, and cinnamon.

2. Trim phyllo sheets into 13" by 9" rectangles, saving trimmings. Cover phyllo with plastic wrap to prevent drying out. In prepared baking dish, place 1 phyllo sheet; brush with some melted butter. Repeat with 5 more layers of phyllo; sprinkle 1 cup walnut mixture over phyllo.

3. Place 1 phyllo sheet in baking dish over walnut mixture; brush with some melted butter. Repeat with at least 6 layers of phyllo. Sprinkle 1 cup walnut mixture over phyllo. Repeat layering 2 more times, ending with walnut mixture. Use phyllo trimmings to make layers when all larger sheets have been incorporated.

4. Place remaining phyllo on top of walnut layer; brush with some melted butter. With sharp knife and cutting only halfway through layers, cut baklava lengthwise into 3 equal strips. Cut each strip crosswise into 4 rectangles; then cut each rectangle diagonally into 2 triangles. Bake 1 hour 25 minutes, or until top is golden brown.

5. Toward end of baking time, in small saucepan, heat honey over medium-low heat until hot but not boiling. Spoon hot honey evenly over hot baklava. Cool baklava in pan on wire rack at least 1 hour, then cover and let stand at room temperature until serving time.

6. To serve, with sharp knife, cut all the way through triangles.

Each serving: about 265 calories, 4g protein, 25g carbohydrate, 18g total fat (5g saturated), 1g fiber, 16mg cholesterol, 115mg sodium

Mini Phyllo Tartlets

A creamy filling is best for these crisp, light shells; see the box below for suggestions. Pop the shells out of the pan carefully, using the tip of a small knife if they don't come out easily.

Active time: 15 minutes
Bake time: 12 minutes
Makes: 12 tartlet shells

2 tablespoons butter or margarine, melted
6 sheets (17" by 12" each) fresh or thawed frozen phyllo

1. Preheat oven to 375°F.

2. Cover stacked phyllo with plastic wrap to prevent drying out and place on work area. Transfer 1 phyllo sheet to work surface and brush with some melted butter. Cover with second phyllo sheet; brush with melted butter. Repeat with third sheet of phyllo and more butter. With long sharp knife, cut phyllo into twelve 4-inch squares. Gently pat 1 square into each cup of standard muffin pan.

3. Repeat buttering, layering, and cutting into squares using remaining 3 phyllo sheets and melted butter. Arrange 1 square at right angle on top of each phyllo square already placed in muffin-pan cups.

4. Bake 12 minutes, or until phyllo is crisp and golden. Cool in pan on wire rack. Carefully remove from pan. Fill just before serving.

Each shell: about 45 calories, 1g protein, 5g carbohydrate, 2g total fat (1g saturated), 0g fiber, 5 mg cholesterol, 65mg sodium

PHYLLO TART SHELLS To make larger tart shells, follow the procedure outlined for tartlets, but use *8 sheets fresh or thawed frozen phyllo* and melt *3 tablespoons butter or margarine.* In step 2, layer only 2 sheets phyllo. Cut layered phyllo crosswise in half, making 2 rectangles. Place 1 rectangle over other, rotating it so that points of second rectangle angle slightly away from points of first. Instead of forming shells in muffin tins, use four 6-ounce custard cups or ramekins. Place one cup right side up, in center of phyllo stack, and gather phyllo up around custard cup. Place shell with cup in 15½" by 10½" jelly-roll pan. Repeat with remaining phyllo sheets and butter. Bake as directed; shells may take 12 to 15 minutes to turn golden. Cool in pan on wire rack 15 minutes, remove cups from shells, and allow shells to cool completely, about 45 minutes.

Each shell: about 190 calories, 3g protein, 20g carbohydrate, 11g total fat (6g saturated), 0g fiber, 23mg cholesterol, 260mg sodium

SWEET TARTLET FILLINGS

After you've baked the tartlet shells, here are some luscious ideas for filling them.

Spoon in a sweetened or flavored whipped cream, pastry cream, or sweetened ricotta. Garnish with berries, sliced fresh fruit, chocolate curls, mini chocolate chips, chopped crystallized ginger, or mint sprigs. Or fill the shells with fresh fruit and pipe whipped cream decoratively on top.

Tomato Phyllo Tarts

These pretty, savory tarts are filled to the brim with Greek favorites like feta, fresh tomatoes, oregano, and black olives. The homemade phyllo shells can be prepared and baked up to 24 hours ahead. Store them, unfilled, in an airtight container—and you'll be ready to prepare a summery meal at a moment's notice.

Active time: 10 minutes
Makes: 4 tarts

¹/₃ cup reduced-fat cream cheese (Neufchâtel), softened
¹/₄ cup crumbled feta cheese
¹/₄ teaspoon dried oregano
1 pound ripe tomatoes, cut into 1-inch chunks
1 small Kirby (pickling) cucumber, not peeled, cut into
   ¹/₂-inch chunks
¹/₄ cup Kalamata olives, pitted and coarsely chopped
1 tablespoon extra-virgin olive oil
1 recipe Phyllo Tart Shells (opposite)

1. In medium bowl, stir cream cheese, feta, and oregano until smooth and spreadable. Cover and refrigerate if not using right away.

2. When ready to assemble tarts, in large bowl, gently stir tomatoes, cucumber, and olives with oil to coat. Spread scant 2 tablespoons cheese mixture in bottom of each cooled phyllo shell. Spoon vegetable mixture over cheese mixture.

Each serving: about 325 calories, 7g protein, 28g carbohydrate, 22g total fat (10g saturated), 3g fiber, 44mg cholesterol, 540mg sodium

Figs in Phyllo

There's no need to fear the phyllo! Making the flaky-crisp crust cups is almost foolproof. Then just finish off this good-for-you Greek treat with yogurt, honey, and sliced figs.

Active time: 5 minutes
Makes: 4 tarts

1 recipe Phyllo Tart Shells (opposite)
1¹/₃ cups nonfat Greek yogurt
4 teaspoons pure honey
12 fresh, ripe Calimyrna figs, cut into quarters
Fresh mint sprigs for garnish

Place cooled phyllo shells on dessert plates. Fill each shell with ⅓ cup yogurt, drizzle with 1 teaspoon honey, and top with quartered figs. Garnish with mint.

Each serving: about 345 calories, 11g protein, 53g carbohydrate, 11g total fat (2g saturated), 6g fiber, 3mg cholesterol, 320mg sodium

Strawberry Napoleons

Instead of the traditional puff pastry and pastry cream, we've swapped in readymade phyllo, whipped cream, and strawberries in this delectable take on the French classic, plus a sprinkling of slivered almonds.

Active time: 45 minutes

Bake time: 10 minutes

Makes: 8 servings

1 large egg white

Pinch salt

1 teaspoon water

4 sheets (17" by 12" each) fresh or thawed frozen phyllo

3 tablespoons butter or margarine, melted

1/3 cup plus 1 tablespoon sugar

1/2 cup sliced natural almonds

3/4 cup heavy cream

1/2 teaspoon vanilla extract

1 container (12 ounces) strawberries, hulled and sliced

1. Preheat oven to 375°F. In small bowl, lightly beat egg white and salt with water. Lay 1 phyllo sheet on surface; brush with some melted butter and sprinkle with about 1 rounded tablespoon sugar. Top with second phyllo sheet; brush with some melted butter and sprinkle with 1 rounded tablespoon sugar. Repeat layering with third phyllo sheet, some melted butter, and sugar. Top with remaining phyllo and brush with egg-white mixture.

2. With sharp knife or pizza wheel, cut phyllo lengthwise into 3 equal strips, then cut each strip crosswise into 4 squares. Cut each square diagonally in half to make 24 triangles. Place phyllo triangles on ungreased large cookie sheet; sprinkle with sliced almonds and 1 rounded tablespoon sugar. Bake 10 minutes or until golden. With wide spatula, transfer to wire racks to cool.

3. Just before serving, in small bowl, with mixer on medium speed, beat cream with vanilla and remaining 1 tablespoon sugar until stiff peaks form.

4. To assemble, place 1 phyllo triangle in center of each of 8 dessert plates. Top each with 1 rounded tablespoon whipped cream and about 1 rounded tablespoon sliced strawberries. Place a second phyllo triangle on top of each, rotating it so the points of second triangle are angled slightly away from points of first triangle. Top triangles with remaining whipped cream and strawberries, dividing them equally; top each dessert with third triangle. Serve immediately.

Each napoleon: About 230 calories, 3g protein, 20g carbohydrate, 16g total fat (8g saturated), 1g fiber, 42mg cholesterol, 125mg sodium

TEST KITCHEN KNOW-HOW

WORKING WITH PHYLLO DOUGH

Made from flour water, oil, and salt, the tissue-thin layers of phyllo must be handled with care.

Working with one sheet of phyllo at a time, gently brush each sheet with melted butter, then fill or shape it as the recipe instructs. Be sure to keep the remaining sheets of phyllo covered with plastic wrap or a damp kitchen towel while you work—dry pastry sheets are too brittle to handle and will tear.

Galatoboureko

This Greek dessert consists of a thick vanilla custard spread between phyllo crusts; the pastry is soaked with lemon syrup while still warm. Farina, a breakfast cereal typically made from semolina, adds substance to the custard.

Active time: 50 minutes plus cooling
Bake time: 35 minutes
Makes: 24 servings

PASTRY

6 cups milk
2 strips (3" by 1" each) orange peel
3/4 cup quick-cooking enriched farina cereal
3/4 cup sugar
4 large eggs
2 teaspoons vanilla extract
16 sheets (14" by 9" each) fresh or thawed
    frozen phyllo
1/2 cup butter or margarine (1 stick), melted

LEMON SYRUP

2 lemons
3/4 cup sugar
1/3 cup water

1. Preheat oven to 350°F. Grease 13" by 9" glass or ceramic baking dish. In 3-quart saucepan, heat milk and orange peel to boiling over medium-high heat. In small bowl, combine farina and sugar; gradually sprinkle into milk mixture, stirring with spoon; heat to boiling. Reduce heat to medium-low and cook, stirring, 5 minutes, or until mixture thickens slightly. Remove saucepan from heat. Discard orange peel.

2. In large bowl, with mixer on high speed, beat eggs and vanilla well. Reduce speed to medium and gradually beat in farina mixture.

3. Cover stacked phyllo with slightly damp kitchen towel and place in work area. Transfer 1 phyllo sheet to prepared baking dish, allowing it to extend up side of dish; brush with some melted butter. Repeat to make 5 more layers, brushing each with melted butter. Pour farina mixture into phyllo-lined dish.

4. Cut remaining phyllo into approximately 13" by 9" rectangles and reserve trimmings. Place 1 phyllo sheet on farina; brush with some melted butter. Repeat with remaining phyllo and butter, overlapping phyllo trimmings to complete rectangles when larger sheets have been incorporated. With sharp knife and cutting only halfway through, cut top phyllo layers lengthwise into 4 equal strips; then cut each strip crosswise into 6 pieces. Bake 35 minutes, or until phyllo is golden and puffy.

5. Meanwhile, prepare lemon syrup: From lemons, cut 4 strips peel, 3" by 1" each, and squeeze 1 tablespoon juice. In 1-quart saucepan, heat sugar, water, and lemon peel to boiling, stirring occasionally. Reduce heat and simmer 8 minutes, or until syrup thickens slightly. Discard peel and stir in lemon juice. (Makes about 3/4 cup.)

6. When pastry is removed from oven, pour hot lemon syrup evenly over dessert. Cool in pan on wire rack at least 2 hours before serving. To serve, with sharp knife, cut along existing lines to divide into portions. Serve warm, or cover and refrigerate to serve chilled.

Each serving (without lemon syrup): about 180 calories, 4g protein, 25g carbohydrate, 7g total fat (4g saturated), 0g fiber, 54mg cholesterol, 140 mg sodium

GREEK DESSERTS

The Greek Islands are known for their pastries, cakes, and cookies, from delicate and fragile to crunchy and chewy,

Often flavored with orange or lemon, honey, or brandy, and studded with walnuts, almonds, or pistachios, these mouthwatering treats will tempt any sweet tooth. Along with Baklava (page 295) and Galatoboureko (above), some other favorites are *kourambiedes* (rich little butter cookies), *yaourtini* (a brandied yogurt cake), and *kadaifi* (filled "bird's nests" made with a shredded phyllo-like dough that resembles shredded wheat).

Spanakopita

Phyllo is filled with spinach and feta and baked to golden flakiness in this popular Greek pastry. You can also use this filling in the smaller appetizers on page 302.

Active time: 1 hour
Bake time: 35 minutes
Makes: 16 servings

6 tablespoons butter or margarine
1 jumbo onion (1 pound), finely chopped
4 packages (10 ounces each) frozen chopped spinach, thawed and squeezed dry
8 ounces feta cheese, crumbled
1 cup part-skim ricotta cheese
1/2 cup chopped fresh dill
1/4 teaspoon salt
1/4 teaspoon coarsely ground black pepper
3 large eggs
10 sheets (17" by 12" each) fresh or thawed frozen phyllo

1. In 12-inch skillet, melt 2 tablespoons butter over medium-high heat until hot. Add onion and cook, stirring occasionally, about 15 minutes, until tender and lightly browned.

2. Transfer onion to large bowl. Stir in spinach, feta, ricotta, dill, salt, pepper, and eggs until combined. (Filling can be prepared a day ahead and refrigerated in an airtight container.) Let filling come to room temperature before proceeding.

3. Preheat oven to 400°F. Melt remaining 4 tablespoons butter. Cover stacked phyllo with plastic wrap to prevent drying out and place in work area. Lightly brush bottom and sides of 11" by 7" glass or ceramic baking dish with some melted butter. Transfer 1 phyllo sheet to sheet of waxed paper and brush with some melted butter. Place phyllo sheet into prepared baking dish, pressing against sides of dish and allowing edges to overhang rim. Lightly brush second phyllo sheet with melted butter; place over first sheet. Repeat buttering and layering 3 more times, for total of 5 sheets. Spread spinach filling evenly over phyllo.

4. Fold overhanging edges of phyllo over filling. Cut remaining 5 phyllo sheets crosswise in half. On waxed paper, lightly brush 1 phyllo piece with some melted butter. Place on top of filling. Repeat with remaining cut phyllo, brushing each piece lightly with butter.

5. Bake 35 to 40 minutes, until filling is hot in center and pastry is golden. Cool slightly.

Each appetizer: about 175 calories, 8g protein, 13g carbohydrate, 10g total fat (6g saturated), 2g fiber, 69mg cholesterol, 380mg sodium

Greek Cheese Pastries

This recipe gives you a choice of three ways to shape these bourekakia me tyri—*tidy rolls, flag-folded triangles, or plump little bundles. Choose one, or follow our instructions to make some of each. Assembling these pastries is a time commitment, but the results are worth it. And you can make them ahead of time (see Tip).*

Active time: 2 hours 30 minutes
Bake time: 15 minutes per batch
Makes: 74 appetizers

1 package (8 ounces) feta cheese
1 cup part-skim ricotta cheese
¼ cup chopped fresh parsley
½ teaspoon coarsely ground black pepper
2 large eggs
16 sheets (17" by 12" each) fresh or thawed frozen phyllo
½ cup butter or margarine (1 stick), melted

1. In medium bowl, with fork, finely crumble feta; stir in ricotta, parsley, pepper, and eggs.

2. Cover stacked phyllo with plastic wrap to prevent drying out and place in work area. With knife, cut phyllo as directed for rolls, triangles, and/or bundles (see right).

3. Grease 15½" by 10½" jelly-roll pans. Prepare appetizers as directed for each shape. Place about 1 inch apart on prepared jelly-roll pans. Brush pastries with some melted butter. If not serving right away, cover with plastic wrap and refrigerate.

4. Preheat oven to 400°F. Bake pastries 15 to 20 minutes, until golden, rotating pans between upper and lower oven racks halfway through.

Each appetizer: about 40 calories, 1g protein, 3g carbohydrate, 3g total fat (2g saturated), 0g fiber, 13mg cholesterol, 75mg sodium

ROLLS Stack 6 phyllo sheets and cut crosswise into 4 strips. Brush 1 strip lightly with some melted butter. Place 1 rounded teaspoon filling on center at end of strip. Roll strip with filling one-third of way, then fold left and right sides over roll; continue rolling to end. Repeat to make 24 rolls.

TRIANGLES Stack 5 sheets phyllo and cut lengthwise into 5 strips. Brush 1 strip lightly with melted butter. Place 1 rounded teaspoon filling at end of strip. Fold 1 corner of phyllo diagonally across filling to opposite edge to form triangle. Continue to fold triangle onto itself to end of strip. Repeat to make 25 triangles.

BUNDLES Stack 5 sheets phyllo and cut lengthwise into 4 strips, then cut each strip crosswise into 5 squares. Stack 2 squares and brush top lightly with melted butter. Layer 2 more squares crosswise over first squares; brush with melted butter. Place 1 rounded teaspoon filling in center; crimp phyllo around filling. Repeat to make 25 bundles. (If bundles brown too quickly during baking, cover loosely with foil partway through cooking.)

TIP To prepare the pastries ahead of time, shape and fill them, then freeze them in the jelly-roll pans until firm. Transfer the frozen pastries to airtight containers, separating the layers with waxed paper. At serving time, bake the unthawed pastries in a 400°F oven for 20 minutes, or until golden.

Spring Vegetable Pie

Celebrate fresh seasonal flavors with this pretty savory pastry that's perfect for brunch or a buffet. Phyllo and a sprinkling of bread crumbs are layered with a luscious asparagus and ricotta filling.

Active time: 35 minutes
Bake time: 40 minutes
Makes: 8 main-dish servings

1/2 cup butter or margarine (1 stick)
6 green onions, thinly sliced (1 cup)
2 pounds thin asparagus, trimmed and cut into
   1-inch pieces
1 teaspoon salt
1 teaspoon dried mint
1 container (32 ounces) part-skim ricotta cheese
2/3 cup freshly grated Parmesan cheese
3 large eggs
1/2 teaspoon ground black pepper
8 sheets (17" by 12" each) fresh or thawed frozen phyllo
10 1/2 teaspoons plain dried bread crumbs

1. In 12-inch skillet, melt 2 tablespoons butter over medium heat. Add green onions and cook 2 minutes, or until tender. Add asparagus, 1/2 teaspoon salt, and 1/2 teaspoon mint and cook, stirring frequently, 10 minutes, or until tender. Cool to room temperature.

2. Preheat oven to 375°F. Butter 13" by 9" baking pan. In large bowl, stir together ricotta, Parmesan, eggs, pepper, and remaining 1/2 teaspoon each salt and mint. Stir in asparagus mixture until combined.

3. In small saucepan, melt remaining 6 tablespoons butter. Cover stacked phyllo sheets with plastic wrap to prevent drying out and place in work area. Fit 1 phyllo sheet into bottom and up sides of prepared pan. Brush with some melted butter and sprinkle with 1 1/2 teaspoons bread crumbs. Repeat layering, buttering, and sprinkling with bread crumbs until 5 layers of phyllo are in pan. Spread ricotta mixture over phyllo.

4. Top with 1 phyllo sheet, brush with butter, and sprinkle with 1 1/2 teaspoons bread crumbs. Top with another sheet of phyllo, brush with melted butter, and sprinkle with remaining 1 1/2 teaspoons bread crumbs. Top with last sheet of phyllo and brush with remaining melted butter. With knife, make several slashes into top layers of pastry, cutting through to filling.

5. Bake 40 to 45 minutes, or until filling is set and phyllo is golden brown. Cool in pan on wire rack 10 minutes before serving.

Each serving: about 420 calories, 23g protein, 23g carbohydrate, 27g total fat (15g saturated), 1g fiber, 154mg cholesterol, 850mg sodium

Samosas

A favorite first course in Indian restaurants, samosas are little fried turnovers filled with spicy ground meat (keema samosa) *or highly seasoned potatoes and peas* (aloo samosa). *In this simplified version, phyllo replaces homemade pastry. To reduce the saturated fat, the filled pastries are baked rather than fried.*

Active time: 35 minutes plus cooling
Bake time: 15 minutes per batch
Makes: 80 samosas

1¹/2 pounds baking potatoes, peeled and cut into
   1-inch chunks
1¹/4 teaspoons salt
1 teaspoon cumin seeds
¹/4 cup olive oil
1 onion, finely chopped
2 large garlic cloves, minced
¹/4 teaspoon ground black pepper
¹/4 teaspoon cayenne (ground red) pepper
¹/8 teaspoon ground turmeric
¹/8 teaspoon ground cardamom
¹/2 cup frozen peas
¹/3 cup low-fat plain yogurt
¹/2 cup butter or margarine (1 stick), melted
1 package (16 ounces) fresh or thawed frozen phyllo

1. In 3-quart saucepan, cover potatoes with *water*, add ¹/2 teaspoon salt, and heat to boiling. Reduce heat and simmer, covered, until tender, about 15 minutes.

2. While potatoes are cooking, toast cumin seeds in 10-inch skillet over medium-low heat, shaking skillet frequently, until fragrant, about 4 minutes. Transfer to small plate.

3. In same skillet, heat 2 tablespoons oil over medium-low heat. Add onion and cook, stirring frequently, until golden brown, about 10 minutes. Stir in remaining ¾ teaspoon salt, garlic, black pepper, cayenne, turmeric, cardamom, and peas. Cook, stirring frequently, 2 minutes. Remove skillet from heat.

4. Drain potatoes well and add while still hot to skillet. With potato masher, mash potatoes, leaving some chunks. Stir in yogurt. Transfer mixture to bowl and cover loosely. Refrigerate about 1 hour, until cool.

5. Preheat oven to 375°F. Stir remaining 2 tablespoons oil into melted butter. Cover stacked phyllo with plastic wrap to prevent drying out and place in work area. Transfer 1 phyllo sheet to work surface. Brush lightly with some butter mixture. Top with second phyllo sheet. With pastry wheel or sharp knife, cut sheets lengthwise into 5 equal strips. Place 1 heaping measuring teaspoon filling at end of strip. Fold 1 corner of phyllo diagonally across filling to opposite edge to form triangle. Continue to fold triangle onto itself to end of strip. Place, seam side down, 1 inch apart, on large cookie sheet. Brush lightly with butter mixture. Repeat with remaining phyllo, butter mixture, and filling, placing triangles 1 inch apart. Use 32 sheets of phyllo in all.

6. Bake 15 minutes, or until golden brown and crisp. With wide metal spatula, transfer to wire rack to cool. Serve warm or at room temperature.

Each samosa: about 40 calories, 1g protein, 5g carbohydrate, 2g total fat (1g saturated), 0g fiber, 3mg cholesterol, 70mg sodium

Mushroom-Potato Strudel

For a tasty appetizer, serve half slices of this savory strudel on a bed of greens. Top with sour cream and fresh chives.

Active time: 45 minutes plus cooling
Bake time: 40 minutes
Makes: 8 main-dish servings

1 1/2 pounds baking potatoes, peeled and thickly sliced
1 1/2 teaspoons salt
9 tablespoons butter or margarine
2 garlic cloves, finely chopped
8 ounces shiitake mushrooms, stems removed and caps coarsely chopped
8 ounces white mushrooms, stems trimmed and caps coarsely chopped
2 tablespoons snipped chives
6 sheets (17" by 12" each) fresh or thawed frozen phyllo
3 tablespoons plain dried bread crumbs

1. In 2 1/2-quart saucepan, combine potatoes and *cold water* to cover by 1 inch. Heat to boiling, add 1 teaspoon salt, and boil 15 minutes, or until potatoes are tender. Drain, reserving *2 tablespoons potato cooking liquid*. Return potatoes to saucepan. Add 2 tablespoons butter and reserved potato cooking liquid; with potato masher, mash until smooth.

2. Meanwhile, in 12-inch skillet, melt 2 tablespoons butter over low heat. Add garlic and cook, stirring frequently, 2 minutes, or until tender. Add shiitake mushrooms, increase heat to medium, and cook, stirring frequently, 5 minutes, or until almost tender. Stir in white mushrooms and remaining 1/2 teaspoon salt and cook, stirring frequently, 5 minutes, or until tender and dry. Stir mushroom mixture and chives into potato mixture.

3. In small saucepan, melt remaining 5 tablespoons butter over low heat. Cool to room temperature.

4. Preheat oven to 375°F. Grease 15 1/2" by 10 1/2" jelly-roll pan. Place stacked phyllo, covered with slightly damp kitchen towel, on work surface. Lay 1 phyllo sheet on second kitchen towel. Brush with some melted butter and top with second phyllo sheet. Brush with some melted butter and sprinkle with 1 tablespoon bread crumbs. Top with 2 more phyllo sheets, brushing each with melted butter. Sprinkle with 1 tablespoon bread crumbs. Top with remaining 2 phyllo sheets, brushing each with melted butter. Sprinkle with remaining 1 tablespoon bread crumbs.

5. Spoon mushroom-potato mixture along 1 long side of phyllo, leaving 1-inch border at top and ends. Flatten mixture slightly. Fold ends over filling. Using towel as guide, roll phyllo up from 1 long side to form log. Roll log, seam side down, off towel onto prepared jelly-roll pan. With serrated knife, make slashes at 1-inch intervals down length of log. Brush with remaining melted butter.

6. Bake 40 to 45 minutes, until golden brown. Cool. To serve, cut into 8 slices.

Each serving: about 235 calories, 4 g protein, 24g carbohydrate, 15g total fat (8g saturated), 2g fiber, 35mg cholesterol, 520mg sodium

Apple Strudel

One of the trickiest jobs in baking is making strudel dough, which includes hand-stretching a piece of dough until it is a sheer, tissue-thin sheet the size of a tabletop. Packaged phyllo eliminates all that intensive labor but does not sacrifice the light, delicate pastry.

Active time: 1 hour plus cooling
Bake time: 35 minutes
Makes: 10 servings

1/2 cup butter or margarine (1 stick)
4 pounds Granny Smith apples, peeled, cored, and cut into 1/2-inch pieces
1/2 cup dark seedless raisins
2/3 cup plus 1/4 cup granulated sugar
1/4 cup walnuts, toasted (see page xxiii) and ground
1/4 cup plain dried bread crumbs
1/2 teaspoon ground cinnamon
1/4 teaspoon ground nutmeg
8 sheets (17" by 12" each) fresh or thawed frozen phyllo
Confectioners' sugar for dusting

1. In 12-inch skillet, melt 2 tablespoons butter over medium heat. Add apples, raisins, and 2/3 cup sugar. Cook, uncovered, stirring occasionally, 15 minutes. Increase heat to medium-high and cook 15 minutes longer, or until liquid has evaporated and apples are tender but not brown. Remove skillet from heat; cool apple filling completely.

2. Meanwhile, in small bowl, stir together remaining 1/4 cup sugar, walnuts, bread crumbs, cinnamon, and nutmeg until thoroughly combined.

3. Preheat oven to 400°F. In small saucepan, melt remaining 6 tablespoons butter; set 1 tablespoon aside. Cut two 24-inch-long sheets of waxed paper; arrange sheets so that two long sides overlap by about 2 inches. Cover stack of phyllo with plastic wrap to prevent drying out. Place 1 sheet of phyllo on waxed paper. Brush phyllo with melted butter. Sprinkle phyllo sheet with 2 scant tablespoons bread-crumb mixture. Top with another

sheet of phyllo and brush lightly with butter; sprinkle with 2 scant tablespoons crumb mixture. Continue layering phyllo, brushing each sheet with melted butter and sprinkling with scant 2 tablespoons crumb mixture.

4. Spoon cooled apple filling along one long side of dough, leaving about 3/4-inch border at edges and covering about one-third of phyllo rectangle. Using waxed paper to help lift roll, starting at filled end, roll up phyllo jelly-roll fashion. Place roll, seam side down, diagonally on large cookie sheet. Tuck in ends of roll. Brush with reserved 1 tablespoon melted butter.

5. Bake 35 to 40 minutes, or until phyllo is golden and filling is hot (cover with foil during last 10 minutes of baking if strudel is overbrowning). Cool on cookie sheet on wire rack about 20 minutes before slicing. Before serving, sprinkle with confectioners' sugar.

Each serving: about 340 calories, 2g protein, 58 g carbohydrate, 13g total fat (6g saturated), 4g fiber, 25mg cholesterol, 190mg sodium

CHERRY STRUDEL Substitute cherry filling for apple filling: In 4-quart saucepan, heat *2 cans (16 ounces each) tart cherries packed in water*, drained, but with ½ cup liquid reserved; *1 cup granulated sugar*; *¼ cup cornstarch*; *1 tablespoon fresh lemon juice*; and *¼ teaspoon ground cinnamon* to boiling over medium-high heat, stirring occasionally. Reduce heat to medium-low; boil 1 minute. Remove saucepan from heat; stir in *½ teaspoon vanilla extract*; cool completely. Proceed as directed.

Each serving: about 230 calories, 2g protein, 40 g carbohydrate, 8g total fat (4g saturated), 0g fiber, 19mg cholesterol, 150mg sodium

APPLE-CRANBERRY STRUDEL Substitute apple-cranberry filling for apple filling: In 12-inch skillet, melt *4 tablespoons butter or margarine* over medium heat. Add *3 pounds Golden Delicious apples*, peeled, cored, and cut into ½-inch pieces; *1½ cups cranberries*; *½ cup dark seedless raisins*; *½ teaspoon ground cinnamon*; and *½ cup granulated sugar*. Cook, uncovered, stirring occasionally, 12 minutes. Increase heat to medium-high and cook about 10 minutes longer, until liquid has evaporated and apples are tender but not brown. Remove skillet from heat; cool completely. Proceed with recipe as directed.

Each serving: about 285 calories, 2g protein, 44g carbohydrate, 13g total fat (7g saturated), 3g fiber, 31mg cholesterol, 190mg sodium

PEAR STRUDEL Substitute pear filling for apple filling: Prepare filling as directed but instead of apples, use *4 pounds Bartlett pears*, peeled, cored, and cut into ½-inch pieces; use only *½ cup granulated sugar*. In step 1, cook pear filling 35 minutes total; cool completely. Proceed as directed.

Each serving: about 320 calories, 3g protein, 52 g carbohydrate, 13g total fat (6g saturated), 5g fiber, 25mg cholesterol, 190mg sodium

CHEESE STRUDEL Substitute cheese filling for apple filling: In large bowl, with mixer on medium speed, beat *1 package (8 ounces) softened cream cheese, ¼ cup granulated sugar,* and *1 tablespoon cornstarch* 1 minute, or until blended. Fold in *1 cup ricotta cheese, 1 teaspoon freshly grated lemon peel*, and *½ teaspoon vanilla extract*. Cover and refrigerate. Proceed as directed, but during baking, place two sheets foil under cookie sheet and crimp edges to form rim to catch any overflow.

Each serving: about 255 calories, 6g protein, 16g carbohydrate, 19g total fat (11g saturated), 0g fiber, 56mg cholesterol, 230mg sodium

STRUDEL: A VIENNESE SPECIALTY

German for "whirlpool," strudel is a Viennese pastry made up of many layers of very thin dough spread with a filling, then rolled and baked until crisp and golden brown. It's popular in Germany, Austria, and much of central Europe, and wherever immigrants from those countries settled in the United States.

Paper-thin strudel dough resembles phyllo, but is more difficult to work with, so we've swapped in phyllo in this recipe and the four delectable variations. Apple strudel is the most famous, but strudel can feature a wide variety of fillings—most typically sweet, but savory too. Try our recipe for Mushroom-Potato Strudel (page 305).

Apple-Berry Hand Pies

Crisp, tart apples and sweet juicy berries are a delicious combo in this healthier version of a much-loved dessert. Premade phyllo dough has 86 percent less fat than piecrust, and the dip made from nonfat yogurt and maple syrup helps keep this recipe skinny, too.

Active time: 30 minutes • Bake time: 10 minutes • Makes: 15 hand pies (7 servings)

1¹/2 cups peeled, chopped Granny Smith apples
³/4 cup blackberries
1 teaspoon fresh lemon juice
1 tablespoon all-purpose flour
¹/4 cup plus 2 teaspoons sugar
⁵/8 teaspoon apple pie spice

10 sheets (14" by 9" each) fresh or thawed frozen
   phyllo dough
Nonstick cooking spray
¹/4 teaspoon kosher salt or coarse sea salt
1 cup plain nonfat Greek yogurt
3 tablespoons maple syrup

1. In medium bowl, mix apples, blackberries, lemon juice, flour, ¼ cup sugar, and ½ teaspoon apple pie spice.

2. Cover stacked phyllo with plastic wrap to prevent drying out and place in work area. Transfer 1 phyllo sheet to work surface; lightly coat with cooking spray. Top with another sheet; spray top. Cut lengthwise into three 3-inch-wide strips. Mound 1 heaping tablespoon fruit filling at end of 1 strip, about 1 inch from corner. Fold 1 corner of phyllo diagonally across filling to opposite edge to form triangle. Continue to fold triangle onto itself to end of strip. Repeat with remaining phyllo sheets and filling.

3. Preheat oven to 400°F. Lightly spray cookie sheet with cooking spray. Place pies seam sides down on prepared sheet; spray tops with cooking spray. In small bowl, mix salt and remaining 2 teaspoons sugar and ⅛ teaspoon apple pie spice; sprinkle over pies.

4. Bake 10 to 12 minutes or until golden brown. Remove to wire racks to cool slightly.

5. For topping, stir together yogurt and maple syrup. Serve pies warm with topping.

Each serving: about 170 calories, 4g protein, 34g carbohydrate, 2g total fat, 2g fiber, 0mg cholesterol, 200mg sodium

Small Cream Puffs (page 314)

CHOUX PASTRY

The "other" puff pastry, choux pastry, or pâte à choux (pronounced "pot-a-shoe") is used for cream puffs and éclairs, as well as for savory gougères. As desserts, choux-pastry shells can hold flavored whipped creams, custard, or ice cream. Or fill them with chicken or crab salad to make tempting hors d'oeuvres.

Choux Pastry

Choux means "cabbages"—a reference to the plump, round shape of cream-puff shells, the most familiar use of this versatile dough.

Active time: 10 minutes
Cook time: 5 minutes
Makes: 8 large cream puffs, 22 small puffs, or 30 éclairs

1 cup water
1/2 cup butter or margarine (1 stick), cut up
1/4 teaspoon salt
1 cup all-purpose flour
4 large eggs

1. In 3-quart saucepan, heat water, butter, and salt to boiling over medium heat until butter has melted. Remove saucepan from heat. With wooden spoon, vigorously stir in flour all at once until mixture forms ball and leaves side of pan.

2. Add eggs, one at a time, beating well after each addition, until batter is smooth and satiny. Shape warm batter as directed in recipes.

MAKING CHOUX PASTRY DOUGH

Choux pastry is simply mixed by hand in a sauce-pan. The trickiest part of it all may be convincing yourself, as you beat in the eggs, that the wet, curdled-looking mixture is going to turn into a thick, satiny dough.

After melting the butter in boiling water, add the flour all at once. Stir vigorously until the dough forms a ball and leaves the sides of the pan.

Add the eggs one at a time. At first the egg won't combine with the dough, but after brief beating, you'll have a smooth mixture.

TOP: CREAM PUFFS; BOTTOM CHOCOLATE PROFITEROLES

Cream Puffs

You can bake these puffs a few days ahead of time, then recrisp them in a preheated 325°F oven for 10 minutes. After cooling, fill them with softened ice cream and drizzle with our decadent hot fudge sauce.

Active time: 30 minutes plus standing and cooling
Bake time: 40 minutes
Makes: 8 large cream puffs

1 recipe Choux Pastry (page 311)
1 quart vanilla ice cream, slightly softened
Sublime Hot Fudge Sauce (page 348)

1. Preheat oven to 400°F. Grease and flour large cookie sheet. Using slightly rounded ¼-cup measure, drop choux pastry dough onto prepared cookie sheet in 8 large mounds, 3 inches apart. With moistened finger, gently smooth tops to round.

2. Bake 40 to 45 minutes, until deep golden. Remove cookie sheet from oven; with knife, poke hole into side of each puff to release steam. Turn off oven. Return cookie sheet to oven and let puffs stand 10 minutes. Transfer puffs to wire rack to cool.

3. With serrated knife, cut each cooled puff horizontally in half; remove and discard any moist dough inside.

4. To serve, place ½-cup scoop of vanilla ice cream in bottom half of each puff; replace tops. Spoon hot fudge sauce over puffs.

Each cream puff: about 630 calories, 9g protein, 56g carbohydrate, 44g total fat (26g saturated), 3g fiber, 215mg cholesterol, 320mg sodium

Chocolate Profiteroles

Delicate, bite-size chocolate pastries stuffed with ice cream and topped with a luscious homemade chocolate sauce make a divine treat for any special occasion.

Active time: 35 minutes plus standing and cooling
Bake time: 35 minutes
Makes: about 28 profiteroles

1 cup cold water
7 tablespoons butter or margarine, softened
1 teaspoon plus 2/3 cup sugar
1 cup all-purpose flour
1/4 cup unsweetened cocoa
4 large eggs
4 ounces unsweetened chocolate, chopped
3/4 cup heavy cream
2 tablespoons light corn syrup
1/4 teaspoon salt
2 teaspoons vanilla extract
Ice cream for serving

1. Preheat oven to 400°F. Line two large cookie sheets with parchment paper.

2. In 4-quart saucepan, combine water, 6 tablespoons butter, and 1 teaspoon sugar. Heat over medium until just boiling. Remove from heat. Add flour and cocoa, stirring vigorously until ball forms. Add eggs, one at a time, beating well after each, until batter is smooth.

3. Drop batter by rounded tablespoons, 2 inches apart, onto prepared sheets. Bake 35 minutes, rotating sheets between upper and lower oven racks halfway through. Turn off oven and remove sheets. With knife, make ½-inch slit on side of each puff. Return sheets to oven; let stand 10 minutes. Remove from oven. Place cookie sheets on wire racks until puffs are cool. (To make puffs ahead, transfer cooled puffs to airtight container and freeze up to 1 month. Reheat in 350°F oven 5 to 10 minutes; cool before proceeding.)

4. In 2-quart saucepan combine chocolate, cream, corn syrup, salt, and remaining 2/3 cup sugar. Bring to simmering over medium heat, stirring. Reduce heat to medium-low. Cook, stirring, 3 to 6 minutes or until chocolate is melted and sauce is thick. Stir in vanilla and remaining 1 tablespoon butter until smooth. Keep warm over low heat. (Chocolate will keep, refrigerated in airtight container, up to 5 days. Rewarm over low heat, stirring constantly, before proceeding.)

5. Cut puffs in half with serrated knife. Place small scoops of ice cream on bottoms; replace tops. Serve with warm chocolate sauce.

Each serving: about 375 calories, 7g protein, 36g carbohydrate, 26g total fat (15g saturated), 3g fiber, 133mg cholesterol, 110mg sodium

Small Cream Puffs

Children adore these bite-size minis, but these are for dessert lovers of any age. Fill the puffs with the pastry cream of your choice, arrange them on pretty plates, and garnish them with Raspberry Sauce (page 350).

Active time: 40 minutes
Bake time: 35 minutes
Makes: 22 mini cream puffs

1 recipe Choux Pastry (page 311)
Vanilla, Chocolate, or Praline Pastry Cream (page 345)
   or Ricotta Filling (page 347), chilled
Confectioners' sugar

1. Preheat oven to 400°F. Grease two large cookie sheets. Drop choux pastry batter by rounded tablespoons onto prepared cookie sheets, making 22 mounds, 1½ inches apart. (Or pipe batter using pastry bag.)

2. Bake 35 minutes, or until deep golden, rotating cookie sheets between upper and lower oven racks halfway through. Transfer puffs to wire racks to cool.

3. With serrated knife, cut each cooled puff horizontally almost in half, leaving one side attached. Whisk pastry cream filling until smooth. Spoon 2 tablespoons filling into bottom half of each puff; replace top of puff and sprinkle with confectioners' sugar.

Each puff with vanilla pastry cream: about 135 calories, 3g protein, 14g carbohydrate, 7g total fat (4g saturated), 0g fiber, 92mg cholesterol, 95mg sodium

Each puff with chocolate pastry cream: about 160 calories, 3g protein, 17g carbohydrate, 9g total fat (5g saturated), 0g fiber, 92mg cholesterol, 95mg sodium

Each puff with praline pastry cream: about 210 calories, 4g protein, 25g carbohydrate, 11g total fat (4g saturated), 0g fiber, 92 mg cholesterol, 95mg sodium

Each puff with ricotta filling: about 175 calories, 6g protein, 13g carbohydrate, 11g total fat (6g saturated), 0g fiber, 71mg cholesterol, 115mg sodium

Cream-Puff Ring

Impress your guests with this wreath-shaped dessert—no pastry bag required. Use chocolate pastry cream instead of vanilla, if you prefer.

Prep time: 45 minutes plus chilling and cooling
Bake time: 40 minutes
Makes: 12 servings

Vanilla Pastry Cream (page 345)
1 recipe Choux Pastry (page 311)
½ cup heavy cream
Chocolate Glaze (page 339)

1. Prepare Vanilla Pastry Cream; cover and refrigerate until ready to use.

2. Preheat oven to 400°F. Lightly grease and flour large cookie sheet. Using 7-inch plate as guide, with toothpick, trace circle in flour on cookie sheet. Prepare Choux Pastry. Drop batter by heaping tablespoons into 12 mounds inside circle to form ring. (Mounds should be touching.)

3. Bake 40 minutes, or until deep golden. Turn off oven. Let ring stand in oven 15 minutes. Transfer ring to wire rack to cool.

4. With long serrated knife, cut cooled ring horizontally in half. In small bowl, with mixer on medium speed, beat cream until soft peaks form. With wire whisk, beat pastry cream until smooth. With rubber spatula, fold whipped cream, one third at a time, into pastry cream; spoon into bottom of ring. Replace top.

5. Prepare Chocolate Glaze. Spoon glaze over ring. Let stand until glaze sets.

Each serving: About 350 calories, 7g protein, 33g carbohydrate, 22g total fat (12g saturated), 1g fiber, 190mg cholesterol, 210mg sodium

Saint-Honoré

Saint Honoré, the patron saint of French bakers, is honored with this lavish creation: a glorious construction of pastry ringed with cream-filled puffs, finished with cream filling in the center, and drizzled with caramel.

Active time: 2 hours
Bake time: 40 minutes
Makes: 16 servings

Pastry for 9-Inch Tart (page 140), formed into disk and
   chilled but not rolled
1 recipe Choux Pastry (page 311)
1 cup heavy cream
Vanilla Pastry Cream (page 345)
1¹/2 cups sugar
¹/4 cup water

1. On lightly floured surface, with floured rolling pin, roll pastry dough into 12-inch circle, trim edges. Place dough on ungreased large cookie sheet, prick with fork, and refrigerate.

2. Preheat oven to 400°F. Grease and flour second large cookie sheet. Spoon choux pastry batter into large pastry bag fitted with ¹/2-inch round tip. Pipe batter into 16 mounds 1¹/2" wide and 1" high, placed 2 inches apart on prepared cookie sheet. With fingertip dipped in water, smooth any peaks. Fill pastry bag with remaining batter and pipe around edge of pastry dough circle to form rim.

3. Bake puffs 40 minutes and pastry circle 25 minutes, until golden, rotating sheets between upper and lower oven racks after 20 minutes of baking. Transfer puffs to wire rack to cool. Leave pastry circle on cookie sheet to cool.

4. In small bowl, with mixer on high speed, beat cream until stiff peaks form. Spoon 1¹/4 cups pastry cream into large pastry bag fitted with a ¹/4-inch round tip. Fold whipped cream into remaining 1¹/2 cups pastry cream; refrigerate.

5. Insert tip of pastry bag into side of each puff and pipe in pastry cream to fill halfway.

6. In 2-quart saucepan, heat sugar and water to boiling over medium-high heat. Boil until mixture turns amber in color. Immediately pour hot caramel into small bowl to stop cooking. Carefully dip bottom of each puff in caramel and attach on top of rim around edge of pastry circle. Drizzle remaining caramel over puffs. Spread pastry-cream mixture evenly in center of circle. Refrigerate up to 6 hours before serving.

Each serving: about 390 calories, 6g protein, 46g carbohydrate, 20g total fat (11g saturated), 1g fiber, 159mg cholesterol, 215mg sodium

CROQUEMBOUCHE

This festive creation is the traditional French wedding cake, a tapering tower of tiny, filled cream puffs "glued" together with warm caramel.

After the caramel sets, the structure stands on its own, and it can be adorned with edible flowers, small berries, candies, and a veil of spun sugar. Croquembouche is also a favorite centerpiece for Christmas buffets.

Éclairs

These cream-filled pastries are topped with a chocolate glaze. Choose between vanilla and chocolate pastry cream—or make some of each.

Active time: 45 minutes plus chilling and cooling
Bake time: 40 minutes
Makes: about 30 éclairs

1 recipe Choux Pastry (page 311)
Vanilla or Chocolate Pastry Cream (page 345), chilled
Chocolate Glaze (page 339)

1. Preheat oven to 400°F. Grease and flour large cookie sheet. Spoon choux batter into large pastry bag fitted with ½-inch round tip. Pipe batter into strips about 3½" by ¾", 1 inch apart on prepared cookie sheet (see right). With fingertip dipped in water, smooth any peaks.

2. Bake 40 minutes, or until deep golden. Transfer pastries to wire racks to cool. Baked, unfilled shells can be frozen, well wrapped, for up to 1 month.

3. With serrated knife, cut each cooled éclair horizontally almost in half, leaving one side attached; alternatively, with small knife, make hole in each end. Whisk pastry cream until smooth; spoon into large pastry bag fitted with ¼-inch round tip. Pipe into bottom halves of split éclairs or pipe into both ends of whole éclairs.

4. Dip top of each éclair into chocolate glaze, smoothing with small metal spatula if necessary. Let stand until glaze sets. Éclairs can be refrigerated for up to 3 hours.

Each éclair with vanilla pastry cream: about 125 calories, 3g protein, 13g carbohydrate, 7g total fat (4g saturated), 0g fiber, 71mg cholesterol, 80mg sodium

Each éclair with chocolate pastry cream: about 140 calories, 3g protein, 15g carbohydrate, 8g total fat (5g saturated), 1g fiber, 71mg cholesterol, 80mg sodium

TEST KITCHEN KNOW-HOW

PIPING ÉCLAIRS

You don't have to visit a patisserie to enjoy éclairs—you can make them yourself! You'll need a pastry bag to create the traditional oblong shape.

Fill a pastry bag fitted with a ½-inch plain tip two-thirds full of choux pastry dough, then pipe the pastry onto the prepared cookie sheet in long, straight strips. Smooth out any peaks with the tip of your finger so these areas do not overbrown in the oven. Cool the éclairs completely before filling and glazing as instructed.

Caramel Christmas Wreath

This special-occasion-worthy wreath of cream-puff pastry is filled with caramel and cream. Find dulce de leche in supermarkets alongside the canned milk.

Active time: 40 minutes plus cooling
Bake time: 45 minutes
Makes: 12 servings

½ cup butter or margarine (1 stick)
1 cup water
¼ teaspoon salt
1 cup all-purpose flour
4 large eggs, at room temperature
1 cup heavy cream
1 can or jar (13 to 14 ounces) dulce de leche
1½ cups sliced almonds, toasted (see page xxiii)
2 tablespoons confectioners' sugar
Raspberries for garnish
Fresh mint leaves for garnish

1. Preheat oven to 425°F. Line large cookie sheet with parchment paper. Using 8-inch plate or cake pan as guide, with pencil, trace circle on parchment and flip over so that pencil marking does not touch food.

2. In 3-quart saucepan, heat butter, water, and salt to boiling over medium-high. Reduce heat to medium-low and add flour. Stir 1 minute or until mixture leaves side of pan and forms ball. Continue stirring 2 minutes or until mixture begins to coat bottom of pan. Transfer to large mixer bowl and cool 2 minutes.

3. With mixer on medium speed, beat dough 1 minute. Continue beating and add eggs, one at a time, then beat 2 to 3 minutes longer or until satiny. Mixture should still be warm and should cling to side of bowl. Transfer dough to large pastry bag fitted with ¾-inch plain tip or to large resealable plastic bag with one corner cut to make ¾-inch hole.

4. Using circle traced on parchment as guide, pipe dough onto parchment on cookie sheet in 1-inch-thick ring just inside circle (see photo opposite). Pipe second ring inside of first, making sure dough rings touch. With remaining dough, pipe third ring on top of first

two rings, covering center seam. With moistened finger, gently smooth dough rings where ends meet.

5. Bake 20 minutes. Reduce oven temperature to 375°F and bake 25 minutes longer or until golden. With tip of small knife, make small slits to release steam. Bake 10 minutes longer. Cool completely on cookie sheet.

6. Whip cream until soft peaks form. In large bowl, with mixer or wooden spoon, beat dulce de leche 5 minutes or until soft; gently fold in almonds. With long serrated knife, slice wreath horizontally in half; remove and discard moist dough from inside. With spatula, spread almond mixture into bottom of wreath; top with whipped cream. Replace top of wreath.

7. To serve, dust wreath with confectioners' sugar and garnish with raspberries and mint leaves.

Each serving: about 370 calories, 8g protein, 31g carbohydrate, 25g total fat (11g saturated), 2g fiber, 113mg cholesterol, 160mg sodium

PIPING A WREATH

A choux pastry wreath makes for an impressive dessert.

Use a large plain tip on your pastry bag to pipe a total of three rings of choux pastry onto the prepared cookie sheet: First you'll make two concentric rings, then add the third ring to cover the center seam on top.

Black Pepper Puffs with Goat-Cheese Filling

These peppery puffs hold a mixture of cream cheese and goat cheese, freshened with chopped parsley. Fans of blue cheese will find a pleasing variation below.

Active time: 30 minutes plus cooling
Bake time: 35 minutes
Makes: about 48 puffs

1 teaspoon black peppercorns
1 recipe Choux Pastry (page 311)
8 ounces goat cheese, softened
1 small package (3 ounces) cream cheese, softened
2 tablespoons milk
1 tablespoon chopped fresh parsley

1. Place peppercorns in resealable plastic bag. Crush with rolling pin.

2. Preheat oven to 400°F. Grease two large cookie sheets. Stir crushed peppercorns into choux pastry batter and drop by rounded teaspoons, 1½ inches apart, onto prepared cookie sheets.

3. Bake 35 minutes, or until deeply golden, rotating cookie sheets between upper and lower oven racks halfway through. Transfer puffs to wire racks to cool.

4. In medium bowl, combine cheeses, milk, and parsley until blended. Spoon filling into pastry bag fitted with ¼-inch round tip. Insert tip into side of each cooled puff and pipe in cheese mixture to fill halfway.

Each puff: about 60 calories, 2 g protein, 1g carbohydrate, 5g total fat (3g saturated), 0g fiber, 29 mg cholesterol, 65mg sodium

BLACK PEPPER PUFFS WITH BLUE-CHEESE FILLING

Prepare puffs as instructed in steps 1 through 3 above. When making filling, substitute *3 ounces crumbled blue cheese* for goat cheese and increase cream cheese to *1 large package (8 ounces) softened cream cheese.* Proceed as directed.

Each puff: about 55 calories, 2g protein, 5g carbohydrate, 5g total fat (3g saturated), 0g fiber, 29 mg cholesterol, 75mg sodium

Cheddar Crab Puffs

These melt-in-your-mouth puffs are sure to be a hit with guests.

Active time: 15 minutes
Bake time: 25 minutes
Makes: about 42 puffs

¾ cup water
4 tablespoons butter or margarine, cut up
¼ teaspoon salt
¼ teaspoon ground black pepper
¾ cup all-purpose flour
3 large eggs
4 ounces extra-sharp Cheddar cheese, shredded (1 cup)
6 ounces lump crabmeat, picked over

1. Preheat oven to 400°F. Line two cookie sheets with parchment paper.

2. In 3-quart saucepan, combine water, butter, salt, and pepper. Heat to boiling on medium. Remove from heat. Add flour and stir until ball forms. Stir in eggs, one at a time, until dough is smooth and shiny. Stir in Cheddar and crab.

3. With tablespoon-size cookie scoop, scoop mixture into balls onto parchment, spacing 1 inch apart. Bake 25 to 30 minutes or until golden brown, rotating sheets between upper and lower oven racks halfway through. Serve warm. (Puffs can be made up to 1 month ahead; place in resealable plastic bag and freeze. Reheat in 400°F oven 8 to 10 minutes.)

Each serving (2 puffs): about 75 calories, 4g protein, 4g carbohydrate, 5g total fat (2g saturated), 0g fiber, 40mg cholesterol, 125mg sodium

Top: Herbed Gougères; Bottom: Cheddar Crab Puffs

Herbed Gougères

You'll be surprised at how easy it is to make these sophisticated-looking appetizers. Fresh chives and lemon zest add bright flavor to traditional choux pastry dough.

Active time: 45 minutes
Bake time: 20 minutes
Makes: about 60 gougères

1 cup water
6 tablespoons butter or margarine, cut into pieces
1/4 teaspoon salt
Pinch cayenne (ground red) pepper
1 cup all-purpose flour
4 large eggs
6 ounces Gruyère cheese, shredded (1 1/2 cups)
1/4 cup fresh flat-leaf parsley leaves, finely chopped
2 tablespoons finely chopped fresh chives
1 teaspoon freshly grated lemon peel

1. Preheat oven to 400°F. Line two large cookie sheets with parchment paper.

2. In 3-quart saucepan, heat water, butter, salt, and cayenne to boiling on medium. Remove from heat. With wooden spoon, vigorously stir in flour all at once until mixture forms ball and leaves side of pan.

3. Add eggs, one at a time, beating well after each, until batter is smooth and satiny. Stir in cheese, parsley, chives, and lemon peel until well mixed. Drop batter by rounded teaspoons, about 1½ inches apart, onto prepared cookie sheets.

4. Bake 20 to 25 minutes, or until puffed and golden brown, rotating sheets between upper and lower oven racks halfway through. Place sheets on wire racks to let puffs cool slightly, 3 to 5 minutes. Serve warm. (Gougères can be made up to 1 month ahead. Cool completely, then transfer to airtight containers and freeze. Reheat in 350°F oven for 10 minutes.)

Each serving (4 gougères): about 140 calories, 6g protein, 7g carbohydrate, 10g total fat (7g saturated), 0g fiber, 84mg cholesterol, 160mg sodium

PUFF PASTRY

The preparation of puff pastry requires careful attention to detail, but the payoff is a light and airy pastry that's tremendously versatile. Use it to make cinnamon-sugar or cheese straws for a cocktail party, elegant tarts filled with whipped cream and berries, or showstopping Napoleons with a luscious ricotta, pistachio, and raspberry filling.

Puff Pastry

Making puff pastry is the crowning achievement of the baker's art. Here, we offer a recipe for demi-feuilletée—sometimes called simple puff pastry. Although it takes some effort to prepare, our step-by-step photos, opposite, will help you through the process.

Active time: 1 hour 30 minutes plus chilling
Makes: about 2½ pounds dough

3 cups all-purpose flour
1 cup cake flour (not self-rising)
1 teaspoon salt
2 cups unsalted butter (4 sticks), chilled
(do not use salted butter or margarine)
1 cup ice water

1. In large bowl, stir together both flours and salt. With pastry blender, two knives used scissor-fashion, or fingertips, work ½ cup butter into flour mixture until coarse crumbs form. With fork, gradually stir in ice water, 1 tablespoon at a time, until soft dough forms, adding more water if necessary. Wrap dough in plastic; refrigerate 30 minutes.

2. Meanwhile, between two sheets waxed paper, with rolling pin, pound and roll remaining 1½ cups butter into 6-inch square; wrap and refrigerate.

3. On lightly floured surface (see Tip), with floured rolling pin, roll dough into 12-inch square; place butter square diagonally in center. Fold corners of dough over butter to meet in center, overlapping slightly (see opposite). Press with rolling pin to seal.

4. Roll dough into 18" by 12" rectangle. From one short side, fold one-third of dough over center, then fold opposite third over first, letter-style, to form 6" by 12" rectangle; press seam to seal.

5. Turn dough 90 degrees. Roll into 15" by 8" rectangle, fold into thirds to form 5" by 8" rectangle. Wrap in plastic; refrigerate at least 1 hour. Repeat, rolling dough into 15" by 8" rectangle and folding into thirds, two more times. Wrap and refrigerate 30 minutes.

6. Repeat process of rolling and folding dough into 5" by 8" rectangle, then refrigerating for 30 minutes, twice more, so that dough has been folded six times in all. After sixth fold, wrap well and refrigerate at least 1 hour or up to 3 days (or freeze up to 1 month) before using.

TIP If you don't have a cool marble slab to work on, chill the countertop by placing an ice-filled jelly-roll pan on top of it before you roll out the pastry.

MAKING PUFF PASTRY DOUGH

This pastry's myriad flaky layers are created by repeatedly folding and rolling a chilled block of butter into a sheet of dough.

1. Flatten the cold butter into a uniformly thick square by rolling it between two sheets of waxed paper.

2. Center the slab of butter diagonally atop the larger square of chilled dough.

3. Fold the four corners of the dough over the butter as if you were creating an envelope. Seal the seams by flattening them with a rolling pin.

4. Roll the packet of butter and dough into an 18" by 12" rectangle (it will be quite thick).

5. Fold the two short sides into the center as if you were folding a letter. Seal the seam together with your fingers.

6. Give the folded dough a quarter turn, then roll it out into a 15" by 8" rectangle. Fold the dough in thirds again, then wrap and chill before continuing.

Puff-Pastry Tarts

These tart shells can be made through step 2 and frozen, then baked straight from the freezer. Use a variety of different berries (or chopped fruit) for the filling.

Active time: 1 hour plus chilling
Bake time: 40 minutes
Makes: 16 tarts

1 recipe Puff Pastry (page 322)
1 large egg, beaten
Sweetened Whipped Cream (page 351)
4 cups assorted fresh berries, cut up if large

1. Cut puff pastry dough crosswise in half. On lightly floured surface, with floured rolling pin, roll 1 piece into 20½" by 10½" rectangle, gently lifting dough occasionally to prevent sticking. With pastry wheel or sharp knife, trim edges to make 20" by 10" rectangle. Cut rectangle into eight 5-inch squares; place on ungreased large cookie sheet. Refrigerate 30 minutes. Repeat with remaining dough half.

2. Shape each tart shell (see photos at right): Fold 1 dough square diagonally in half to form triangle. Cut ½-inch-wide border strip parallel to both sides of triangle, without cutting through either fold or tip of triangle, so strips remain attached. Unfold triangle. Lift up 1 loose border strip and bring across base, gently pulling to match corner of border to corner on base. Bring second loose border strip over first and into same position on opposite side. Attach points with drop of water. Refrigerate on cookie sheet 30 minutes.

3. Preheat oven to 400°F. Bake tarts 20 minutes. Reduce oven temperature to 375°F; brush top of borders with beaten egg. Rotate sheets between upper and lower racks; bake 20 minutes longer, or until centers of shells are lightly browned. Cool pastries on wire rack.

4. To serve, fill tarts with whipped cream; top with berries of choice.

Each tart: about 440 calories, 5g protein, 34g carbohydrate, 32g total fat (20g saturated), 1g fiber, 106mg cholesterol, 160mg sodium

ROLLING AND SHAPING PUFF PASTRY TARTS

Follow these easy steps to create tarts that look like they were made by a professional pastry chef.

Fold one square diagonally in half. Starting near the fold, make a cut ½ inch from the edge without cutting through either the fold or the tip of the triangle.

When you unfold the dough, it should look like this. Lift up one border strip and cross it over, aligning it with the opposite edge.

Cross the other border strip over dough and match it to opposite edge. Brush a drop of water under the point of each strip and press gently to help the two layers adhere.

Raspberry-Pistachio Napoleons

This lavish dessert looks like a gourmet treat, but it can be put together with surprising speed, thanks to readymade frozen puff pastry.

Active time: 15 minutes plus cooling
Bake time: 17 minutes
Makes: 2 servings

1/2 sheet frozen puff pastry (6" by 12"), partially thawed
3/4 cup ricotta cheese
3 tablespoons confectioners' sugar plus more for dusting
1/4 teaspoon vanilla extract
Pinch freshly grated orange peel
1/4 cup roasted salted pistachios, shelled and chopped
1 container (6 ounces) raspberries

1. Preheat oven to 400°F. Line small cookie sheet with parchment paper.

2. Cut pastry into four 3" by 6" rectangles; place on prepared cookie sheet, spacing 2 inches apart. With fork, pierce pastry all over. Cover with second sheet parchment paper and small cookie sheet. Bake 15 minutes. Remove top cookie sheet and parchment paper. Bake 2 to 5 minutes, or until golden brown. Cool completely on wire rack. Pastry can be kept uncovered at room temperature up to 3 hours.

3. While pastry bakes, in medium bowl, stir together ricotta, 3 tablespoons sugar, vanilla, and orange peel; set aside. Ricotta mixture can be covered and refrigerated up to 1 hour.

4. To assemble: Spread ricotta mixture on 2 rectangles pastry. Sprinkle with pistachios. Arrange raspberries in single layer on pistachios and ricotta. Top with remaining 2 rectangles pastry. Dust tops with confectioners' sugar.

Each serving: about 640 calories, 18g protein, 54g carbohydrate, 40g total fat (12g saturated), 6g fiber, 47mg cholesterol, 270mg sodium

Cinnamon-Sugar Straws

A variation on the French pastry twists known as sacristains, these pretty sweets emerge from the oven with a coating of caramelized cinnamon sugar.

Active time: 20 minutes plus chilling
Bake time: 15 minutes
Makes: about 20 straws

1/2 cup sugar
2 teaspoons ground cinnamon
1/4 recipe Puff Pastry (page 322), or 1 sheet thawed frozen puff pastry (half of 17 1/4-ounce package)

1. Preheat oven to 400°F. Line two large cookie sheets with foil. Mix sugar and cinnamon. Sprinkle half of sugar mixture on work surface. Lay dough out on sugar. Roll into 15" by 10" rectangle, sprinkling remaining sugar mixture under and over dough to prevent sticking.

2. With sharp knife, cut dough crosswise into 3/4-inch-wide strips. Twist each strip two or three times, and place 1/2 inch apart on prepared cookie sheets. Bake 15 minutes, or until sugar has caramelized, rotating sheets between upper and lower oven racks halfway through. With wide metal spatula, loosen straws and set cookie sheets on wire racks until pastries cool completely.

Each straw: about 85 calories, 1g protein, 10g carbohydrate, 5g total fat (3g saturated), 0g fiber, 12mg cholesterol, 30 mg sodium

RASPBERRY-PISTACHIO NAPOLEONS

Puff Pastry Cheese Straws

Always a party favorite, paprika and a little cayenne pepper give these cheesy twists a kick. Instead of the usual Cheddar, we've used aged Gouda or Parmesan for more sophisticated flavor. For easy party prep, feel free to substitute store-bought puff pastry for homemade.

Active time: 30 minutes
Bake time: 15 minutes per batch
Makes: 48 straws

1 tablespoon paprika
1/2 teaspoon cayenne (ground red) pepper
1/4 teaspoon ground nutmeg
1/4 teaspoon salt
1/2 recipe Puff Pastry (page 322), or 1 package
    (17 1/4 ounces) thawed frozen puff pastry sheets
1 large egg white, lightly beaten
8 ounces aged Gouda or Parmigiano-Reggiano cheese,
    at room temperature, finely shredded (2 cups)

1. Preheat oven to 375°F. Grease two large cookie sheets. In small bowl, combine paprika, cayenne, nutmeg, and salt.

2. Unfold 1 puff pastry sheet. On lightly floured surface, with floured rolling pin, roll pastry into 14-inch square. Lightly brush with some egg white. Sprinkle half of paprika mixture on pastry. Sprinkle half of cheese on half of pastry. Fold pastry over to cover cheese, forming rectangle. With rolling pin, lightly roll over pastry to seal layers together. With knife, cut pastry crosswise into 1/2-inch-wide strips.

3. Place two-thirds of strips, 1 inch apart, on one prepared cookie sheet, twisting each to form spiral and pressing ends against cookie sheet to prevent strips from uncurling. (Do not crowd; strips puff while baking.) Half fill second cookie sheet with remaining strips; set sheet aside. Bake first sheet of strips 15 to 20 minutes or until golden. (For even cooking, bake only one sheet of strips at a time.) With spatula, transfer to wire rack to cool.

4. Meanwhile, form remaining pastry into straws, using remaining egg white, paprika mixture, and Gouda. Place one-third of strips on second cookie sheet, to fill sheet completely; bake as above. When first cookie sheet is cool, wash and grease again; use to bake remaining strips. Store in airtight container up to 3 days.

Each serving: about 75 calories, 2g protein, 5g carbohydrate, 5g total fat (2g saturated), 0g fiber, 5mg cholesterol, 75mg sodium

TIP These cheese straws make delightful holiday gifts; present them in a tall jar tied with a bow. You can shape and freeze the unbaked straws up to one month ahead, but bake them only a day or two before you need them, or they may lose their crispness.

Classic Palmiers

The step-by-step photographs at right will help you form these scrolled "palm leaves." Serve palmiers with fresh berries and coffee or tea.

Active time: 30 minutes plus chilling
Bake time: 14 minutes per batch
Makes: about 60 palmiers

⅓ cup sugar
¼ recipe Puff Pastry (page 322), or 1 sheet thawed frozen
   puff pastry (half of 17¼-ounce package)

1. Sprinkle sugar on work surface and place puff pastry on sugar. With floured rolling pin, roll dough into 16" by 10" rectangle, incorporating as much sugar as possible into dough. Using side of hand, make indentation lengthwise down center of dough. Starting at one long side, roll dough tightly up to indentation. Repeat with other long side until it meets first in center. Wrap scroll in plastic and refrigerate 30 minutes, or until sugar has dissolved and pastry is cold enough to slice easily.

2. Preheat oven to 400°F. Line large cookie sheet with foil. With knife, cut scroll crosswise into ¼-inch-thick slices. Place slices, 1 inch apart, on prepared cookie sheet. Bake 7 minutes. Turn pastries over and bake 7 minutes longer, or until sugar has caramelized and palmiers are deep golden. Cool 1 minute on cookie sheet. With wide metal spatula, transfer to wire rack to cool.

3. Repeat with remaining dough.

Each palmier: about 25 calories, 0g protein, 3g carbohydrate, 2g total fat (1g saturated), 0g fiber, 4mg cholesterol, 10 mg sodium

MAKING PALMIERS

These curliqued pastries are sure to impress, but rolling and slicing them is not difficult if you follow our step-by-step instructions. Just be sure to chill as instructed so your palmiers will hold their shape.

After rolling the sheet of puff pastry into a 16" by 10" rectangle, use the side of your hand to make a shallow indentation down the middle of the dough.

Roll one long side of the dough sheet inward toward the center, then roll the other side in until they meet. Wrap and chill the scroll so that it holds its shape.

After chilling, slice the dough crosswise into ¼-inch-thick slices. When baked, the rolls of dough will become crisp, delicate double scrolls coated with caramelized sugar.

Frostings, Fillings & Flourishes

Small-Batch Butter Frosting

FROSTINGS

Whether you need buttery icings to spread or pipe on cupcakes, fluffy frostings to fill layer cakes, or a smooth glaze to drizzle on cream puffs or éclairs—the recipes are all here.

Small-Batch Vanilla Butter Frosting

The variations at right offer three different frosting flavors for a standard (8- or 9-inch) layer cake, such as our classic Yellow Cake (page 80).

Active time: 10 minutes
Makes: about 2⅓ cups

1 package (16 ounces) confectioner's sugar
½ cup butter or margarine (1 stick), softened
3 to 6 tablespoons milk or half-and-half
1½ teaspoons vanilla extract

In large bowl, with mixer on medium-low speed, beat sugar, softened butter, and 3 tablespoons milk until smooth and blended. Beat in additional milk as needed for easy spreading consistency. Increase speed to medium-high, add vanilla, and beat until light and fluffy.

Each tablespoon: about 70 calories, 0g protein, 12g carbohydrate, 3g total fat (2g saturated), 0g fiber, 7mg cholesterol, 25mg sodium

LEMON OR ORANGE BUTTER FROSTING Prepare frosting as instructed, but add *2 tablespoons fresh lemon or orange juice* and use only *1 to 2 tablespoons milk* (as needed for easy spreading consistency); beat in *1 teaspoon fresh grated lemon or orange peel.*

Each tablespoon: about 70 calories, 0g protein, 12g carbohydrate, 3g total fat (2g saturated), 0g fiber, 7mg cholesterol, 25mg sodium

BURNT BUTTER FROSTING In small skillet, cook *½ cup (1 stick) butter* over medium heat until lightly browned; cool. Prepare frosting as instructed, using cooled browned butter instead of plain butter.

Each tablespoon: about 70 calories, 0g protein, 12g carbohydrate, 3g total fat (2g saturated), 0g fiber, 7mg cholesterol, 25mg sodium

CHOCOLATE BUTTER FROSTING Melt either *4 ounces bittersweet chocolate* or *3 ounces semisweet chocolate plus 1 ounce unsweetened chocolate*; allow to cool. Prepare frosting as instructed, but beat in chocolate. Makes about 2¾ cups.

Each tablespoon: about 75 calories, 0g protein, 12g carbohydrate, 3g total fat (2g saturated), 0g fiber, 6mg cholesterol, 20mg sodium

---

FIGURING FROSTING

Here's how much frosting you'll need for the following cake sizes:

8-inch round, two layers	2¼ cups
8-inch round, three layers	2¾ cups
9-inch round, two layers	2⅔ cups
8-inch square, one layer	1⅓ cups
9-inch square, one layer	2 cups
13- by 9-inch sheet cake	2⅓ cups
10-inch tube cake	2¼ cups
24 cupcakes	2¼ cups

Big-Batch Vanilla Butter Frosting

This makes a cup and a half more frosting than the small-batch version, enough to fill and frost a large special-occasion cake.

Active time: 10 minutes
Makes: about 3¾ cups

1 cup butter or margarine (2 sticks), softened
6 cups confectioners' sugar
½ cup half-and-half or light cream
1 tablespoon vanilla extract

In large bowl, with mixer on low speed, beat all ingredients just until blended. Increase speed to medium; beat until frosting is smooth and fluffy, about 1 minute, scraping bowl constantly with rubber spatula.

Each tablespoon: about 75 calories, 0g protein, 11g carbohydrate, 3g total fat (2g saturated), 0g fiber, 9mg cholesterol, 30mg sodium

Silky Vanilla Butter Frosting

This fine-textured frosting is made by beating together softened butter and a thick, saucelike base. The base should be completely cool before the two are combined.

Active time: 10 minutes plus cooling
Cook time: 8 minutes
Makes: about 3¼ cups

1 cup sugar
½ cup all-purpose flour
1⅓ cups milk
1 cup butter or margarine (2 sticks), softened
1 tablespoon vanilla extract

1. In 2-quart saucepan, stir together sugar and flour until evenly combined. Gradually stir in milk until smooth. Cook over medium-high heat, stirring often, until mixture thickens and boils. Reduce heat to low; cook 2 minutes, stirring constantly. Remove saucepan from heat; cool completely.

2. In large bowl, with mixer on medium speed, beat softened butter until creamy. Gradually beat in milk mixture and vanilla.

Each tablespoon: about 55 calories, 0g protein, 5g carbohydrate, 4g total fat (2g saturated), 0g fiber, 10mg cholesterol, 40mg sodium

Silky Chocolate Butter Frosting

Our basic "silky" frosting in an intense chocolate mode. Cocoa replaces some of the flour, and there's a quarter pound of semisweet chocolate in the recipe, too. For a classic combo, use it on Yellow Cake (page 80) or, for a special occasion, spread it on Checkerboard Cake (page 94).

Active time: 10 minutes plus cooling
Cook time: 8 minutes
Makes: about 3 cups

¾ cup sugar
¼ cup all-purpose flour
3 tablespoons unsweetened cocoa
1 cup milk
1 cup butter or margarine (2 sticks), softened
1 tablespoon vanilla extract
4 ounces semisweet chocolate, melted and cooled

1. In 2-quart saucepan, stir together sugar, flour, and cocoa until evenly combined. Gradually stir in milk until smooth. Cook over medium heat, stirring, until mixture thickens and boils. Reduce heat to low; cook 2 minutes, stirring constantly. Remove saucepan from heat; cool completely.

2. In large bowl, with mixer on medium speed, beat softened butter until creamy. Gradually beat in cooled milk mixture, vanilla, and melted chocolate.

Each tablespoon: about 65 calories, 0g protein, 6g carbohydrate, 5g total fat (3g saturated), 0g fiber, 11mg cholesterol, 40mg sodium

Swiss Meringue Buttercream

This icing is created by heating sugar and egg whites, then whisking over heat. The results are featherlight and fun to pipe.

Active time: 30 minutes plus cooling
Cook time: 15 minutes
Makes: about 4 cups

1¹/2 cups sugar
³/4 cup water
4 large egg whites
¹/4 teaspoon cream of tartar
2 cups unsalted butter (4 sticks), softened
  (do not use salted butter or margarine)
1¹/2 teaspoons vanilla extract
Pinch salt

1. In 2-quart saucepan, heat 1 cup sugar and ½ cup water to boiling, without stirring. Cover and cook 2 minutes longer. Remove cover; set candy thermometer in place and continue cooking, without stirring, until temperature reaches 248°F to 250°F, or hard-ball stage.

2. Meanwhile, in top of double boiler or in large stainless-steel bowl set over 4-quart saucepan filled with *1-inch simmering water,* with handheld mixer on high speed, beat egg whites, remaining ½ cup sugar, remaining ¼ cup water, and cream of tartar until soft peaks form, about 5 minutes. Reduce speed to low; slowly pour hot sugar syrup in thin stream into egg-white mixture. Increase speed to high; beat until meringue forms stiff peaks and mixture reaches 160°F on thermometer. Remove double-boiler top or bowl from saucepan, and beat until cool to touch, about 10 minutes.

3. When meringue is cool, reduce speed to medium. Gradually incorporate softened butter, 1 tablespoon at a time, beating after each addition. (If buttercream appears to curdle, increase speed to high and beat until mixture comes together, then reduce speed to medium and continue adding softened butter.) When buttercream is smooth, reduce speed to low and beat in vanilla and salt.

Each tablespoon: about 70 calories, 0g protein, 5g carbohydrate, 6g total fat (4g saturated), 0g fiber, 16mg cholesterol, 5mg sodium

BASIC TOOLKIT FOR PIPING FROSTING

Depending on how much decorating you do, you may want to invest in a whole set of tips or just buy a plain writing tip and a star tip.

DECORATING BAG Polyester or plastic-coated canvas is best; disposable plastic is good for bright icings, which can stain. (Uncoated canvas bags are clumsier to use, and the fat from frosting or whipped cream can ooze right through the fabric.) Buy 8- or 10-inch bags, which accept all standard decorating tips.

COUPLER This two-piece device lets you switch tips without changing bags. It forms a tight seal between the bag and the decorating tip.

TIPS These cone-shaped metal nozzles have a design cut out of the point to form various shapes and textures as the frosting is pushed through. Do some practice piping onto waxed paper before you start on a cake: you can always spoon the frosting back into the bag and use it again. Your results will vary depending on your angle and pressure on the bag (see page 337).

Wash bag, couplers, and tips in hot soapy water after using, turning bags inside out. Rinse well. Dry tips immediately to prevent rusting.

Amaretto Buttercream

This meringue-based buttercream is flavored with almond liqueur (substitute almond extract if you'd rather not use alcohol). Try it on a chocolate cake or any layer cake made with nuts.

Active time: 35 minutes plus cooling
Cook time: 5 minutes
Makes: about 4 cups

1 cup sugar
1/2 cup water
4 large egg whites
2 cups unsalted butter (4 sticks), softened
   (do not use salted butter or margarine)
1/4 cup amaretto (almond-flavored liqueur),
   or 1/2 teaspoon almond extract
Pinch salt

1. In 1-quart saucepan, heat ¾ cup sugar and water to boiling over high heat, without stirring. Cover and cook 2 minutes longer. Remove cover; set candy thermometer in place and continue cooking, without stirring, until temperature reaches 248°F to 250°F, or hard-ball stage. Remove saucepan from heat.

2. Just before syrup is ready (temperature will be about 220°F), in large bowl, with mixer on high speed, beat egg whites until foamy. Gradually beat in remaining ¼ cup sugar and continue beating until soft peaks form.

3. With mixer on low speed, slowly pour hot syrup in thin stream into beaten egg-white mixture. Increase speed to high; beat until meringue forms stiff peaks and mixture is cool to the touch, about 15 minutes.

4. When meringue is cool, reduce speed to medium. Gradually add softened butter, 1 tablespoon at a time, beating after each addition. (If buttercream appears to curdle, increase speed to high and beat until mixture comes together, then reduce speed to medium and continue adding softened butter, 1 tablespoon at a time.) When buttercream is smooth, reduce speed to low; beat in amaretto and salt until incorporated.

Each tablespoon: About 65 calories, 0g protein, 3g carbohydrate, 6g total fat (4g saturated), 0g fiber, 16mg cholesterol, 5mg sodium

Coconut-Pecan Frosting

This sweet and nutty cooked frosting is an absolute must for German's Chocolate Cake (page 92). Of course, you can also spread it on any chocolate layer or sheet cake.

Active time: 5 minutes
Cook time: 15 minutes
Makes: about 3 cups

1/2 cup butter or margarine (1 stick), cut up
1 cup heavy cream
1 cup packed light brown sugar
3 large egg yolks
1 teaspoon vanilla extract
1 cup sweetened flaked coconut
1 cup pecans (4 ounces), chopped

In 2-quart saucepan, combine butter, cream, and brown sugar. Heat almost to boiling over medium-high heat, stirring occasionally. Meanwhile, place egg yolks in medium bowl. Slowly pour about ½ cup sugar mixture into egg yolks, whisking. Reduce heat to medium-low. Add egg-yolk mixture to saucepan and whisk until thickened (do not boil). Remove saucepan from heat. Stir in vanilla, coconut, and pecans until combined. Cool to room temperature.

Each tablespoon: about 80 calories, 1g protein, 6g carbohydrate, 6g total fat (3g saturated), 0g fiber, 25mg cholesterol, 30mg sodium

A BEGINNER'S GUIDE TO CAKE ART

A special occasion calls for an equally special cake. After you've frosted the top and sides of your cake (see page 81), fill up a pastry bag and try your hand at the following decorating techniques. Buttercream is the most versatile and easiest to work with—pipe it at cool room temperature—but you can also pipe ganache or very cold whipped cream frosting.

Filling a Decorating Bag

With coupler and tip in place, position the bag in a tall glass; fold the top half of the bag down to form a cuff. Using a rubber spatula, fill the bag halfway with frosting, gently pushing the frosting down as you go. After you unfold the cuff, shake the frosting down (to eliminate air pockets), twist the top of the bag, and you're ready to pipe. (For best results when piping any design, hold the bag with the twisted end between the thumb and index finger of your writing hand; use the other hand to guide and squeeze the lower part of the bag.)

Plain Tip

Pipe dots, lines, squiggles, or messages. For dots: Hold the bag directly upright, with the tip slightly above the surface of the cake. Squeeze the bag, without lifting the tip, until the dot is the size you like. Stop squeezing and pull bag away. If dot gets a little "tail" at the top, smooth it gently with a finger dipped in confectioners' sugar or cornstarch. For lines, squiggles, or written messages: Hold the bag at a 45-degree angle. Squeeze it with steady, even pressure while piping. Stop squeezing before lifting the bag.

Star Tip

To make stars: Hold the bag directly upright, with the tip slightly above the surface of the cake. Squeeze to form a star, then stop squeezing and pull the bag away. The size of the star depends on the amount of pressure applied, as well as on the size of the tip opening. To make a rope: Hold the bag at a 45-degree angle and pipe a partial S shape (just don't drag the tail down to complete the S); tuck the tip under the top portion of the S curve and repeat, joining the curves to form a twisted pattern like rope.

Ganache

Ganache is the richest of all chocolate frostings—virtually a spreadable fudge. It's traditionally used to complement a not-so-rich cake, such as Chocolate Génoise (page 124). Use a fine-quality chocolate for this recipe, because it's the chocolate that will make or break the frosting. If the ganache is too thick to spread when you take it out of the refrigerator, let it stand at room temperature until softened.

Active time: 5 minutes plus cooling
Cook time: 5 minutes
Makes: about 2 cups

1 cup heavy cream
2 tablespoons sugar
2 teaspoons butter or margarine
10 ounces semisweet chocolate, coarsely chopped
1 teaspoon vanilla extract
1 to 2 tablespoons brandy, or orange- or almond-flavored
    liqueur (optional)

1. In 2-quart saucepan, combine cream, sugar, and butter and heat to boiling over medium-high; remove saucepan from heat.

2. Add chocolate to cream mixture and whisk until melted and smooth. Stir in vanilla and brandy, if you like. Pour into jelly-roll pan and place in refrigerator to cool.

Each tablespoon: about 75 calories, 1g protein, 7g carbohydrate, 6g total fat (3g saturated), 1g fiber, 11mg cholesterol, 5mg sodium

WHIPPED GANACHE Prepare ganache and cool as above. Bring to room temperature; spoon into medium bowl. With handheld mixer, whip ganache until mixture is light in color and takes on spreadable consistency.

Milk Chocolate Frosting

If you like the combo of peanut butter and chocolate, smear some of this on Peanut Butter and Jelly Cupcakes (page 104).

Active time: 15 minutes
Makes: about 2³/₄ cups

4¹/₂ ounces milk chocolate, melted and cooled
³/₄ cup butter (1¹/₂ sticks), softened
1¹/₂ cups confectioners' sugar
3 to 4 tablespoons milk

In large bowl with mixer on low speed, beat melted chocolate and softened butter until blended. Add confectioners' sugar and 3 tablespoons milk. Beat until smooth, adding remaining 1 tablespoon milk as needed. Increase speed to medium-high and beat 1 minute, or until fluffy.

Each tablespoon: about 70 calories, 0g protein, 6g carbohydrate, 5g total fat (3g saturated), 0g fiber, 12mg cholesterol, 45mg sodium

White Chocolate Butter Frosting

You can't tell that this is a chocolate frosting until you taste it. But, oh, what a scrumptious surprise! Swirl it on our Rich Chocolate Cupcakes (page 107).

Active time: 15 minutes
Makes: about 3¹/₂ cups

1 cup butter (2 sticks), softened (do not use margarine)
3 tablespoons milk
2 cups confectioners' sugar
6 ounces white chocolate, Swiss confectionery bars,
    or white baking bars, melted and cooled

In large bowl, with mixer on low speed, beat softened butter, milk, confectioners' sugar, and melted white chocolate just until blended. Increase speed to high; beat 2 minutes, or until light and fluffy, scraping bowl often with rubber spatula.

Each tablespoon: about 60 calories, 0g protein, 6g carbohydrate, 4g total fat (3g saturated), 0mg fiber, 9mg cholesterol, 35mg sodium

Chocolate Glaze

Pour or spread this glaze over Boston Cream Pie (page 120) and Éclairs (page 317), or a Bundt cake while it's still warm. The glaze will thicken and set as it cools.

Active time: 5 minutes
Cook time: 3 minutes
Makes: about ½ cup

3 ounces semisweet chocolate, coarsely chopped
3 tablespoons butter
1 tablespoon light corn syrup
1 tablespoon milk

In heavy 1-quart saucepan, heat chocolate with butter, corn syrup, and milk over low heat, stirring occasionally, until smooth.

Each tablespoon: about 100 calories, 1g protein, 9g carbohydrate, 8g total fat (5g saturated), 1g fiber, 12mg cholesterol, 50mg sodium

RICH CHOCOLATE GLAZE Prepare recipe as instructed, but substitute *3 ounces milk chocolate*, broken into pieces, for the semisweet chocolate.

Each tablespooon: About 110 calories, 1g protein, 9g carbohydrate, 8g total fat (3g saturated), 1g fiber, 16mg cholesterol, 60mg sodium

Mocha Glaze

Drizzle this intensely coffee-flavored glaze over our Chocolate Bundt Cake (page 110), allowing it to drip down the sides.

Active time: 5 minutes
Makes: about 1½ cups

1 teaspoon instant espresso powder (see Tip)
1 tablespoon hot water
3 tablespoons unsweetened cocoa
3 tablespoons dark corn syrup
1 tablespoon coffee-flavored liqueur
1 cup confectioners' sugar

In medium bowl, stir espresso powder and hot water until dissolved. Stir in cocoa, corn syrup, and coffee-flavored liqueur until blended. Add confectioners' sugar; stir until smooth.

Each tablespoon: 30 calories, 0g protein, 8g carbohydrate, 0g total fat, 0g fiber, 0mg cholesterol, 4mg sodium

TIP Espresso powder is very dark and strong instant coffee that can be found in the coffee aisle at the grocery store or purchased online.

Two-Tone Brandied Butter Frosting

The addition of brandy makes for a thoroughly grown-up buttercream. Half the batch is vanilla flavored, the other half chocolate; use one for the filling and the other to frost the cake.

Active time: 15 minutes plus cooling
Cook time: 10 minutes
Makes: about 1½ cups of each flavor

1 cup sugar
½ cup all-purpose flour
1 cup milk
1 ounce semisweet chocolate
1 ounce unsweetened chocolate
1 cup butter or margarine (2 sticks), softened
2 tablespoons brandy
1 teaspoon vanilla extract

1. In 2-quart saucepan, combine sugar and flour. With wire whisk, mix in milk until smooth. Cook over medium-high heat, stirring often, until mixture thickens and boils. Reduce heat to low and cook 2 minutes, stirring constantly. Cool completely, about 45 minutes. Meanwhile, melt both chocolates over low heat, stirring frequently; cool slightly.

2. In large bowl, with mixer on medium speed, beat butter until creamy. Gradually beat in cooled flour mixture. When mixture is smooth, beat in brandy and vanilla until blended. Spoon half of frosting into small bowl; stir cooled chocolate into frosting remaining in large bowl.

Each tablespoon vanilla frosting: about 60 calories, 0g protein, 5g carbohydrate, 4g total fat (2g saturated), 0g fiber, 11mg cholesterol, 40mg sodium

Each tablespoon chocolate frosting: about 70 calories, 0g protein, 6g carbohydrate, 5g total fat (3g saturated), 0g fiber, 11mg cholesterol, 40mg sodium

Caramel Frosting

With a lighter caramel flavor than Butterscotch Frosting, at right, this is a great match for the Tweed Cake (page 80). The frosting is a bit sticky—grease the icing spatula with a little oil or nonstick vegetable cooking spray, and it will be easier to spread.

Active time: 5 minutes
Cook time: 5 minutes
Makes: about 1½ cups

1¾ cups sugar
½ cup butter (1 stick), cut up (do not use margarine)
¾ cup milk, plus additional if needed

1. In heavy 3-quart saucepan, heat sugar and butter over high heat, stirring occasionally, until sugar has dissolved. Stir in milk. Set candy thermometer in place and continue cooking until temperature reaches 240°F on candy thermometer, or soft-ball stage (when small amount of mixture dropped into very cold water forms a soft ball that can be pressed flat when removed from water).

2. Transfer mixture to small bowl and, with mixer on high speed, beat 2 to 3 minutes, until frosting thickens and takes on spreadable consistency. If frosting remains too thick to spread, stir in additional milk, 1 teaspoon at a time, until desired consistency is achieved.

Each tablespoon: about 95 calories, 0g protein, 15g carbohydrate, 4g total fat (3g saturated), 0g fiber, 11mg cholesterol, 45mg sodium

Butterscotch Frosting

This old-fashioned frosting is wonderful on banana or spice cake. It makes enough to fill and frost the top of an 8- or 9-inch layer cake, but not enough to cover the sides. But that's the old-fashioned way to ice a cake.

Active time: 5 minutes
Cook time: 5 minutes
Makes: 1 cup plus 2 tablespoons

1 cup packed brown sugar
1/3 cup butter or margarine, cut up
1/3 cup heavy cream

1. In 1-quart saucepan, heat brown sugar, butter, and cream to boiling over high heat, stirring occasionally. Set candy thermometer in place and continue cooking until temperature reaches 240°F, or soft-ball stage (when small amount of mixture dropped into very cold water forms a soft ball that can be pressed flat when removed from water).

2. Transfer mixture to small bowl. With mixer on medium speed, beat 3 minutes, until frosting thickens and takes on spreadable consistency.

Each tablespoon: about 90 calories, 0g protein, 12g carbohydrate, 5g total fat (3g saturated), 0g fiber, 15mg cholesterol, 40mg sodium

Maple Frosting

For a change of pace, try this fluffy frosting on Applesauce Spice Cakes or Banana Cupcakes (pages 89 and 103). Use real maple syrup; the lower grades, if you can get them, have a more pronounced maple flavor.

Active time: 10 minutes
Cook time: 10 minutes
Makes: about 6 cups

2 large egg whites
1 1/2 cups maple syrup
1/8 teaspoon salt
1 teaspoon vanilla extract

In top of double boiler, over simmering water, combine egg whites, maple syrup, and salt. Using handheld mixer on high speed, beat 7 to 10 minutes, until soft peaks form. Remove double-boiler top from saucepan. Add vanilla and beat 1 to 2 minutes, until frosting thickens and takes on spreadable consistency.

Each tablespoon: about 15 calories, 0g protein, 3g carbohydrate, 0g total fat, 0g fiber, 0mg cholesterol, 5mg sodium

Peanut Butter Frosting

Here's how to make a dessert lover's dreams come true. Serve up Cocoa Brownies with Mini Chocolate Chips (page 53) or Banana Layer Cake (page 81) lavished with this creamy frosting.

Active time: 10 minutes
Makes: about 2 3/4 cups

1/2 cup butter or margarine (1 stick), softened
1/2 cup creamy peanut butter
1 small package (3 ounces) cream cheese, softened
1 teaspoon vanilla extract
2 cups confectioners' sugar
2 to 3 tablespoons milk

1. In large bowl, with mixer on medium speed, beat softened butter, peanut butter, cream cheese, and vanilla until smooth and fluffy.

2. Add confectioners' sugar and 2 tablespoons milk. Beat until blended. Increase speed to medium-high; beat 2 minutes, or until fluffy, adding remaining 1 tablespoon milk as needed for easy spreading consistency.

Each tablespoon: about 65 calories, 1g protein, 6g carbohydrate, 4g total fat (2g saturated), 0g fiber, 8mg cholesterol, 40mg sodium

Cream Cheese Frosting

The favorite of many cake lovers, cream cheese frosting is the traditional topping for Carrot Cake and is delicious on Banana Layer Cake, too (pages 86 and 81).

Active time: 10 minutes
Makes: about 2½ cups

3 cups confectioners' sugar
6 ounces cream cheese, slightly softened
6 tablespoons butter or margarine, softened
1½ teaspoons vanilla extract

In large bowl, with mixer on low speed, beat confectioners' sugar, cream cheese, softened butter, and vanilla just until blended. Increase speed to medium; beat 1 minute, or until smooth and fluffy, scraping bowl often with rubber spatula.

Each tablespoon: about 65 calories, 0g protein, 9g carbohydrate, 3g total fat (2g saturated), 0g fiber, 9mg cholesterol, 30mg sodium

Whipped Cream Frosting

This makes enough to fill and frost a two-layer cake, a tube cake, a standard sheet cake, or two dozen cupcakes. Keep the frosted cake refrigerated until serving time. The coffee whipped cream variation would make a tasty filling for Whoopie Pies (page 98).

Active time: 5 minutes
Makes: about 4 cups

2 cups heavy cream
¼ cup confectioners' sugar
1 teaspoon vanilla extract

In large bowl, with mixer on medium speed, beat cream, confectioners' sugar, and vanilla until stiff peaks form.

Each tablespoon: about 30 calories, 0g protein, 1g carbohydrate, 3g total fat (2g saturated), 0g fiber, 10mg cholesterol, 5mg sodium

COFFEE WHIPPED CREAM FROSTING Dissolve *2 teaspoons instant coffee powder* in *2 teaspoons hot water*; let cool and beat into frosting along with vanilla.

Each tablespoon: about 30 calories, 0 g protein, 1g carbohydrate, 3g total fat (2g saturated), 0g fiber, 10mg cholesterol, 5mg sodium

COCOA WHIPPED CREAM FROSTING Prepare frosting as instructed, but use *½ cup confectioners' sugar* and add *½ cup unsweetened cocoa*.

Each tablespoon: about 30 calories, 0g protein, 1g carbohydrate, 3g total fat (2g saturated), 0g fiber, 10mg cholesterol, 5mg sodium

CRÈME FRAICHE WHIPPED CREAM FROSTING Prepare frosting as instructed, but use 1 cup confectioners' sugar and, in addition to the heavy cream, add ⅓ cup crème fraiche or sour cream.

Each tablespoon: about 40 calories, 0g protein, 2g carbohydrate, 3g total fat (2g saturated), 0g fiber, 12mg cholesterol, 4mg sodium

Fluffy White Frosting

This classic American "seven-minute frosting" has a marshmallow-like texture. If you're using it on a chocolate cake (and we recommend that you do!), omit the lemon juice.

Active time: 15 minutes
Cook time: 7 minutes
Makes: about 3 cups

2 large egg whites
1 cup sugar
1/4 cup water
1 teaspoon light corn syrup
1/4 teaspoon cream of tartar
2 teaspoons fresh lemon juice (optional)

1. Combine egg whites, sugar, water, corn syrup, cream of tartar, and lemon juice (if using) in top of double boiler or in medium stainless-steel bowl set on top of 3- to 4-quart saucepan filled with *1 inch simmering water* (double-boiler top or bowl should be about 2 inches above water). Using handheld mixer on high speed, beat until soft peaks form and temperature reaches 160°F on candy thermometer, about 7 minutes.

2. Remove double-boiler top or bowl from saucepan; beat mixture 5 to 10 minutes longer, until stiff peaks form.

Each tablespoon: about 15 calories, 0g protein, 4g carbohydrate, 0g total fat (0g saturated), 5g fiber, 0mg cholesterol, 5mg sodium

Ornamental Frosting

This smooth frosting is perfect for decorating holiday cookies, including Classic Sugar Cookies and Gingerbread Cutouts (pages 34 and 38).

Active time: 10 minutes
Makes: about 3 cups

1 package (16 ounces) confectioners' sugar
3 tablespoons meringue powder
1/3 cup warm water, plus more if needed
Assorted food colorings (optional)

1. In bowl, with mixer on medium speed, beat sugar, meringue powder, and water until ingredients are blended and mixture is very stiff, about 5 minutes.

2. Tint frosting with food colorings if desired; keep surface of frosting covered with plastic wrap to prevent drying out. With small spatula or decorating bags fitted with small writing tips, decorate cookies with frosting. (You may need to thin frosting with small amount of warm water to obtain proper consistency.)

Each tablespoon: about 40 calories, 0g protein, 10g carbohydrate, 0g total fat (0g saturated), 0g fiber, 0mg cholesterol, 0mg sodium

COLORING FROSTING

For tinting frosting and icing, the pros prefer paste food colorings (also called icing colors).

Paste food colors do not dilute the frosting as liquid colors can. They also create extremely intense colors; add them to the frosting a tiny bit at a time, using the tip of a toothpick.

BOSTON CREAM PIE (PAGE 120)

of pastry cream to keep skin from forming. Cool to room temperature. Refrigerate at least 2 hours, or overnight.

Each tablespoon: about 30 calories, 1g protein, 5g carbohydrate, 1g total fat (0g saturated), 0g fiber, 21mg cholesterol, 5mg sodium

CHOCOLATE PASTRY CREAM Prepare as for vanilla pastry cream, but add *3 ounces semisweet chocolate* and *1 ounce unsweetened chocolate*, both melted, along with vanilla. Makes about 3 cups.

Each tablespoon: about 40 calories, 1g protein, 6g carbohydrate, 2g total fat (1g saturated), 0g fiber, 19mg cholesterol, 5mg sodium

FILLINGS

Recipes for luscious lemon curd, silky pastry cream, and creamy ricotta filling are all provided here.

Vanilla Pastry Cream

Use this classic custard or the chocolate variation to fill Small Cream Puffs or Eclairs (pages 314 and 317).

Active time: 5 minutes plus chilling
Cook time: 10 minutes
Makes: 2³⁄₄ cups

2¹⁄₄ cups milk
4 large egg yolks
²⁄₃ cup sugar
¹⁄₄ cup cornstarch
¹⁄₄ cup all-purpose flour
2 teaspoons vanilla extract

1. In 3-quart saucepan, heat 2 cups milk to boiling over high heat. Meanwhile, in large bowl, with wire whisk, beat egg yolks, remaining ¼ cup milk, and sugar until smooth; whisk in cornstarch and flour until combined. Gradually whisk hot milk into egg-yolk mixture.

2. Return mixture to saucepan; cook over medium-high heat, whisking constantly, until mixture thickens and boils. Reduce heat to low and cook, whisking, 2 minutes.

3. Remove saucepan from heat; stir in vanilla. Pour pastry cream into shallow dish. Press plastic wrap onto surface

Praline Pastry Cream
This sweet and nutty twist on Vanilla Pastry Cream is made with toasted slivered almonds.

Active time: 15 minutes plus chilling and cooling
Cook time: 25 minutes
Makes: about 3³⁄₄ cups

Vanilla Pastry Cream (above)
1 cup sugar
¹⁄₃ cup water
1 cup slivered blanched almonds (4 ounces), toasted
  (see page xxiii)

1. Grease jelly-roll pan. In 2-quart saucepan, heat sugar and water, stirring gently, over low heat until sugar dissolves. Increase heat to medium and boil rapidly. With pastry brush dipped in water, occasionally wash down side of pan to prevent sugar from crystallizing. Cook, swirling pan occasionally, about 7 minutes, until syrup turns light amber.

2. Working quickly, stir in almonds. Spread mixture in thin layer on prepared jelly-roll pan; cool until hardened. Break praline into small pieces.

3. In food processor with knife blade attached, process praline until finely ground. In medium bowl, stir together pastry cream and praline until blended.

Each tablespoon: about 55 calories, 1g protein, 8g carbohydrate, 2g total fat (0g saturated), 0g fiber, 18mg cholesterol, 5mg sodium

Pastry Cream for 9-Inch Tart

Spread this firmer pastry cream in a tart shell, then top it with sliced fruit or whole berries. This is also the traditional filling for Boston Cream Pie (page 120).

Active time: 5 minutes plus chilling
Cook time: 8 minutes
Makes: about 1½ cups

1 cup plus 2 tablespoons milk
2 large egg yolks
⅓ cup sugar
2 tablespoons all-purpose flour
2 tablespoons cornstarch
1 tablespoon butter or margarine
1 teaspoon vanilla extract

1. In 1-quart heavy saucepan, heat 1 cup milk to boiling over medium heat. Meanwhile, in large bowl, with wire whisk, beat egg yolks, remaining 2 tablespoons milk, and sugar until smooth; whisk in flour and cornstarch until thoroughly combined. Gradually whisk hot milk into egg-yolk mixture.

2. Return mixture to saucepan; cook over medium heat, whisking constantly, 4 minutes, or until mixture thickens and boils. Reduce heat to low and cook, whisking, 2 minutes.

3. Remove saucepan from heat; stir in butter and vanilla. Pour pastry cream into shallow dish. Press plastic wrap directly onto surface of pastry cream to keep skin from forming. Cool to room temperature. Refrigerate at least 2 hours, or overnight.

Each tablespoon: about 30 calories, 1g protein, 4g carbohydrate, 1g total fat (1g saturated), 0g fiber, 21mg cholesterol, 10mg sodium

Lemon Curd

A time-honored teatime tradition in Britain, where it is often served on toast, lemon curd is a smooth, velvety citrus custard that also makes a wonderful filling for tarts. Lemon curd cream is a super-rich variation.

Active time: 5 minutes plus chilling
Cook time: 12 minutes
Makes: about 1 cup

2 lemons
½ cup sugar
6 tablespoons butter or margarine
3 large egg yolks

1. From lemons, grate 1½ teaspoons peel and squeeze ⅓ cup juice. In 1-quart saucepan, cook lemon peel and juice, sugar, butter, and yolks over low heat, stirring constantly with wooden spoon, until mixture thickens and coats back of spoon, or candy thermometer registers 140°F, about 5 minutes. (Do not boil, or yolks will curdle.)

2. Pour mixture into medium bowl. Press plastic wrap directly onto surface of curd to keep skin from forming. Cool to room temperature. Refrigerate 1 hour, or up to 2 days.

Each tablespoon: about 75 calories, 1g protein, 7g carbohydrate, 5g total fat (3g saturated), 0g fiber, 52mg cholesterol, 45mg sodium

LEMON CURD CREAM Prepare lemon curd as directed. Once curd has cooled, beat *¼ cup heavy* cream to soft peaks. Fold into curd. Makes about 1⅔ cups.

Each tablespoon: about 55 calories, 0g protein, 4g carbohydrate, 4g total fat (2g saturated), 0g fiber, 35mg cholesterol, 30mg sodium

Lemon Filling

This "sturdier" cornstarch-thickened version of lemon curd works as a filling for a layer cake or in our old-fashioned Jelly Roll (page 126).

Active time: 15 minutes plus chilling
Cook time: 8 minutes
Makes: about 1 cup

3 large lemons
1 tablespoon cornstarch
6 tablespoons butter or margarine
3/4 cup sugar
4 large egg yolks

1. From lemons, grate 1 tablespoon peel and squeeze 1/2 cup juice. In 2-quart saucepan, with wire whisk, mix cornstarch and lemon peel and juice until smooth. Add butter and sugar. Heat to boiling over medium heat; boil 1 minute, stirring constantly.

2. In small bowl, beat egg yolks lightly. Into egg yolks, beat small amount of hot lemon mixture; pour egg mixture back into lemon mixture in saucepan, beating rapidly. Reduce heat to low; cook, stirring constantly, 5 minutes, or until thick (do not boil).

3. Pour mixture into medium bowl. Press plastic wrap directly onto surface to keep skin from forming. Cool to room temperature. Refrigerate 3 hours, or up to 3 days.

Each tablespoon: about 95 calories, 1g protein, 11g carbohydrate, 6g total fat (3g saturated), 0g fiber, 65mg cholesterol, 45mg sodium

Ricotta Filling

While this super-quick filling is delicious plain, you can dress it up by stirring in chopped dried fruit, finely chopped semisweet chocolate, or chocolate mini chips. Use it to fill the Mini Phyllo Tartlets (page 296); finish with grated chocolate or fresh fruit.

Active time: 5 minutes
Makes: about 4 cups

1 container (32 ounces) ricotta cheese
1 1/3 cups confectioners' sugar
1 teaspoon freshly grated orange peel
2 teaspoons vanilla extract
1/8 teaspoon ground cinnamon

In food processor with knife blade attached, pulse ricotta until smooth. Add confectioners' sugar, orange peel, vanilla, and cinnamon; pulse to combine.

Each tablespoon: about 35 calories, 2g protein, 3g carbohydrate, 2g total fat (1g saturated), 0g fiber, 7mg cholesterol, 10mg sodium

Streusel Topping

Sprinkle this buttery, crumbly topping over the batter before baking muffins, coffee cakes, and quick breads. Or use it as a topping for fruit pie in place of a crust.

Active time: 10 minutes
Makes: about 3/4 cup

1/2 cup all-purpose flour
1/3 cup packed brown sugar
4 tablespoons cold butter or margarine, cut up

In medium bowl, combine flour, brown sugar, and butter. With pastry blender or two knives used scissor-fashion, cut in butter until mixture is crumbly. The crumbs should be the size of small peas. Use fingers to sprinkle the topping over batter.

Each tablespoon: about 75 calories, 1g protein, 10g carbohydrate, 4g total fat (2g saturated), 0g fiber, 10mg cholesterol, 40mg sodium

SAUCES & SYRUPS

Drizzle these dessert sauces over everything from cakes and puddings to pastries and, of course, scoops of your favorite ice cream.

Apple-Rum Sauce

Brown sugar and a splash of rum contribute rich flavor to this dessert sauce, which is as luscious served over Bread-and-Butter Pudding (page 208) as it is on a sundae.

Active time: 15 minutes plus cooling
Cook time: 10 minutes
Makes: about 1¹/₂ cups

1 large Granny Smith apple
1 large Fuji or Gala apple
4 tablespoons butter or margarine
¹/₃ cup packed light brown sugar
1 tablespoon rum

1. Peel and core apples, then cut each into ¼-inch-thick slices. In 12-inch skillet, melt butter over medium heat. Add apples and cook 7 minutes or until tender, stirring occasionally. Add sugar and cook 2 minutes or until sugar melts, stirring occasionally. Stir in rum and simmer 1 minute.

2. Remove from heat and cool 5 minutes. Serve warm.

Each tablespoon: 35 calories, 0g protein, 5g carbohydrate, 2g total fat (0g saturated), 0g fiber, 0mg cholesterol, 25mg sodium

Sublime Hot Fudge Sauce

This homemade fudge sauce is simple but superb. We like to pour it over ice-cream-filled cream puffs (312) or chocolate profiteroles (313).

Active time: 5 minutes
Cook time: 10 minutes
Makes: about 1³/₄ cups

1 cup heavy cream
³/₄ cup sugar
4 ounces unsweetened chocolate, chopped
2 tablespoons light corn syrup
2 tablespoons butter or margarine
2 teaspoons vanilla extract

1. In heavy 2-quart saucepan, heat cream, sugar, chocolate, and corn syrup to boiling over medium heat, stirring occasionally. Cook 4 to 5 minutes, stirring constantly, until sauce thickens slightly and is gently boiling.

2. Remove saucepan from heat. Stir in butter and vanilla until smooth and glossy. Serve immediately, or let sauce cool completely, then cover and refrigerate. (If condensation collects inside container, it will make sauce grainy.)

Each tablespoon: about 85 calories, 1g protein, 8g carbohydrate, 6g total fat (4g saturated), 1g fiber, 14mg cholesterol, 15mg sodium

TIP Store fudge sauce in an airtight container, refrigerated, for up to one week—just spoon out as much as you need and heat it in the microwave.

CHOCOLATE PROFITEROLES (PAGE 313)

Raspberry Sauce

Here's a classic dessert sauce that's perfect for topping everything from puddings to cheesecake. Drizzle it over our Flourless Chocolate Hazelnut Cake (page 96).

Active time: 5 minutes plus chilling
Cook time: 5 minutes
Makes: about 1 cup

1 container (10 ounces) frozen raspberries in syrup, thawed
2 tablespoons red currant jelly
2 teaspoons cornstarch

1. Press thawed raspberries through sieve into 2-quart saucepan. Stir in jelly and cornstarch. Heat to boiling over medium, stirring; boil 1 minute.

2. Pour sauce into bowl; cover and refrigerate.

Each tablespoon: about 25 calories, 0g protein, 7g carbohydrate, 0g total fat (0g saturated), 0g fiber, 0mg cholesterol, 0mg sodium

Hard Sauce

This sauce is firm enough to scoop up in a spoon, but melts on contact with warm pudding or pie. Never serve a Christmas pudding without it. Try it on Persimmon-Date Pudding (page 212), a holiday classic.

Active time: 10 minutes
Makes: about 2/3 cup

1 cup confectioners' sugar
1/3 cup butter or margarine, softened
1/2 teaspoon vanilla extract or 1 tablespoon brandy

In small bowl, with mixer on medium speed, beat confectioners' sugar with softened butter until creamy; beat in vanilla. Spoon into serving bowl; refrigerate, covered, if not needed immediately.

Each tablespoon: about 100 calories, 0g protein, 12g carbohydrate, 6g total fat (4g saturated), 0g fiber, 16mg cholesterol, 60mg sodium

Butterscotch Sauce

This old-fashioned favorite is, of course, delicious on a scoop of vanilla ice cream, but it's also a wonderful way to liven up a slice of apple pie. Drizzle the sauce on the pie while it's still warm, adding ice cream on the side for a cool contrast if you want to really indulge.

Active time: 5 minutes
Cook time: 5 minutes
Makes: about 1 1/3 cups

1 cup packed brown sugar
1/2 cup heavy cream
1/3 cup light corn syrup
2 tablespoons butter or margarine
1 teaspoon distilled white vinegar
1/8 teaspoon salt
1 teaspoon vanilla extract

1. In heavy 3-quart saucepan, combine brown sugar, cream, corn syrup, butter, vinegar, and salt; heat to boiling over high heat, stirring occasionally. Reduce heat and simmer 2 minutes. Remove saucepan from heat and stir in vanilla.

2. Serve warm, or cover and refrigerate up to 1 week. Gently reheat before using.

Each tablespoon: about 85 calories, 0g protein, 14g carbohydrate, 3g total fat (2g saturated), 11mg cholesterol, 38mg sodium

Custard Sauce (Crème Anglaise)

Spoon this classic pouring custard over a slice of plain cake, a wedge of fruit pie, or a serving of apple crisp.

Active time: 5 minutes
Cook time: 15 minutes
Makes: about 1 3/4 cups

1 1/4 cups milk
4 large egg yolks
1/4 cup sugar
1 teaspoon vanilla extract

1. In 2-quart saucepan, heat milk to boiling over medium heat. Meanwhile, in medium bowl, whisk egg yolks with sugar until smooth. Gradually whisk hot milk into egg yolk mixture.

2. Return mixture to saucepan; cook over medium heat, stirring constantly, just until mixture thickens slightly and coats back of wooden spoon (finger run across custard-coated spoon leaves track). Do not boil, or mixture will curdle.

3. Remove saucepan from heat. Strain custard through sieve into clean bowl. Stir in vanilla. Serve warm, or cover and refrigerate up to 2 days to serve chilled.

Each tablespoon: about 20 calories, 1g protein, 2g carbohydrate, 1g total fat (0g saturated), 0g fiber, 32mg cholesterol, 5mg sodium

Sweetened Whipped Cream
This whipped cream is flavored with vanilla or your liqueur of choice.

Active time: 10 minutes plus chilling
Makes: about 3 cups

1 1/2 cup heavy or whipping cream (preferably not ultrapasteurized), well chilled
3 tablespoons sugar or to taste
1 1/2 teaspoon vanilla extract, 1/8 teaspoon almond extract, or 1 1/2 tablespoon brandy, rum, or orange-flavored liqueur

1. Chill medium bowl and beaters 20 minutes.

2. In chilled bowl, with mixer on medium speed, beat cream, sugar to taste, and vanilla or other flavoring until soft, fluffy peaks form. Do not overbeat, or cream will separate.

Each tablespoon: about 30 calories, 0g protein, 1g carbohydrate, 3g total fat (2g saturated), 10mg cholesterol, 3mg sodium

Flavored Simple Syrup
Brush this syrup over fine-grained cakes (such as Génoise, page 124) to add flavor and moistness. For this recipe, choose a liqueur that is clear and pale in color, not a creamy one.

Active time: 2 minutes
Cook time: 5 minutes
Makes: about 1/3 cup

1/4 cup sugar
1/4 cup water
2 tablespoons brandy or liqueur of choice

In 1-quart saucepan, heat sugar and water over high heat, stirring occasionally, until sugar dissolves. Remove saucepan from heat and stir in liqueur.

Each tablespoon: about 55 calories, 0g protein, 10g carbohydrate, 0g total fat (0g saturated), 0g fiber, 0mg cholesterol, 0mg sodium

2. Remove chocolate from pan. Using vegetable peeler, draw blade across surface of chocolate to make large curls. If chocolate is too brittle to curl, let stand at room temperature 30 minutes. (It's easiest to shave long curls if the chocolate is slightly warm.) To avoid breaking curls, use toothpick to lift and transfer.

FLOURISHES

Chocolate curls, wedges, leaves, and hearts make sophisticated garnishes for desserts. To keep the chocolate looking shiny after it cools, we melt it with a little vegetable shortening.

Chocolate Curls

We used this to decorate our Black-Bottom Chocolate Cream Pie (page 173).

Active time: 15 minutes plus chilling
Cook time: 5 minutes
Makes: enough to cover top of 9-inch cake

6 ounces semisweet chocolate
2 tablespoons vegetable shortening

1. In heavy 1-quart saucepan, heat chocolate and shortening over very low heat until melted and smooth, stirring often. Pour mixture into foil-lined 5¾" by 3¼" loaf pan. Refrigerate until set, 2 hours.

White Chocolate Hearts

These open designs are very striking when used on a rich, dense chocolate tart or cake. Try them with on our dramatically dark Chocolate Truffle Cake (page 97).

Active time: 15 minutes plus standing
Cook time: 3 minutes
Makes: 12 hearts

1¹/2 ounces white chocolate, coarsely chopped

1. With pencil, draw outline of 12 hearts, each about 1½" by 1½", on piece of waxed paper. (You can also draw other simple, open shapes or abstract squiggles.) Place waxed paper, pencil side down, on cookie sheet; tape to sheet.

2. In top of double boiler over simmering water, melt white chocolate, stirring, until smooth. Spoon warm chocolate into small decorating bag fitted with small writing tube; use to pipe heart-shaped outlines following patterns on waxed paper. Let hearts stand until set, then gently peel away waxed paper.

Chocolate Wedges

Stand these wedges atop a frosted cake or a whipped-cream-topped pie to add an extra dimension to the dessert.

Active time: 10 minutes plus chilling
Cook time: 5 minutes
Makes: enough to decorate 9-inch cake

¹/₂ cup semisweet chocolate chips
2 teaspoons vegetable shortening

1. In heavy 1-quart saucepan, heat chocolate chips and shortening over very low heat until melted and smooth, stirring frequently.

2. On 10-inch-long sheet of waxed paper, with toothpick, trace circle using bottom of 9-inch round cake pan; cut out circle. Place cake pan, bottom side up, on work surface; moisten slightly with water. Place waxed-paper circle on damp pan (water will keep paper from sliding). With large metal spatula, evenly spread melted chocolate mixture on waxed paper. Refrigerate until chocolate is firm, about 30 minutes. Heat blade of long knife in hot water; wipe dry. Quickly but gently, cut chocolate into as many wedges as desired and use to garnish cakes and pies.

Chocolate Leaves

These decorations are made by spreading melted chocolate onto real leaves. We used lemon, but leaves from many plants are safe (nontoxic) and sturdy enough to be suitable. You could try gardenia, grape, magnolia, nasturtium, rose, and wood violet. Before using the leaves, wash them with warm, soapy water, then rinse and dry them thoroughly.

Active time: 20 minutes plus chilling
Cook time: 5 minutes
Makes: 6 chocolate leaves

¹/₂ cup semisweet chocolate chips
2 teaspoons vegetable shortening
6 medium lemon leaves

1. In heavy 1-quart saucepan, heat chocolate chips and shortening over very low heat until melted and smooth, stirring frequently. Meanwhile, rinse lemon leaves and pat dry with paper towels.

2. With pastry brush or small metal spatula, spread layer of melted chocolate mixture on underside of leaves (underside will give more distinct leaf design). Refrigerate chocolate-coated leaves until chocolate is firm, about 30 minutes.

3. With cool hands, carefully peel each lemon leaf from chocolate; discard lemon leaf. Use chocolate leaves to garnish cakes and pies.

METRIC EQUIVALENTS

The recipes in this book use the standard United States method for measuring liquid and dry or solid ingredients (teaspoons, tablespoons, and cups). The information on this chart is provided to help cooks outside the U.S. successfully use these recipes. All equivalents are approximate.

Metric Equivalents for Different Types of Ingredients

A standard cup measure of a dry or solid ingredient will vary in weight depending on the type of ingredient. A standard cup of liquid is the same volume for any type of liquid. Use the following chart when converting standard cup measures to grams (weight) or milliliters (volume).

Standard Cup	Fine Powder (e.g., flour)	Grain (e.g., rice)	Granular (e.g., granulated sugar)	Liquid Solids (e.g., butter)	Liquid (e.g., milk)
1	140 g	150 g	190 g	200 g	240 ml
3/4	105 g	113 g	143 g	150 g	180 ml
2/3	93 g	100 g	125 g	133 g	160 ml
1/2	70 g	75 g	95 g	100 g	120 ml
1/3	47 g	50 g	63 g	67 g	80 ml
1/4	35 g	38 g	48 g	50 g	60 ml
1/8	18 g	19 g	24 g	25 g	30 ml

Equivalents for Liquid Ingredients by Volume

1/4 tsp	=	=	=	1 ml
1/2 tsp	=	=	=	2 ml
1 tsp	=	=	=	5 ml
3 tsp	= 1 tblsp	=	= 1/2 fl oz	= 15 ml
	2 tblsp	= 1/8 cup	= 1 fl oz	= 30 ml
	4 tblsp	= 1/4 cup	= 2 fl oz	= 60 ml
	5 1/3 tblsp	= 1/3 cup	= 3 fl oz	= 80 ml
	8 tblsp	= 1/2 cup	= 4 fl oz	= 120 ml
	10 2/3 tblsp	= 2/3 cup	= 5 fl oz	= 160 ml
	12 tblsp	= 3/4 cup	= 6 fl oz	= 180 ml
	16 tblsp	= 1 cup	= 8 fl oz	= 240 ml
	1 pt	= 2 cups	= 16 fl oz	= 480 ml
	1 qt	= 4 cups	= 32 fl oz	= 960 ml
			33 fl oz	= 1000 ml 1 L

Equivalents for Dry Ingredients by Weight

(To convert ounces to grams, multiply the number of ounces by 30.)

1 oz	=	1/16 lb	=	30 g
4 oz	=	1/4 lb	=	120 g
8 oz	=	1/2 lb	=	240 g
12 oz	=	3/4 lb	=	360 g
16 oz	=	1 lb	=	480 g

Equivalents for Cooking/Oven Temperatures

	Farenheit	Celsius	Gas Mark
Freeze Water	32°F	0°C	
Room Temperature	68°F	20°C	
Boil Water	212°F	100°C	
Bake	325°F	160°C	3
	350°F	180°C	4
	375°F	190°C	5
	400°F	200°C	6
	425°F	220°C	7
	450°F	230°C	8
Broil			Grill

Equivalents for Length

(To convert inches to centimeters, multiply the number of inches by 2.5.)

1 in	=		=	2.5 cm
6 in	= 1/2 ft		=	15 cm
12 in	= 1 ft		=	30 cm
36 in	= 3 ft	= 1 yd	=	90 cm
40 in	=			100 cm = 1 m

VOLUME EQUIVALENTS

Small Volume

Tablespoons	Cups	Fluid Ounces
1 tablespoon = 3 teaspoons		1/2 fluid ounce
2 tablespoons	1/8 cup	1 fluid ounce
4 tablespoons	1/4 cup	2 fluid ounces
5 tablespoons + 1 teaspoon	1/3 cup	2 2/3 fluid ounces
6 tablespoons	3/8 cup	3 fluid ounces
8 tablespoons	1/2 cup	4 fluid ounces
10 tablespoons +2 teaspoons	2/3 cup	5 1/3 fluid ounces
12 tablespoons	3/4 cup	6 fluid ounces
14 tablespoons	7/8 cup	7 fluid ounces
16 tablespoons	1 cup	8 fluid ounces

Larger Volume

Cups	Fluid Ounces	Pints/Quarts/Gallons
1 cup	8 fluid ounces	1/2 pint
2 cups	16 fluid ounces	1 pint
3 cups	24 fluid ounces	1 1/2 pints = 3/4 quart
4 cups	32 fluid ounces	2 pints = 1 quart
6 cups	48 fluid ounces	3 pints = 1 1/2 quarts
8 cups	64 fluid ounces	2 quarts = 1/2 gallon
16 cups	128 fluid ounces	4 quarts = 1 gallon

Pan Volumes

Pan Size	Approximate Volume
2 1/2" by 1 1/2" muffin pan cup	1/2 cup
8 1/2" by 4 1/2" by 2 1/2" loaf pan	6 cups
9" by 5" by 3" loaf pan	8 cups
8" by 8" by 1 1/2" baking pan	6 cups
9" by 9" by 1 1/2" baking pan	8 cups
9" by 1" pie plate	4 cups
11" by 7" by 1 1/2" baking pan	8 cups
13" by 9" by 2" baking pan	15 cups
15 1/2" by 10 1/2" by 1" jelly-roll pan	16 cups

EMERGENCY BAKING SUBSTITUTIONS

Baking powder, 1 teaspoon
Use ½ teaspoon cream of tartar and ¼ teaspoon baking soda (make fresh for each use).

Buttermilk, 1 cup
Place 1 tablespoon vinegar or lemon juice in cup and stir in enough milk to equal 1 cup; let stand 5 minutes to thicken. Or use 1 cup plain yogurt or sour cream thinned with ¼ cup milk (there will be some left over).

Cake flour, 1 cup
Place 2 tablespoons cornstarch in cup and add enough all-purpose flour to fill to overflowing; level off top; stir well before using.

Chocolate, semisweet, melted 1 ounce
Use ½ ounce unsweetened chocolate plus 1 tablespoon granulated sugar.

Chocolate, unsweetened, melted, 1 ounce
Use 3 tablespoons unsweetened cocoa plus 1 tablespoon vegetable oil, shortening, butter, or margarine.

Cornstarch (for thickening), 1 tablespoon
Use 2 tablespoons all-purpose flour, quick-cooking tapioca, or arrowroot.

Corn syrup, light or dark, 1 cup
1¼ cups granulated or packed brown sugar plus ¼ cup liquid (use whatever liquid the recipe already calls for).

Half-and-half, 1 cup
Use ⅞ cup whole milk plus 1½ tablespoons butter, or ½ cup light cream plus ½ cup whole milk.

Light brown sugar, 1 cup
Use 1 cup granulated sugar and 1 tablespoon molasses, or use dark brown sugar.

Milk, whole, 1 cup
Use 1 cup nonfat milk plus 2 teaspoons butter or margarine or ½ cup evaporated whole milk plus ½ cup water.

Pine nuts
Use walnuts or almonds.

Sour cream, 1 cup
Use 1 cup plain yogurt, or ¾ cup sour milk, buttermilk or plain yogurt plus ⅓ cup butter, or 1 tablespoon lemon juice plus evaporated whole milk to equal 1 cup.

Yeast, active dry, ¼-ounce package
Use 0.6-ounce cake, or use one third of 2-ounce cake compressed yeast.

Vanilla extract
Use brandy or an appropriately flavored liqueur.

Whipping Cream (36–40% fat), 1 cup
Use ¾ cup whole milk plus ⅓ cup melted butter. Use this for baking purposes, not for topping.

INDEX

Note: Page numbers in *italics* indicate Healthy Makeover recipes.

PHOTOGRAPHY CREDITS

Antonis Achilleos : 189

James Baigrie: xviii, 60, 225, 265 (stollen), 297, 308, 327

Chris Bain: xvi, 50, 76, 137, 195, 237, 293, 331

Monica Buck: 41, 44

Corbis Images: Ocean, 28, Christian Kargi, 339; Radius Images, 62 (peanut butter bars)

Tara Donne: 113, 256

Getty Images: James Baigrie, 306; Bayside, 250; Lauren Burke, xxiv (sugar); Chris Cole, 101 (frosting); Michael Lamotte/Cole Group, 165; Angus Fergusson, 168; Food Collection, xiv (brush), xvi, 36 (cookie dough with stars); Dan Goldberg, 321 (Gougères); Dennis Gottlieb, 19; Martin Harvey, 343; Image Source, 315; Paul Johnson, 296; Dorling Kindersley, 238; Jessica L, 273; Alison Brian Macdonald, 253; Miksch, 81; MIXA, 108; David Murray; 166; Victoria Pearson , 282; Kathryn Russell, 102 (chocolate cupcake); William Shaw,197, 265 (irish soda bread); Howard Shooter, xv (spoon); Joy Skipper, 247; Smneedham, 301; SOT, 310; Stockfood, 279; Kevin Twomey, 55

Brian Hagiwara: 18, 30 (tulipes), 31

Lisa Hubbard: 134 (chocolate cheesecake), 154

iStock photo: 4kodiak , xvii (cup), 182; Alphacat, xiv (egg); Sedneva Anna , xxiv (butter); Images by Barbara, x; Ugurhan Betin, xii (whisk); Bluestocking, 204, 303; Cathy Britcliffe, 336; Jill Chen; 61; Creativeye99, 240; Donald Erickson, 45 (coconut macaroon); Ermingut, xxiii (nuts); Floortje, 305, 313; Ekaterina

Fribus, 8; Gvictoria, 22; Red Helga, 149; Oliver Hoffmann, 215; Hue Photography, xx; Joe Lena, 88; Peng Li, xv (spatulas); Lizcen, 152, 164; Lujing, 347; Photo Maru,158; Milan Foto, 155; Pichunter, xii (cups); Samohin , 111; Debbi Sharky1, xxiv (oil); Smirnoff, xxii; Supermimicry, viii; Unalozmen, xvii (chocolate), 355; Venakr, xii (peeler); Valentyn Volkov, 200; Matka Wariatka, 307; wdstock, 340; Carolyn Woodcock, xiii (spoons); xxmmxx, 269

Frances Janisch: 26, 43, 134 (ricotta cheesecake), 162

Yunhee Kim: 2, 25, 37, 46, 68, 146

Kate Mathis: 13 (macaroon sandwiches), 16, 21, 32, 33, 38, 39, 43, 48, 52, 62, 65, 73, 85, 114, 116, 127, 128, 147, 151, 161, 174, 177, 185, 202, 206, 216, 226, 232, 234, 255, 266, 319, 321 (cheddar crab puffs), 328

Steven Mark Needham: 4, 6, 10, 15, 29, 40, 58, 121, 125, 129, 153, 156, 217, 231, 233, 244, 251, 271, 274. 275, 276, 281, 291, 197, 311, 317, 318, 323, 325, 329, 337, 352, 353

Con Poulos: iv, xxi, 23 (cookie pizza), 75, 86 (gingerbread), 90, 92, 96 (chocolate hazelnut cake), 99, 148, 157, 170 (ganache tart), 172, 193, 209, 213, 219, 312 (chocolate profiteroles), 349

David Prince: 83, 110 (tangerine pound cake)

Alan Richardson: xv, 95 (checkerboard cake)

Kate Sears: 130, 170 (chocolate macaroon tart), 180, 220, 245

Shutterstock: Bonchan, xiv (peppercorns); Olga Miltsova, xv (honey); Yuliya Rusyayeva, 191

StockFood: Chris Alack, 45 (macaroon sandwich); Klaus Arras, 324; Noel Barnhurst, 285 (calzone); Mary Ellen Bartley, 246; Oliver Brachat, xiv (sugar), 289; Angie Norwood Browne, 139; Steve Buchanan, 78; Alain Caste, 316; Elisabeth Cölfen, 258; Michael Cogliantry, 243; Shaun Cato-Symonds, 30 (madelines), 101 (icing); Colin Cooke, 6 (molasses cookies); Eising Studio, 142; Ken Field, 222; Foodcollection, 351, 356; Beth Galton, 120, 344; Michael Grand, 179; Dean Hannas, 57; A. Hbrkova, 13 (coconut macaroons); ISTL, 286; Valerie Janssen, 71, 109 (lemon pound cake); Richard Jung, 102 (carrot cupcake); Keller & Keller, 123, 342; Kent Lacin, ix, 198; Studio Lipov , 294; Rita Maas, 96 (chocolate truffle cake); Alison Miksch, 143; Gareth Morgans, 211; Michael Paul, xi; Ewa Rejmer, 335; Tina Rupp, 106; Paul Schiefer Photography, xiii (cupcake); Charles Schiller , 312 (cream puffs); Joy Skipper, 66; Snowflake Studios, xxiii (biscuits), 86 (carrot cake), 110 (chocolate pound cake); Yelena Strokin, 109 (poppy seed pound cake); Anthony Tieuli, 249; Ngoc Minh & Julian Wass, 100; Tanya Zouev, 261

Ann Stratton: vi, 23 (hermits), 228, 263

Studio D: Studio Philip Friedman, vii, xii (melon baller, dough), 36 (rolling pin, colored sugar), 141

Think Stock: MichaelJay, xv (zester)

Mark Thomas: 35, 54, 56, 95 (piping), 97, 118, 126, 235

Anna Williams: ii, 186, 285 (pizzettes)

Front cover: Front: Philip Friedman/Studio D
Spine: Kate Mathis
Back: Noel Barnhurst/StockFood (top), Kathryn Russell (middle), Con Poulos (bottom)
Inside flap: Francis Janisch

THE GOOD HOUSEKEEPING TRIPLE-TEST PROMISE

At *Good Housekeeping*, we want to make sure that every recipe we print works in any oven, with any brand of ingredient, no matter what. That's why, in our test kitchens at the **Good Housekeeping Research Institute,** we go all out: We test each recipe at least three times—and, often, several more times after that.

When a recipe is first developed, one member of our team prepares the dish and we judge it on these criteria: It must be **delicious, family-friendly, healthy,** and **easy to make.**

1 The recipe is then tested several more times to fine-tune the flavor and ease of preparation, always by the same team member, using the same equipment.

2 Next, another team member follows the recipe as written, varying the brands of ingredients and kinds of equipment. Even the types of stoves we use are changed.

3 A third team member repeats the whole process using yet another set of equipment and alternative ingredients. By the time the recipes appear on these pages, they are guaranteed to work in any kitchen, including yours.

We Promise.

HEARST BOOKS
New York

An Imprint of Sterling Publishing
387 Park Avenue South
New York, NY 10016

ISBN 978-1-61837-131-7

GOOD HOUSEKEEPING

Jane Francisco
EDITOR IN CHIEF

Courtney Murphy
CREATIVE DIRECTOR

Susan Westmoreland
FOOD DIRECTOR

Sharon Franke
KITCHEN APPLIANCES & FOOD
TECHNOLOGY DIRECTOR

BOOK DESIGN by Jon Chaiet
PROJECT EDITOR Sarah Scheffel
PHOTOGRAPHY CREDITS on page 372.

Distributed in Canada by Sterling Publishing
c/o Canadian Manda Group, 165 Dufferin Street
Toronto, Ontario, Canada M6K 3H6
Distributed in the United Kingdom by GMC Distribution Services
Castle Place, 166 High Street, Lewes, East Sussex,
England BN7 1XU
Distributed in Australia by Capricorn Link (Australia) Pty. Ltd.
P.O. Box 704, Windsor, NSW 2756, Australia

ALL RECIPES
· GOOD ·
HOUSEKEEPING
Since ★ 1909
COOKBOOKS
Triple TESTED

The Good Housekeeping Cookbook Seal guarantees that
the recipes in this cookbook meet the strict standards
of the Good Housekeeping Research Institute. The
Institute has been a source of reliable information and a
consumer advocate since 1900, and established its seal
of approval in 1909. Every recipe has been triple-tested
for ease, reliability, and great taste.

www.goodhousekeeping.com

For information about custom editions, special sales,
and premium and corporate purchases, please contact
Sterling Special Sales at 800-805-5489 or specialsales@
sterlingpublishing.com.

Manufactured in China

2 4 6 8 10 9 7 5 3 1

www.sterlingpublishing.com